British Fortifications Through
the Reign of Richard III

ALSO BY JEAN-DENIS G.G. LEPAGE
AND FROM McFARLAND

Vauban and the French Military Under Louis XIV (2010)

Aircraft of the Luftwaffe, 1935–1945: An Illustrated Guide (2009)

French Fortifications, 1715–1815: An Illustrated History (2009)

Hitler Youth, 1922–1945: An Illustrated History (2009)

The French Foreign Legion: An Illustrated History (2008)

*German Military Vehicles of World War II:
An Illustrated Guide to Cars, Trucks, Half-Tracks,
Motorcycles, Amphibious Vehicles and Others* (2007)

The Fortifications of Paris: An Illustrated History (2006; paperback 2010)

*Medieval Armies and Weapons in Western Europe:
An Illustrated History* (2005)

*Castles and Fortified Cities of Medieval Europe:
An Illustrated History* (2002; paperback 2011)

British Fortifications Through the Reign of Richard III

An Illustrated History

JEAN-DENIS G.G. LEPAGE

McFarland & Company, Inc., Publishers
Jefferson, North Carolina, and London

LIBRARY OF CONGRESS CATALOGUING-IN-PUBLICATION DATA

Lepage, Jean-Denis.
British fortifications through the reign of Richard III :
an illustrated history / Jean-Denis G.G. Lepage.
 p. cm.
Includes bibliographical references and index.

ISBN 978-0-7864-5918-6
softcover : acid free paper ∞

1. Fortification — Great Britain — History.   2. Siege warfare —
Great Britain — History.   3. Great Britain — History, Military.   I. Title.

UG429.G7L47 2012   725'.18 — dc23   2011041026

BRITISH LIBRARY CATALOGUING DATA ARE AVAILABLE

©2012 Jean-Denis G.G. Lepage. All rights reserved

*No part of this book may be reproduced or transmitted in any form
or by any means, electronic or mechanical, including photocopying
or recording, or by any information storage and retrieval system,
without permission in writing from the publisher.*

Front cover image © 2012 Shutterstock

Manufactured in the United States of America

*McFarland & Company, Inc., Publishers
Box 611, Jefferson, North Carolina 28640
www.mcfarlandpub.com*

Acknowledgments

The author wishes to express his gratitude to Jeannette à Stuling, Anne Chauvel, Michèle Clermont, Véronique Janty, Antoinette-Anna Genessey and Nicole-Juliette Lapaux, Jan à Stuling, Siepje Kroonenberg, Eltjo de Lang and Ben Marcato, and Simone and Bernard Lepage. Also great thanks to the artists Alan Sorell, Peter Fraser and Andrew Spatt, whose excellent works have been the inspiration for some of the illustrations.

Table of Contents

Acknowledgments v
Introduction 1

Part 1. Prehistoric Fortifications

The Celts 5
Hill Forts and Oppida 8
Hill Forts in England
    and Wales 25
Hill Forts in Scotland 25
Hill Forts in Ireland 33
Other Forms of Fortifications 38
Aftermath 51

Part 2. Roman Fortifications in Britain A.D. 43–409

The Roman Empire
    and Its Army 53
Roman Engineering Corps 55
Britannia 62
Camps and Forts 64
Roman Urban Fortifications 89

Part 3. Early Medieval Fortifications A.D. 409–1066

Anglo-Saxon Invasion 99
Danish Invasions 102
Dikes 104
Burhs 108
Siege Warfare 115
Aftermath 116

Part 4. Norman Castles 1066–1154

The Normans and England 117
Norman Military Architecture .. 122
Motte-and-Bailey Castles 124
Shell-Keeps 129
Stone Keeps 133
Aftermath 158

Part 5. Early Plantagenet Fortifications 1154–1327

Historical Background 161
Siege Warfare 173

Evolution of Castles in the 12th
and 13th Centuries 178

Edwardian Castles 202

Aftermath 230

Part 6. Late Plantagenet Fortifications 1327–1485

Historical Background 231

Development of Castles in the
14th and 15th Centuries 238

Urban Fortifications 252

Tower Houses in the North 281

Conclusion 291

Appendix 1: Maps of the Main Castles in the British Isles   295

Appendix 2: Conservation Organizations   301

Appendix 3: Kings and Queens (from A.D. *802 to 1485)*   304

Bibliography   305

Index   307

Introduction

From the most remote past man's building efforts and resources have been devoted to meeting his most important needs, such as accommodation (houses), worship (temples), and burial (tombs), as well as defense, which has occupied a prominent place in all periods of the history of mankind. Indeed, one of man's first needs is security and its pursuit is among the most ancient of human endeavors. An area of protection for the family hearth, tribe and social group has always been necessary to preserve survival, food stores, stored goods, institutions, language and culture. Aggression, by an opposite if not always equal reaction, stimulates defense.

A strategic position, a convenient anchorage or harbor, the availability of water, the arability of land and mineral deposits all added to the value of certain locations and made them worth the extra effort to defend and attack. Fortifications appeared in the earliest stage of urbanization at Jericho in Palestine in c. 7000 B.C., and ever since have been recorded in all areas of the world.

Many countries have experienced internal unrest at some time in their past, and Great Britain is certainly no exception. Its turbulent history has seen battles between the Irish and the English, the House of York and the House of Lancaster, the Royalists and the Parliamentarians, and Jacobites and Hanoverians. To internal unrest has been added the danger of foreign invasion. From the time the Romans first landed on British shores the islands have lived with the constant threat of invasion, although the last successful invader was William the Conqueror in 1066 (some would argue William of Orange in 1689, but he was formally "invited"). Since that time, varying types of fortification have been created around the coasts to repel further invasions from the Spanish, French, Dutch and, most recently, Germans. The British Isles cannot claim the full span of more than 9000 years, but they have participated fully in the history of fortifications. Defensive works were needed because the waters around Britain, the Channel and the North Sea far from being a protective moat, were invasion highways tempting intruders to penetrate to the very vitals of the nation. This had been the case for thousands of years before the Norman invasion of 1066. Ever since Julius Caesar first set foot on England's shore in 55 B.C., a constant stream of invaders has inexorably followed. The Romans returned in A.D. 43, followed by north German barbarian tribes after A.D. 400, and lastly the Vikings from the 8th century. The physical memorials to these ancient invaders are still numerous and architecturally significant, embracing such varied structures as Iron Age hill forts, Roman castra and Hadrian's Wall, and Anglo-Saxon burhs. Eventually Norman castles, as well as Edwardian castles, Irish tower houses and many more, were erected when the fragile notions of nationhood and national identity were established.

The purpose of this book is to present the rather complex issue of British fortifications to a wider public in an accessible form. The focus is on England, but attention is also paid to Irish and Scottish castles, as well as to medieval fortifications built by the English in France. The book covers the development of British fortifications from the Iron Age until the end of the Wars of the Roses (1455–1485), and the reign of Richard III (1483–1485), the last Plantagenet king. This period marked the decline of the classical medieval castle, soon replaced with elaborate forts adapted to artillery and firearms built by the new Tudor dynasty.

The word castle has become a generic term used to describe many types of fortification. Unlike most other buildings, such as churches, houses or temples, castles served more than one purpose. It is now admitted that a medieval proper castle was a home for its owner and family, a place where guests could be received and entertained, and the local center for administration and justice. A castle was naturally built strong enough to defend its occupants from aggression while acting as a base from which attacks on neighbours or more distant enemies could be launched. Originating from a private initiative directly connected to feudalism, castles played a central role in medieval history. They were living structures that evolved over time, according to political situations, military conditions and social evolution. They were besieged, destroyed, and eventually rebuilt and re-occupied, and as techniques of siege warfare improved, they grew in size, height and strength to meet the increased threats from attacks. No two castles are the same; they are all different depending on the natural site and material used, the period, and the rank, fortune and ambitions of those who built them. The thought of castles conjures up images of adventure, romance and intrigue, a majestic castle standing on top of a sunny hill or cliff. We are apt to think of the medieval castles as bustling with glamorous life, with armored knights at every merlon and archers at each loophole, and blaring trumpets and colorful heraldic insignias spattered everywhere. In reality, most castles presented a rather different kind of picture, with the stench from garde-robes and sewage, stagnant water in a moat half-filled with decaying refuse, the strong smell of farm, the discomfort of the cold rooms and drafty hall, window-slits boarded up, the harsh clank of iron on stone, and the wind sweeping along the walls. Because by their very nature defensive works needed to be strong, and they tend to survive in greater number than other types of structures, and medieval castles are very familiar to us. Although exact numbers are hard to come by, there are thousands of fortifications of all types still visible in the British Isles, even if not all of them are as prominent and as easy to find as the Castles at Dover, Kidwelly, Conway, Harlech, Rhuddlan, Beaumaris, or the White Tower in London. Although many have not withstood the violence of war and the attrition of time, Britain is indeed strewn with castles either well preserved or in ruins, rubble from the centuries of her existence. Castles are tangible relics of a remarkable past, a lengthy heritage etched in stone, and stained with the blood and sweat of those who built, labored, fought, and died in their shadows. Ruins stir up in us a profound awareness of those past lives. Castles have a timelessness that is awe-inspiring. That they have endured centuries of warfare and the effects of weather is a testimony to the creativite skill and power of their medieval builders and owners.

PART 1

Prehistoric Fortifications

The Celts

HISTORICAL BACKGROUND

The Celts' origin is obscure. They came from central Europe or farther east, from Russia, moving slowly westward and establishing themselves in much of western Europe. The somewhat obscure and generic term Celt was applied to a variety of related tribal societies in Iron Age Europe. About 700 B.C., the first Celts went across the English Channel from Europe. Whether or not the arrival of the Celts in the British Isles was an actual invasion, or a more gradual process, is an open question. However their coming did not mean a total take-over overnight. Immigrants from the Continent came more as an intermittent flow than as a sudden torrent. Britain was not taken by storm culturally, and the infusion of new elements continued a movement already begun, allowing the British Iron Age to develop a certain insular character. Thus the period known as the Iron Age lasted in Britain for about 800 years (from c. 750 B.C. to A.D. 43). The changes and technological innovations that occurred during this time were every bit as significant as those that have occurred in the last 800 years, from the 13th century to the present day. One thing is certain: the "barbarian" Celtic civilization was a great deal more advanced than some (Roman) writings would have us believe. By the end of the Iron Age, amongst other things, coinage had been introduced, wheel-thrown pottery was being made, there was an increased interest in personal appearance, people had started to live in larger and more settled communities, and the mortuary rites of society had changed. The newcomers were indeed lovers of personal finery and ostentatious display, which is reflected in finds of elaborate jewelry, weapons and the remains of chariots in graves. The Celts were organized into tribes consisting of enlarged family units headed by a hereditary king or an elected leader. Celtic society was divided into four main classes: the warrior aristocracy, the Druids, who were the religious leaders, the free commoners, and the slaves. Interestingly women were regarded highly amongst the Celts, which was unusual during ancient times. Celtic society was indeed more equal in terms of

Left: *Celtic warrior. The Celts had a warrior class drawn from what we would describe as the middle and upper classes. They were warriors in the heroic sense, living for war, and their glorification of bravery often led them to recklessness. Most Celts scorned the use of body protection but chiefs and the wealthiest Celts often did wear armor and helmets.*

Right: *Pict warrior. Ordinary Celtic soldiers, sometimes naked, worked themselves into a fury before entering battle and then fought like wild beasts. Their weapons included axes, javelins and spears (approx. 2.5m long), and Caesar noted the use of slings, and occasionally bows and arrows. The Celts often carried for protection an oval (or round) wooden, leather-enclosed, brightly decorated shield that was 5 to 8 feet long.*

gender roles. Women were on more or less equal footing with men, being extremely dexterous in domestic skills but also sometimes accomplished warriors, merchants and rulers. Some, like the famous Boudica and Cartimandua, even became tribal queens.

The progression from the Bronze Age to the Iron Age is not as clear as the approximate dates given above. Iron was a far superior metal to bronze, being stronger and more durable. It helped in improving the practices of farming, making tilling easier. On the other hand, it required much hotter fires to extract it from its ore and so it took a fair degree of skill to produce iron. None of this is to be taken to mean that bronze fell out of use overnight. Rather, iron simply became an alternative metal; many bronze objects have been found that were made in the Iron Age. It should be noted that, in spite of their common language, religious beliefs, customs and arts, social organization and lifestyle, the Celts never formed a united nation in Britain, or a centralized realm or empire in Europe. Tribal particularities and clannic desire for independence always prevented the formation of any large political, economic or military entity, which made them vulnerable to their enemies. This in the end caused their defeat, and subjugation. Had they been strongly united they would probably have been invincible.

CELTIC TRIBES IN BRITAIN

One of the main sources of information about the Celtic world are Roman writers, notably Tacitus, and much of our information about the tribes of Scotland derives

Celtic tribes in Britain c. 120 B.C.

from the geographical writings of Claudius Ptolemaeus or Ptolemy (A.D. 90–168). However, all authors were writing from a Roman viewpoint and their works have to be treated with some caution when it comes to their descriptions of the tribes and their beliefs and attributes. The Celtic tribes of southern England (e.g., Durotriges, Belgae, Regni, and Cantiaci) had close contact with other Celtic tribes established in northern France (Caletes, Atrebates, Morini, and Menapi). By 150 B.C. there was a substantial commerce between Britain and the rest of Europe. This involved trade in tin, silver, gold, pottery, wine, coins and slaves. Apart from trading across the Channel, the British tribes were even able to send military aid to their "cousins" in France against the Romans, one reason for the first attempt to conquer them by Julius Caesar in 55–54 B.C. By the time the Romans arrived for the second time in A.D. 43, Celtic Britain was organized into small independent kingdoms.

As technology improved and its use in agriculture and hunting increased, so the human population increased too. It was inevitable that these expanding communities would eventually start to compete for resources, which led to the building of defensive works around the settlements. The Celts lived in tribes divided into extended family groups. These families controlled certain areas of the country, occupying villages, and some tribes constructed defensive positions known as *hill forts*.

Hill Forts and Oppida

Generalities

Early Celtic settlements were farms or small villages sometimes defended by a simple timber palisade, showing little change from the agricultural settlements of the Middle Bronze Age, but gradually new structures appeared. The so-called hill fort, in one form or another, is one of the most typical field monuments of the Celtic world in the Iron Age.

Technically defined, a hill fort was a continuous fortified enclosure considered as protection against wild animals and thieves, and helping to fulfill man's fundamental psychological need to secure himself and his property with some kind of wall or fence. They did not necessarily have military or strategic significance, and as the name implies the enclosure was often (but not always) located on a hill or high ground in order to exploit a rise in elevation for defensive advantage. The natural site was reinforced by one, two or more man-made lines of concentric earthworks. Each earthwork consisted of a rampart preceded by an external ditch. These multiple walls described a complete circuit (often irregular or oval in plan as it followed the contours of the hill), except on sites situated adjacent to a particularly steep slope or precipice. Most hill forts followed the same pattern, and the alternating concentric embankments, palisades and ditches were intended to enable a defense in depth and to exhaust and delay any attacking force before they got to the settlement at the top.

Some of these elevated and fortified sites originated in the late Neolithic period, but were common during later periods.

In spite of their important numbers, hill forts in the British Isles are only a part of a much larger picture embracing many parts of central and western Europe. Hill forts, under variant local designations, were indeed used from the Late Bronze Age (c. 1200–800 B.C., the period when this alloy of copper and tin replaced stone in the manufacture of some tools and weapons) in many Celtic areas, notably in Scandinavia, Russia, Lithuania and Estonia, Portugal, Spain, Germany, Gaul (France) and central Europe. In spite of the fact that these structures display similarities in detail, it would be unwise to try to correlate them or to suggest a common and direct derivation. The idea of digging a ditch and piling up earth to form a rampart probably occurred independently to widely dispersed people, and subsequent refinements and additions sprang from equally random inspiration. It should also be pointed out that, certainly in Britain, many earthworks classed as "hill forts" (a generic term, coined by archaeologists) are not actually on hills, nor were they garrisoned and defended, so there is room to question whether these works were forts at all. A more accurate and descriptive term would be *defensive enclosure*, but the word hill fort has stuck for convenience.

It must also be emphasized that hill forts were not occupied simultaneously. Detailed studies of individual sites reveal intermittent periods of disuse, and at any one time only a fraction of the total number may have been in commission.

Julius Caesar described the large Late Iron Age hill forts he encountered during

A dolmen (also known as a cromlech) is a type of single-chamber megalithic tomb, usually consisting of three or more upright stones supporting one or more large flat horizontal capstones. Most of these astonishing structures date from the early Neolithic period, and they were usually covered with earth or smaller stones to form a barrow or tumulus, a mound raised over a grave.

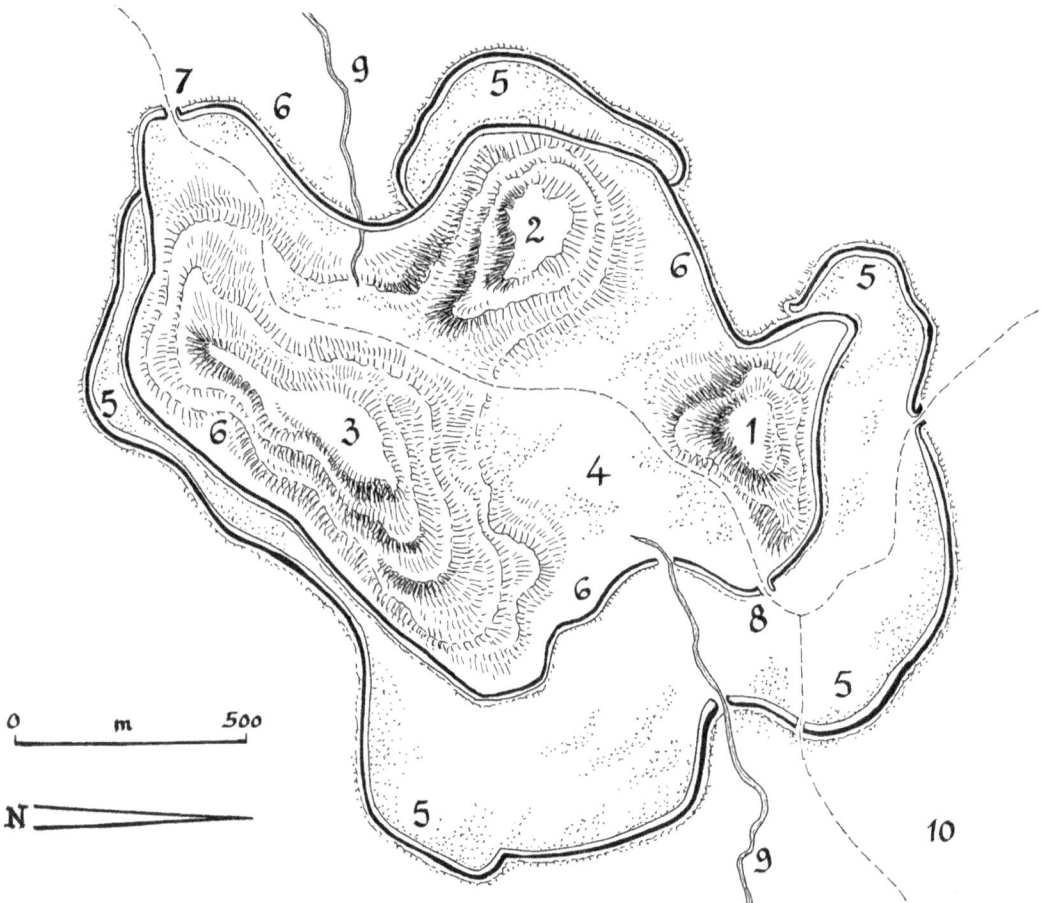

Bibracte, a Gaulish oppidum (fortified settlement), was the capital of the Aedui tribe and one of the most important hill forts in Gaul. Situated on Mont Beuvray near modern Autun in Burgundy, France, Bibracte was a fortified economic, political and religious center. At its height it sheltered an estimated population of 5,000. A few decades after the Roman conquest of Gaul in 52 B.C., Bibracte was abandoned in favor of Autun, 25 kilometers distant. Today Bibracte is open to the public and houses an archaeologist research center for the study of Celtic civilization. The site occupies three hills with an average height of 700 m: in the north, Pierre de la Wivre (1); in the west, Theurot de la Roche (2); in the south, Le Parrey (3); and a lower valley called Pature du Couvent (4). The oppidum was enclosed by a first outer wall and ditch (5), and a second inner wall and ditch (6). The perimeter was crossed by a main road with two gates: Grandes Portes (7) in the south and Porte du Rebout (8) in the north. Two small brooks (9) provided water. A necropole (10) was placed outside the perimeter.

his campaigns in Gaul as *oppida* (singular: *oppidum*). By the time of the Roman conquest some of them, the larger ones and the best situated, became more like cities than fortresses; many were the origins of later Roman towns. Hill forts were indeed frequently occupied by conquering armies, but on other occasions they were destroyed, the local people forcibly evicted, and the forts left derelict. For example, Solsbury Hill was sacked and deserted during the invasions of southern Britain in the first century B.C. Abandoned forts were sometimes re-occupied, re-used, and re-fortified under renewed threat of foreign intruders during the successive invasions of Britain by Saxons, Danes and Vikings.

Iron Age hill forts, although many originated from Late Bronze Age defensive enclosures, are thus the youngest of the prehistoric remains to be seen in the British Isles. Iron Age men experimented with a variety of techniques and it is not always easy to see what they were aiming at. Before them earthworks and stoneworks of different sorts were built, not only in Britain but throughout Europe, many for mysterious or unclear purposes. These Neolithic and Bronze Age causewayed camps, long barrows, passage graves, tumuli, and stone circles (henges) seem to indicate a pervading atmosphere in prehistoric Britain, a stable society which — benevolent or authoritarian — enabled isolated communities to farm, mine, trade, live and worship in peace. Perhaps the Bronze Age in Britain was not the golden time of peace and plenty that has often been suggested; perhaps it was as faction-ridden as later societies, but apparently there was no fear of attack by foreign invaders or aggressive local outlaws, enabling collective social energies to be devoted to the construction of spiritual and ritual burial and worship structures rather than defense works with a military character. It seems that it was the arrival of the Hallstatt culture (named after the Austrian region where it originated), with its knowledge of ironworking, about 500 B.C., which ended this supposed prehistoric idyll. Advances in metal processing meant the introduction of a highly dangerous combination: coins (thus money) and better weapons. As a result the British Isles would have become a land of perpetual wars waged by a patchwork of little kingdoms, each with its own hilltop fortress set behind ramparts and ditches. From 500 B.C. onward, the hill fort became a permanent feature of the British landscape. Favored sites, which had been occupied intermittently from the Neolithic period, became fortified settlements. When threats of invasion from Europe were eventually renewed, hill forts were rebuilt with additional defenses of increased complexity.

Structure and Appearance

Beyond the simple definition of hill fort, there was a wide variation in types and periods from the Bronze Age to the early Middle Ages. Size, general appearance and topology, as well as time of occupation, function and purpose varied a lot. Although hill forts and oppida had many common features, they were all different and no two of them were the same. As a result it is rather difficult to discuss them in broad terms because of the very large numbers involved, the variations from region to region and the very long period of time considered.

Some enclosures had a footprint of 20 hectares, and sometimes more, offering accommodations for a large population and domesticated cattle, but being rather diffuse to defend. The large sprawling examples at Bindon Hill and Bathampton Down are more than 50 acres (20 hectares). Others were only one hectare or less and

N
0 Feet 300

AVON RIVER
N
0 Feet 400

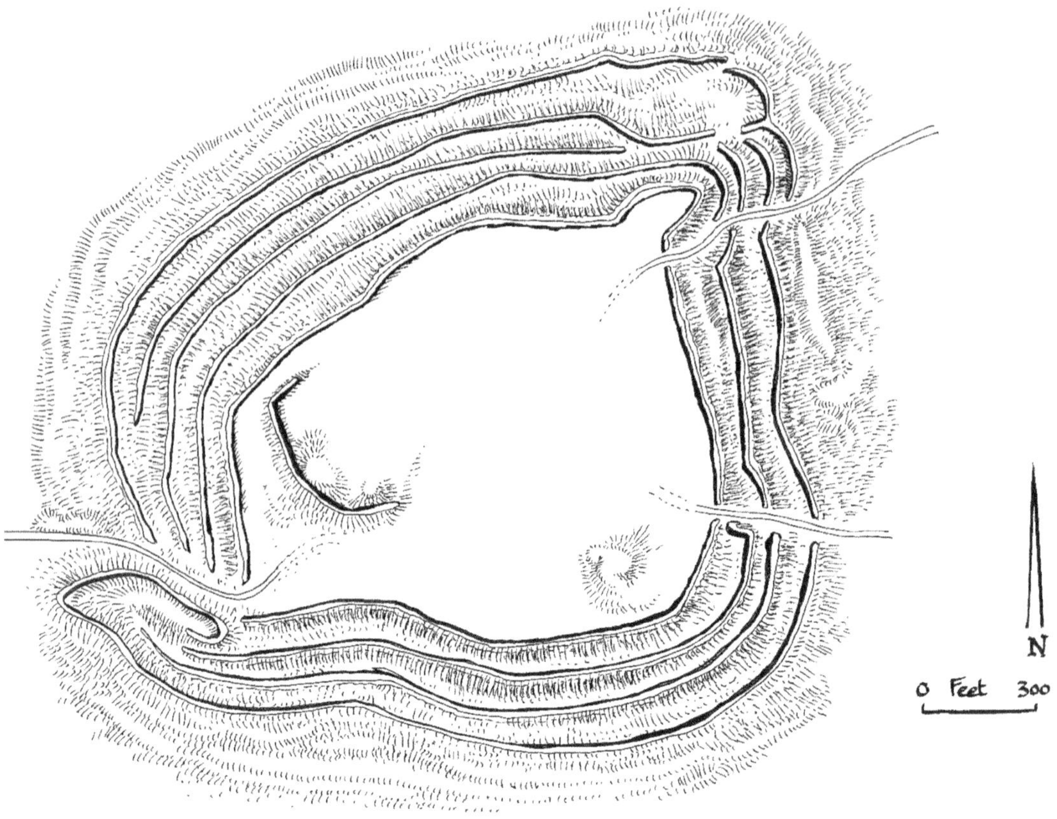

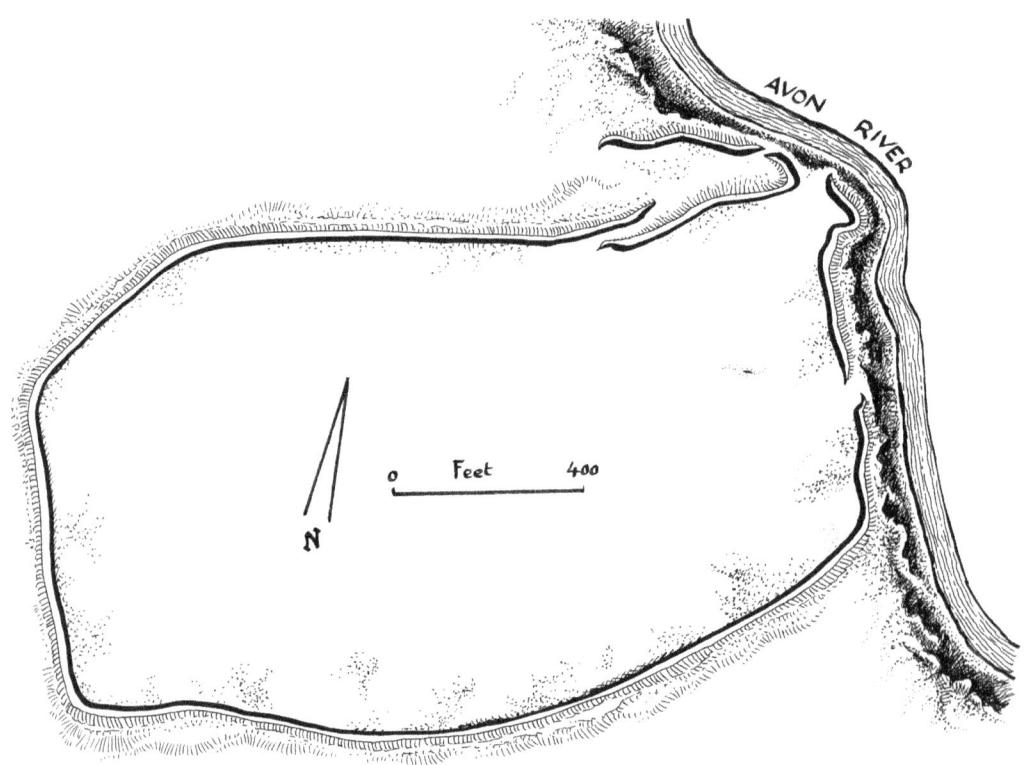

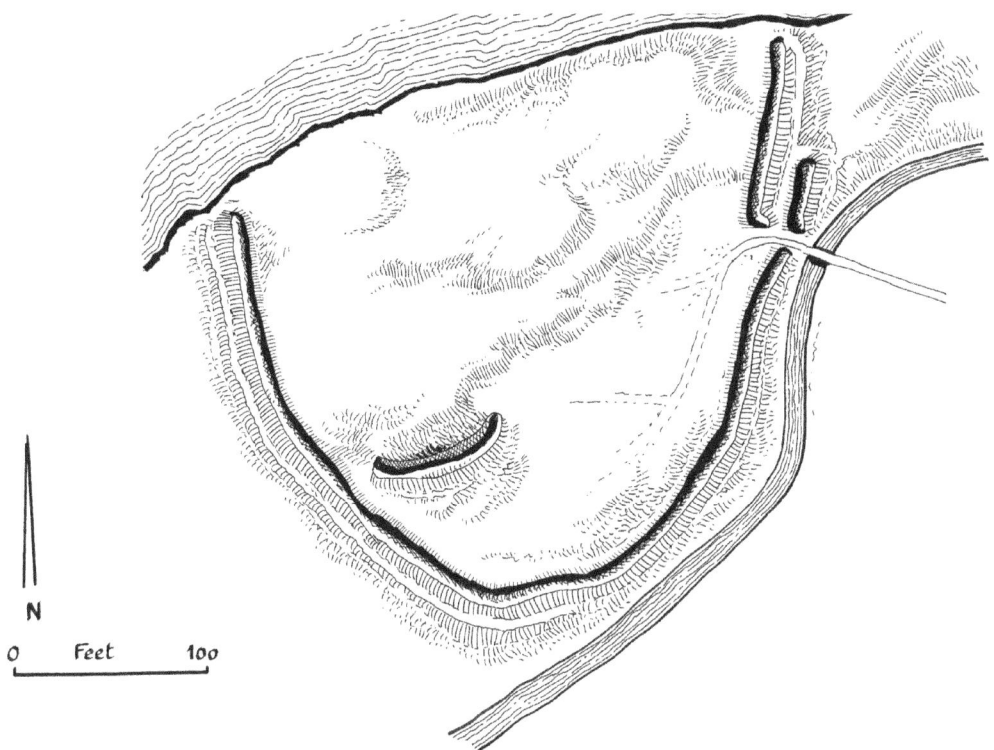

Above: *Daw's Castle (or Dart's Castle or Dane's Castle), located just west of Watchet, a port town in Somerset, England, is an excellent example of a sea cliff fort. The enclosure is situated on an east-west cliff about 80 m above the sea, on a tapering spur of land bounded by the Washford River to the south and east, as it flows to the sea at Watchet, about 1 km east. The ramparts of the fort would have formed a semicircle backing onto the sheer cliffs, but coastal erosion has reduced the size of the enclosure, and later destruction by farming, limekilns, and the contruction of the B3191 road has left only about 300 m of ramparts visible today. The fort may be of Iron Age origin, but it was rebuilt and fortified as a burh by King Alfred, as part of his defense against Viking raids from the Bristol Channel around A.D. 878. It would have been one of a chain of forts and coastal lookout posts, connected by the Herepath, or military road, which allowed Alfred to move his army along the coast, covering Viking movements at sea.*

Opposite top: *The Iron Age Cadbury Castle is located in the parish of Congresbury near the village of Yatton in North Somerset. Cadbury is a good illustration of a multivallate hill fort featuring four terraced earthwork banks and ditches and a stand of trees enclosing an area of about eight and a half acres. The hill fort was refortified on several occasions as its occupation extended into the post–Roman period.*

Bottom: *Bathampton Down, located east of Bath in Somerset, England, is a pre–Roman enclosure on a 669-feet-high (204 m) flat plateau in a bend of the River Avon. The univallate enclosure is roughly rectangular in shape. On the northeast side the ground falls down steeply into a meander of the River Avon, 558 feet (170 m) below, and there is a single rampart and flat-bottomed ditch on the other three sides. The date of these earlier earthworks is unknown. The total area enclosed is about 80 acres (32 hectares), but no evidence of human settlement within the site has ever been found. The extended perimeter, the poor univallate wall and gentle slope to the south mean it would have been difficult to defend. So it is generally accepted that Bathampton Down was an enclosure for animals, not a defended hill fort. This clearly illustrates that not all pre–Roman earth enclosures were fortified villages. The site is now part of a golf course behind the University of Bath.*

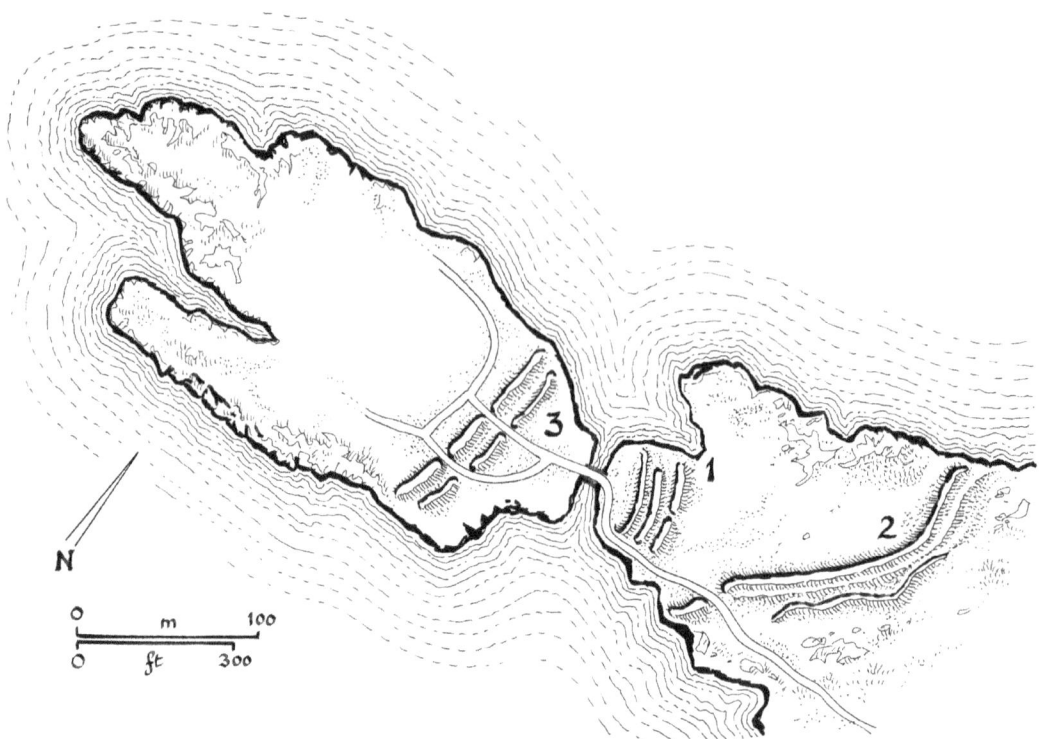

The Celtic fortress of Trevelgue Head, located to the north of Newquay in Cornwall, is a typical example of an island/promontory fort. This site must have been of major importance in prehistoric times because it sheltered a port used by merchants trading the local tin during the Bronze Age. The earthworks that are visible today, however, belong to the Iron Age. On the landward side three pairs of banks and ditches (1) guarded the approach, a fourth earthwork (2) lying further to the east and cutting off nearly 600 feet of the head. A second group of three banks and ditches (3) defended the eastern end of the island. These rock-cut ditches and banks are all massive, the outermost being 12 feet deep and its bank 6–8 feet high. They enclose an area of nearly 6 acres. Within, a series of dry-stacked stone huts has been excavated. The site was occupied from about the third century B.C. until the early Middle Ages.

rather likely to have been merely individual farmsteads or animal pens. When it came to constructing hill forts, whether in Britain, France or elsewhere in Europe, the procedure was quite similar. First of all, a suitable site was selected, sometimes one which was already of some significance to the people in the area. Many hill forts were built on a hilltop with artificial defensive ramparts adapted to and following the steep natural slopes, but other designs existed. For example, placement on top of an inaccessible ridge or spur with precipitous slopes on two or three sides, and artificial man-made fortifications only on the side facing the level approaches. A variant location could be a promontory above the confluence of two rivers, or in the sharp bend of a river's meander (e.g., Caer Alyn in Wales). Another location could be on top of a cliff overlooking a seacoast or the shore of a lake with semi-circular crescent-shaped ramparts backing onto the straight slope. Similarly a sea promontory could offer excellent natural defenses, only demanding a strong linear earthwork across the narrow neck of land leading to the peninsula if there were steep cliffs or rocky shores on the three other sides. These dispositions were common on rocky and indented coasts in Ireland, Scotland, Cornwall, Brittany and Wales. The ramparts could be reinforced with thorny bushes, or with a fence of wooden stakes, a palisade, but on a good natural site this was hardly necessary. So natural cliffs, precipitous slopes, and promontories not only enhanced the defenses, but saved a lot of hard and long labor. Placing a fortress or a refuge on a high and naturally protected location presented several main advantages. The defenders could see the approach of danger, have time to prepare to counter it, and, from the summit, have command of the surrounding area. The high position placed attackers at a disadvantage. After having scaled the hill, they would be fatigued and submitted to projectiles thrown and dropped by the rested defenders. But if natural inaccessibility favored defenses in the case of crisis, such sites, however, were inconvenient for the purpose of permanent peacetime dwelling. Being remote from a supply of water and far from grazing lands, they greatly complicated the daily life of a community. Hill forts and promontory and cliff castles also had another major demerit; it must have been impossible to escape or retreat from them if an enemy did manage to break in. So fortified settlements and large enclosures for cattle were often built in lowlands on top of gently sloping hills or on top of flat plateaus with limited natural protection. There, one could possibly take advantage of a marsh or a riverbed, for example, but in low locations strong artificial defensive positions were always badly required.

Walls and Ditches

Early Iron Age hill forts were univallate (with a single circuit of ramparts and ditches), following the contours around the crown of a hill, but they became more complicated or multivallate (with more than one defensive earthwork, ditch, or additional outer work protecting the weakest approaches). As time passed at least some of them were enlarged. One reason, it seems, for the addition of new ramparts and ditches alongside the existing ones was the introduction of the sling as a throwing weapon. It is thought that it became necessary for the defenders to put a greater distance between themselves and the attackers to keep out of the weapons' range. Indeed, in dry weather, slingers could throw red-hot clay pellets to set afire the thatched houses within the defenses. Curiously, the bow was known but only used for hunting. The strengthening of the defenses might also have been a response to increasing inter-tribal tensions leading to armed conflicts, and the coming of new raiders and invaders.

While the hill forts' outline was generally very simple (in most cases just following the contour of the hill), the earth- and stoneworks piled up, the palisades erected and the ditches dug were often quite massive and impressive, and the necessitated enormous efforts on the part of their builders. Today remnants of hill forts' banks are gently sloping grassy mounds or tumbled masses of loose stones, but when occupied they were formidable, almost vertical walls. Whatever their size, wherever their location, hill fort defenses were basically similar, simple and effective. First a trench was dug all the way around the intended perimeter, the soil being thrown up on the inner rim of the excavation. When an appropriate height had been reached, one had obtained a fundamental feature of fortification: a deep outer ditch and a high inner rampart. From prehistory until today, the ditch has always been an essential element of fortification, forming a passive but nonetheless extremely effective obstacle in its own right. In military terms, the inner side of the ditch at the foot of the rampart is called the *scarp*. The opposite outer side is called the *counterscarp*. With the exception of rock-cut ditches, which tended to be somewhat irregular, ditches were typically V-shaped in cross-section and from 20 to 30 feet wide and 8 to 12 feet deep, although the shape, width and depth could vary. Between the ditch scarp and the front of a revetted rampart a space, known as a *berm*, was usually left, most probably to prevent the undermining of the rampart by erosion of the ditch edge.

The rampart consisted of a simple earth wall, or a raised mass of earth reinforced with wooden beams. Dimensions varied considerably. At their largest hill fort ramparts could be up to 20 feet high, although the majority were shorter. If the region was rocky, loose stones and boulders were sometimes manhandled into position; the wall was made vertical and consolidated with rough masonry or *dry stone* (or *rock fence*, a building method by which structures are constructed from carefully selected interlocking stones without any mortar to bind them together). In certain cases the wall could also be revetted with wooden poles, wattle hurdles or planks, depending upon the right sort of wood or rock being available, the stone and/or pole reinforcement acting as buttresses. The top of the wall was leveled in order to form a walkway (probably covered by a duckboard or flat pounded-stone), and surmounted by a continuous man-high palisade forming a breastwork intended to protect the defenders. The rear of the bank would be finished off in various ways, either by a sloping ramp, a series of steps or an inner back revetment giving the rampart a box-like cross-section. Finally, the ground beyond the walls and ditches was cleared of vegetation, thus forming a bare slope (called in military engineering a *glacis*) on which any attacker was exposed to killing missiles during the whole of his approach to the actual defenses.

Inevitably due to weather erosion and the attrition of time, the timbers rotted, the earth crumbled, and the berms, scarps and counterscarps sagged and became overgrown with vegetation. Therefore the ramparts had to be constantly checked and maintained and periodically cleared, repaired and rebuilt, and the ditches cleaned out from debris and collapsed materials.

The construction method used was coined by archaeologists *murus gallicus*. The *murus gallicus* (Gallic wall), encountered in Gaul by Julius Caesar during his campaigns of 52 B.C., is described in Caesar's work entitled *De Bello Gallico* (*On Gallic Wars*, Book VII, § 23). A rather similar method of building defensive walls for Iron Age hill forts and oppida in Europe was the so-called *Pfostenschlitzmauer* (meaning post-slot wall in German). This manner, used in central Europe, including northern Germany, Bavaria and the Czech Republic, was characterized by vertical wooden beams set into the front stone facing. The rampart was constructed from a timber

1. Prehistoric Fortifications   17

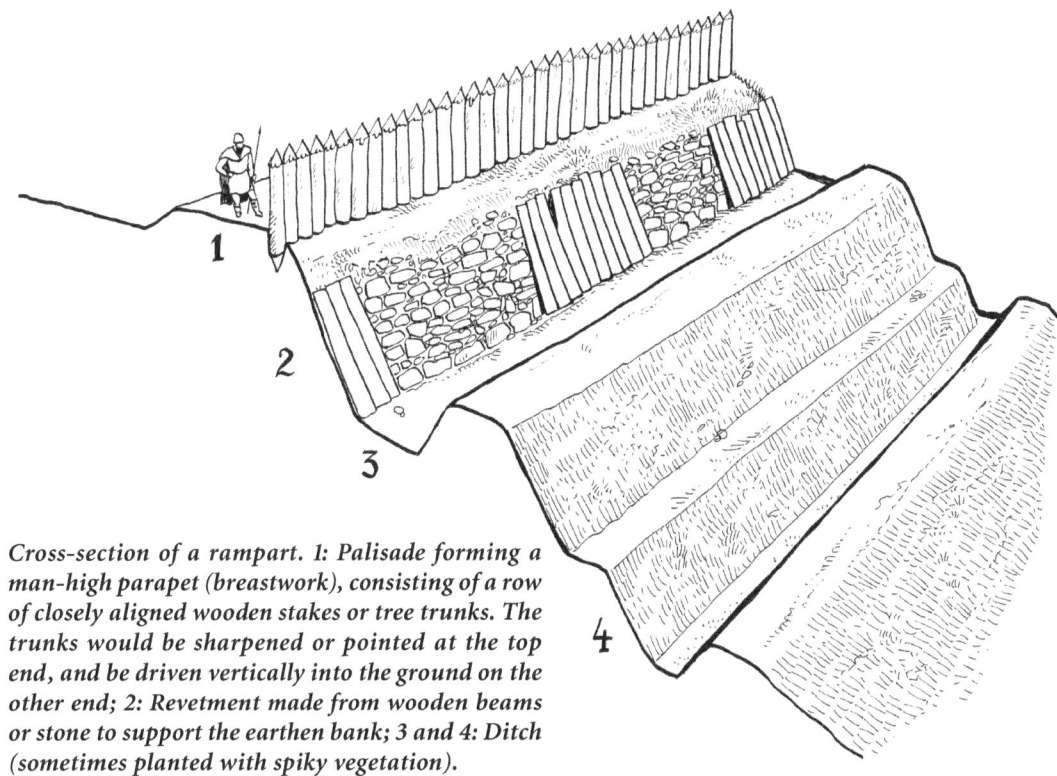

Cross-section of a rampart. 1: Palisade forming a man-high parapet (breastwork), consisting of a row of closely aligned wooden stakes or tree trunks. The trunks would be sharpened or pointed at the top end, and be driven vertically into the ground on the other end; 2: Revetment made from wooden beams or stone to support the earthen bank; 3 and 4: Ditch (sometimes planted with spiky vegetation).

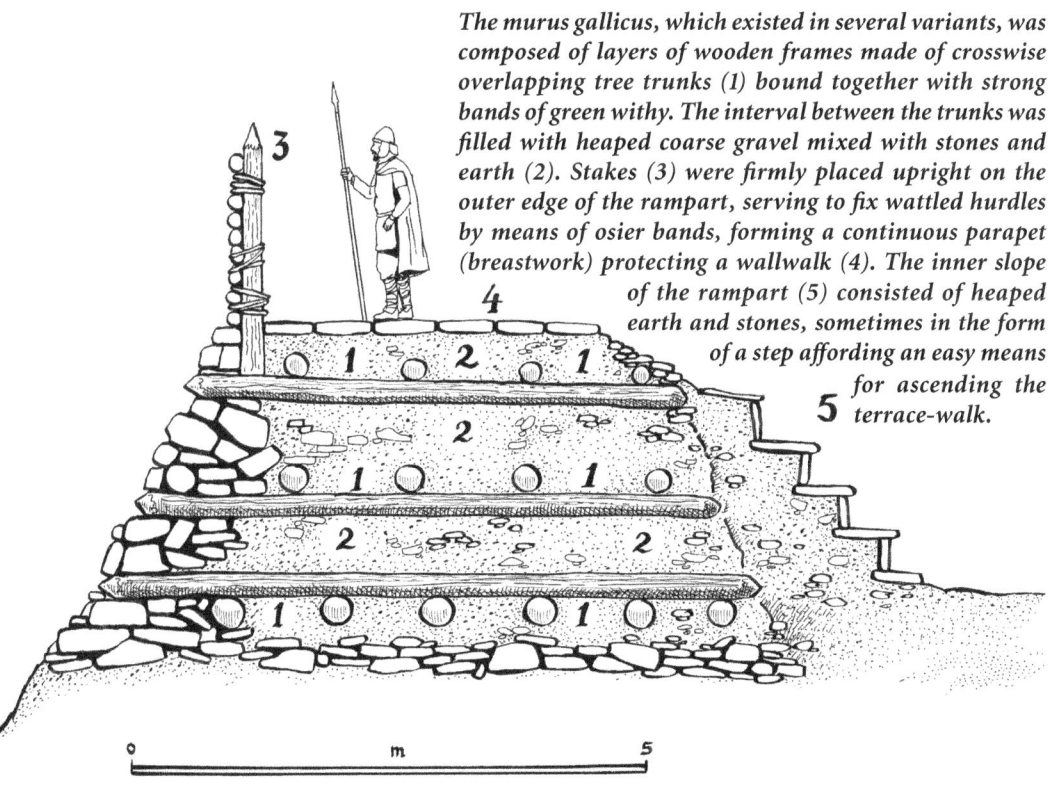

The murus gallicus, which existed in several variants, was composed of layers of wooden frames made of crosswise overlapping tree trunks (1) bound together with strong bands of green withy. The interval between the trunks was filled with heaped coarse gravel mixed with stones and earth (2). Stakes (3) were firmly placed upright on the outer edge of the rampart, serving to fix wattled hurdles by means of osier bands, forming a continuous parapet (breastwork) protecting a wallwalk (4). The inner slope of the rampart (5) consisted of heaped earth and stones, sometimes in the form of a step affording an easy means for ascending the terrace-walk.

Cross-section of a Pfostenschlitzmauer. The profile of the Celtic wall could of course vary, including either a sloping dump or glacis with palisade; or an earth rampart piled behind a wooden beam revetment, forming a palisade; or a timber-laced murus gallicus filled with earth and stone with stone revetment.

lattice filled with earth or rubble. The transverse crossbeams could also protrude through the stone facing, as with *murus gallicus* used in Gaul and western Germany. The construction method is also known as *Kelheim-style*, named after the extensive ramparts at the oppidum of Kelheim, Bavaria (south Germany). Pfostenschlitzmauer, murus gallicus and Kelheim existed in numerous variants and adaptations to local conditions, so one should not be too dogmatic about wall and ditch construction. Many later hill forts in Britain were built without timber or stone reinforcements.

To an outsider a hill fort revetted with stone must have had from a distance all the appearance of a massive stone wall rather than an earthen bank. This would have radiated an impression of strength and pride intended to overawe the leader's own subjects as well as to deter the enemy.

As can be easily imagined, the amount of labor involved in the construction of a hill fort was colossal, and completion took years. Slaves, but also the whole tribe, including free men, women and children, were put to work with tools, which were ridiculously rudimentary by modern standards, such as deer antler picks to break up the soil, shoulder blades of oxen to shovel it out, and wicker baskets to carry it to the bank, while heavy stones and tree trunks were carried by hand. The construction method also required men with skill in carpentry and by implication some form of long-term forestry management. Modern calculations have estimated that the volume of wood used for the construction of the ramparts of Cadbury Castle (a perimeter of 1,100 m) would have involved about 21 kilometers of planking, plus some 900 vertical support beams. The architects who designed the hill forts are, of course, unknown. It may be argued that the term "architect" is an inappropriate word to use of unlettered designers. The fact remains that all these impressive works were laid out (without any writing, papers, plans, mathematics, or surveying instruments) under the direction of builders who, we may assume, had to keep the general layout in their head and do all their calculations by a combination of mental arithmetics and inspired guesswork. Hill forts form one of the most substantial monument remnants of the prehistoric period, and even today their visible remains are eloquent testimony to the tenacity and building capabilities of the early inhabitants of the British Isles.

Entrances

The entrances were the weakest spots in the system, especially vulnerable to a rush assault. Therefore they received special attention, and were fitted with more or less elaborate defensive works. A large number of hill fort entrances were only narrow openings fitted with a timber gate at some convenient point in order to give access to the interior. When only a gap in the wall, it indicated an enclosure, rather than a properly defended position. Genuine fortified sites would have had wooden gates perhaps with overhead guardhouses and lookouts to check on incoming and outgoing traffic, coupled with more or less sophisticated arrangements. An elaborate and common approach was to have the main ramparts turn inward or outward, and to have them widened and raised for controlling and dominating the entrance. Sometimes there was a linear hallway consisting of a straight parallel pair of ramparts dominating and restricting the entrance, and projecting either inward or outward, or occasionally overlapping along the main rampart. There was a relentless tendency toward elaboration and doubling-up. Sometimes entrances were complex structures with bending corridors and multiple overlapping or convoluted outer works, staggered or interwoven multivallate ramparts planted with spiky vegetation, narrow zigzag entranceways twisting and turning between additional mounds which masked the entrance. These had timber gates and often included a sort of gatehouse fitted with a guardhouse or a tower-like structure featuring raised combat platforms with well-planned lines of fire. When the ditch was continuous, there was probably some form of bridge, perhaps nothing more than some tree trunks or beams with planks, which could be quickly removed when all occupants were safely inside. Clearly, elaborate defenses were intended to defend the weakest part of the hill fort by preventing direct approach, lengthening the time the attackers took to reach the gateway, and channeling them into a narrow front where they would be more than normally vulnerable. Archaeological investigations have revealed that elaborate entrances were additional features, built after the original fortifications, when some advances in tactics had been made.

No doubt necromancy was invoked. Druids may have performed human

Top: *Hill fort entrances. Gateway with protruding sides in rampart.* Middle: *Inturned type in revetted rampart.*

Below: *Entrance at Moel Y Gaer (Llandedr), Clwyd. The constricted access featured an overlapping arrangement, the rampart on one side passing in front of the rampart on the other in the entrance area.*

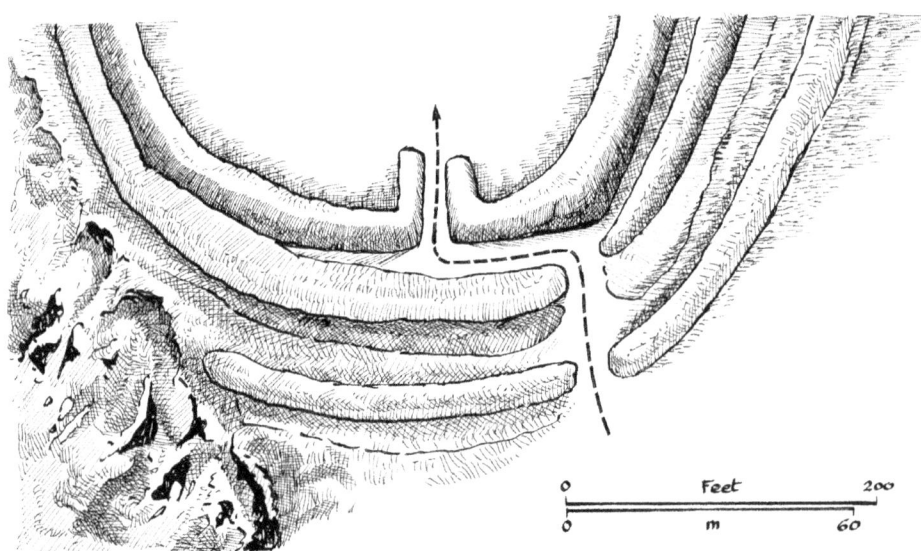

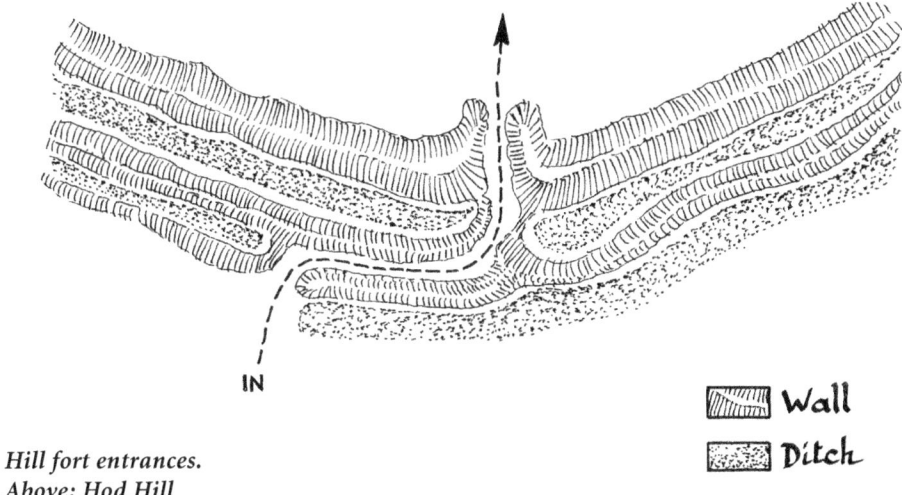

Hill fort entrances.
Above: Hod Hill
Below: Maiden Castle

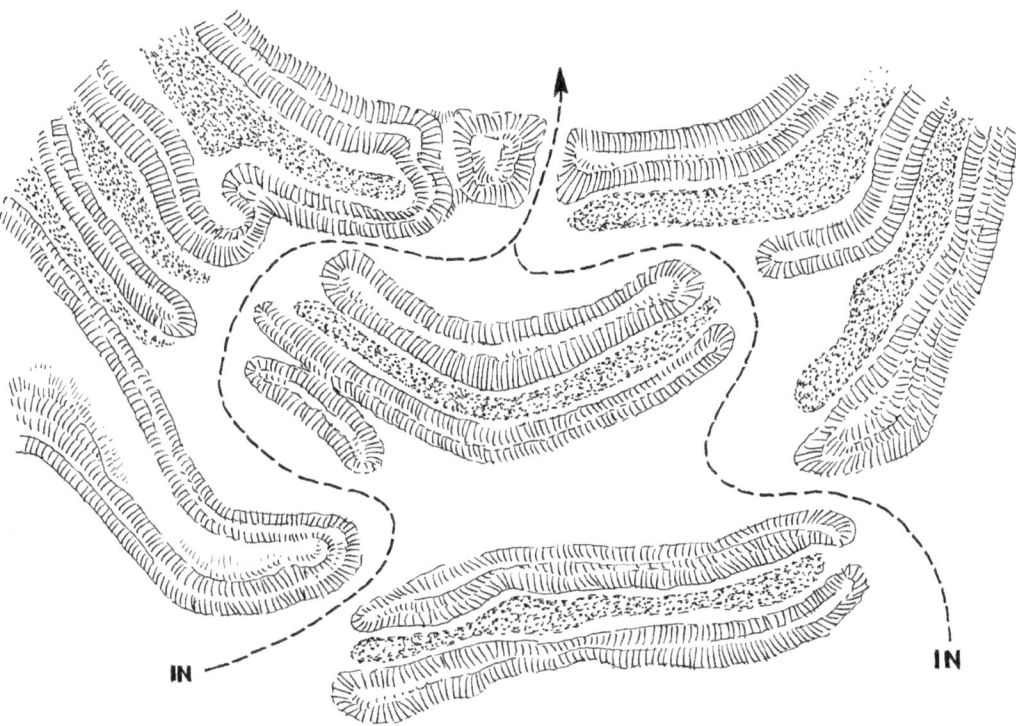

sacrifices to ensure the protection of the gods, the corpse then being buried within the earth walls, especially near the entrances. At both Maiden Castle and Hod Hill sacrificial skeletons have been found within the ramparts.

Functions of Hill Forts

The idea of building hill forts, these spectacular monuments, which dominate the highest points of the blocks of chalk in downland Sussex, Hampshire, Wiltshire or Dorset, came to Britain as a continental influence. The reason for their emergence in Britain, and their purpose, has been a subject of debate. Two main functions are traditionally attributed to hill forts: fortifying a permanent settlement, and providing temporary refuge in time of danger.

In favor of the first function, it has been argued that hill forts could have been military sites constructed in response to invasion from continental Europe, sites built by invaders, or sites that were a military reaction to social tensions caused by an increasing population and consequent pressure on agriculture. The dominant view since the 1960s has been that the increasing use of iron led to social changes in Britain. Deposits of iron ore were located in different places than the tin and copper ore necessary to make bronze. As a result, trading patterns shifted, and the old elites lost their economic and social status. Power passed into the hands of a new group of people. It is also believed that population increase played a role and that the hill forts provided defensive possibilities for the community at those times when the stress of an increasing population burst out into conflict and open warfare. Hill forts would have been functional as defensive strongholds when there were tensions and some of them were attacked and destroyed, but undoubtedly those erected in fertile lands were also used to control agricultural land to support a large community. Monumental defenses such as Maiden Castle indicate that the land was disputed and communities fought each other for control. Some hill forts were therefore permanent fortified settlements, which would have been tribally important centers where the chief, leader, or king of the area would live with his extended family, enjoying the accumulated and increasing wealth of his people, safe from attack, and forming a base for launching his warriors upon his enemies. Permanent hill forts were true strongholds; however, they were not proper towns, and cannot be considered truly urban because they were so closely related to agriculture and storage. They were rather more protected villages, or fortified "town-like settlements," a form of proto-urbanism. The (often large) size of open ground enclosed strongly suggests the provision of accommodation not only for people, but for flocks and herds as well. Without doubt a permanently occupied hill fort was a self-contained unit living in autarchy. It included the usual Celtic living accommodation, a circular hut having a single room with walls made from mud and a thatched roof; workshops for the making of goods and a forge for the working of metal; enclosures and corrals for cattle, as well as fields, meadows and orchards; corn-drying racks, granary huts, sheds, pits, underground souterrains (in Ireland and Scotland), and fogous (in Cornwall) for food storage; water in the form of a well, spring, cistern, brook or river in sufficient supply to meet the needs of the occupants and their animals; and an ample supply of javelins, rocks and projectiles for slings—in time of war or when a conflict was likely. In addition a hill fort would have included religious places for worship, rituals and offerings, a dwelling for the druids surrounded by a sacred enclosure, as well as burial sites, necropoles, and graves typically located outside the ramparts.

Across Britain, many hill forts fell out of use in the 100 years around the turn of the millennium. It has been suggested that this, and the contemporary change in material culture of the Britons (e.g., an increase in craft industries), was caused by frequent and gradually more important interaction with the Roman Empire. The introduction of coinage and the development of long-range trade have been taken as evidence for increasing relationships with groups of people over large areas and the emergence of tribal identities. The developing industries may have resulted in a shift away from the hill fort warrior elites, whose power was based on agriculture. Such change is not obvious everywhere in Britain, but there was a trend of abandonment of hill forts in some areas and a proliferation of small, less-protected or undefended farmsteads, indicating a possible migration of population.

The second main function attributed to hill forts was that of a place of temporary refuge. Hill forts were not necessarily intended for permanent occupation, but only occupied seasonally, or in times of strife. Some were refuges into which the local population could withdraw in time of unrest, upheaval, or threat of enemy raids, to emerge when danger was gone. When such a place was intended to be occupied only for a short while, it would probably have no well, relying on rainwater collected in cisterns. Such a refuge would also be difficult to keep supplied as it was likely to be difficult to access, and therefore would not be able to withstand a long attrition siege by determined and numerous aggressors. The expectation was that attackers would be simply raiders from the neighboring area who would rush through the land stealing anything movable and then return to their own territory before any large force could be gathered to oppose them. The fortified refuge's main usefulness was thus to protect inhabitants from the neighboring villages for short periods against small enemy gangs and passing raiders.

This being said, it is probably unwise to be too dogmatic about what prehistoric sites were used for. The size, number and types involved, the widespread distribution, and the very long period (eight centuries) during which they were built, used, destroyed, rebuilt, enlarged, re-used and eventually abandoned make any single function unlikely. History and life are never black-or-white and a lot of events can occur in a timespan of 800 years. It is indeed unlikely that a huge, heavily fortified and complex hill fort enjoyed the same function as a small univallate site. There was probably a whole range of functions, which varied from area to area, from period to period and indeed from type to type. A few large and well-situated hill forts would have been important meeting places combining numerous functions. In economic terms they were probably market and trading centers, in military terms important bases, and in political terms they were without doubt provincial capitals. Many others were much too small to have housed even a village. Others must surely have been connected in some way with livestock, separating people from animals, being large cattle pounds used as safe grazing ground, but also used as a refuge for people in time of danger. Some coastal promontory hill forts look much too bleak and exposed for permanent settlement, although they could still be temporary refuges, but at the same time, their location near an accessible shore along a major sea route makes another function plausible, that of trading place, perhaps used seasonally when weather conditions suited. There may well be other functions, which we cannot yet perceive, and which will emerge only as a result of future archaeological discoveries.

SIEGE WARFARE

As for siege warfare, it was without doubt rudimentary. Attackers would use various techniques to force the defenders to surrender. They could employ treachery, and take advantage of quarrel and dissention between the defenders. They could display their force in order to impress and deter them, they could threaten them of terrible retaliation and finally obtain capitulation by means of negotiation under heavy pressure.

The sheer length of the perimeter of a hill fort was actually a weakness; the defenders could not man the whole wall so attackers could use surprise, attacking at dawn when the guards were tired after a night's watch, crossing the ditches and climbing the wall in silence, neutralizing sentries and then pouring into the fortification.

The technique of blockade — encircling and isolating a fortified place and waiting until the defenders are forced to surrender when they run short of supplies — was probably impossible due to the limited number of attackers, the length of the defended perimeter and the fact that such a place would probably have enough supplies to hold on for a long period.

Until the coming of gunpowder and efficient siege artillery in the late 15th century, all attacks on strongholds had to be mounted at close range. In the case of a direct assault, attackers often concentrated on the entrance, attempting to demolish the gate with a battering ram, or tried to destroy the wooden palisade by fire. In the meantime another party would try to scramble over the top of the palisade with scaling ladders, very insecure footing for hand-to-hand combat. Sophisticated hurling machines like the catapult were unknown, but slingers and warriors would try to cover the assaulting party by throwing pieces of rock and javelins. Projectile-throwing, however, rarely repaid the effort, as stout palisades and thick ramparts easily absorbed the energy directed against them. The besieged, on the other hand, taking advantage of their elevated position, would defend themselves by repulsing the ladders, slinging stones, throwing down javelins and spears, dropping rocks, stones and other projectiles upon the attackers below them. The siege could also take the form of a bloody pitched battle fought on horse, on foot or with chariots outside the walls.

For both the besiegers and the defenders, inspired and charismatic leadership, good overall morale and a good sense of collective cohesion were extremely important, but in actual combat individual factors, like determination, pugnacity and physical fitness, played a central role. But bravery was not always enough against greater odds.

The causes of such inter-tribal wars were as numerous as mankind's imperfections. Greed, ruthless egoism, conflicts of economic and political interest, desire for dominance and power, imperialism, personal or collective vendettas, the brutish cult of force and violence, group aggression, ignorance, religious extremism, lack of cooperativeness, and social disintegration and disruption were as devastating, bloody and pointless in the Iron Age as they are today.

Hill Forts in England and Wales

There are about 3,000 hill forts in England, concentrated in the south and west, with especially high numbers in the southwest peninsula (Devon and Cornwall have a total of 285 large hill forts). There are also about 570 hill forts in Wales. Although some originated in the Bronze Age, the general consensus is that the majority of hill forts in Britain were constructed during the Iron Age (between 700 B.C. and the Roman conquest of Britain in A.D. 43). By the 8th century B.C. only a few existed, but gradually the numbers increased and existing ones were strengthened. The further development seems to have occurred in the last century before the Roman conquest. In many cases, however, it is difficult to say which are prehistoric and which are of later periods, and this rough timetable applies for England only. Events in western and northern regions, as well as in Ireland, were probably delayed by a century or so, possibly more.

There are also variations from area to area in the size, type and density of sites. The largest numbers of the sites are in the western counties, namely in Dyfed and Cornwall with a majority of small univallate sites enclosing only one or two acres. Larger hill forts are found in southern England, the Cotswolds and the Welsh borderland. The Wessex region (Dorset, Wilshire, Hantshire and Berkshire) is one of the classic hill fort areas in Britain, with about 150 sites, a number of them very large and spectacular, including the most famous hill fort of all, Maiden Castle.

The Romans eventually occupied some of the hill forts, such as the military garrison at Hod Hill and Brean Down, but others were destroyed and forsaken. Some of the place names of these sites bear the suffix "-bury" (e.g., Cadbury), meaning fort. Where the Roman influence was less strongly felt, such as in uninvaded Ireland and in the unsubdued northern parts of Scotland, hill forts and other forms of fortified settlements were still built and used for several more centuries. Some hill forts were reoccupied following the end of Roman rule in the early 5th century, to defend against pirate raids and the Anglo-Saxon invasions in the 6th century. Some hill forts were reoccupied by the Anglo-Saxons during the period of Viking raids in the 9th century.

Hill Forts in Scotland

There are about one thousand hill forts in Scotland, mostly below the Clyde/Forth line, with particular emphasis on the southeast in the *(continued on page 31)*

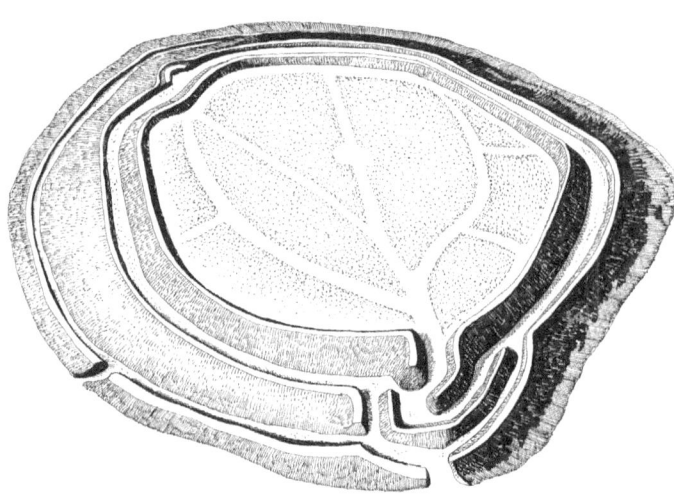

Left: *The Iron Age hill fort Danebury is located about 4 km northwest of Stockbridge and about 19 km northwest of Winchester in Hampshire. The site was built in the 6th century B.C., and remained in use for almost 500 years. Danebury was remodeled several times, making it more complex and resulting in its becoming a developed hill fort covering 12 acres (5 hectares). Today the site is protected as a Scheduled Ancient Monument and a Site of Special Scientific Interest.*

Bottom: *Dowsborough Camp (or Danesborough or Dawesbury) is an Iron Age hill fort on the Quantock Hills near Nether Stowey in Somerset, England. The site is at a height of 340 m on an easterly spur from the main Quantock ridge, with views north to the Bristol Channel, and east over the valley of the River Parrett. The oval-shaped earthwall features only a single rampart and ditch (univallate) following the contours of the hilltop, enclosing an area of 2.7 hectares. The main entrance is to the east, towards Nether Stowey, with a simpler opening to the northwest, aligned with a ridgeway leading down to Holford. A pass to the south links the hill to the main Stowey ridge, where a linear earthwork known as Dead Woman's Ditch cuts across the spur. This additional rampart was probably intended to provide an extra line of defense against attack from the main Quantock ridge to the west, and at the same time it could have marked a tribal boundary.*

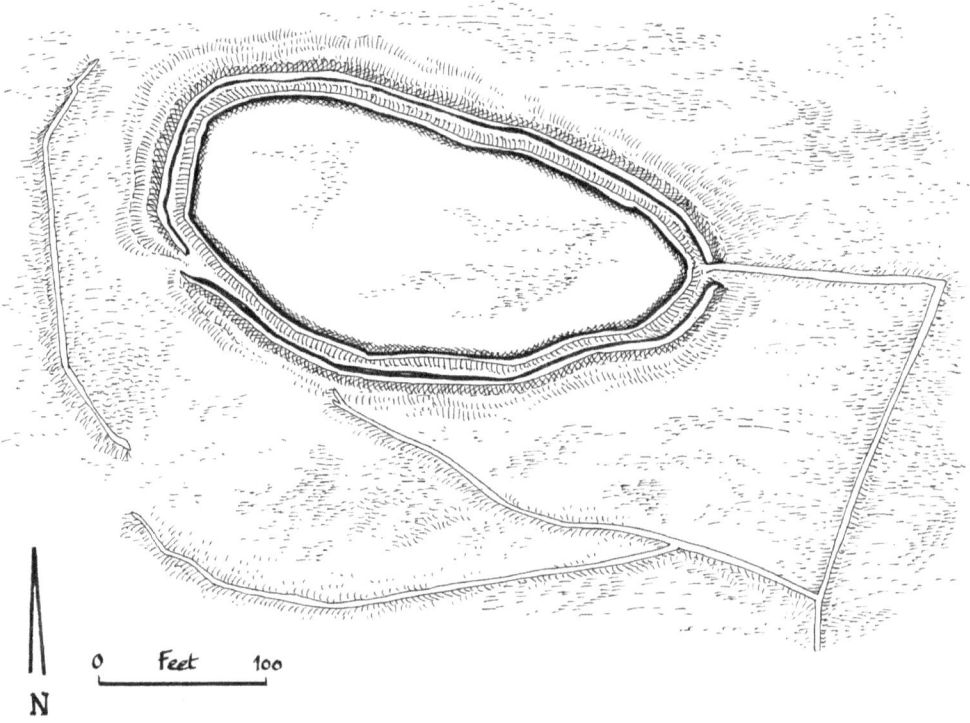

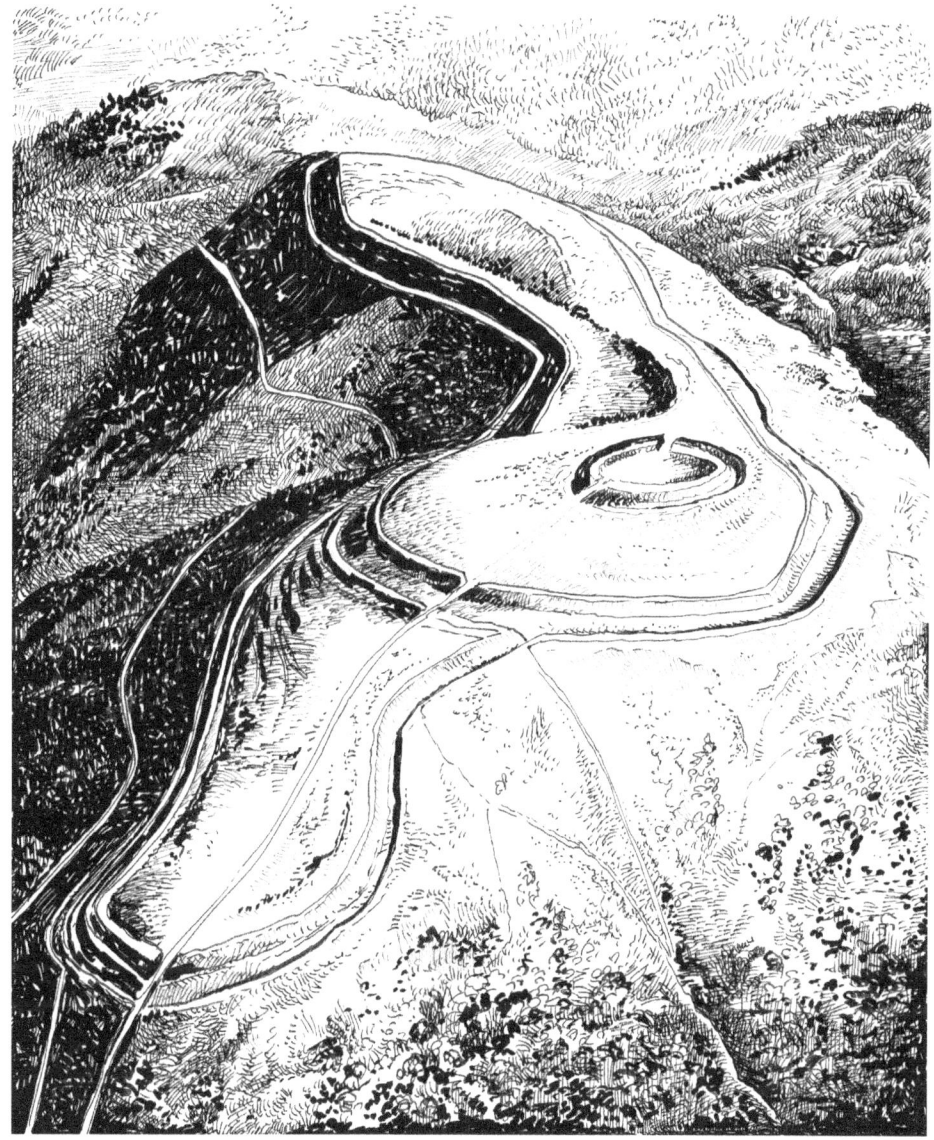

British Camp at Herefordshire Beacon. The Herefordshire Beacon is one of the Malvern Hills, a volcanic ridge running north/south for about 9 miles (13 km) in the counties of Worcestershire, Herefordshire and a small area of northern Gloucestershire, dominating the surrounding countryside and the towns and villages of the district of Malvern. Officially designated an Area of Outstanding Natural Beauty, the Herefordshire Beacon is 1,109 feet (338 m) high, and its top is crowned with an impressive Iron Age earthwork known as British Camp. This was constructed in c. 200 B.C. and in the centuries following, more earth banks and ditches were built lower down the hillside. This hill fort is one of a remarkable series of such sites that extend in a belt from the Dorset coast into northeast Wales. British Camp is long, about ⅝ mile (1 km), and large (32 acres) and also one of the most imposing of these ancient structures. The function of the remote and difficult to access British Camp remains unclear. But for its central section, it is unlikely that it could have withstood a long-sustained siege due to its large size and the absence of a natural water supply within its defenses. It is thought to have been originally built as a ritual site and a temporary refuge, but it might also have had something to do with the salt industry at the time. The site ceased to be used about A.D. 50 at the time of the Roman invasion.

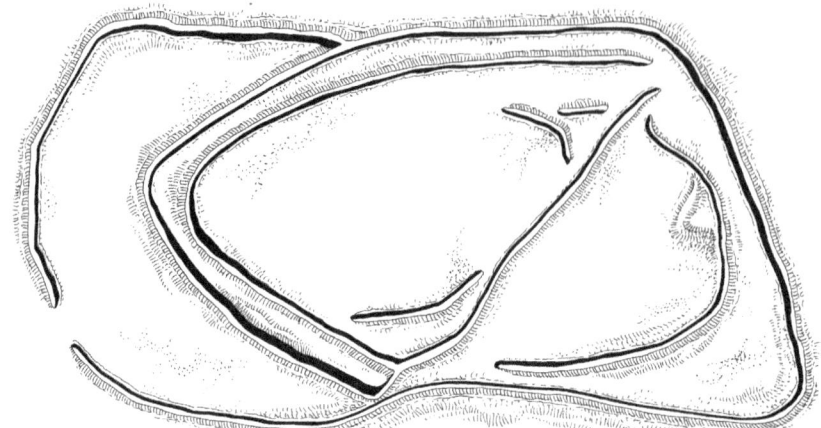

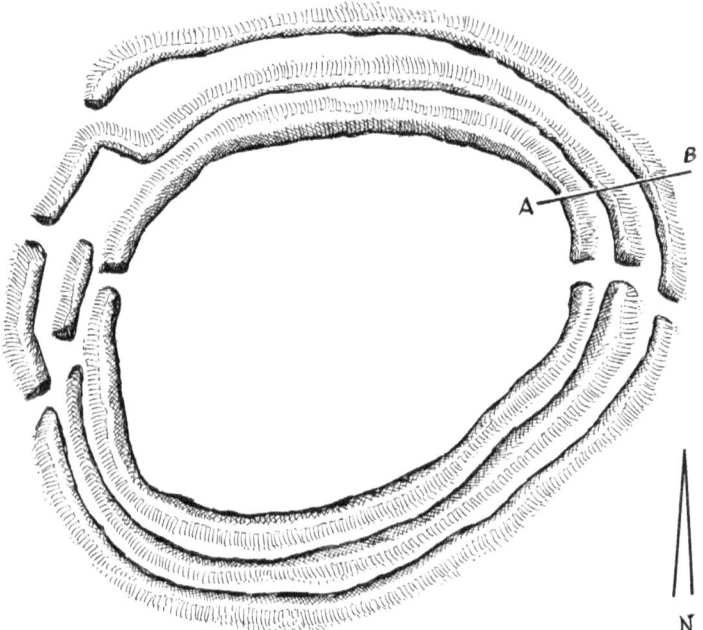

Above: *Stonea Camp*, located near March in Cambridgeshire, is situated on a low gravel island in the fens. The site was fortified with earth banks and ditches during the Iron Age to make a hill fort enclosing an area of approximately one quarter square mile, but little occupation evidence has been found. It is possible that Stonea Camp may have been the site of conflict between the Iceni and the Romans in A.D. 44, and human bones showing clear evidence of sword marks were found in one of the ditches during excavations in 1991. Excavation by the British Museum in 1980 suggested there had been some deliberate destruction by the Romans, who further asserted their authority by establishing a tower and town just to the north of Stonea Camp. The outer ditches had been levelled by agriculture in the 1970s and 1980s, but were carefully reinstated in 1991. Visible today are the earthworks remains of the defensive banks and ditches which surrounded the hill fort.

Bottom: *Badbury Rings*. This Iron Age concentric multivallate hill fort, situated near the village of Shapwick in east Dorset, dates from c. 800 B.C., and according to archaeologists was built to stem an invasion from the northeast of the country. The hill fort consists of three 40-feet-high concentric rings of banks and ditches enclosing an area of 7 hectares. There were two entrances to the site: one in the east, which is staggered to make it more difficult to attack, and one in the west. The site may have been deemed strategic in Roman times because two important roads, between Dorchester, Old Sarum (Salisbury), Bath and Hamworthy (Poole) formed a junction here.

1. Prehistoric Fortifications   29

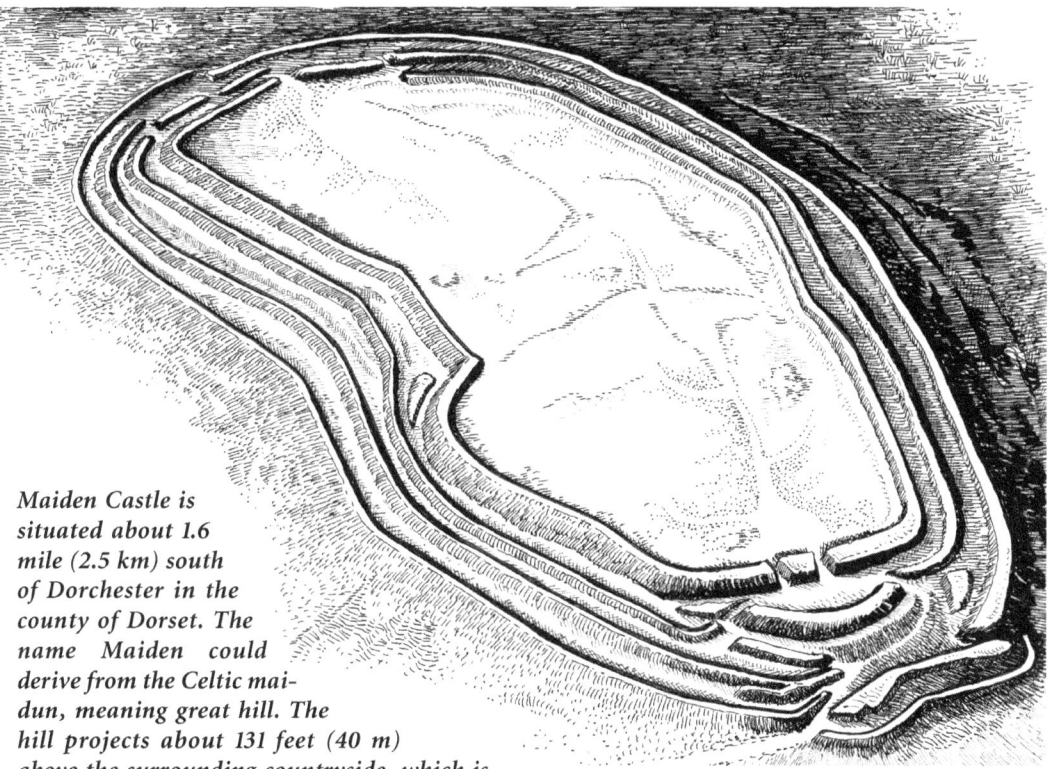

Maiden Castle is situated about 1.6 mile (2.5 km) south of Dorchester in the county of Dorset. The name Maiden could derive from the Celtic mai-dun, meaning great hill. The hill projects about 131 feet (40 m) above the surrounding countryside, which is generally about 295 feet (90 m) above sea level. The earliest archaeological evidence of human activity on the site consists of a Neolithic causewayed enclosure and bank barrow built around 4000 B.C. This was an oval area, enclosed by two small ditches, which seemed to have had a symbolic function, separating the interior of the enclosure and its activities from the outside. As the interior of the enclosure has been disturbed by later habitation and farming, the early function of the site remains obscure. The site does not appear to have been inhabited; it rather was possibly a sanctuary for rituals related to death, and a place of religious meeting, or simply a boundary marker. The enclosure was abandoned around 3400 B.C., and arrowheads discovered in the ditches suggest that activity at Maiden Castle met a violent end. In about 1800 B.C., during the Bronze Age, the site was cleared and used for growing crops before being abandoned when the soil was exhausted. Maiden Castle itself was built in about 600 B.C. In the early phase it was a simple and unremarkable site, similar to many other hill forts in Britain. Maiden Castle was one of over 100 hill forts of similar size built around the same time in the area that now forms the counties of Berkshire, Dorset, Hampshire, and Wiltshire. The defenses consisted of the V-shaped ditch and a rampart enclosing an area of 16 acres (6.4 hectares). The earthwork was probably only timber-faced around the entrances in order to impress visitors. The site was accessed by an entrance in the northwest and a double entrance in the east. The double entrance is unique in hill forts in the British Isles. The reason for a double entrance is unclear, but it has been suggested that it was a form of segregation. It is likely that several farming communities lived in the hill fort and wanted different entrances. The defenses of the early Maiden Castle were rebuilt on at least one occasion. The ditch was deepened by 4.9 to 23 feet (1.5 to 7 m). The déblai (spoil) from re-digging the ditch was deposited on the back of the rampart. At the same time, the protection around the eastern entrances was made more elaborate. A bank and ditch were constructed outside the two entrances, and an earthwork was built between them. The bank had a wall faced with limestone, which originated over 2 miles (3 km) away. It is believed that this would have created an impressive gateway, demonstrating the settlement's high status. By that time

Maiden Castle was probably densely occupied, with separate areas for habitation and storage, but unfortunately a lack of finds does not allow us to determine with certainty the inhabitants' activity on the site. About 450 B.C. the site underwent major development. The enclosed area expanded westwards, and the ditch was extended to enclose the neighboring Hog Hill. The site nearly tripled in size to 47 acres (19 hectares), making it the largest hill fort in Britain and one of the largest in Europe. At the same time, Maiden Castle's defenses were made more elaborate with the addition of further ditches and earthwalls heightened to 11 feet (3.5 m). The southern defenses were then made up of four ramparts and three ditches, but because of the steepness of the northern slope of the hill the fourth rampart did not extend all the way around, and the northern side was less defended. At the same time, the eastern entrance was again made more complex through the addition of further outer earthworks, lengthening the approach to the site. The multiple rings of ditches and earth banks were likely not just defensive but also an expression or a statement of power and authority. The expansion of Maiden Castle and the construction of monumental defenses indicate that its inhabitants, the Celtic Durotrige tribe, had become important possibly through warfare, and prosperous through economic growth and long-distance trade. Around 100 B.C. habitation at the hill fort went into decline and became limited to the eastern end of the site. Maiden Castle was occupied until the Roman conquest of Britain in A.D. 43. It is unclear whether the site was conquered by force by the Romans during Vespasian's campaigns in A.D. 43–47. After the Roman conquest the eastern part of the hill fort remained in use for a few decades, although the duration and nature of habitation is uncertain. It has been suggested that Maiden Castle was occupied as a Roman military outpost or fort and the settlement discontinued, as there is no known fort in the area and it was not uncommon for hill forts in the southwest of England to have been occupied by Roman forces. The site appears to have been totally abandoned by the end of the first century, when Durnovaria (Dorchester) rose to prominence as the civitas (regional capital) of the Durotrige tribe. In the late 4th century A.D., a Romano-Celtic temple with ancillary buildings was constructed, but this gradually fell into disuse. In the 6th century A.D. Maiden Castle was entirely abandoned and for centuries was used only for open pasture and agriculture. The site has been thoroughly investigated in the end of the 19th century and methodically excavated and surveyed in the 1920s and 1930s. Today Maiden Castle is maintained by English Heritage and open to the public all year round.

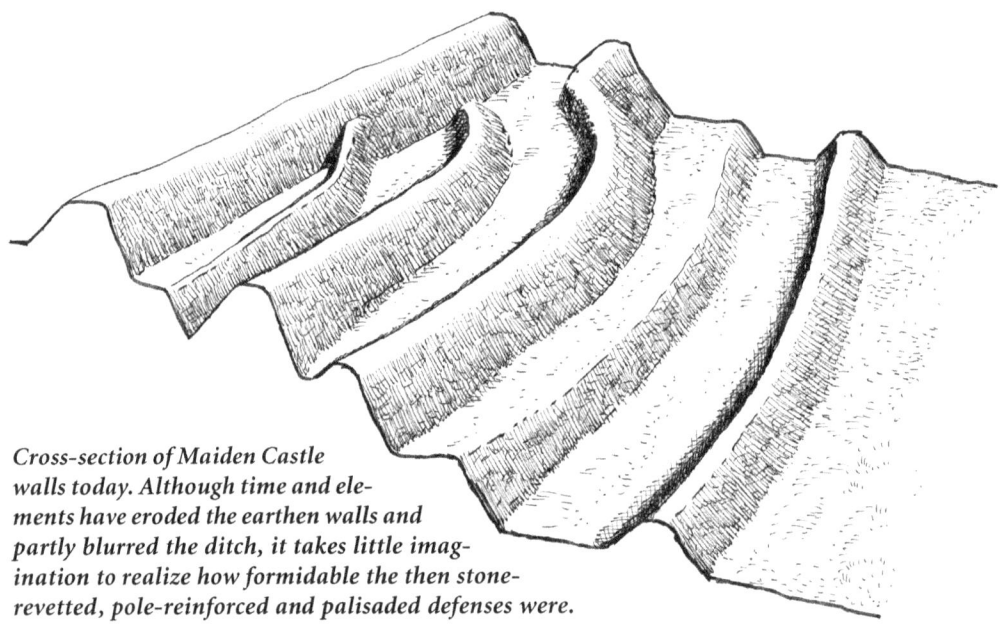

Cross-section of Maiden Castle walls today. Although time and elements have eroded the earthen walls and partly blurred the ditch, it takes little imagination to realize how formidable the then stone-revetted, pole-reinforced and palisaded defenses were.

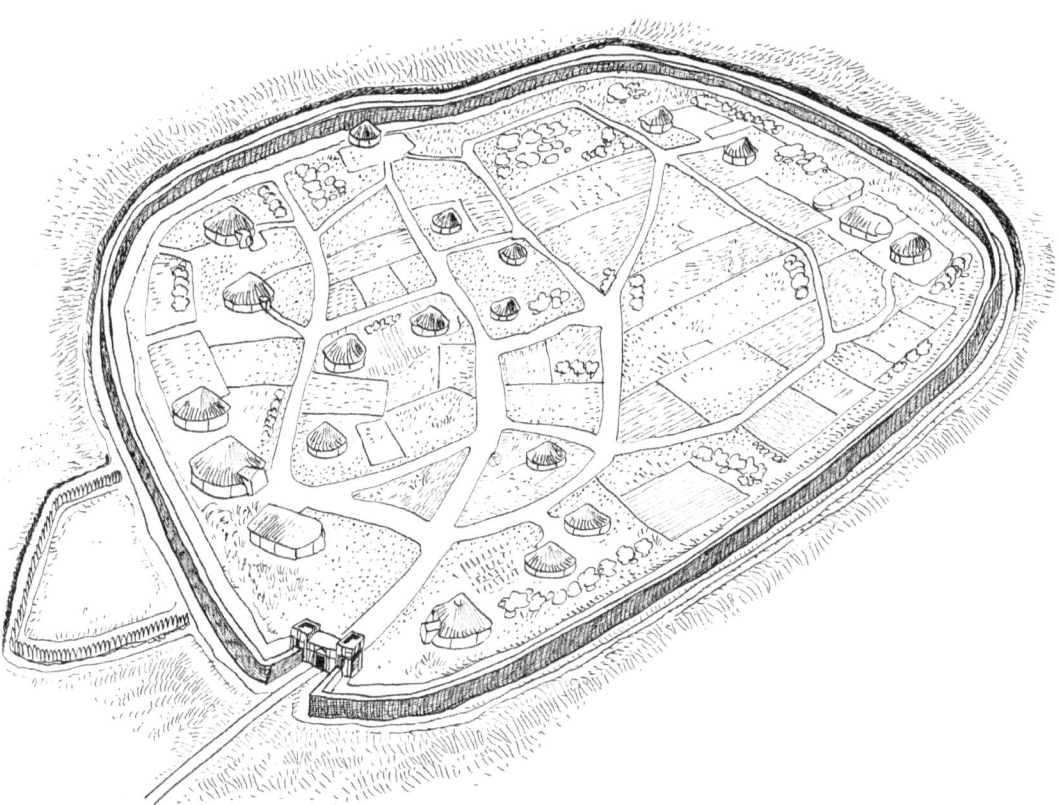

Caer Drewyn hill fort (conjectured reconstruction) is located on a hill overlooking the valley of the Afon Dyfrdwy (River Dee) near Corwen, Denbighshire, in Wales. The site is first mentioned in c. 1600 B.C. when its construction is attributed to the hero or giant Drewyn Gawr. The hill fort measures overall approximately 192 m north to south by 215 m east to west, enclosing 3.36 hectares. Unlike other Iron Age hill forts in the area, Caer Drewyn does not have earthen banks (ramparts), but a large dry-stacked stone wall which was then probably fitted with a wallwalk and breastwork. It is also hemmed with a ditch, the remains of which can still be seen today. The hill fort interior would probably have contained roundhouses constructed of stone and wood, providing shelter and safety for the occupants. The northeast inturn entrance had a sort of gatehouse with guardchambers built into it. A triangular-shaped enclosure was added to the side of the fort at a later date, probably during the Romano-British or Dark Age period, which strongly suggests that Caer Drewyn continued to be used long after the Iron Age had ended.

(*continued from page 25*) counties adjacent to the English border. In their range of sizes and types hill forts in Scotland tend to follow the tradition of southwest England and Wales rather than that of Wessex and the Marches. A high proportion of the sites are small, one acre or two, circular or nearly circular, with univallate defenses. There are, however, a small number of sites of greater size and complexity (e.g., Castle O'er, Birrenwark, Cademuir, Cardrona, White Meldon). In southwest Scotland sites are less numerous, about 100, again mostly small and often circular in plan except in promontory situations, which are fairly common in the region.

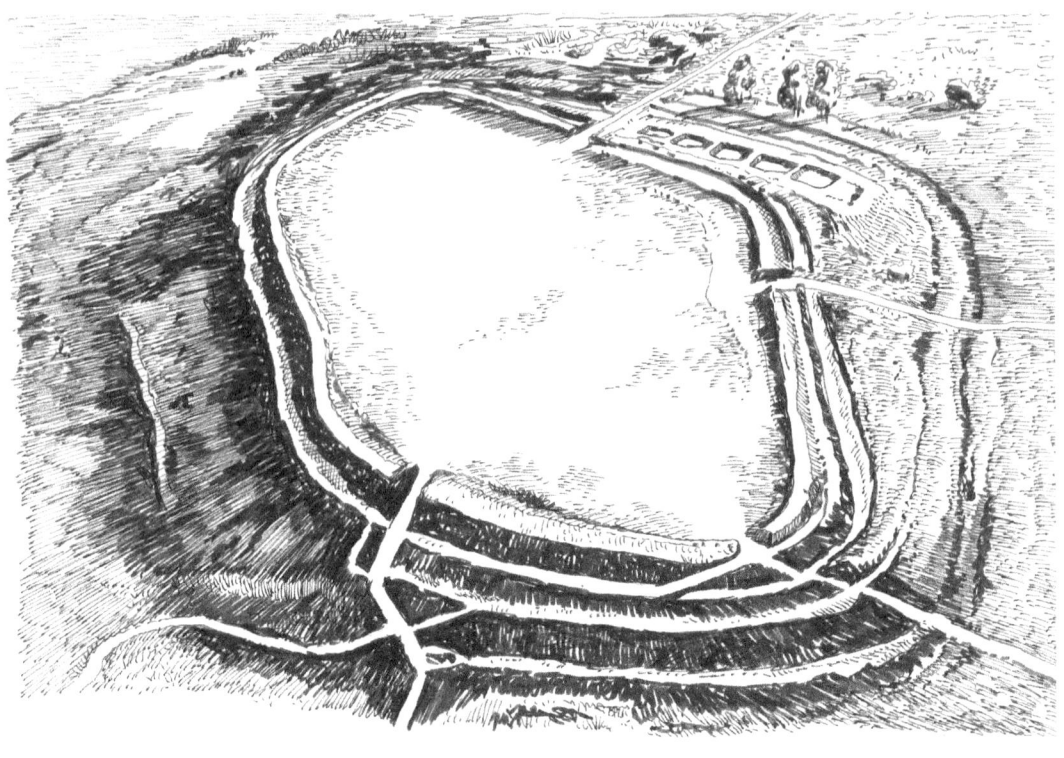

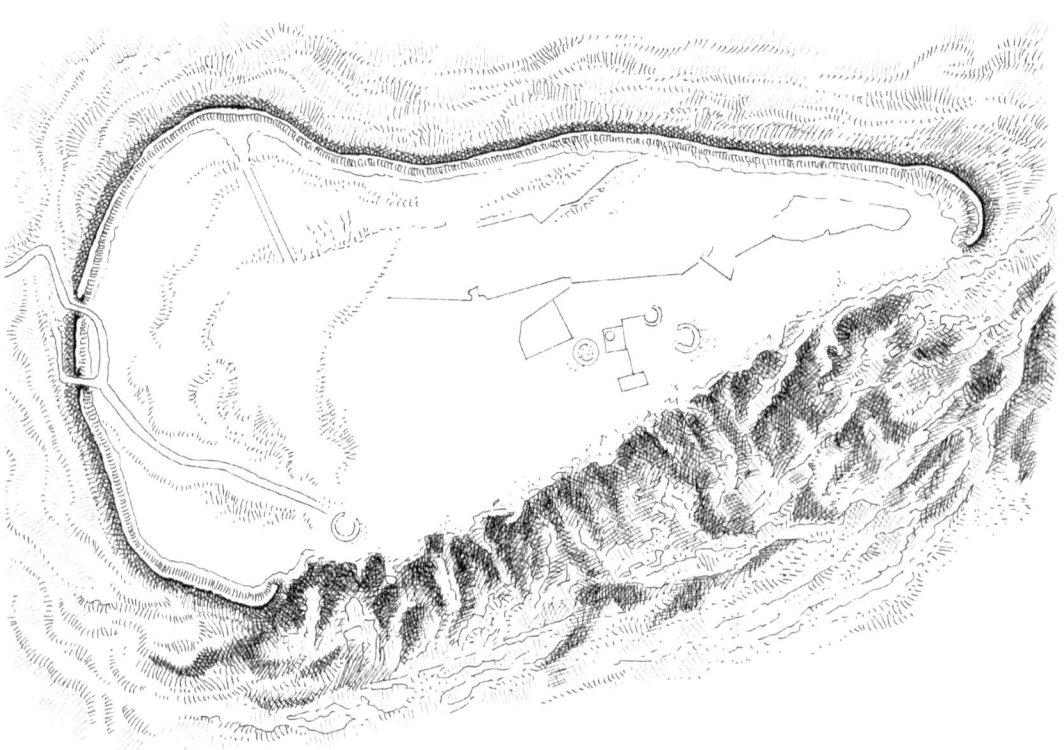

Hill Forts in Ireland

There are about 500 Iron Age hill forts in Ireland, particularly numerous in the southern half of the island. There are also thousands of *ringforts* (duns), which are smaller and a different form of settlement, and which are described separately below. A few Irish hill forts of general small univallate type, up to 20 acres, including such sites as Navan, Tara, and Freestone Hill, as well as strongly multivallate sites, clearly indicate links with hill forts in other parts of the British Isles. On the south and southwest coasts, distribution is often dictated by geology and some 200 promontory forts are recorded with defenses across the neck of the peninsula—very much the same pattern as in southwest England and southwest Wales. Some Irish hill forts have *cairns* (human-formed piles of rocks or stone constructed as monuments, tributes, and astronomical markers or landmarks) inside their boundaries and there are many speculations and theories about them.

(Continued on page 38.)

Opposite top: *Located about one mile north of Oswestry on the Welsh border in northwest Shropshire, Old Oswestry is an impressive Iron Age hill fort, covering 40 acres (6 hectares), with formidable multiple ramparts. The complexity of its defenses suggests several phases of development. The undefended site was originally occupied by a few round huts, and eventually these were enclosed by a double bank and ditch. These defenses were later rebuilt and a third bank added on all sides except the southeast, where the hill's steep slope made further strengthening unnecessary. There were two entrances through which Iron Age inhabitants would have accessed the interior, one on the western side and one on the eastern side. The western entrance is the most obvious because of a series of deep rectangular hollows. This feature cannot be found at any of the other hill forts around Shropshire, or indeed anywhere else. They also help to make the hill fort entrance one of the most elaborate in Britain. There have been many suggestions as to what these hollows would originally have been used for, including: stock-pens, storage areas, quarries, water reservoirs or simply additional defensive outworks. There is no evidence that the Roman Legions ever tried to besiege the formidable hill fort, and it is unknown whether the Old Oswestry hill fort was occupied again in Roman time.*

Bottom: *Traprain Law (also known as Dunpendyrlaw, and locally referred to as Dunpelder) is a hill about 724 feet (221 m) in elevation situated 4 miles (6 km) east of Haddington in East Lothian, Scotland. It is the site of an oppidum or hill fort, which covered at its maximum extent about 40 acres (16 hectares). Whether it was a seasonal meeting place or a permanent settlement is a matter for speculation. The site was already a place of burial in c. 1500 B.C., and showed evidence of occupation with fortifications after 1000 B.C. The ramparts were rebuilt and re-aligned many times in the following centuries, and Traprain Law a good example of a hill fort in which the designers have taken advantage of the natural defense of a steep precipice on one side and created artificial fortifications on the gentle slope on the other side. Excavations have shown the place was occupied in the late Iron Age from about A.D. 40 through the last quarter of the 2nd century. In the 1st century the Romans recorded the Votadini as a British tribe in the area, and Traprain Law is generally thought to have been one of their major settlements. They emerged as a kingdom under the Brythonic version of their name Gododdin and Traprain Law is thought to have been their capital before it was moved to Din Eidyn (Edinburgh). After the Romans withdrew behind Hadrian's Wall it was occupied from about A.D. 220 almost uninterruptedly until about 400, when an impressive new rampart was built, then within a few decades the site was abandoned.*

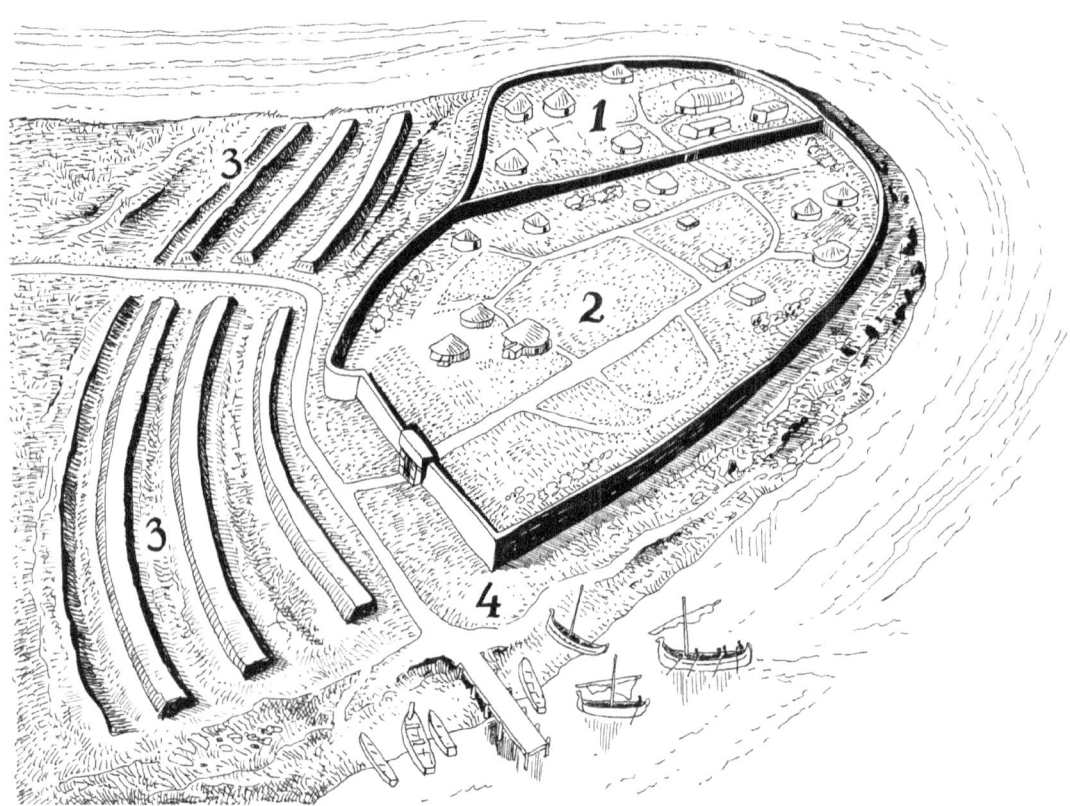

Burghead (conjectured reconstruction). The village of Burghead stands on a narrow promontory of land projecting northwest into the outer Moray Firth a little over seven miles northwest of Elgin, Scotland. The tip of the promontory was occupied by a Celtic fortress. The promontory fort at Burghead was large, covering an area of 3 hectares or 7.5 acres. It seems to have been occupied from the the early Iron Age, and settlement here dates back even further, to the Bronze Age. The fortress had two distinct areas. The smaller, higher area occupying the southwest side of the promontory has been variously described as the upper ward or the citadel, which provided the high status accommodation of the king and his retainers, while the larger area on the northeast side of the promontory tends to be called either the lower ward or the annex. The fortress was surrounded by a massive rampart up to 25 feet (8 m) thick and nearly 20 feet (6 m) high, with a similar rampart dividing the citadel from the annex. The landward side of the fortress was additionally defended by three chevron-shaped ramparts on the landward side. A significant harbor (both a commercial and a military base) was built on the northwest side of the promontory, outside the annex but within the protection afforded by the triple outer ramparts. The illustration shows the following features: 1: Citadel; 2: Lower ward; 3: Triple defensive wall; 4: Port.

1. Prehistoric Fortifications   35

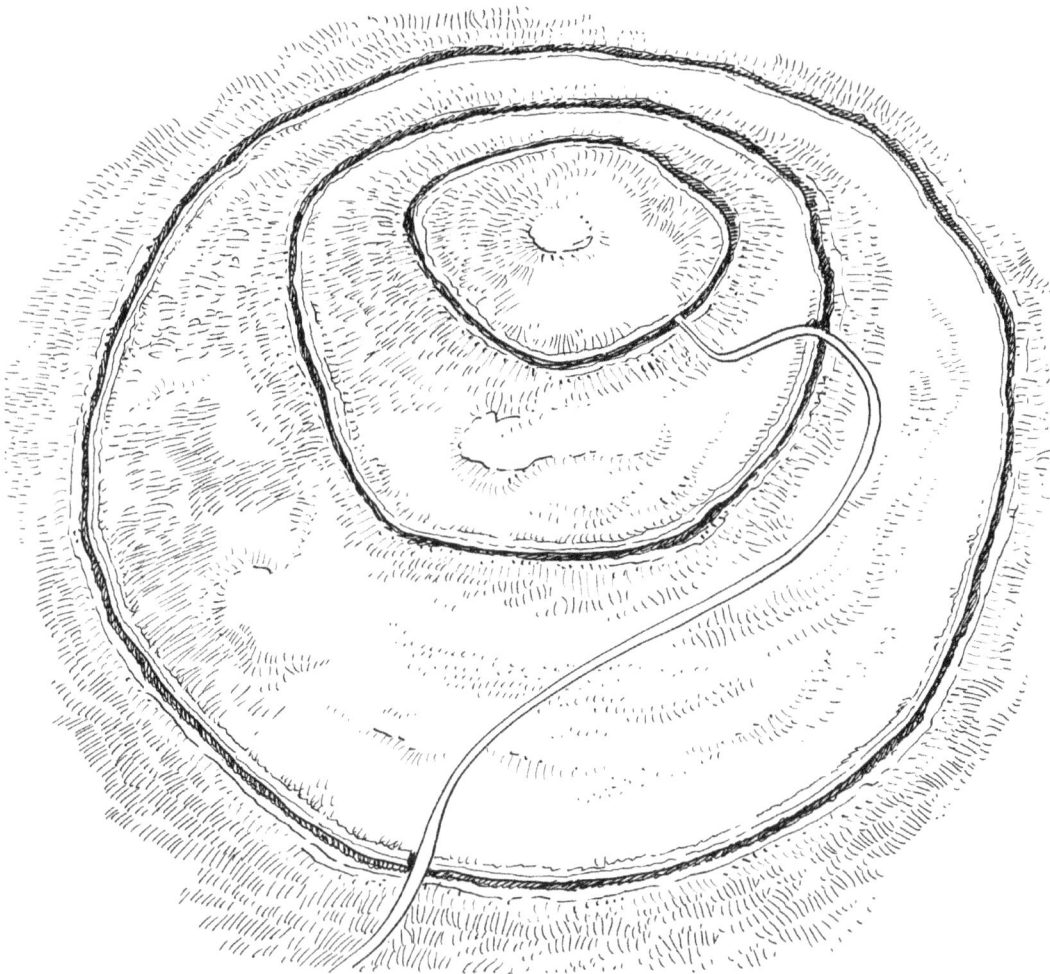

The trivallate hill fort (three almost-concentric enclosures) at Mooghaun North, county of Clare, is thought to be the largest hill fort in Ireland. Built just about 930 B.C., it is situated on a low hillock in a fairly gently undulating landscape of good agricultural land dotted with many small lakes. It has widely spaced ramparts, the outermost of its impending stone walls covers an area of about 27 acres (12 hectares). The ramparts could be as much as 12 m wide in some places and over 2 m in height. All of the walls were made of limestone and appear to be constructed so as to take advantage of the natural contours of the landscape.

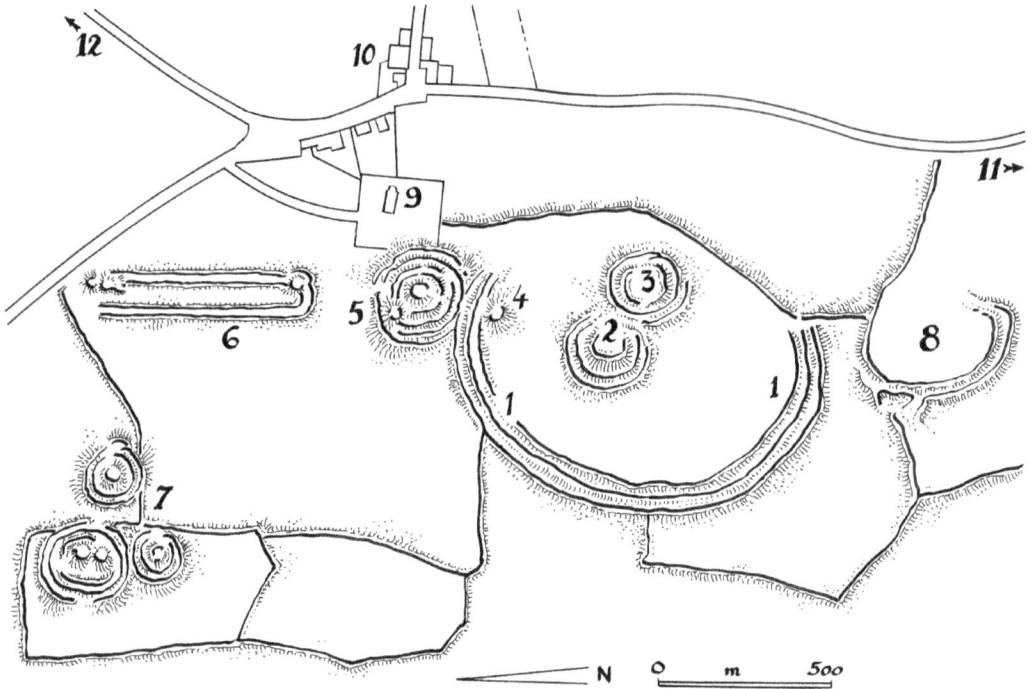

The Hill of Tara (meaning Hill of the Kings) is located near the River Boyne about 30 miles north of Dublin. It is an archaeological complex that extends for miles around between Navan and Dunshaughlin in County Meath, Leinster, Ireland. Tara can be described as a collection of both sites and monuments, but it is also a single unified cultural landscape. At the summit of the hill, to the north of the ridge, is an oval Iron Age hill fort, measuring 1,043 feet (318 m) north-south by 866 feet (264 m) east-west and enclosed by an internal ditch and external bank, known as the Royal Enclosure. The most prominent earthworks within are the two linked enclosures, a bivallate ring fort (known as Cormac's House) and a bivallate ring barrow called the Royal Seat. In the middle of the barrow is a standing stone, which is believed to be the Stone of Destiny, where the Irish kings were crowned. To the north of the ringforts is a small Neolithic passage tomb known the Mound of the Hostages, which was constructed around 3400 B.C. To the north, there is another ringfort with three banks known as the Rath of the Synods. Further north is a long, narrow rectangular structure known as the Banqueting Hall, although it is more likely to have been a ceremonial avenue or cursus monument approaching the site, and three circular earthworks known as the Sloping Trenches and Grainne's Fort. All three are large ring barrows, which may have been built too close to the steep and subsequently slipped. To the south of the Royal Enclosure lies a ringfort known as Laoghaire's Fort, where the eponymous king (said to be the last pagan king of Ireland) would have been buried in an upright position. Half a mile south of the Hill of Tara is another hill fort known as Rath Maeve. For many centuries, historians worked to uncover the site's mysteries, and they have suggested that the most familiar role played by the Hill of Tara in Irish history is as the seat of the kings of Ireland until the 6th century. This role extended until the 12th century, albeit without its earlier splendor. Regardless, the significance of the Hill of Tara predates Celtic times. The ceremonial complex dates back to the Neolithic period around about 4000 B.C., and was used in prehistory as a burial ground, a sanctuary and as the site where the king was publicly proclaimed. The king of Tara was the most important sacred king in prehistoric Ireland and was probably regarded by society as "the king of the world." The map shows the following features. 1: Royal Enclosure; 2: Cormac's House; 3: Royal Seat; 4: Mound of the Hostages; 5: Rath of the Synods; 6: Banqueting Hall; 7: Sloping Trenches and Grainne's Fort; 8: King Loaghaire's Fort; 9: Saint Patrick Church; 10: Hamlet; 11: Road to Maeve hill fort; 12: Road to Navan and Dublin.

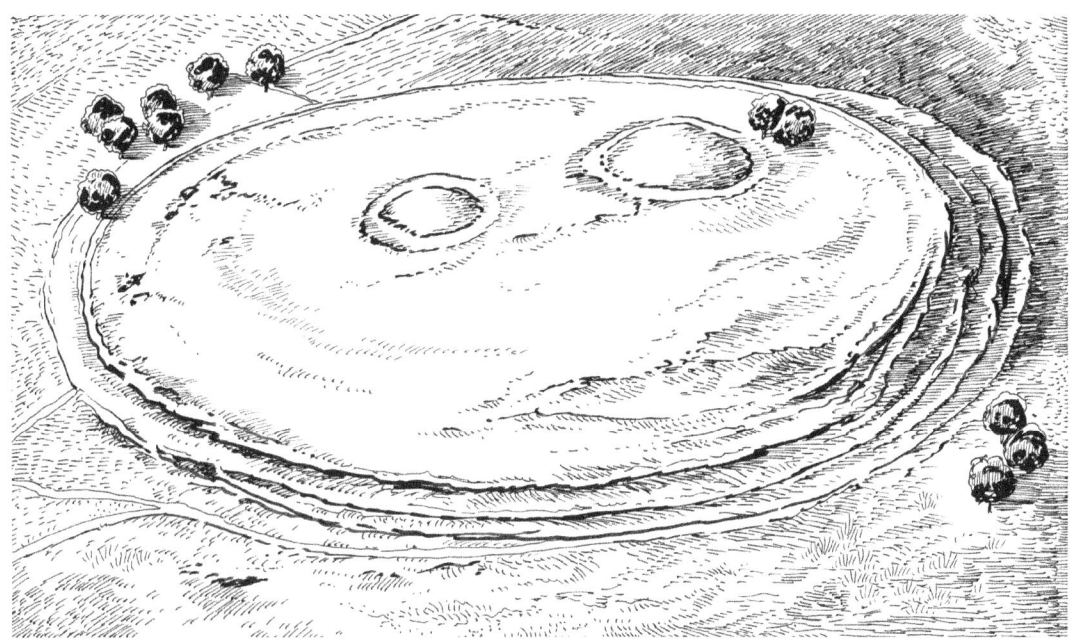

Enaim Macha hill fort, also called Navan Fort, is situated at Navan, 2 miles west of Armagh, Northern Ireland. The site includes a circular bank, now defaced, and a ditch enclosing a number of earth- and stoneworks. At the summit rests a univallate tumulus, once a residential site subsequently used for ceremonial purposes. Emain Macha is probably identical with the Isamnion mentioned in Ptolemy's geography (2nd century A.D.). The site was destroyed, or abandoned some time before the advent of Christian evangelization, perhaps in the 5th century. The abandoned hill fort continued, however, to be the site of an annual feast through medieval times.

Rathgall, situated west of Tullow, county of Carlow, Ireland, is a trivallate hill fort, consisting of three more-or-less concentric stone ramparts enclosing a fourth, well-preserved wall of polygonal masonry. The last is clearly a two-period construction and at least in its primary phase is likely to date to the medieval period. The enclosing ramparts are probably prehistoric, but it is not clear if they represent a single phase, or several phases of building activity. The total area of the hill fort is 18 acres (7.5 hectares).

Other Forms of Fortifications

Duns

Hill forts of the type described above are rare, although not entirely absent, in northern and western Scotland. Their place is taken, in part, by stone-built fortifications known as duns or ringforts. Dating from protohistoric time, these sites, of which about 350 are scattered down the western side of Scotland, including the Inner

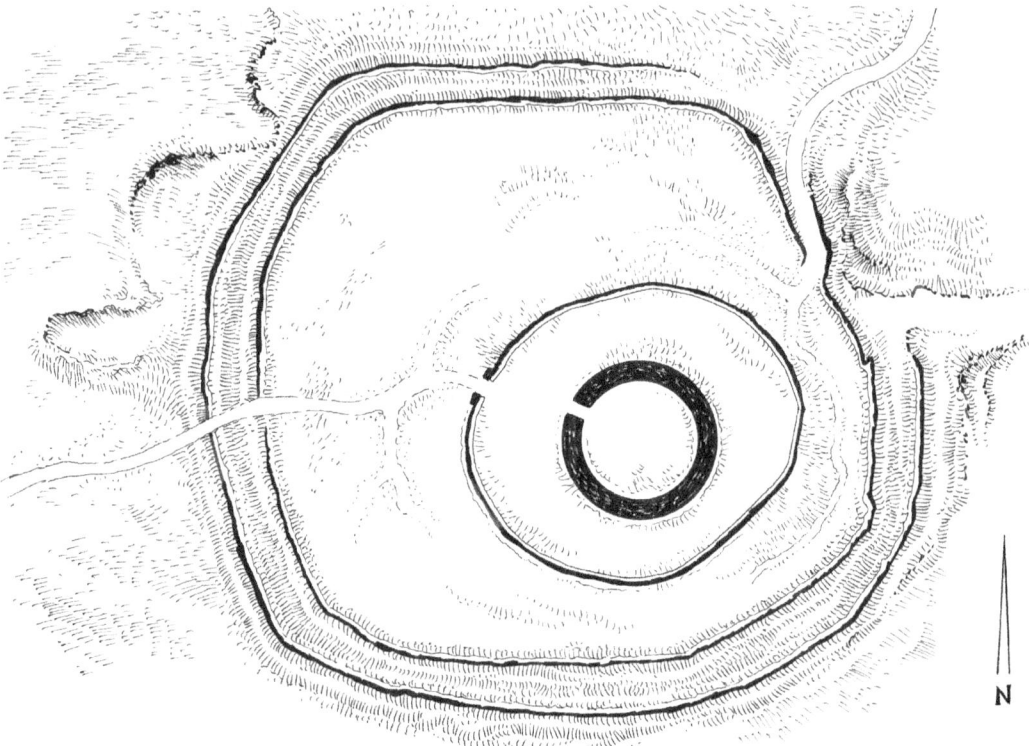

Situated 7 km west of Derry, Ireland, Grianan of Aileach is an impressive stone ringfort with surrounding earthworks perched on the summit of Greenan Mountain, allowing excellent views from the fort across Lough Swilly, Lough Foyle and the Inishowen Peninsula. Although heavily restored between 1874 and 1879, there are no doubts as to the antiquity of the site, as it is thought to have been built in the late Bronze Age or Iron Age. The ramparts of the hill fort have been eroded by time and only hints of their former stature remain, but recent accurate surveys show that there were two sets of ramparts, an inner and an outer. Both of the ramparts comprised a pair of banks and the total area enclosed by the outer boundary is about 5 acres. Grianan of Aileach is the only multivallate example to be found in the north of Ireland. The inner stone ringfort, also known as a cashel, is thought to have been built in the early years A.D. The cashel is of well-fitted dry-stacked stone construction and the the outer surface of the 5-meter-high walls has a graceful curved, or battered form. The interior of the structure today has a diameter of 23.6 m and is reached through a lintel-covered entrance passage 4.65 m long and 1.86 m high. The entrance passage originally had recesses let into each sidewall. The interior of the walls has three terraces, or walkways, which are reached by several inset stairways. Within the walls are two passages which extend almost to the entrance passage itself; they are accessed by two small doorways.

Inside Grianan of Aileach ringfort.

and Outer Hebrides islands, form a varied and heterogenous group of defended settlements. The main concentration of duns is from the northern end of Skye to the southern end of Kintyre. Also found in Ireland (and only a few in England), they differed from the rather large tribal hill forts by the fact that they consisted of a fairly small, usually oval or circular area up to about 60 feet in internal diameter enclosed by earth or stone ramparts. Ringforts were generally small, family farmsteads. They typically enclosed a group of homes and farming buildings with great variations in size: only one acre at Dunbeg and forty acres at Dun Ailinne. They were built by wealthy families who had both the need and the means to construct strong defenses. Ringforts had thus more of an economic function than a military one. Some were simple univallate sites enclosed by an earthbank or a stone wall and were built in lowlands, with or without an accompanying ditch. Others had multivallate defenses and were placed in dominant or commanding positions, on top or on the slopes of rounded glacial hills in lowland areas or backed up to bodies of water, which gave them a certain level of added security through better visibility as well as better draining soils. The rampart was usually 10 to 15 feet thick and consisted of a solid rubble core and well-built inner and outer face, often neatly coursed and with a noticeable batter or inward slope. Of course, particular attention was paid to the entrance passage, which narrowed in angular fashion to provide door checks, which were secured by a bar housed in sockets on either side. Access to the rampart was provided by a staircase in the thickness of the wall or by steps projecting from the inner face. There was sometimes a gallery running lengthwise along the wall at ground level, providing accommodations. There were also more elaborate timber galleries built against the inside of the wall, above ground level, in a number of duns. Some or all of the

Conjectured reconstruction of the entrance to a dun

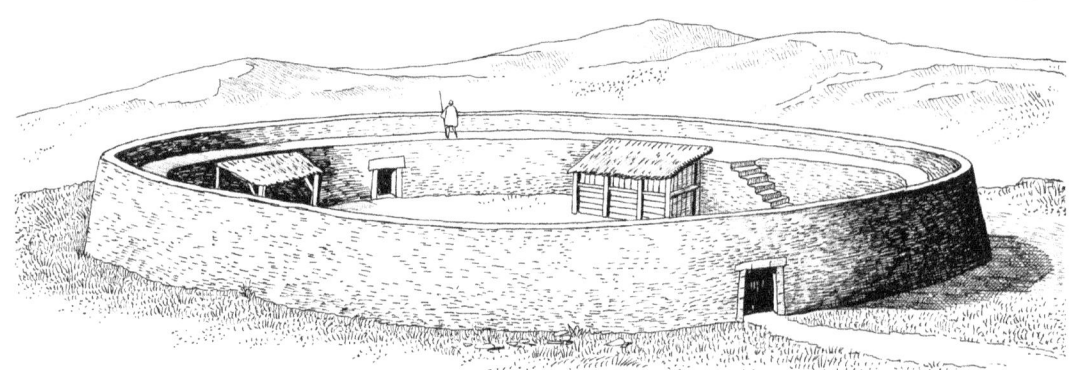

Above and below: *Duns made of dry-stacked stone, which means that the stones were put together without what is known today as mortar. It has been suggested from the high quality of this type of work at certain dun sites that there may have been dry-stacked stone specialists. This would suggest a high level of craft specialization because dry masonry is certainly not a subsistence activity.*

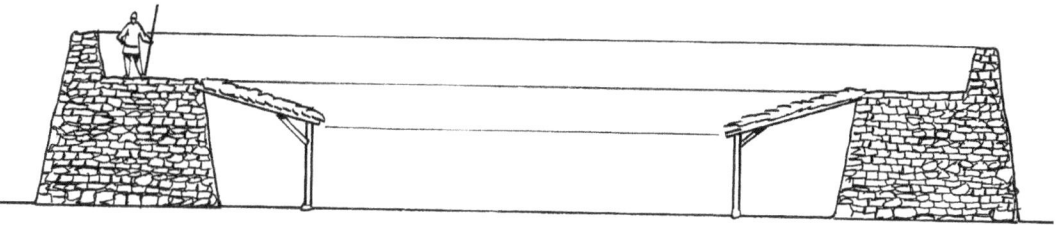

Cross-section of a one-story galleried dun

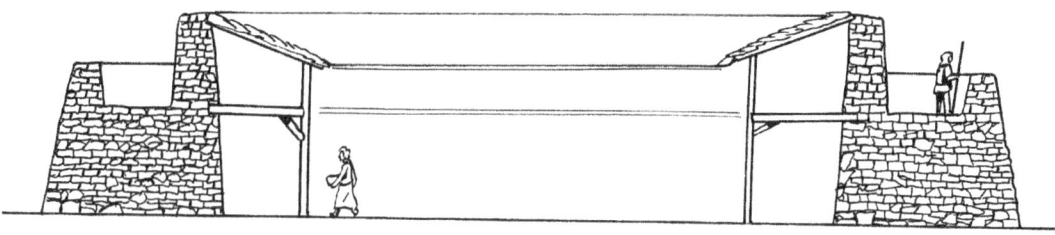

Two-story gallery

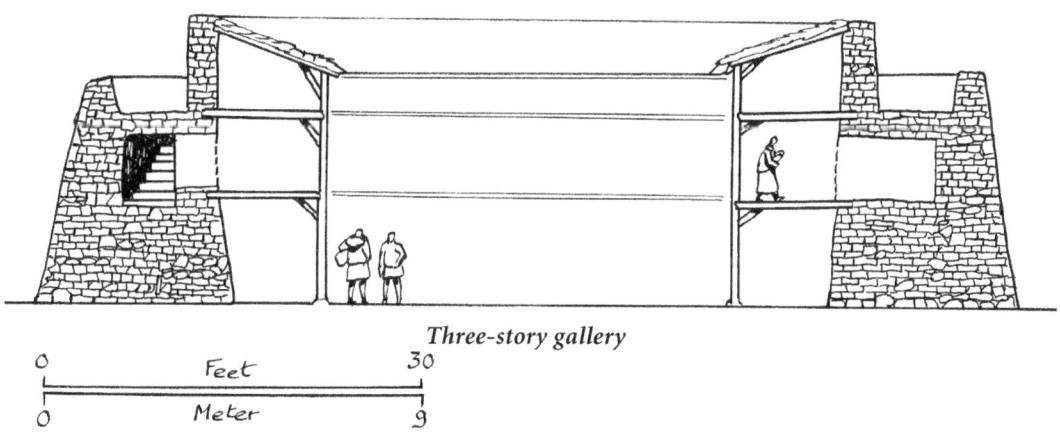

Three-story gallery

features just described appear in a number of small hill forts, and there is in fact no hard and fast dividing line between the types. A dun may appear to be a specialized form of hill fort, its main distinguishing feature being its small size. Variations from this standard pattern are generally the result of particular situations. On promontories, for example at Dunbeg Fort, where the defense was partly provided by cliffs or precipitous slopes, the fortifications were simply a straight or curving length of rampart facing the landward side. In the south and west of Ireland, stone ringforts (known

Ruins of Staigue ringfort, located inland of the Kenmare River in County Kerry about 3 km northeast of Castlecove, Ireland, was probably built in 500 B.C. and seems to have been occupied until A.D. 800. The dry-stacked stone walls of the circular settlement were 10 to 18 feet in height and 13 feet thick at the base. The diameter of the whole structure is 90 feet (30 m).

as cashels) are situated on the tops of steep-sided rocky outcrops (e.g., Leacanabuaile near Cahirciveen, or Carraig Aille near Lough Gur, Cashlaungar, county of Clare). Others were placed in sea-girth promontories.

Duns (particularly galleried duns) and brochs (see below) certainly have features in common, although this does not prove that one was derived from the other. They could well have developed in parallel from some source common to both.

Brochs and Wheelhouses

Away from lowland Britain and into the highland zone, notably in Scotland, the Iron Age settlement structures take on a different aspect and are not easy to connect directly with southern cultures or groups. The units of settlement are most often small, as appropriate to a harsher terrain, and the lowland timber buildings with earthen ramparts are largely replaced by structures with walls of stone, known as brochs. Brochs, one of the most distinctive types of monument to be found in Scotland and the Outer Hebrides, were massive dry-stacked stone towers built from 500 B.C. onward. The tendency to build upwards rather than outwards reflected a need for fortifications with a short perimeter that could be defended by many fewer people than a hill fort's rampart or a dun's stone wall.

There are about 500 brochs remaining in Scotland, mostly distributed in the Orkney, Hebrides, Northern Isles, and the north and west coasts of the Scottish Highlands. They had various functions, serving as an imposing home for the leading family of the area, a farmhouse, a central focus for the locality (in the same way a medieval castle did in later times), and as a demonstration of the strength and power of the individual who lived there. Within their enclosing area, they also were used as a place of possible refuge for the immediate community and its animals in extreme circumstances, notably during raids by Scandinavian Viking pirates.

The tower-like structures of the brochs are particularly distinctive, although they varied somewhat in design. A more compact and elevated version of the dun, brochs were circular in plan, generally between 12 and 19 m in diameter, with massively thick lower walls usually incorporating several chambers. Some were ground-galleried, not solid-based. Some were encircled by outlying walls. Some had guardrooms beside the constricted entrance, which was usually only 1.5 m high and 60 cm wide. This tunnel was sometimes surmounted by a chamber with holes in the floor, through which occupants could drop projectiles upon the cramped and crawl-

Mousa broch. Of all Scotland's brochs, this one quite literally stands supreme: it rises to 13 m high and is both magnificent and awe-inspiring. The broch stands on the now uninhabited island of Mousa, a mile or so off the east coast of Shetland's mainland. Today access is by a passenger ferryboat from Sandwick, some 15 miles south of Lerwick. At its base the broch is 15 m in diameter, but the interior is only 6 m in diameter. Within the huge thickness of the base of the walls are several chambers, probably used for storage, while at higher levels passages run between the inner and outer skins of the wall. Many mysteries remain about this impressive 2000-year-old tower. It is unclear whether, like many brochs, Mousa was the focus of a settlement that surrounded it or if it has always stood alone.

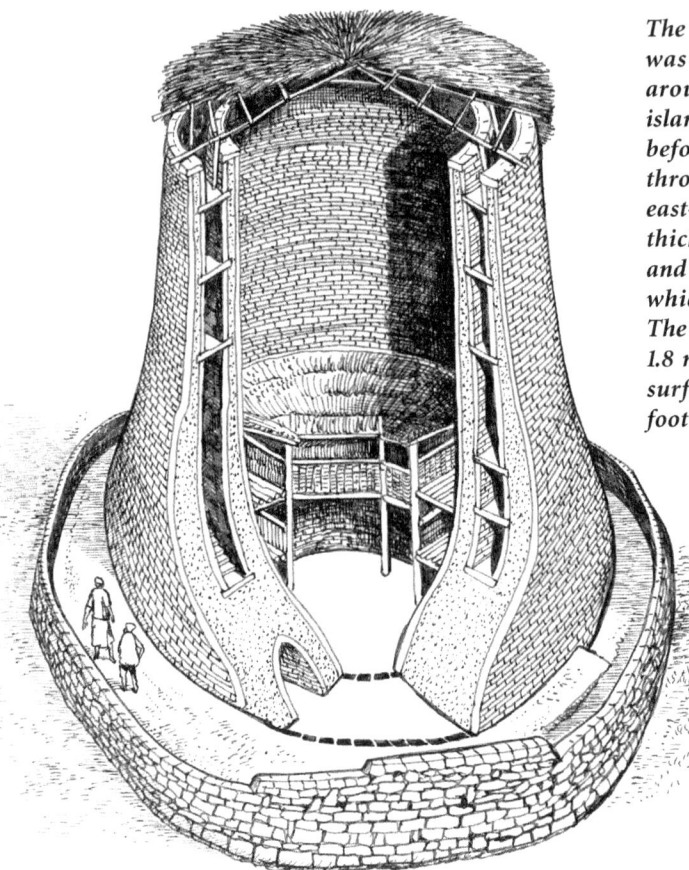

The Iron Age broch of Dun Mhulan was a large tower-like house built around 150 B.C., originally on an island within a freshwater loch, long before the open sea had broken through. It is 19 m across, with an east-facing doorway. The massively thick wall was built with an inner and outer face divided by a passage, which partly survives on one side. The broch's original ground level is 1.8 m below the present day ground surface, and the flat slabs underfoot in the doorway are the roof of the original passage into the building. This passage led into the ground floor of the broch. There was also an upper floor, resting on a row of stones jutting out from the edge of the north wall. The upper room may have been the main living area of the broch, perhaps with storage space below, and there is uncertainty about the nature of the roof. A doorway in the south side led into a small oblong chamber (no longer visible) from which a stone staircase ascended clockwise within the wall. Subsidence soon after construction caused this staircase to crack and this part of the wall fell down within a few centuries. A small settlement grew up around Dun Mhulan in the early centuries A.D. It included a small house and two rectangular, stone-flagged barns. Around A.D. 400 the interior of the ruined broch was rebuilt as a roundhouse, with entry over the doorway's roof slabs, past a small sideroom on the south side and into the main, circular room of the house. By the time the Vikings arrived, from 795 onwards, Dun Mhulan was abandoned.

ing attackers. If they were successful, attackers could only emerge one at a time, and thus were very vulnerable. The tunnel-like entrance shows that brochs were indeed places of refuge and not bases for offensive military operations. Above ground, floor-level brochs are built of two separate concentric walls, with a staircase and passageways between, tied together at intervals with stone slabs. The interior space of the broch comprised the mural chambers and main rooms, with storage on the ground floor, and the main living area above. Inevitably the uppermost parts have not been preserved, but brochs were likely to have been covered with a conical roof, although perhaps resting on the interior wallhead to allow a parapet walkway for observation and active defenses. But archaeologists have not determined if or how they were roofed, and therefore cannot gauge with precision their original height—perhaps between 30 and 50 feet.

1. Prehistoric Fortifications   45

Carloway, or Dun Charlabhaigh, is a remarkably well-preserved broch in a stunning location overlooking Loch Roag on the west coast of Lewis, Scotland. Carloway was probably built sometime in the last century B.C. It would have served as an occasionally defensible residence for an extended family, complete with accommodation for animals at ground level. It would also have served as a visible statement of power and status in the local area. Inside the broch a number of chambers are accessible at ground level, an area which would probably have been used to house farm animals. The human residents would have lived 2 m higher, above wooden flooring. As in other brochs, stairs are fitted within the thickness of the walls, and there would probably have been several floors of accommodation beneath a conical roof. Carloway broch was severely damaged in the 16th century but its double-skinned construction is all the more clearly shown by its current ruinous condition.

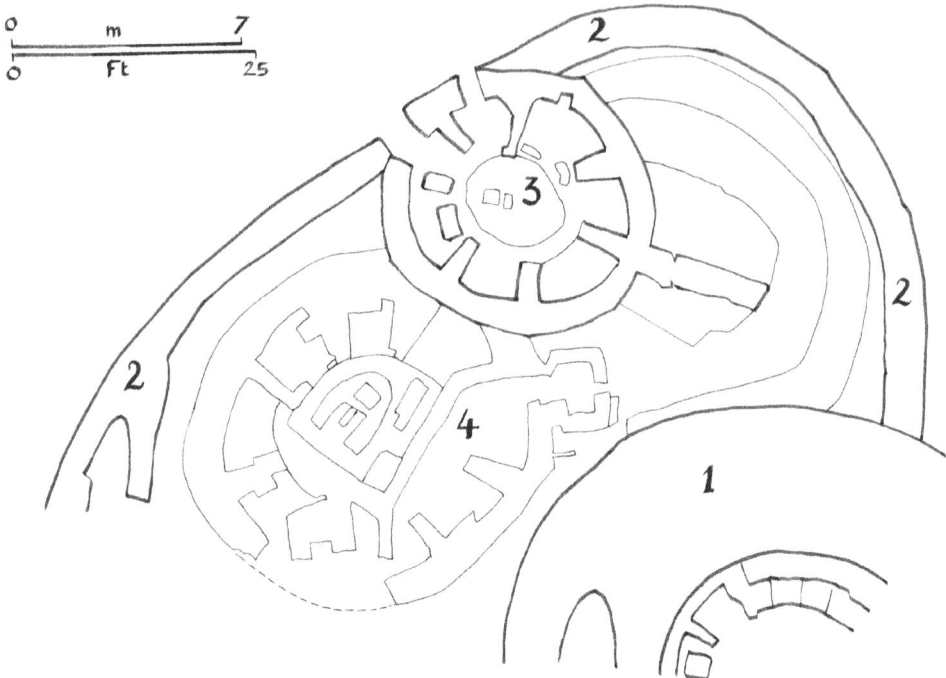

Jarlshof broch, situated in Shetland, had a diameter of 60 feet, walls 17 feet thick and an interior diameter of 25 feet. It had a roughly D-shaped walled courtyard on its west side, approximately 130 feet long and 75 feet wide, in which wheelhouses were eventually built. 1: Broch; 2: Enclosure of broch; 3 and 4: Wheelhouses later erected within the broch's yard.

The best-preserved broch in the Outer Hebrides is at Dun Carloway on the west side of Lewis, standing in parts to 6.7 m high, although its original height may have been as much as 9 m. Other good examples are at Dun Cuier, Barra, Dun Mhulan in South Uist, Dun an Sticar in North Uist, and Dun Boranais and Dun Borgh in Lewis, although at some sites they only survive as a robbed-out footprint, as at Rubha' an Teampuill, Harris.

Much of our knowledge comes from two brochs in the Outer Hebrides, which have been extensively although not completely excavated: Dun Mhulan in South Uist; and Beirgh Broch in Uig, Lewis. At Beirgh broch, however, all the deeply stratified excavated levels related to later re-occupation. The most complete broch in Scotland is on Mousa in Shetland, reaching 13 m.

Brochs can occupy a wide variety of settings, from hilltops to sheltered islands within lochs, and often their surrounding landscape has changed dramatically, such as in the case of Dun Mhulan, which started out on an island in a protected freshwater loch, and now lies on a storm-battered Atlantic shore. In the early centuries A.D., the classic way of life in many of the brochs seems to have come to an end, and smaller, humbler houses were built inside the shells of the grand, old brochs. Re-occupation generally continued until the eve of the Viking incursions at the end of the 8th century, after which the sites were commonly abandoned. It was *(continued on page 49)*

1. Prehistoric Fortifications   47

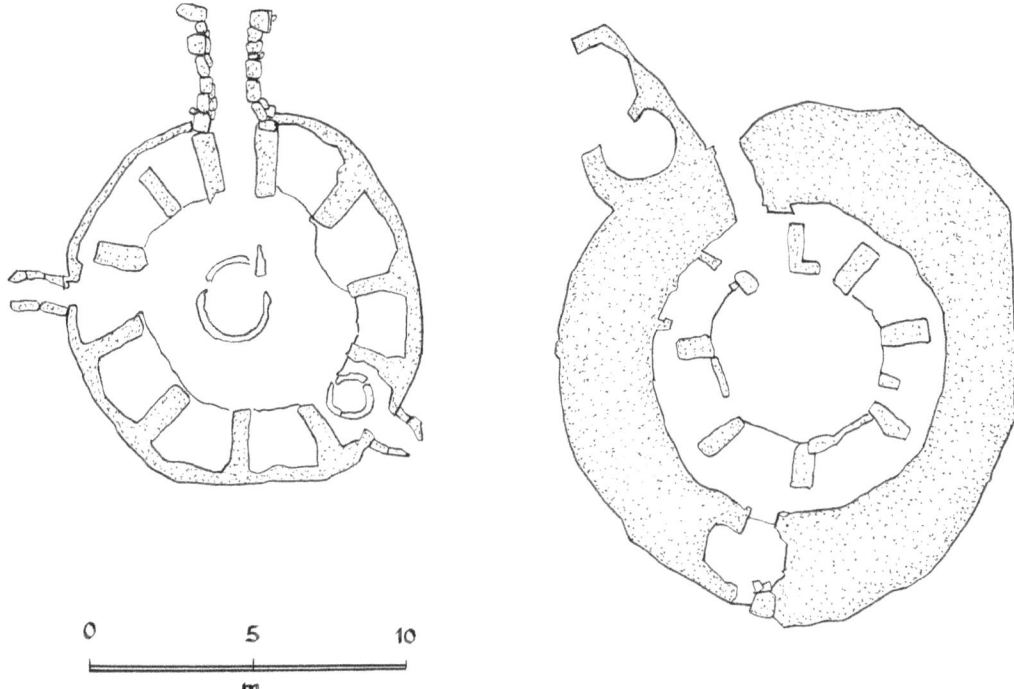

Wheelhouses. Left: *Kilpheder (South Uist)* Right: *Clettraval (Northern Uist)*.
Below: *Cross-section of a wheelhouse (Conjectured reconstruction)*.

Clickhimin Broch (conjectured reconstruction) occupies what is today a promontory in the freshwater Clickimin Loch, on the outskirts of Lerwick. Originally, however, it was an island reached by boat, as denoted by the landing stage just outside the ringfort defenses on the south side. It was inhabited from c. 1000 B.C. to A.D. 500. Accommodation in the fort, pre-dating the broch, is represented by a low cellular structure of late Bronze Age or early Iron Age date. In the broch period the island was accessed by a stone causeway. Once through the ringfort entrance visitors were expected to duck through the blockhouse doorway. This has a door jamb and could be barred, and the structure is usually interpreted as a defensive tower with a fighting platform. It certainly had stairs to a second floor, but does not seem to have had much defensive functionality as it does not articulate with the ringfort. The essentially symbolic function of this structure is reinforced by the insertion in the later Iron Age of a shrine or small temple. Access to the broch itself is via an entrance on the western side, not immediately apparent from the main entrance. The broch entrance passage is long and low, with a blocked guard cell entrance on the right side just inside the door jamb. The design is usually interpreted as defensive but it also has the effect of making visitors bow as they enter the house, which may have been the most important intended consequence—a sign of respect. The tower is 65 feet in overall diameter, with walls 17 feet thick at the base and a central space 30 feet in diameter. There are cells in the wall's thickness at ground level, but the main accommodation would have been in the circular central space that was roofed. In fact the prestigious accommodation was probably on the first floor, which must have been reached by an internal ladder or stair. The stairs both start at the first rather than ground floor level. As with many brochs, they ascend in a clockwise/sunwise direction. Over the centuries of occupation debris gradually raised the ground surface and the structure ceased to be an impressive tower, becoming more of a settlement mound. However, the site evidently remained prestigious.

(*continued from page 46*) not uncommon in the later Middle Ages, however, for the broch shells to once more become the residences of local chieftains.

Brochs are only one type in an impressive range of related buildings. Another version of the same theme is the wheelhouse, unique so far to the Outer Hebrides and Shetland. A total of 62 sites have been identified in the Northern and Western Isles, and on the north coast of Caithness and Sutherland. The wheelhouse, sometimes referred to as an "aisled roundhouse," takes its name from the radial piers inside the circular stone wall, probably designed to support the roof structure. The interior was divided by a number of stone piers, arranged like the spokes of a wheel. The chambers thus created around the wall of the house were each roofed with a small, corbelled stone dome, and only the central, open area over the earth needed to be spanned with scarce timber, which would be covered over with turf. Wheelhouses were adapted for the Hebridean environment; they could be built as subterranean structures in sand or machair coastal areas with only the roof projecting above the ground, the small doorway giving little clue to the spacious house within, which might be from 4 to 10 m in diameter and about 6 m high. Wheelhouses could be built as free-standing structures, such as on the moorland where it was difficult to dig down. In those cases, a thick blanket of midden material was built against the outer wall. Wheelhouses, however, were lower and much less massive than brochs, and were probably farmhouses or dwellings, although many sites incorporate animal burials beneath the floor, tending to support the hypothesis that the primary purpose of these buildings was ritualistic. The highly restricted nature of their geographical locations suggests that they may have been contained within a political or cultural frontier of some kind. The co-incidence of their arrival and departure being associated with the period of Roman influence in Scotland is a matter of ongoing debate.

In the Northern Isles many wheelhouses are often found associated with brochs, the former taking advantage of the strong thick shell of the latter. At Clickhimin, a wheelhouse was built inside the disused broch, and at Jarlshof, also in the Shetland, wheelhouses were inserted into the broch courtyard. No sites in the west have such an association, an as yet unresolved enigma.

The material culture associated with the brochs and wheelhouses has local elements as well as those derived ultimately from southern Britain. Like Ireland, the north of Scotland lay beyond the frontier of Roman Britain, and the local Iron Age substantially outlasted the Roman occupation of Britain. The Scottish and Irish Iron Ages must be regarded as loose and rather remote variants of that combination of native and intrusive elements. Even the term "pre–Roman Iron Age" loses meaning in these areas. However, in spite of their elaborate structure, broch towers appear to have had a relatively short history. By c. A.D. 80–100 many of them seem to have gone out of use, while open settlements developed around their remains. The less elaborate duns may have persisted somewhat longer, as they were less specialized and more easily adaptable to peaceful activities.

Loch Tay crannog.

CRANNOG

The term *crannog* refers to small artificial islands, which can be found in the majority of Scotland's lochs and inland waters. The name is derived from the Irish word *crann*, meaning a tree. Originally the term may have been applied to the timber palisades that surrounded such sites, the timber buildings within them, or the timber foundations on which they were erected. The same name is used in Scotland, where similar sites occur. These lake villages on small islands—it is believed—were dwellings of prominent families or groups of families and the crannog also served as a refuge in times of attack. Most crannogs are to some extent artificial. This means that it has taken a certain amount of human activity to create them. In some cases, small islands or natural bedrock outcrops were only slightly enlarged, requiring relatively less effort. In other cases, crannogs were created from scratch by piling up vast amounts of material on the loch bed or in a marshy area in a bog. This obviously required substantial effort and considerable time. Regardless of the effort the product is always very similar—a small island, its surface protruding above the water, which owes its existence to human activity. Other features also found on crannogs include vertical wooden piles set into the bed of the lake or river, middens of discarded domestic waste, and sometimes a small harbor and jetties. Access to the crannog was normally by boat but when times became more settled, causeways or bridges were used. Although lake villages and crannogs may not have been of military intent originally, their very location must have made them difficult to approach, so that they became defensive places of refuge in times of crisis. Crannogs had a variety of forms. Most were circular or oval, but all differed greatly in size. Average surface diameters range between 15 and 30 m, although there were notable exceptions both larger and smaller. The materials used to build crannogs also varied throughout Scotland. Crannogs found in the Hebrides seem to have been built primarily of stone, whereas those found in the mainland were predominantly built of wood. Most of this variation has been ascribed to differences in local environments. Obviously people used materials which were easy to come by or immediately at hand. Evidence suggests that crannogs have been used as habitation sites for a period longer than any other type of structure in Scotland's history. Archaeological excavations have shown that crannogs were used during various periods ranging from the Neolithic (4000–2000 B.C.), the Bronze Age (c. 2000–500 B.C.), the Iron Age and Roman times. Literary evidence indicates that crannogs were still being used in remote areas of Scotland until the seventeenth century. This extensive time range makes it hard to know when a particular crannog was in use. Crannogs offer an unparalleled opportunity to recover information about Scotland's past. Because Scotland's lochs are so cold and relatively bacteria-free, organic materials such as wood, seeds and plant fiber are often well preserved. Such preservation helps archaeologists piece together what life on a crannog was actually like, in a way that cannot be achieved on dryland sites.

A few lake villages also existed in England, for example at Glastonbury, where a settlement was reclaimed in bogs and marshes, while farmers raised crops on high ground in the area. Worthy of mention is the Craggaunowen crannog, situated near Kilmurry, about 10 miles (16 km) from Ennis, county of Clare, in southern Ireland. This is a full-scale reconstruction of a crannog in its typical lake setting. Inside the crannog are several thatched roundhouses of wattles and mud surrounded by a protective fence. A gatetower stands over the entrance and a causeway connects the island to the mainland. The site is actually an archaeological open-air museum centered around a 16th-century towerhouse. A park of 50 acres of woodland with a picturesque lake is host to several examples of early historic places. Next to the crannog there is a small ringfort; a Bronze Age cooking and industrial site; a dolmen (Neolithic portal tomb); a standing stone; and a reconstruction of a leather hulled boat that is reputed to have been sailed by Saint Brendan from Ireland to Newfoundland in Canada in the mid–6th century A.D. Another reconstruction is the Loch Tay crannog at Kenmore, Perthshire, Scotland, based on the excavation evidence from a 2,600-year-old site.

Aftermath

Although primitive and unformalized, Celtic fortification had made some significant advances. The Celts had well understood the fact that a fortified place could enable a small body of defenders to resist a superior attacking force. They did not invent, but understood and developed several fundamental principles of fortification, notably the vital importance of taking advantage of height, of natural defense, and of the efficient combination of ditch/rampart. They put in practice the essential *principle of command*, a law of fortification by which the vertical elevation of one work over another or above the surrounding country provides the defenders with superior fire positions, and enables the fortification to dominate an area by virtue of its height. The broch, for example, would later reappear in the history of British fortifications, albeit in varying forms: Roman towers, medieval keeps and wall-towers, post-medieval tower houses, and 19th-century Martello towers. Although designed to serve different purposes, the broch and all these later structures basically use elevation as a safety device. The Celts also applied with success the so-called principle of *defense in depth*, characterized by several lines of defense and outworks. Defense in depth is a military tactic that in modern terminology is referred to as elastic defense or deep defense. Its purpose is to delay rather than prevent the advance of an attacker, buying time and causing additional casualties by slowly yielding space. Defense in depth requires that a defender deploy his fortifications in several lines. When attackers breach one line, they continue to meet resistance as they advance, and one captured work or line does not mean the collapse of the whole defense.

Owing to the combination of fortifications and warrior-heroes, the British Celts were convinced that they could defeat any invader, even the Romans, of whom much had been heard in the last century of the pre–Christian era.

Despite their elaboration and the titanic efforts of the multitudes which went into their creation, Iron Age hill forts, were of little use against the superior Roman material culture and military power. In 55 B.C. the Romans set foot on British shores. They were repulsed but returned in A.D. 43. They came bearing — no doubt without realizing it — the accumulated lore of a variety of cultures reaching back over 2000 years. The Romans had acquired considerable technical and military knowledge, they had their own ideas on how to deal with other people, and they had developed their own concepts about military architecture. After A.D. 43 a new and much clearer phase of British fortification began.

PART 2

Roman Fortifications in Britain A.D. 43–409

The Roman Empire and Its Army

Rome grew from a small Italian village to a city-state and into a large empire, the most powerful state of the ancient world, that ruled the shores of the Mediterranean and much of western Europe. The Roman state began as a kingdom (753 B.C. is the traditional date), then continued as a republic (509–27 B.C.) and then as an empire (27 B.C.–A.D. 476). The Roman Empire reached its greatest extent in the early second century A.D. Rome ruled Europe west of the Rhine River and south of the Danube, as well as present-day Romania. To the east, Rome ruled Asia Minor, Mesopotamia, Turkey, and Palestine; to the south, it ruled Egypt and the entire northern coast of Africa, in fact all lands bordering the Mediterranean Sea, which was called Mare Nostrum ("Our Sea"). Once the empire was established, Rome gave it two centuries of relative peace, called Pax Romana ("Roman Peace," approximately from 29 B.C. to A.D. 192 between the reigns of Augustus and Commodus). Roman civilization, largely influenced by Greek culture, spread throughout the empire, and the language of Rome — Latin — and the legal system established by the Romans remain important parts of Western culture. The Romans also introduced Christianity, after emperor Constantine converted to Christianity in 312, and made it the official religion in the empire. In A.D. 395 an administrative division of the empire into eastern and western parts was made permanent. The western part entered into a gradual decline and collapsed in A.D. 476 under the invasion of Germanic tribes. The eastern part, later called the Byzantine Empire, flourished and lasted until 1453.

Roman conquest and occupation of these large territories was accomplished by the Roman army — one of the most successful and long-lived armies of antiquity. The Roman army developed standards of discipline, organization and efficiency that would not be seen again in Europe until the 18th century. It began as a small non-permanent militia drawn from rich citizens, designed only for short campaigns.

By the late 4th century B.C., it took the form of the familiar and famous legions, which proved very effective in battles. The Roman army was predominantly a force of heavy infantrymen equipped with body armor, helmets, and shields, and armed with spears, javelins, and swords. Each legion included a squadron of mounted men, usually 120 strong, for use as reconnaissance, orderlies or dispatch riders rather than as combat cavalry. However, in the 3rd century, large cavalry units gradually superseded the infantry legions as Rome's most important force, many of them attested in the 4th and early 5th centuries, in order to increase mobility.

In early times the free Roman citizen-soldier's morale was civic and patriotic, but prolonged campaigning caused important reforms traditionally associated with general Marius Gaius (157–87 B.C.). The early Roman citizen militia appeared unsuitable for long service, so increasingly the Roman army became a permanent force consisting of professional soldiers and volunteers drawn from the poor social classes. The growth of professionalism and the permanence of units improved the army's overall quality and more particularly helped develop specialist tasks such as engineering and siege-craft. However, professionalism eventually broke the allegiance of the army to the state that had previously been the main source

This map shows the Roman Empire at the height of its power in circa A.D. 117 during Emperor Trajan's reign.

of political stability. The army of the Roman Empire remained in the form of strong professional legions assisted by mercenary auxiliaries until the 3rd century A.D. The 25 legions that defended the empire during the reign of Augustus each numbered more than 5,000 soldiers. They were the backbone of the Roman army, supported by auxiliary troops. However the fighting spirit, which had made the fortune of the Republic, deserted the Italians by the age of Hadrian (76–A.D. 138). In the old republican days, war was a national duty and a fruitful pastime, as fighting was for the most part under the blue Mediterranean sky, in a land of vines and olives. Campaigns were short, and—most important—plunder was good. But the boring garrison life in a legionary camp in the cold north, on the Danube or the Rhine, or on the Roman walls in Britain was a different matter. This sort of soldiering did not attract the Italians. So when the people of Italy became unwilling to volunteer in sufficient numbers for the rigors of army life, the force needed to defend the borders came to be recruited principally from the remote provinces. The Romans fell back on the expedient of recruiting into the legions the very barbarians from whom the empire had to be defended from. As the defending force came in the end to be composed and commanded by foreigners—mainly by German barbarians—this inevitably led to disaster. Indeed the emperor in Rome was often merely a name to them, and their loyalty came to be concentrated on their immediate leaders. When the barbarians wanted to involve themselves in Roman politics, when they revolted, and when they marched into the Roman Empire, there was thus very little opposing force to drive them back.

Roman Engineering Corps

Each legion included a body of professional engineers, workers, craftsmen or artisans (called fabri) for siege work and the construction of bridges, roads, fortifications and other projects, placed under an officer called the *praefectus fabrum*. Fortification construction was the responsibility of special engineering units to which specialists of many types belonged, officered by *architecti* (architects and engineers) and *mensores* (surveyors), from a class of troops known as *immunes* since they were excused from regular duties. These engineers might requisition manual labor from the soldiers at large as needed, and therefore each Roman legionary was equipped with a *dolabra* (pickaxe), and a *pala* (spade), alongside his *gladius* (sword) and *pilum* (javelin). Other specialized trades included the *hydraularius* (responsible for water supply and drainage), the *naupegus* (shipwright), *ballistarius* (catapult maker and artilleryman), *specularius* (glazier), *sagittarius* (arrow maker), and several others like the woodsmen in charge of tree felling, for example. Roman military engineering fulfilled both routine and extraordinary roles, the former a standard military defensive procedure, and the latter the offensive nature of siege warfare.

A legion's engineer unit could throw up a camp in as little as a few hours. Judging from the names, they probably used a repertory of camp plans from a set textbook, selecting the one appropriate to the strength and length of time a unit would spend in it, e.g., *tertia castra* (a camp for three days), *quarta castra* (camp for four days). In wartime Roman engineers designed, built and operated siege machines. Although most Roman siege engines were adaptations from earlier Greek designs, the Romans were adept at engineering them swiftly and efficiently, as well as innovating variations such as the onager. Owing to knowledge and experience gained through routine peacetime and civilian engineering they also developed siege techniques. One of the most famous of such extraordinary constructions was the circumvallation of the entire oppidum of Alesia, defended by the Gallic leader Vercingetorix in 52 B.C., within a massive length of double-wall — one inward-facing to prevent escape or offensive sallies from the city, and one outward-facing to prevent attack by Celtic reinforcements. This wall was estimated to be over 13 miles (20 km) long. Another successful example would be the large circumvallation and massive 30 feet (9.1 m) assault ramp built at the seige of Massada (Palestine) during the Jewish Revolt in 72–73. It was constructed by order of Luvius Flavius on a natural spur of bedrock and used tons of stones and beaten earth. The ramp went up to the invested city of Masada (Palestine) in the Jewish Revolt in 72–73.

Roman siege works in Britain are scant, and issues concerning Roman attacks on Celtic hill forts are still disputed today. Finds at Maiden Castle and Hod Hill in Dorset, southern England, suggest siege being laid to these Celtic hill forts. At Brunswark in southern Scotland, archaeological evidence has revealed the existence of two Roman siege camps, but scholars now think they were training camps intended for practicing mock attacks and simulating siege techniques. Archaeologists are still debating whether the Roman siege works dug near the hill fort of Woden Law, Roxburgh, in Scotland were actually used to lay siege or rather served as a training ground just like Brunswark.

The Roman engineer corps also built roads and bridges. When invading enemy territories, and later when countries were conquered, the Roman army would improve or create means of communication in order to allow swift reinforcement and resupply, as well as a path for easy retreat if necessary. Roman road-making skills were such that some Roman roads survive to this day. Bridges were made from both timber and stone depending on required permanence and time available. Stone bridges were made possible by the innovative use of the keystone to allow an arch construction, and some have come down to us. An excellent example of a remarkable masterwork of engineering is the Alcantara Bridge located near the city of Alcantara (in Arabic "bridge") in western Spain (province of Caceres) near the border with Portugal. Still existing today, it was built between A.D. 104 and 106, under Emperor Trajan. Other remarkable engineering works were, for example, the road built in the Petit-Saint-Bernard pass in the Alps between Gaul and the Aosta Valley in northern Italy, as well as the 900-meter-long tunnel designed by engineer Lucius Coccelus Auctus and dug during the reign of Augustus under the Monte Grillo Ridge between Baies and Cumes in Italy.

The Roman army was also involved in building projects for civilian use such as the construction of town walls, the digging of shipping canals, aqueducts, and harbors, the drainage of land, even the cultivation of vineyards. In some cases soldiers were even used in mining work, prospecting for metal veins, operating dewatering machines, and building reservoirs to hold the water at the minehead.

There were sound reasons for using the army in both military and civilian building projects. Primarily, when they were not directly engaged in military campaigns, the legions were largely unproductive, costing the Roman state large sums of money. Besides, the involvement of soldiers in building works kept them not only well accustomed to hard physical labor, but also busy, since it was well understood that idleness could undermine discipline. Roads and bridges as well as permanent fortifications and other civilian buildings had the additional advantage of impressing the conquered people, who had little experience with engineering, to emphasize the superiority of Roman culture, and to display the conqueror's power and glory.

(Continued on page 62.)

Caesar's bridge across the Rhine. The first two bridges to cross the Rhine River were built by Julius Caesar and his legionaries during the Gallic War in 55 B.C. and 53 B.C. Strategically successful, they were considered masterpieces of military field engineering. Caesar's first bridge was most likely erected between Andernach and Neuwied, downstream of Koblenz. Two years later, close to the site of the first bridge, possibly at today's Urmitz (near Neuwied), Caesar ordered the construction of a second bridge.

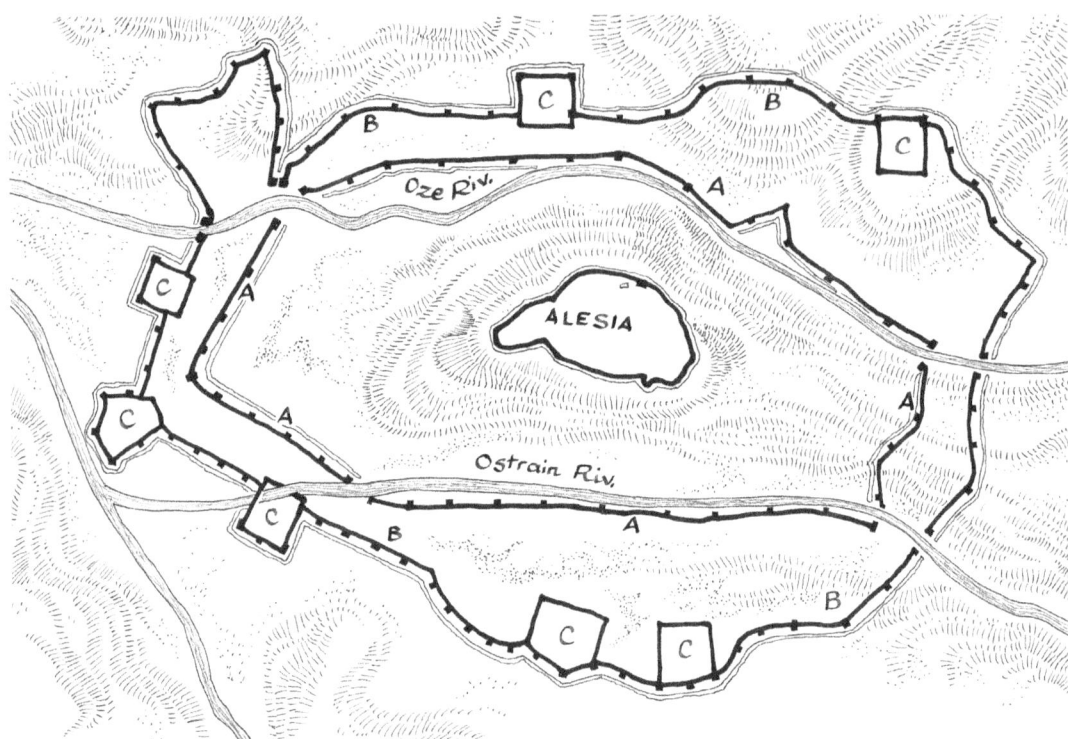

Siege of Alesia, 52 B.C. The siege of the major Gallic oppidum of Alesia led by Julius Caesar (and described in his commentaries on the war in Gaul, book VII, chapters 63–90) took place in late 52 B.C. It marked the turning point of the Gallic Wars in favor of Rome. The siege is considered one of Caesar's greatest military achievements, and is still one of the classic examples of siege warfare. Alesia was probably situated atop Mont Auxois, above modern Alise-Sainte-Reine in France, but this location is still disputed. An alternative would be Chaux-des-Crotenay (in the Jura Mountains). As the Romans were outnumbered by five to one by a coalition of Gallic tribes commanded by the leader Vercingetorix, Caesar ordered the construction of an encircling set of fortifications, or circumvallation, around Alesia in order to blockade the Gallic force. The circumvallation was about 18 kilometers in length, and consisted of a 4-meter-high earth wall and two 4.5-meter-wide ditches, about 1.5 m deep, and regularly spaced timber watchtowers equipped with artillery. These fortifications were supplemented with mantraps and obstacles in front of and in the ditches, creating a dangerous killing zone. Anticipating that a relief force of 258,000 would be sent to release the besieged, Caesar ordered the construction of a second line of fortifications, the contravallation, facing outward. The second line, intended to protect the besiegers, was identical to the first in design and extended for 20 km, including infantry and cavalry camps. Although the Gauls launched massive attacks, the Romans, well entrenched in their field fortifications, ultimately could both repulse the relief army and obtain the surrender of Vercingetorix by starving his troops. A: Countervallation; B: Circumvallation; C: Roman infantry and cavalry camps.

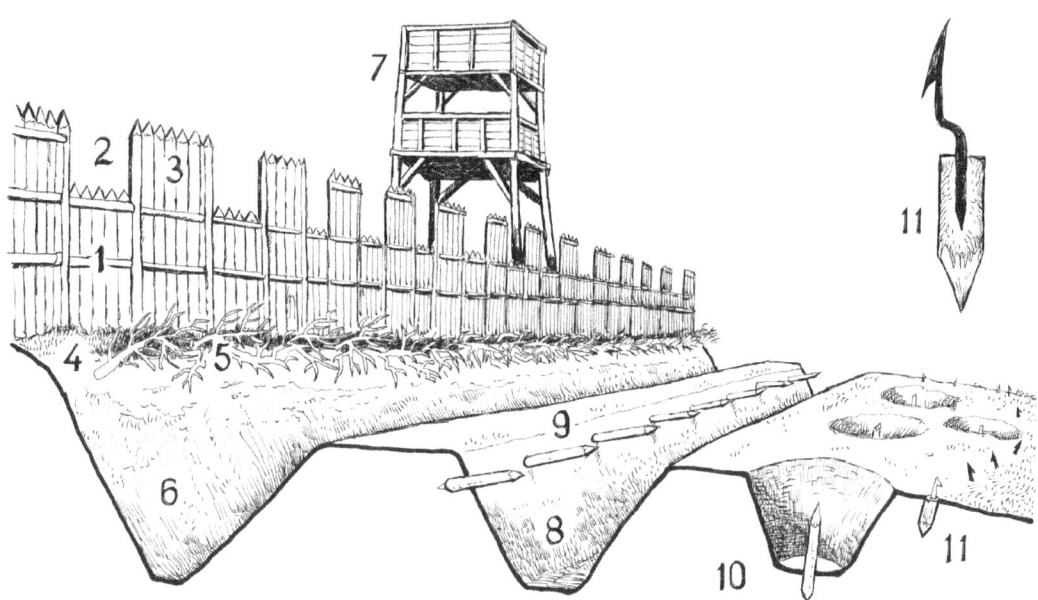

Top: *Cross-section of the Roman fieldworks at Alesia: 1: Lorica (parapet) made of palisade poles; 2: Pinna (crenel or void); 3: Merlon (upstanding solid sections of a parapet between the crenels, behind which the defenders could shelter); 4: Vallum or agger (earth wall); 5: Cervi (sharpened tree branches acting as obstacle); 6: Fossa (ditch) 7: Turris (tower with artillery); 8: Second ditch; 9: Cippe (sharp poles); 10: Lilium (wolf's pit—concealed interlocking conical excavations about 2 meters in diameter and 2.5 meters deep in which one or more dangerous sharpened stakes or spikes were placed); 11: Stimulus (a sharp barbed iron hook fixed on a short stake stuck in the ground, concealed in grass and planted in great number around a position, intended to injure attacking enemy infantrymen and horses).*

Bottom: *Kantara bridge (Algeria). The Roman bridge near the village of Kantara (called in Roman time Calceus Herculis) in Algeria, halfway between Biskra and Batna in the Aures Mountains, still exists today.*

Left: *Tools.* The sudis (plural sudes) was the name given to a stake, pictured to the left, carried by Roman legionaries for employment as a field fortification. Each stake was made of hardwood, usually oak, about 150-180 cm (5-6 feet) long and about 50-100 mm (2-4 in) wide at the thickest point. Square in section, the shape tapered to a point at both ends. The central part was narrowed in a way that suggests the function of a handle, or to facilitate lashing—although this remains unclear. The actual purpose might have been that sudes were used to form a temporary defense, a barrier and incorporated into the ramparts of a Roman marching castrum. It is also believed that sudes lashed in pairs at intervals along a log or beam could form a sort of moveable frizzy horse.* Alternatively, three sudes might have been roped together into a sort of anti-cavalry obstacle—in modern parlance a Czech hedgehog. Engineering tools included spades, pollaxes, and pick-axes.

Right: *The groma* was one of the principal Roman surveying instruments. It comprised a vertical staff with horizontal cross pieces mounted at right angles on a bracket. Each crosspiece had a plumb line hanging vertically at each end. It was used by engineers and architects to survey straight lines and right angles, thence squares or rectangles, and to trace on the ground simple and orthogonal alignments, necessary to the construction of camps, roads, cities, temples and agricultural land subdivisions.

*The frizzy horse was employed as early as the 16th century (probably employed for the first time in 1594 at the siege of Groningen in Friesland—hence its name). The frizzy horse (in German spanischen reiter, in American knife stand, in French cheval de frise) was a mobile obstacle composed of a baulk of timber about 13 feet (4 m) long with pointed stakes protruding from the side. The stakes act as legs while the remainder form an effective obstacle against infantry and cavalry. A modern version consists of a wooden frame resting on crossbars. Dimensions are varied (generally 2 m long, 1 m high and perhaps 50 cm wide). The obstacle is now often wrapped with barbed wire around it and has handles on each side. It is mobile and thus used to block a road, a passage or a gap in a barbed-wire network.

Roman pentaspastos. During the Roman Empire construction activity soared and buildings reached enormous dimensions. The Romans adopted the Greek crane and developed it further. The simplest Roman crane, the trispastos, consisted of a single-beam jib, a winch, a rope, and a block containing three pulleys. It has been calculated that a single man working the winch could raise 150 kg. Heavier crane types featured five pulleys (pentaspastos) or, in the case of the largest one, a set of three by five pulleys (polyspastos), and came with two, three or four masts, depending on the maximum load. The polyspastos, when worked by four men at both sides of the winch, could lift up to 3,000 kg.

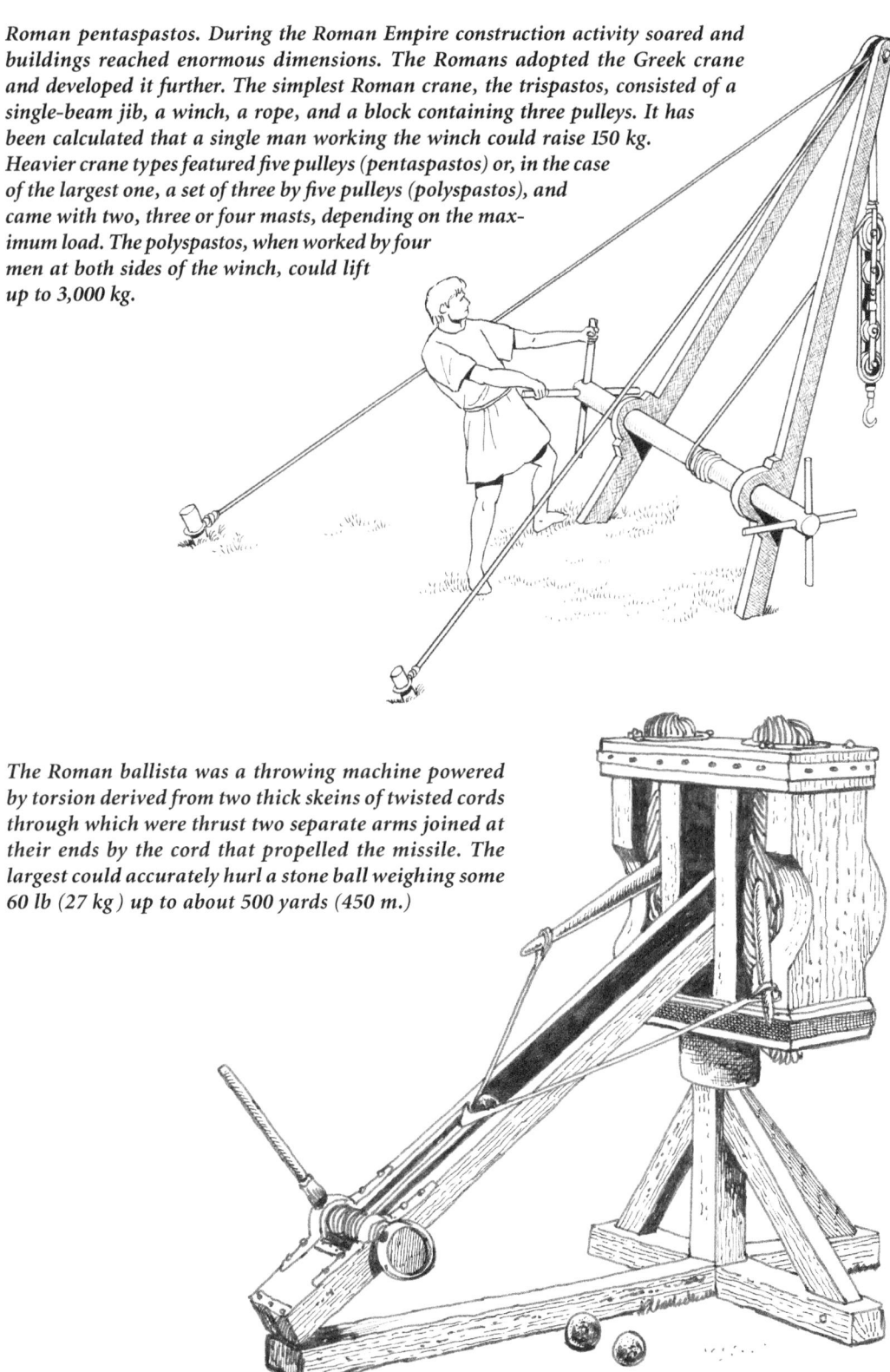

The Roman ballista was a throwing machine powered by torsion derived from two thick skeins of twisted cords through which were thrust two separate arms joined at their ends by the cord that propelled the missile. The largest could accurately hurl a stone ball weighing some 60 lb (27 kg) up to about 500 yards (450 m.)

Britannia

The name Britain comes from the word Pretani, the Greek term for the inhabitants of the British islands, but the Romans mispronounced it and called the people Briton and the country Britannia. The Romans invaded Britannia because military and political leaders had an eye on glory, fame and booty, because the British Celts had supported the Celts of Gaul against them, and also because they could make excellent use of British-produced goods such as corn, animals, metal ores and slaves.

Map of Britannia in c. A.D. 369.

Julius Caesar first came to Britain in 55 B.C. for a reconnaissance en force, but was repulsed. It was not until almost a century later, in A.D. 43, that the Romans were determined to conquer Britain, and sent an army composed of Legion II Augusta, XX Valeria Victoria, XIV Gemina Martia Victoria, and IX Hispana, totaling some 50,000 men. As they possessed artillery machines, siege devices and skilled engineers, the Romans could successfully lay siege to the Celtic hill forts, but they had some difficulty in defeating the high-spirited and quick-for-battle Celtic warriors. Ultimately the lack of unity among tribes led to Roman victory. By the beginning of the second century all the rich plains across the southern half of Britain, from the River Humber to the River Severn, were in subjection. Beyond that line were the upland areas where Roman control was not developed. These areas were watched from the town of York in the north, Chester and Caerleon in the western peninsula of Britain — the area that later became known as Wales. The Romans, however, never managed to subdue Caledonia (Scotland) although they tried over a century to do so.

The Romans came to trade, rule, exploit the land, and levy taxes, but the Italian immigration was never large enough to be overwhelming. However, the few traders and moneylenders, functionaries, officers, and active and discharged soldiers managed to establish a Romano-Celtic culture with methods of occupation that varied little from other parts of the Empire. Provided the subdued populations accepted the servitude of an alien power and payed tributes and taxes, the Romans treated them reasonably. They respected the local religions and customs, built excellent roads enabling their occupation forces to move swiftly from place to place, and fortified centers to hold fixed-occupation garrisons, towns and marketplaces. They introduced the skills of reading and writing, and also brought a new monotheist religion when the emperor Constantine converted to Christianity in 312 and made it the official faith of the empire. By employing a double policy of ruthless annihilation of rebels and dissidents, and favorable treatment of friendly factions, the Romans guaranteed peace throughout their empire for 400 years. There were occasional periods of internal violence, but these were generally the struggles for power between rival emperors or riots and rebellions resulting from temporary breakdown of law and order during such interregna. In some ways life in Roman Britain seemed civilized, but the Romans were indeed too few in number to change the language and customs of the early British people as they successfully did in France and Spain. Only a small fringe of the British population was directly involved with the Roman civilization. Britannia, located much too far away from the Mediterranean basin, was for the Romans very much of a peripheral importance. Indeed this cold island brought them rather little economic advantage. The Romans were forced to leave remote Britain in the early 5th century, as troops were badly needed elsewhere. They left behind a leaderless and quasi-defenseless population, and these were no match for the fierce Germanic tribes that poured into the island. The use of Latin completely disappeared when the Jutes, the Angles and the Saxons invaded the British Islands.

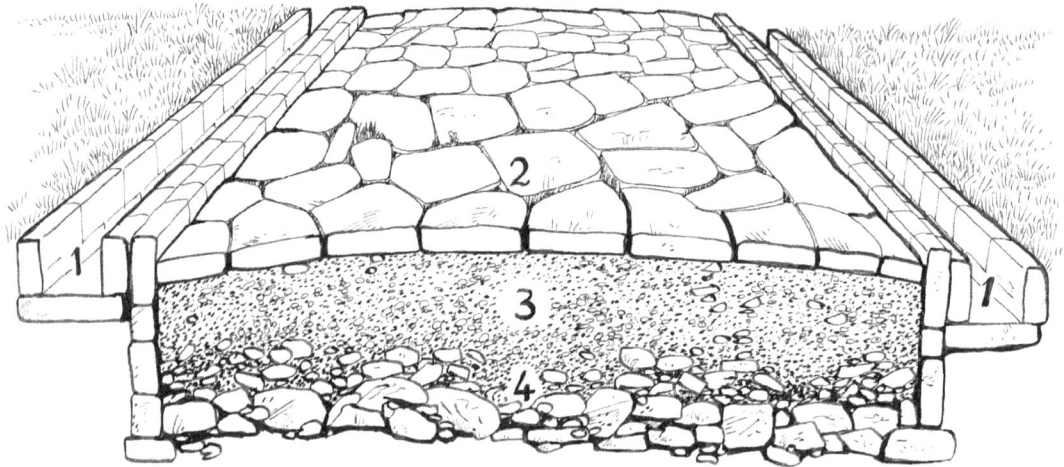

Cross-section of a Roman road. 1: Drainage ditch; 2: Paving stone; 3: Pebbles, gravel and sand; 4: Foundation of rubble stones. Well-metalled roads were, however, more the exception than the rule. Many dirt-tracks existed in the English countryside, choking and dusty in the summertime and quagmire in the autumn.

Camps and Forts

The Roman conquest of A.D. 43 marked the introduction to Britain of a whole new range of fortifications, quite different from the hill forts, duns and brochs of the previous Celtic period. As the conquest progressed, Celtic strongholds were gradually reduced. They were sometimes re-used but generally new fortifications were built by the conquerors. As we have just seen, these new fortified works were made by an efficient, highly organized, well-disciplined army of professionals who constructed fortifications according to standard patterns. No matter where in the Roman Empire, fortifications (but also urban organization, bath-houses, amphitheaters, arenas, official buildings, religious temples, and roads) tended to follow a regular uniformity. Although there were indeed many variations from site to site, and from land to land, general patterns and regular designs were endlessly repeated throughout the empire. For fortifications, the basic shape was a rectangle with rounded corners, often described by archaeologists as a playing-card form. This basic Roman military enclosure was represented in several main types, all of which were seen in Roman Britain: the temporary or semi-permanent (tented) camp; the legionary fortress; and the fort. Other more or less standardized works included fortlets and watchtowers, frontier works and lines, coastal forts, and urban fortification.

TEMPORARY AND SEMI-PERMANENT CAMPS

The Romans were not the first army to build defended camps on the march, but they took the construction of temporary defense works to the point of obsession. It was indeed standard practice for Roman units in hostile territory to construct a defensive earth wall around every *castellum* (non-permanent camp, plural *castella*), even for a single night's bivouac. The playing-card form was always the goal, but it could happen that the engineers and surveyors, whose mission it was to mark out the castellum in advance of the main body of the legion, had to make do with the natural surroundings. Castella diverging from the standard pattern thus existed, but a Roman army's camp on the march was never untidy or totally irregular in shape, and it always displayed an impression of order and discipline. Surveyors and engineers, men with plenty of experience who had an eye for the ground, always attempted to establish the camp on a slightly sloping hillside, a place well-drained and fairly open, if possible with easy access to water, firewood and fodder for the animals. Once such a place had been selected, the survey party would sometimes flatten the ground and before starting the ditch and wall construction, an agrimensor (land surveyor) would draw the locations of the streets and of the wall, beginning from the center of the field, by staking out the center line of the camp (*decumanus maximus*) crossed by its axis (*cardo maximus*). These two lines formed the basis of a broad pathway bisecting the camp, the *via principalis* about 30 m wide. The corners of the square or rectangular camp were marked out, as well as the various *strigae* (spaces where tents were to be erected). As soon as the main body of the army arrived, the legionaries took off their weapons and equipment, grasped their spades and started to dig a *fossa* (ditch) generally 6 feet wide and 3 feet deep, with the *deblais* (excavated soils) thrown inwards to form a *remblais* of similar size, which constituted the agger (rampart). Wooden stakes called sudes— of which one or two were carried along by each legionary, probably for this purpose (or locally felled trees cut into stakes) — were driven into the top of the wall to constitute a vallum (palisade). Strictly speaking a vallum designated only a single stake in the palisade, but in due course it came to designate a palisade and eventually the rampart itself. According to its importance and size, such a tented camp had four or six entrances all guarded by sentries, and the internal space was occupied by troops' tents, commanders' and officers' tents, granaries, workshops, cavalry quarters and so forth. Entrances were defended by a titulus, a free-standing length of bank and ditch constructed directly in front of the opening in order to prevent a direct approach. An alternative disposition was the clavicula, a curving extension of the wall projecting inwards or outwards that provided a simple measure of security for troops under canvas. The standard disposition of the Roman camp was very practical. Indeed once a soldier was inside, he always knew where everything was whether it was, a temporary camp with tents or a permanent fort with buildings.

Of course the size of a temporary camp varied according to the unit it had to house. A legion of 5,000–6,000 men required a camp about 900 feet square. However, where large-scale operations were carried out, larger camps were required. For example, the camp at Featherwood West (Northumbria), was about 1,600 feet by 1,100 feet and could accommodate two legions. The camp at Raedikes (Grampian, southwest of Aberdeen) had an irregular outline: it was approximately 2,620 feet by

1,750 feet (800 by 530 m), covered an area of about 110 acres (44.5 hectares) and could house five legions. The northern and eastern defensive ditch was quite substantial, around 15 feet across and about 7 feet deep (4.6 by 2.1 m), and the rest of the perimeter was markedly less significant. In the same region, there were similarly sized temporary marching camps at Normandikes (106 acres), Kintore (110 acres), Ythan Wells (111 acres) and Muiryfold (109 acres). There were naturally smaller camps for small units, namely for cohorts of 480 men. There were also temporary camps that were built by troops in peacetime as part of their training so that on actual active service legionaries would have the experience necessary to erect a fortified overnight bivouac as a matter of routine. There is no doubt that the Romans were obsessed with digging, perhaps partly to keep the men in physical shape, and partly to give them something to do, as boredom could undermine discipline.

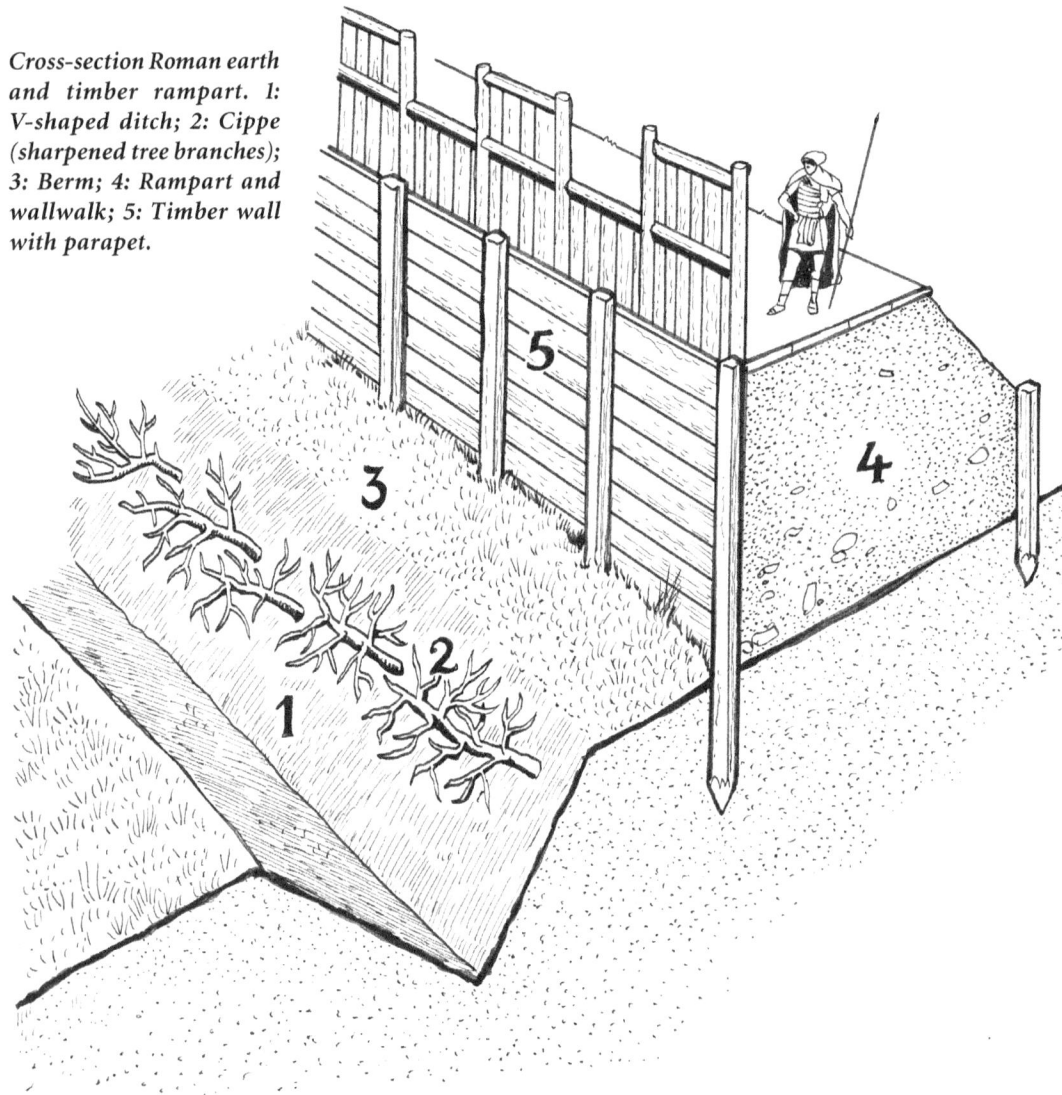

Cross-section Roman earth and timber rampart. 1: V-shaped ditch; 2: Cippe (sharpened tree branches); 3: Berm; 4: Rampart and wallwalk; 5: Timber wall with parapet.

Wattlework parapet. The lorica, also called the parapet or breastwork, was a man-high defensive screen, often fitted with open parts, called crenels or pinnea (1), and standing parts, named merlons (2), placed along the upper outer edge of a wall (3), and protecting the wallwalk (4). The parapet could be an earth bank or a palisade (stakes) or made of wattle (interwoven twigs).

In addition there were semi-temporary camps, which were occupied for longer than one night, or which acted as supply bases for a campaign. In the latter case not all of the space within the camp was used to accommodate troops, but instead featured stores and supplies for units on the move. Semi-permanent camps were built according to the same playing-card design, but they had slightly more elaborate defenses as more time was available. The tents were also replaced with wattle-and-daube, thatched-roofed timber huts for more comfort, particularly when the camp was to be occupied over the winter. Good examples of semi-permanent camps have been discovered at Chew Green in Northumbria (19 acres) and Cawthorn in Yorkshire (5.25 acres). Semi-permanent camps were also used in the case of a siege, and then were part of siege works, for example the camps of Dumfries and Galloway, built during the siege of the Celtic hill fort of Birrenswark. These supply bases and camps were often only maintained for a short period before the military unit would move on to another location. However, if the site was suitable, temporary and semi-temporary camps and supply bases could become permanent camps used for more or less long

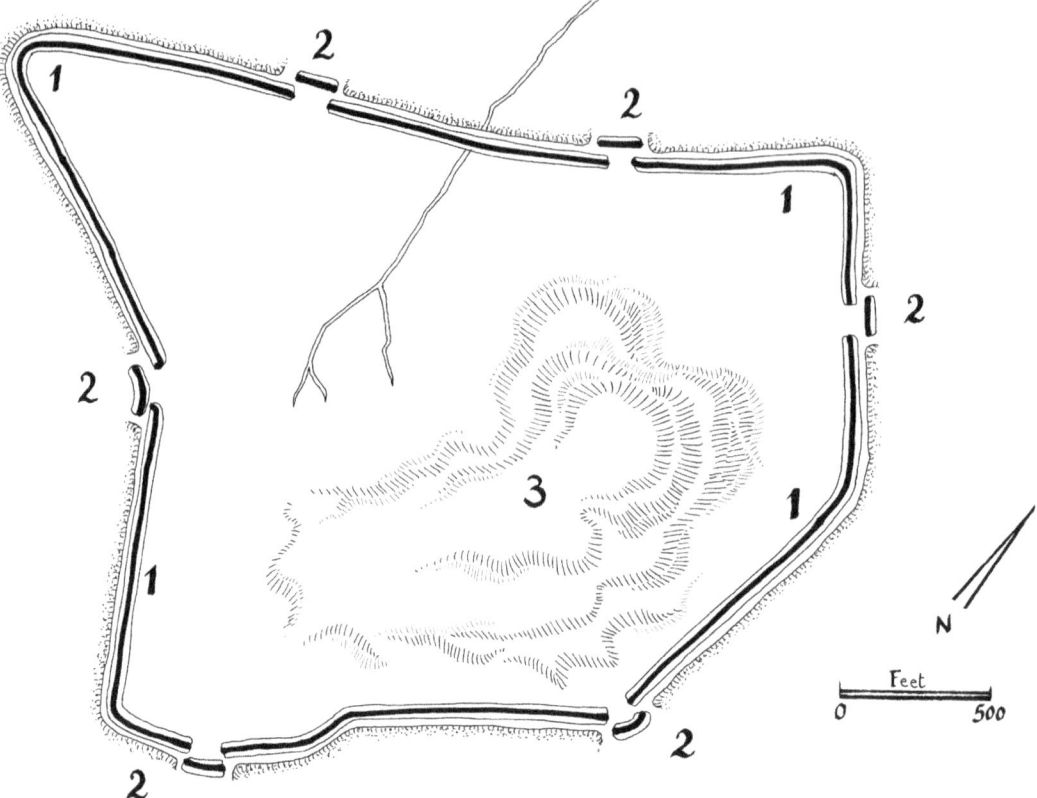

Raedikes: 1: Enclosure; 2: Gates with titulus; 3: Garney Hill (also known as Garrison Hill).

term, when occupation duty replaced active offensive. Whether originating from a semi-permanent camp or a totally new foundation, the structure remained the same, but the defenses of the semi-permanent camps were more elaborate. The surrounding ditch was deeper and the earth wall was higher, up to 8 feet, and up to 20 feet wide, with a proper timber palisade and rampart walk at the top. Tituli and claviculae were stronger, and small wooden watchtowers and obstacles added. When the camp became a permanently occupied position, earth ramparts and timber towers were replaced with stone walls, gatehouses and masonry towers, and all buildings and structures inside the camp were equally built with stone.

Legionary Fortresses

Once the initial conquest of Britain was achieved three legions were stationed in camps called legionary fortresses. The term fortress suggests a formidable defensive structure, something like a medieval castle with high walls and formidable towers, or a fort bristling with weapons and outworks, but in fact the defensive capacity of the legionary fortresses was not particularly impressive, mainly because the fortresses were not intended for passive defense. As a rule, Roman soldiers, when attacked, would not wait inside their walls, but instead would sally en force. Relying on their mobility, strength and discipline, they would rather fight and defeat enemies on the open field. The legionary fortresses were therefore more fortified barracks than defensive structures. Although they had to secure against the possibility of a surprise attack, they were primarily designed to provide permanent and tolerably comfortable quarters for the garrisons. The term "legionary fortress" is probably now too well established by scholars, experts and archaeologists to be changed, but the offensive rather than defensive role of these legionary bases should always be kept in mind. After the reign of Emperor Domitian (A.D. 81–96), legionary fortresses were reduced in size to approximately 10–15 hectares, and accommodated only one legion, or they were even smaller and housed only one or more cohorts. A legionary fortress included a number of buildings of more or less standardized design.

The *principia* or headquarters block was the administrative and spiritual center of the fortress. It faced onto the junction of the two main roads through the fort, often with a portico in front, perhaps carrying an inscription recording construction or renovation. The entrance to the principia proper opened onto a colonnaded courtyard. The presence of altars and *tribunalia* (saluting bases) indicate that ceremonies and parades must have been customarily held there. Ranges of rooms sometimes flanked this courtyard, perhaps serving as stores, especially for weapons (*armamentaria*) or workshops. Behind the courtyard stood the covered crosshall or basilica — a multi-purpose government building. After the Roman Empire became officially Christian, the term basilica came by extension to specifically refer to a large church. The basilica, with its two rows of massive columns flanked by aisles, probably looked like its archictectural successor: the Norman church. It often rose above the courtyard portico and the rooms to its rear, so that clerestory windows could admit light. The whole building was of monumental proportions, dwarfing the barrack blocks and most of the other adjacent constructions. The crosshall at Chester, for example, was about 240 feet long and 80 feet in width; the span of the nave was 40 feet and each aisle 20 feet. It would have been possible to assemble the bulk of the legion here, providing the soldiers stood shoulder to schoulder, and the commander or a visiting dignitary could have spoken to them, read an order of the day or issued special instructions. These assemblies may have been associated with the legionary shrine that stood in the center. The regimental shrine (called the *sacellum* or *aedes*) was the symbolic heart of the fort, where the standards, silver eagles, flags and emblems were kept. At the west end of the crosshall was a dais (tribunal), from which the garrison commander could preside at meetings or ceremonies and dispense justice. To the rear of the basilica were smaller administrative rooms and offices where the administration of the legion was carried out, correspondence was received, answered and filed, accounts were kept by the *cerasii* (administrators), and the *librarii* (clerks) and the *exactores* (accountants) worked out the many deductions from the soldiers' pay.

The *praetorium* (commander's residence) was a building almost as large as the principia, and was usually adjacent to it, either along the via principalis or the via quintana. It reflected the difference in class and status between officers and the rank and file. The fort prefect and his household had the best appointments and most spacious of all the accommodation, showing not only his military senior rank but also his superior social status as a member of the equestrian class. The praetorium, based on Roman townhouses in the Mediterranean, of the type preserved in Pompeii, for example, was composed of a range of heated rooms around a courtyard, sometimes including a private bath, offering the commanding officer a comfortable private space removed from the fort's bustle. The senior officers or tribunes' houses were smaller versions of the above.

The *valetudinarium* was the hospital where the sick and wounded could be segregated and treated. It comprised a range of wards around a central courtyard. At the entrance was a large reception hall and at the end an operating theater with running water. Sick and wounded soldiers were attended to by a variety of medical personnel. Each regiment had its doctor (*medicus ordinariu*), a pharmacist (*seplasiarius*), medical orderlies (*medeci*), and dressers (*capsarii*). Knowledge of medicines and drugs was elementary and highly empirical. Nevertheless, natural antiseptics such as pitch and turpentine were used and much employ was made of herbal lore which has, regrettably, been lost. A number of ancient treatises on medicine and surgery have survived, which throw much light on methods used by the Romans. In wartime, for the army doctors the commonest treatments were the extraction of foreign bodies and amputations.

Horrea (granaries, food and supply stores) were essential buildings ensuring the soldiers' effectiveness as a fighting force and preventing any discontent. Their size and capacity were calculated for adequate provisioning of the soldiers housed in the fort. Granaries generally could store two years' supply of grain. It was vital that the basic food supplies should be given maximum protection to ensure the smallest possible loss. The worst danger was fire, and therefore granaries were solidly constructed, and usually placed near the center of the fortress to be as far as possible from enemy incendiary missiles. Often built in pairs, their floors were raised on wooden posts or stone walls to allow air to circulate beneath in order to keep the grain, as well as other foodstuffs, cool and dry. External walls were normally massively built and buttressed to withstand the lateral pressure of the stored grain (although it remains uncertain whether the grain was stored in bulk or in barrels and also if other kinds of food, such as meat, were housed there as well) and to support the tiled roof. This was given a large overhang, so that the rainwater was carried well clear of the building, and this also offered greater shade from the sun's heat in summer. Slots pierced the external walls to assist ventilation.

Barrack blocks took up much of the space within a fort. Their numbers, size and type depended on the garrison's size and composition. The narrow buildings (on average 10 m wide and 40–50 m long) housed a *centuria* (80 infantrymen) or a *turma* (32 cavalrymen). Arranged in pairs, and placed back to back, forming a complete striga (allotted space in a fort) with little space separating them from one another, the rather gloomy barracks included a series of paired rooms (*contubernia*), as well as the living and storage space for ordinary soldiers. Eight men occupied each room. Its name, the *papilio*, was the same as that of the folding leather tent which sheltered soldiers on campaign and bivouac. There were bunk beds (with straw mattresses) and lockers, shelves and pits for storage. Hearths provided light and heat for warmth and cooking, since there were no central canteens. Floors were of beaten earth, or clay, perhaps carpeted with bracken or straw or occasionally covered with flagging. Often a verandah ran the full length of the barrack. Communal latrines were installed outside the barrack. Living conditions must have been pretty crowded, as the eight legionaries also shared their room with wives, comcubines and children, and some soldiers may also have owned slaves. However given the likely difference between the strength of the unit on paper and its actual strength, barracks were not always fully occupied and more space was generally available.

At the end of the long barrack block were the officers' accommodations, separated by a stone wall from the soldiers' contubernia. The accommodation for the centurions included several rooms grouped around a central corridor. Often this block was wider than the rest of the barrack. Stone flagged floors, separate drainage, latrines and washplaces, glazed windows and plastered walls made these rooms more comfortable as well as more spacious than the rank and file's. These quarters may have been shared with NCOs (junior officers). In cavalry barracks two turmae of 32 men each were assigned to each block. Horses were sometimes stabled in separate blocks, long narrow buildings with an interior drain running them of the building to remove waste. Drainage (sewers) and fresh water supply (springs, cisterns and wells) were very important features, closely associated with the health of the army, and the Roman military engineers always went to considerable lengths to see that both were adequate.

Fabrica (workshops) were built for engineers and practitioners of several craft, including builders, plumbers, leather-workers, smiths and weapon-smiths, carpenters and cartwrights. These fabrica were varied in shape and form, sometimes buildings around a courtyard, sometimes included as the service wing of the praetorium.

Beyond the fort too, the landscape was likely to be dotted with the signs of legionaries' industry, such as kilns for pottery, bricks and lime burning, stone quarries, annexed spaces providing additional accommodation for soldiers and animals, parade and training grounds, and civilian settlements. Other extramural buildings included a bathhouse, amphitheater, and cemetery. The baths were housed in a building with specialized functions. They were shared with one's colleagues and involved physical exercise, massage and indoor games, and were in fact a social club where one normally spent some time, stripping off the cares of daily life as well as its toil and sweat. Roman bathing (a mix between the Scandinavian sauna and the Turkish bath) was encouraged by the army since personal hygiene and social relaxation were important factors in the physical and mental health of the soldiers. The baths were placed outside the fort for two good reasons. First, the furnaces presented a serious fire hazard, and second, units on the move spending the night under the shelter of the fort generally pitched their tents in the annex and could make use of the bathhouse independently of the usual garrison.

The amphitheater was a large open arena, oval in plan, with a massive, heavily butressed outer wall which supported tiers of seats. At Chester the structure stood outside the southeast corner of the fortress and was about 300 by 350 feet with an outer wall 8 feet thick. The amphitheater was designed to accommodate the full garrison for religious celebrations, military parades and commemorations, training and tactical demonstrations, and games associated with gladiator combat and wild beast shows.

Under their law, the Romans were not permitted to bury their dead inside towns or military fortresses, so it was customary to establish the cemeteries along the roads entering the fortress. Both cremation and burial were practiced. The former was universal in the first century but gradually gave place to the latter until that, in turn, was more popular by the late second century.

In the early years of the occupation of Britain legionary fortresses were established at Lincoln and Gloucester, later at York, Chester and Caerleon, and another at Inchtuthil north of Perth in Scotland.

Inchtuthil fortress, located on an isolated plateau, was built in A.D. 83 and abandoned in A.D. 86 as it was probably too far advanced in hostile land. It was occupied for only three years by Legio XX Valeria Vitrix. It featured a 13-feet-thick earth wall (later with stone facing), with a ditch 20 feet wide and 7 feet deep in front. It had four gateways consisting of timber-built flanking towers. Nearly square in plan (1,565 by 1,529 feet), the large fortified enceinte enclosed a perimeter of 53 acres (21 hectares). The space inside was divided into quarters for nearly 6,000 men, stores, a military hospital, a bathhouse, workshops, a drill hall, and granaries and supply stores, as well as barracks and stables for a cavalry unit in the classic Roman military fashion.

The fortress of Lincoln, occupied only for 20 or 30 years in the early period of the conquest, consisted of a rectangular earth wall revetted with timber, enclosing an area of 42 acres. In A.D. 71, Lincoln was abandoned as a legionary fortress and became a colonia for retired *emeriti* (veterans), and the IXth legion left Lincoln in order to subdue the Celtic tribe of Brigantes in northern England. For this purpose a new fortress was founded at Eburacum (York), which remained one of the several permanent bases during the centuries of the Roman occupation. The legionary fortress of York measured 1,590 feet by 1,370 feet. Originally an earth and timber work, it was fortified with a stone wall and an earth bank in A.D. 107–8. In c. A.D. 300 the enclosure was reinforced with eight large projecting towers. The inside of the fortress included a stone-built headquarters, four large barrack blocks, and the usual service buildings as described above.

The legionary fortress of Chester, created in c. A.D. 78, measured some 1,950 feet by 1,360 feet and covered 56 acres. It housed infantry and cavalry, but also some naval personnel for operation on the River Dee. The internal buildings included five groups of barrack blocks, a headquarters, granaries, a bathhouse and an amphitheater.

Like Lincoln, the legionary fortress of Glevum (Gloucester) was transformed into a colonia in c. A.D. 64–5, and its garrison was transferred to a new site at Isca

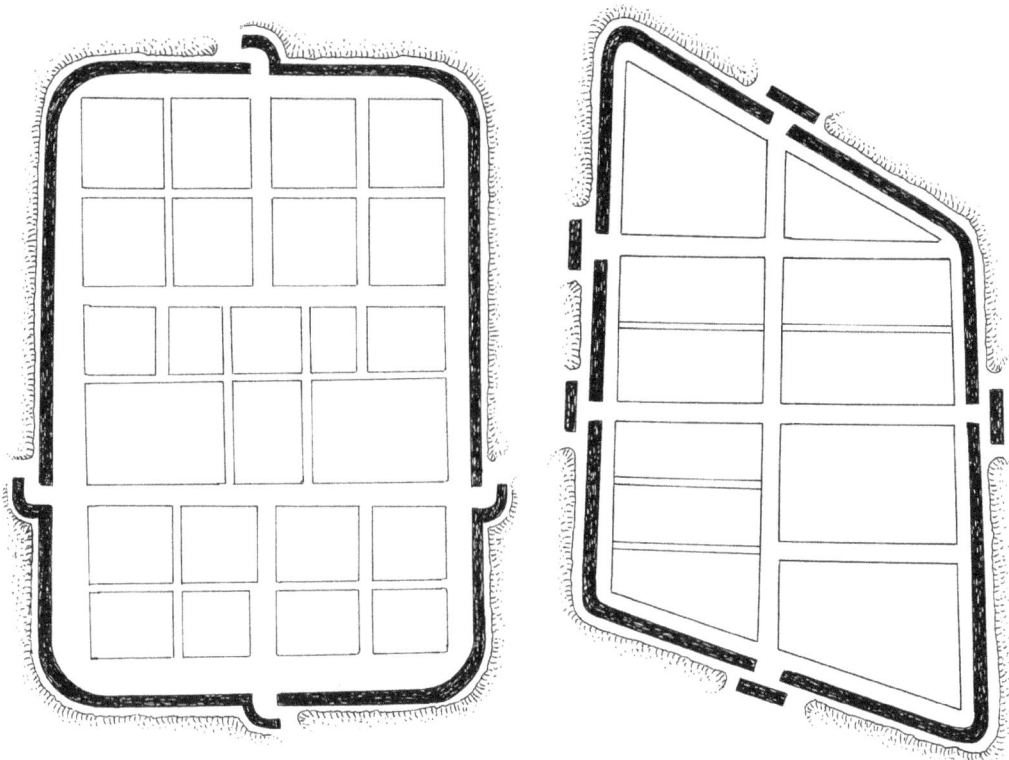

Outline of Roman camps. The shape of a Roman fort was similar to a playing card—at least whenever possible—with an entrance on each side. Inside the fort there were two main streets that divided the camp. The via praetoria led from the front gate to the headquarters building (principia) in the center of the fort. The via principalis joined the two side gates and passed in front of the principia. The commanding officer's house (praetorium) was next to the headquarters building, and the rest of the fort was divided into strigae filled with rows of barracks, workshops and stores. Left: *Regularly-designed legionary fortress (based on Chester).* Right: *Irregularly-shaped marching camp (based on Featherwood West, Northumberland).*

(Caerleon near Cardiff). Originally defended by a clay wall revetted with timber, Gloucester later included a 5-feet-thick stone wall with a ditch in front, enclosing the usual Roman standard premises.

The building of the fortress of Caerleon started around A.D. 75. Its location, selected by the then governor of Britain, Sextus Julius Frontinus, who had been given the task of settling the remaining unconquered areas of Britain, was inside enemy (Silurian) territory, but close enough to the mouth of the River Usk to be reached by seagoing ships should urgent reinforcements or other supplies be required. The original defenses of Isca were of turf, clay and timber, these being replaced sometime around A.D. 100 by stone walls and towers. Inside the defenses, the buildings were laid out in the standard pattern for legionary fortresses of that time. Isca remained the headquarters of Legio II Augusta for more than 200 years. It is unlikely, however, that during all of this time it would have remained at full garrison strength.

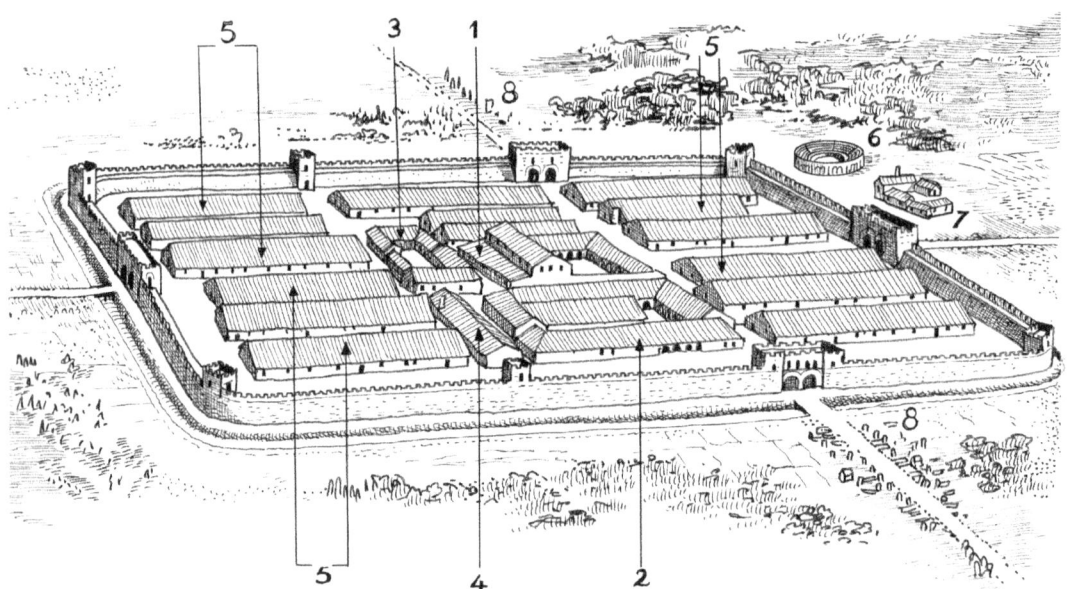

Roman legionary fortress. 1: Principia; 2: Praetorium; 3: Valetudinarium; 4: Horrea; 5: Barracks; 6: Amphitheater; 7: Bathhouse; 8: Cemetery.

Detachments would have undoubtedly been transferred all over the empire. The political turmoil and revolts that happened in the late third century would finally see an end to Isca, somewhere between A.D. 287 and 296.

Auxiliary Forts

As time went by the Roman occupation army in Britain featured fewer and fewer genuine Italian legionaries and more and more *peregrini* (non–Roman citizens), e.g., locally recruited auxiliaries and hired foreign mercenaries. Auxiliaries included infantrymen, archers and light cavalrymen from all parts of the empire. After 25 years of service, they would become Roman citizens upon discharge. By contrast, legionaries were citizens upon enlistment. The places housing these units, called auxiliary forts, were much smaller than the legionary fortresses, being on average 5 acres in area as opposed to the fortress's 50 acres. On the other hand they were much more numerous, over 200 being recorded in Britain. The auxiliary forces were composed of both cavalry and infantry, so their forts included accommodation for horses and varied in size. A fort 400 by 400 feet could accommodate an infantry cohort of about 480 men, a fort 600 by 400 feet could house an *ala* (plural *alae*) including 480 cavalrymen and their mounts. Although there were variations on the standard basic theme, the general layout, plan and structure of the auxiliary forts displayed a scaled-down variant of the legionary fortress with the same playing-card plan, the same arrangement of gates, internal streets, and the same location for the headquarters, commander's house, barracks, stables, workshops, and supply stores.

For example, the auxiliary camp of Gelligaer (Mid-Glamorgan, Wales), built in A.D. 13–12 and intended for 480 men, was 400 by 400 feet. Its enclosure was made of a mass of clay held by inner and outer revetments with an overall width of 20 feet. It included a ditch 20 feet wide and 7 feet deep, four double gateways set between twin towers, and twelve wall- and cornertowers.

The auxiliary camp of Balmuidy (Strathclyde) was one of the two stone-built forts on the Antonine Wall (see below). Its enclosure (460 by 413 feet) was a stone wall 7 feet thick at the base, strengthened by an earth rampart 20 feet wide, with three ditches facing the enemy. Its interior space included the usual standard buildings: headquarters, barracks, and supply stores. Rather roomy for a single cohort, it might have accommodated a garrison of 800 men.

The auxiliary fort of Housesteads in the Hadrian's Wall was long and narrow (610 by 367 feet) and could accommodate some 800 infantrymen. The fort did not feature a ditch since it stood above a steep natural slope. Its enclosure, which formed a part of the Hadrian's Wall, was made of a stone wall 5 feet thick backed by a clay rampart 15 feet wide. The fort obviously contained the usual standard buildings: barracks, supply store and so forth. Other auxiliary forts like Fendoch (Tayside, built in A.D. 78–84), Chesters, Gwynedd, Caerhun, Caernarvon, and Pen Llystyn, for example, conformed to standard unit sizes with slight variations here and there.

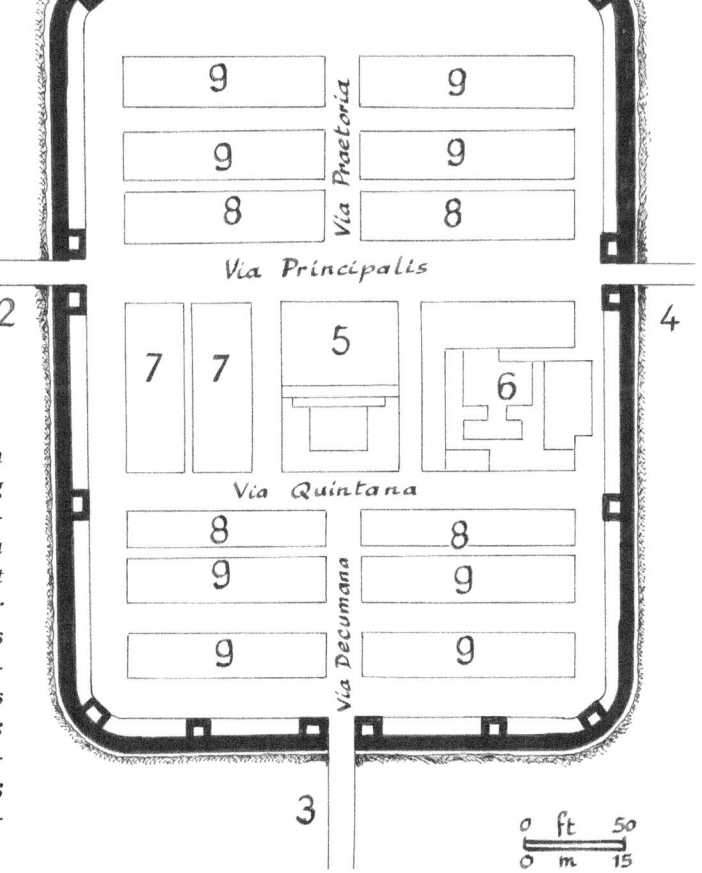

This auxiliary fort, based on Chesters, included the following standard elements. 1: Porta Praetoria (or North Gate); 2: Porta Principalis Sinistra (or West Gate); 3: Porta Decumana (or South Gate); 4: Porta Principalis Dextra (or East Gate); 5: Principia (headquarters, religious and administrative buildings); 6: Praetorium (commander's residence); 7: Horrea (supply stores); 8: Fabricae and stabuli (workshops and stables); 9: Barracks.

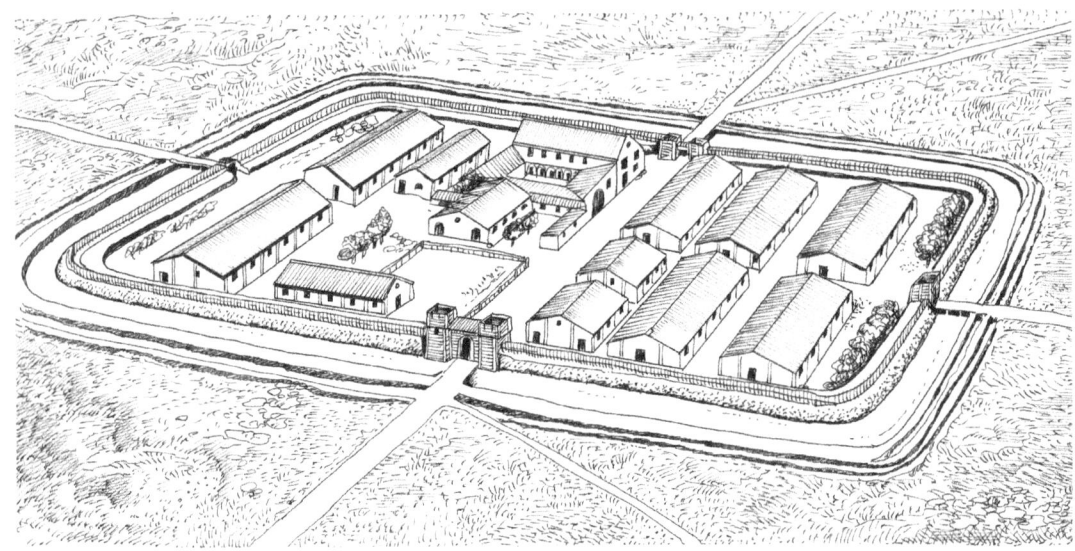

Roman fort

No civil community was allowed within a Roman military camp or fort, but civilians settled outside the walls. Indeed a fort often had an associated civilian settlement outside, forming the nucleus of a township, called a *vicus*. Roman soldiers were one of the groups in society that had a regular wage and, as has often been the case throughout history, these men with money to spend attracted a range of people providing different civilian services who settled nearby and took advantage of soldiers' requirements. These commodities included inns, taverns, gambling dens and brothels, and eventually craftsmen, merchants, and traders. So around a fort could develop a settlement, which could easily become a village and possibly a town.

Frankish auxiliary in Roman service. The depicted auxiliary wears a Roman helmet but no body armor. He is armed with a spear, a short sword and an oval wooden shield.

Fortlets and Watchtowers

Small standard units known as fortlets existed. Generally less than a quarter of an acre in area, they included only one or two small barrack blocks for the accommodation of a *centuria* (80 men), or even a smaller garrison. Fortlets were placed along a road or a river crossing, could be incorporated into border fortifications (e.g., Gask Ridge, Hadrian's Wall) and were often called milecastles because they were spaced at intervals of one Roman mile (1.48 km or 1,618 yards). Fortlets could also be used as signal stations or beacons along the east coast as occurred during the fourth century. In that case they included a signal tower possibly 100 feet high and 50 feet square. An example of such a signal station has been found at Goldsborough in Yorkshire. Dated from the late 4th century, it was part of a group that included similar works at Filey, Ravenscar, Scarborough and Huntcliffe.

Isolated watchtowers also existed. They were made of timber or stone, very often square in plan, two or three stories high, often with an observation balcony, and set within a low earth wall topped with a palisade or a wattlework parapet and hemmed with a ditch. They could accommodate only an outposted contubernia (eight men, the smallest unit of the Roman army), and were spaced out along a coastline, a road or river or along a border to observe traffic and population movement. The first floor of the tower was used as a storage space for food and equipment. Off-duty members of the guard detachment slept and cooked on the second floor, while their

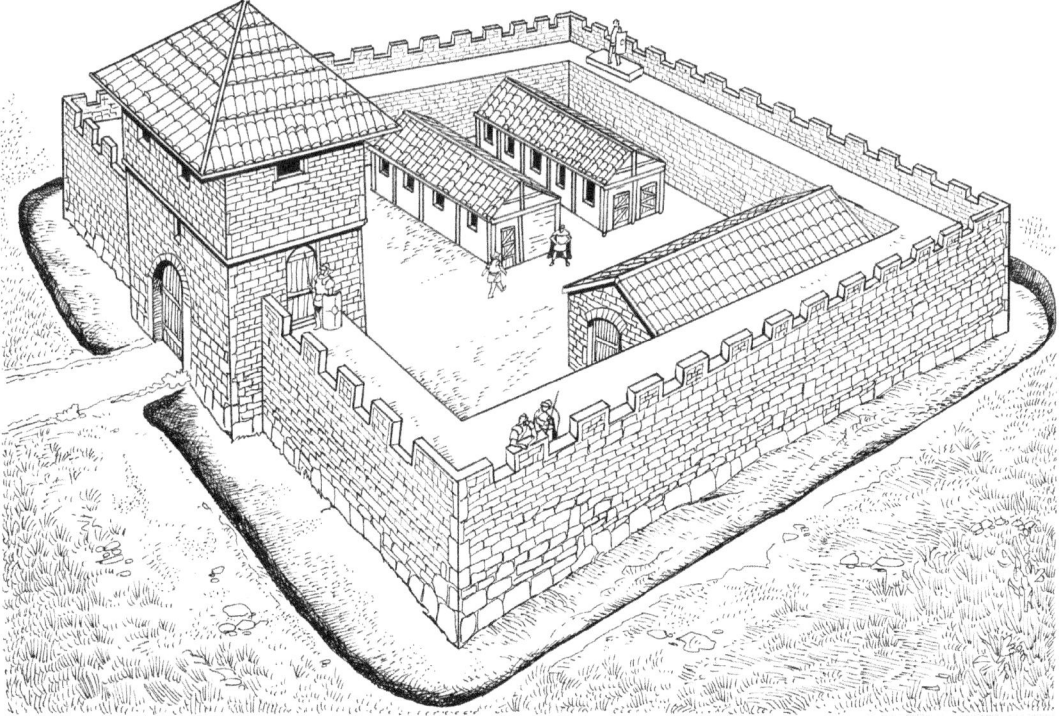

Roman fortlet.

comrades observed the area around them from the third-story guardroom or the balcony all around it. When built in a line at a border like the Gask Ridge, for example, watchtowers were within sight of each other, but not always within actual supporting distance. Fortlets and watchtowers had a twofold role: to see and be seen. They were, in modern parlance checkpoints fulfilling a control, observation, and also deterrent function, as they were physical reminders of Rome's omnipresent power.

Roman timber watchtower. Isolated watchtowers were often protected by a V-shaped ditch and a palisade.

Roman stone watchtower.

Frontier Works

As the first century matured, the frontiers of the Roman Empire became increasingly fixed, and what were once temporary limits became definitive borders. As a result, the function of the legions was no longer conquest but policing the border tribes, mounting punitive raids, and preventing tax evasion and livestock rustling. For this purpose the Romans established frontier defensive works known as *limes* (plural *limites*). The first limes was established in Germany, along the rivers Rhine and Danube, under the reign of the Emperor Dominien (81–96). The defensive program was continued by Trajan (97–117), Hadrien (117–138) and many of their successors. The frontiers of the Roman Empire were largely based on natural features (e.g., rivers, mountains, deserts, forested areas), which were reinforced with artificial defenses. In what later would become England, the Romans made a section of limes fortification, known as the Gask Frontier. This artificial border placed under permanent military surveillance included forts, fortlets and watchtowers linked by a military road. This was built between A.D. 80 and 90, thus about 40 years before the famous Hadrian's Wall. The Gask line started at Glenbank just to the north of Dunblane and reached to Bertha, just upstream of Perth on the Tay. It ran for most of its length along the prominent 70 m high east-west oriented Gask Ridge (hence its name) on the northern side of Strathearn in Perthshire, between the Highland massif and the peninsula of Fife.

The most striking remnant of the Roman presence in Britain is without doubt the fortified frontier line known as Hadrian's Wall, built, as the name implies, by order of Emperor Hadrian. South and central Britain were parts of the empire, but in northern Caledonia (Scotland) the Romans made no headway. On the edge of rough heather moorlands lived the half-savage tribe of the Brigantes, and still farther north the fearsome Picts, both equally refractory to any peaceful penetration. After disappointing and disastrous attempts, the Romans abandoned the idea of subduing the north, and instead fortified the frontier in order to hold them back, hereby showing that they no longer had the offensive initiative. Hadrian's Wall was intended to clearly and physically mark the border of the empire, impose Roman order, repulse Scottish raiders, improve economic stability and provide peaceful conditions in the frontier zone.

The defensive system was an extraordinary feat of engineering. It had a length of 73.5 miles (117 km), and stretched across the width of northern England between the mouth of River Tyne and Newcastle-upon-Tyne in the east to Carlisle, Bowness and the shore of the Solway Firth in the west. Construction started in A.D. 122 and six years later was largely completed. Hadrian's Wall consisted of a continuous stone or turf wall. At intervals of one Roman mile (1.48 km or 1,618 yards) there was a small fort (called a milecastle) abutting the rear of the wall, and between two milecastles, there were two watchtowers built at intervals of 540 yards. In front of the wall was a V-shape ditch and a glacis, except where the ground was very steep. The garrison to man this defensive system totaled some 10,000 men, who were housed in a series of auxiliary forts like the previously discussed Vercovicum (Housesteads) and Cilurnum (Chesters). Forts, fortlets, and towers were linked by a military road that ran parallel to the wall. The garrison of Hadrian's Wall suffered serious attacks, notably in A.D. 180, and also in A.D. 196 and 197, which were followed by long periods of calm. However, Hadrian's Wall would be misunderstood if it were regarded as a kind of Maginot Line protecting a peaceful province. It was rather a means of separating the friendly tribes in the south from northerners hostile to Rome as diplomacy also played its part. The wall remained occupied by Roman troops until their withdrawal from Britain in the late fourth century, when barbarian invasions, economic decline, and military coups loosened the empire's hold on Britain. By A.D. 410, the Roman administration and its legions were gone.

Hadrian's Wall was the first of two fortification lines built across Great Britain, the second being the Antonine Wall in what is now southern Scotland. Pressure from the Caledonians may have led the Roman Emperor Antoninus Pius (reign 138–161) to send the empire's troops farther north. The Antonine Wall was a stone and turf fortification built across the Central Belt of Scotland, between the Firth of Forth and the Firth of Clyde, bringing Lowland Scotland within the Roman province of Britannia. The northernmost frontier barrier of the Roman Empire, it ran approximately 63 km (39 miles), was about ten feet high and fifteen feet wide, and was fronted by a deep ditch on the north side. Construction began in A.D. 142, and took about twelve years to complete. The wall was protected by sixteen forts, with a number of small fortlets and watchtowers between them. Troop movement was facilitated by a road linking all the sites known as the Military Way. Despite this auspicious start the wall was abandoned around A.D. 163 after only twenty years, and the garrisons relocated back down south to Hadrian's Wall. In 208 Emperor Septimius Severus re-established legions at the wall and ordered repairs, and this has led to the wall being referred to as the Severan Wall. However, the occupation ended only a few years later, and the wall was never manned and fortified again. The highland vastness of Scotland remained a free refuge for the Celtic people of Britain. Most of the turf-built Antonine Wall and its associated fortifications have been destroyed over time, but some remains are still visible today, although they are much less evident than the better known Hadrian's Wall to the south.

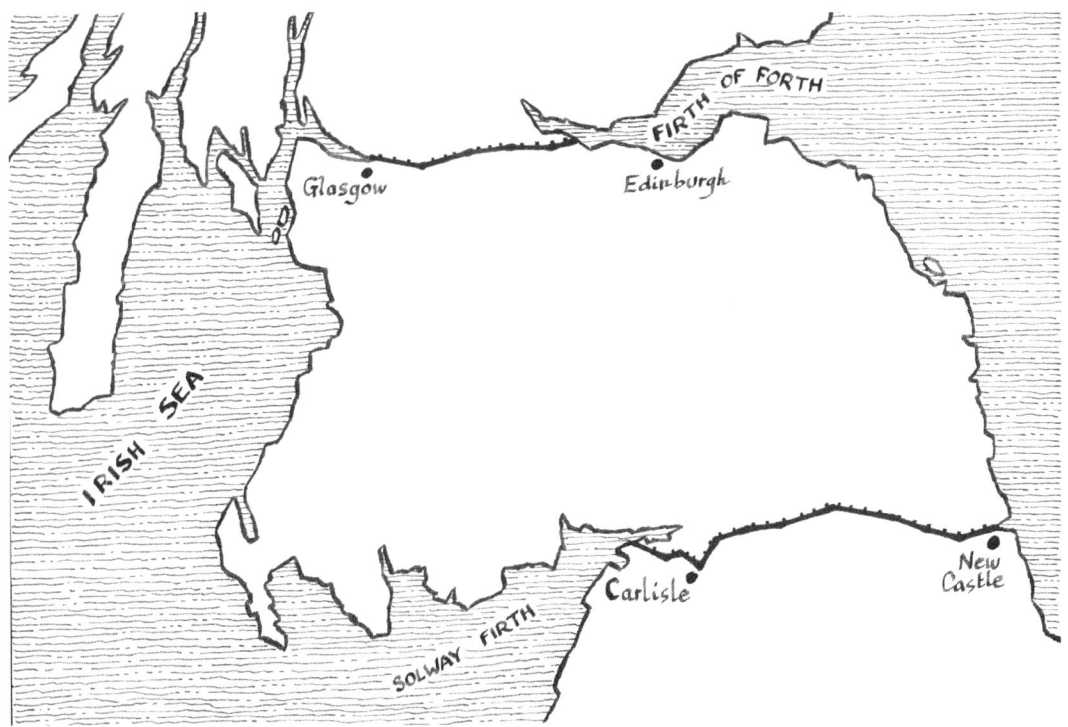

Hadrian's Wall. The map shows Antonine's Wall (top) and Hadrian's Wall (bottom).

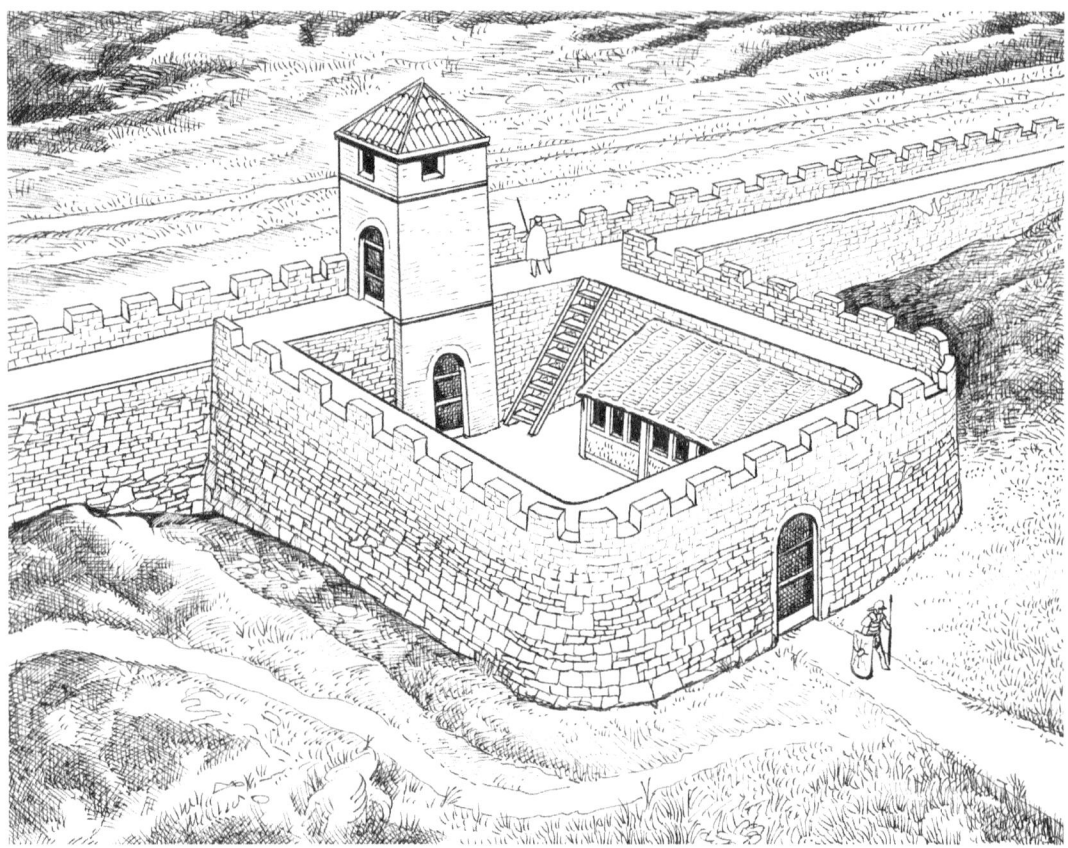

Milecastle in Hadrian's Wall. Spaced at intervals of one Roman mile regardless of natural conditions, each milecastle included a crenallated enceinte with watchtower, a lavatrina (latrine), and a barrack block divided into one dormitory for 16 men and a supply and equipment store.

Saxon Shore Forts

The so-called Forts of the Saxon Shore (Litus Saxonicum in Latin) were a girdle of fortified ports built by the Romans along the southern coast of Britain from the actual county of Norfolk to Hampshire. There were originally at least ten of them, possibly eleven, of which nine survive in varying states of preservation. Most were built towards the end of the 3rd century A.D., though some (e.g., Richborough and Reculver) incorporated parts of earlier fortified buildings. In the 3rd and 4th century a threat appeared in the form of Germanic raiding along the vulnerable and hitherto undefended south and east coasts. The origin and purpose of the Litus Saxonicum were to dispose of powerful military and naval installations in order to protect trade and communication between Gaul (France) and Britannia, to keep watch against Saxon raiders (from northern Germany) and Frisian pirates (from the present day Netherlands), to drive them away if they landed, and to pursue them when they had attacked and looted a Romano-British settlement on the coast. There was thus a provincial naval force called Classis Britannica (Britain Fleet), whose primary task was the secure ferrying of goods, supplies and troops, and the guarding of the commercial shipping lanes between Gaul and Britannia. As is often the case in coastal defense, the forts also played a deterrent role, as the fact that well-trained forces were at constant readiness was often sufficient to deter raiders and pirates. The Roman fleet included two sorts of ships: the military oared galley and the merchant sailing vessel. The nine preserved Saxon fortified ports are: Branodunum (modern day Branscaster); Gariannonum (Burgh Castle); Othona (Bradwell); Regulbium (Reculver); Rutupiae (Richborough); Dubris (Dover); Lemanis (Lympne); Anderida (Pevensey); and Portus Adurni (Portchester). The Litus Saxonicum, placed under command of a naval officer who bore the resounding title Comes litoris Saxonici per Britannia (Count of the Saxon shore of Britain), formed a defensive system. Although there were considerable variations within the group of Saxon Shore forts, they all had certain similar characteristics. They were all on or near the sea, placed at strategic points—harbors or river-mouths—guarding the natural waterways which seaborne raiders or invaders of southeastern Britain might attempt to force. Each fort held harbor installations from which a Roman fleet could operate, and a substantial garrison including naval personnel (officers, sailors and oarsmen), marines (who were employed in amphibious operations against pirate ships and bases), and cavalrymen (who would fight raiders ashore). In other words, the Saxon shore forts were intended to keep what would become the English people out of what would become England. No doubt that these combatants included large numbers of non–Roman auxiliaries, hired local men, and mercenaries. Few of the Saxon shore forts were on or near important Roman roads, so communication between them must have been by sea. The general structure was basically similar to other forts, and the plan used was the rectangular playing-card enceinte, except Pevensey, which has an irregular oval layout fitting the natural configuration of the site. The main variations were in size. The Saxon forts, noticeably larger than the auxiliary forts, had an average size of about 7 acres. They had thick walls (up to 14 feet), which were not always backed by an earth rampart, that is they were free-standing walls made of stone in the manner and dimensions of later medieval castles. The walls' height varied. For example, Pevensey's walls were 28 feet high, Richborough 25 feet, and Lympne 23 feet. In many cases entrances consisted of twin-towered gates, fairly regular in type. Walls included projecting D- or U-shaped towers flanking wide ditches. Towers were usually roofed and adapted to the mounting of light artillery machines like the ballista and the scorpion. Very little is known about the buildings inside the forts but they were likely to have had standard accommodation for a strong garrison and naval personnel, as well as workshops for shipwrights and granaries and stores in addition to the usual headquarters and commander's quarters as described above.

There were also fortified harbors on the other side of the Channel in Gaul, including Mardyk near Calais, Boulogne, Rouen (inlands on the River Seine), Bayeux, Coutances and Avranches (in what later would become Normandy), Saint-Servan near Saint-Malo, Carhaix and Brest (in Armorica, present day French Britanny). Whether these ports were part of the Litus Saxonicum remains unclear, as they guarded places well worth defending in themselves, but they did not seem to have been designed to prevent seaborne invaders from penetrating into the hinterland. Obviously the Saxon shore forts failed to fulfill the task for which they had been established. They were indeed invulnerable when garrisoned at the planned level, but by the beginning of the 5th century the Roman Empire, weakened by internal power struggles and threatened at its very heart, could no longer spare soldiers to defend the remote northern island. When the troops, who had defended Britain for some four hundred years, sailed from the Channel ports, never to return, the system became unworkable. Pevensey, for example, was taken by assault in 491, something which had never happened under the Romans. Other forts fell to the Germanic invaders without a fight.

Most of the Saxon shore forts slowly rotted away. First to go were the timber and fittings, then the roofs, until at last only the massive stone walls, rubble and iron-hard cement remained to defy 2,000 years of British weather. The Saxon shore forts of Pevensey, Dover and Portchester were later reused and adapted by the Norman and Plantagenet kings, and the Roman enclosures were used as baileys to subsequently-built medieval castles.

(Continued on page 89.)

The map shows the Saxon shore forts in southern England and the main sea harbors in Gaul.

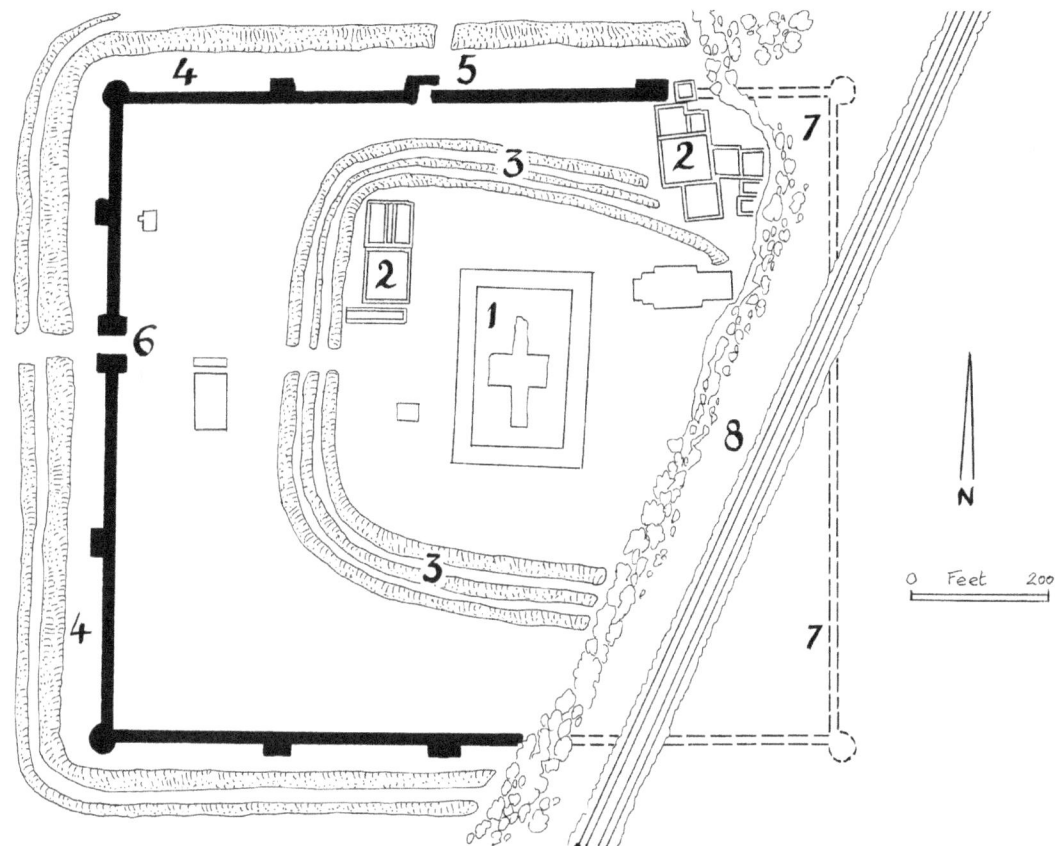

Richborough (Rutupiae) can claim to be, with Hadrian's Wall, the most important Roman fortification in Britain in regard to its preservation, archaeological finds and historical interest. The Roman invasion of Britain in A.D. 43 was led by Senator Autus Plautius, with an army of some 50,000 men. Archaeological evidence suggests that Richborough was the bridgehead for this invasion. As the conquest of Britain rapidly advanced Richborough soon became an important naval supply base, as evidenced by the laying of new roads, and the erection of several timber buildings believed to be storehouses. By A.D. 85 the site underwent a substantial change. The central timber buildings were demolished, and a monumental four-way arch was constructed, the walkways beneath which formed the shape of a large cross that can still be clearly seen today. As Richborough's status grew, so did the settlement around it. However, towards the middle of the 3rd century, military considerations had again come to the fore. A large percentage of the central buildings were demolished and the central monument was ringed with a series of triple ditches, suggesting that this had become a useful lookout tower. These excavated triple ditches are still a striking feature of the site today. By the end of the 3rd century the earth fortifications were dismantled and the ditches backfilled to prepare for the construction of a much more substantial fortification enclosed by a stone perimeter. These massive walls with their corner towers, which were up to 11 feet (3.5 m) thick in places, surrounded by a double ditch, are the most impressive part of the ruins as seen today. Little is known of the internal buildings, as these were most likely constructed of timber. The changes are believed to have been completed by A.D. 286. By the end of the 4th century Richborough Roman fort had ceased to be garrisoned by regular Roman troops, but the site retained its status until approximately A.D. 402. The map shows the following. 1: Archway; 2: Second-century ruined houses; 3: Third-century earth fort; 4: Late 3rd century stone enclosure with towers; 5: North postern; 6: West gate; 7: Parts of the fort that have collapsed and disappeared; 8: Present railway track.

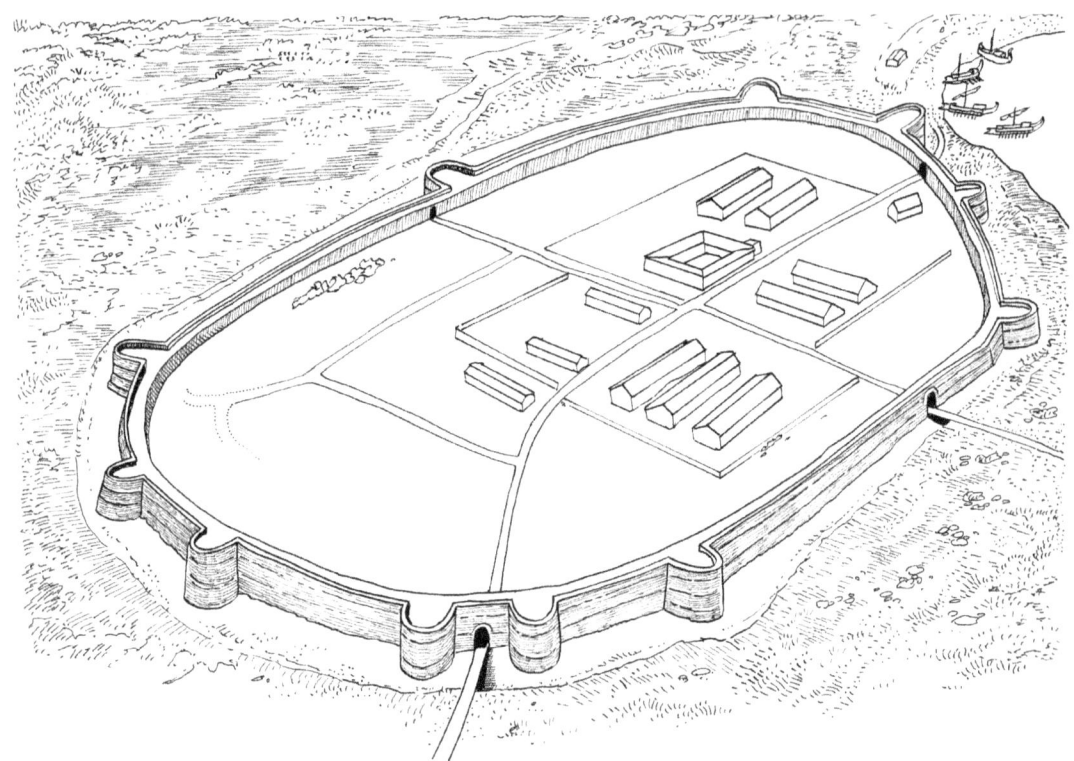

Top: *Roman Pevensey. A part of the Saxon shore forts, Pevensey, then named Anderida, was egg-shaped in plan and quite untypical of Roman fortification, in which the rectangle was the usual pattern. The site was well-chosen, approachable by land only from the southwest. There was an east gate, which led to the harbor where a squadron of galleys or other scouting boats was stationed. The enclosed area is about 8 acres with walls 25 feet high and 12 feet thick; the rubble core was faced with green sandstone and iron-stone. Anderida was probably connected with its neighboring Saxon forts by a series of signal towers. The sea has long since receded from Pevensey but up to the early Middle Ages it could be reckoned as a port. The interior of the Roman fort was filled with rows of barracks, a supply store, and administrative buildings, all presumably of timber construction since no trace of stone foundations has been found. The fort was later reused by the Normans.*

Left: *Tower at Pevensey (reconstruction).*

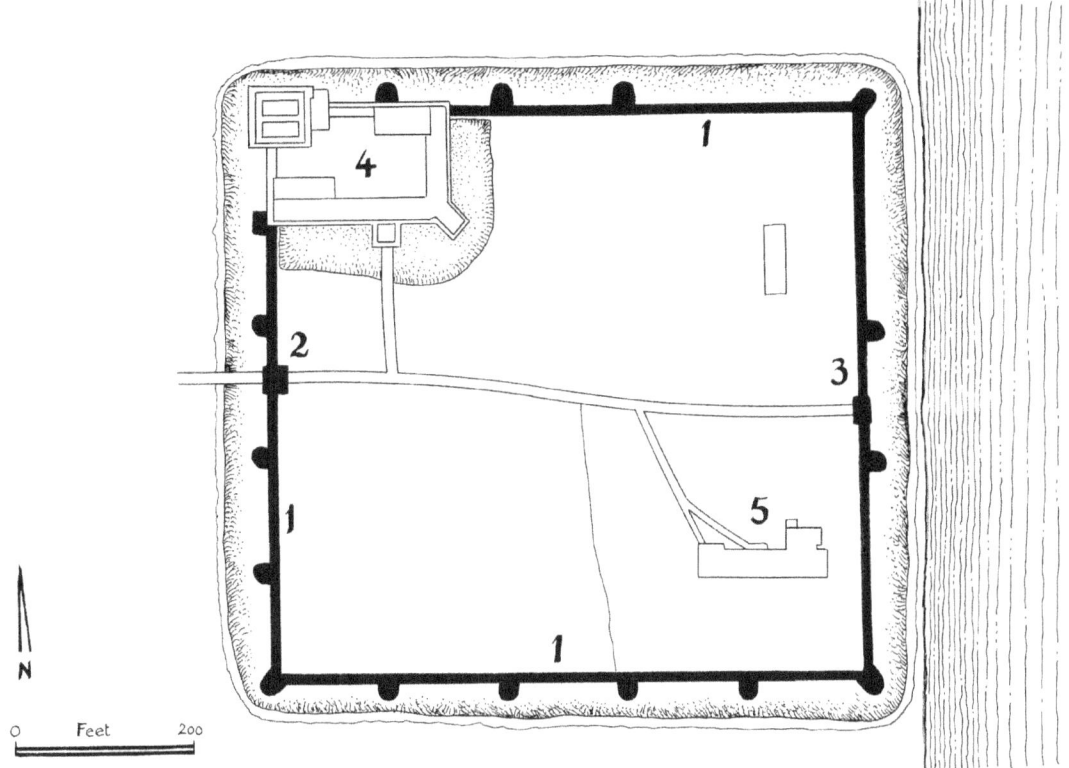

The most impressive and best-preserved of the Roman Saxon shore forts, Portchester Castle (Hampshire) was originally built in the late 3rd century. It forms a vast square, some 200 yards each way, covering 10 acres. Midway in the east and west sides are gateways, in each of the north and south sides is a postern, and the whole enclosure was reinforced by 20 towers, of which 14 are preserved. Portchester is the only Roman stronghold in northern Europe whose walls still mainly stand to their full 6 m height, complete with most of their original towers. Subsequently housing an Anglo-Saxon settlement after the departure of the Romans, the huge waterside fortress became a Norman castle in the 12th century, when a formidable tower-keep was built in the northwest corner. 1: Roman stone wall with towers and ditch; 2: West gate; 3: East gate; 4: Norman castle with keep; 5: Medieval Norman church.

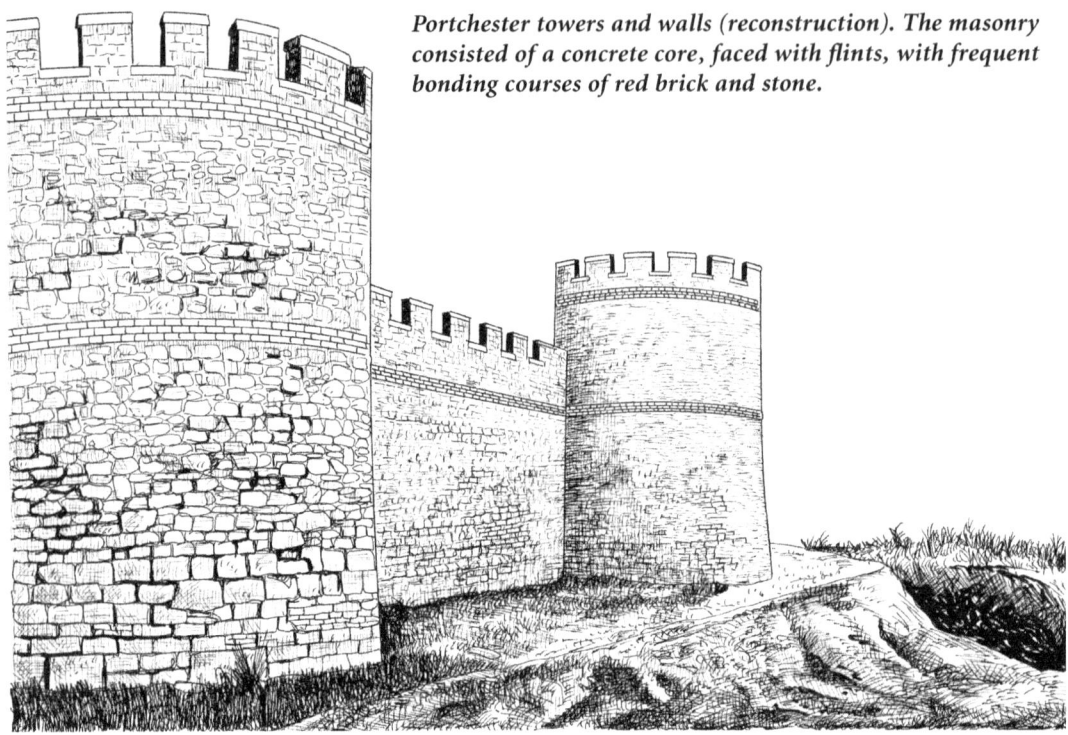

Portchester towers and walls (reconstruction). The masonry consisted of a concrete core, faced with flints, with frequent bonding courses of red brick and stone.

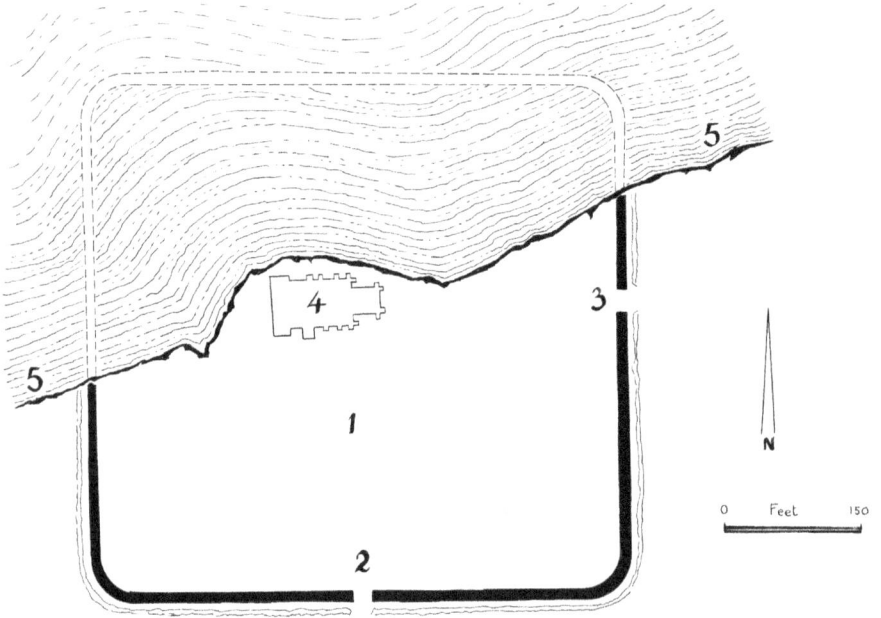

Built between A.D. 180 and 185 as Regulbium, Reculver was one of the Saxon shore forts. It was a location for a fort with lighthouse and watchtower, presumably because of its strategic position at the northern entrance to the important Wantsum Channel, and covered the mouths of both the River Thames and the River Medway. Owing to coastal erosion, half the fort has now disappeared into the sea and the later-built Saxon church ruins are now on the edge of a steep cliff. 1: Site of 3rd-century headquarters building; 2: South gate; 3: East gate; 4: Saxon church built c. A.D. 669; 5: Present coastline.

Roman Urban Fortifications

The most obvious characteristic of Roman Britain was the development of towns, which were the basis of Roman administration and civilization. Many grew out of previous Celtic Britton settlements, but also from Roman military camps or market centers. Basically there were three different sorts of towns in Britain: a few *coloniae*—towns peopled by a majority of Roman settlers and discharged veterans; the *municipiae*—a number of cities in which the whole native population was given Roman citizenship; and a majority of *civitates* (singular *civitas*), which included the old Celtic tribal communities, their towns, villages and settlements, through which the Romans

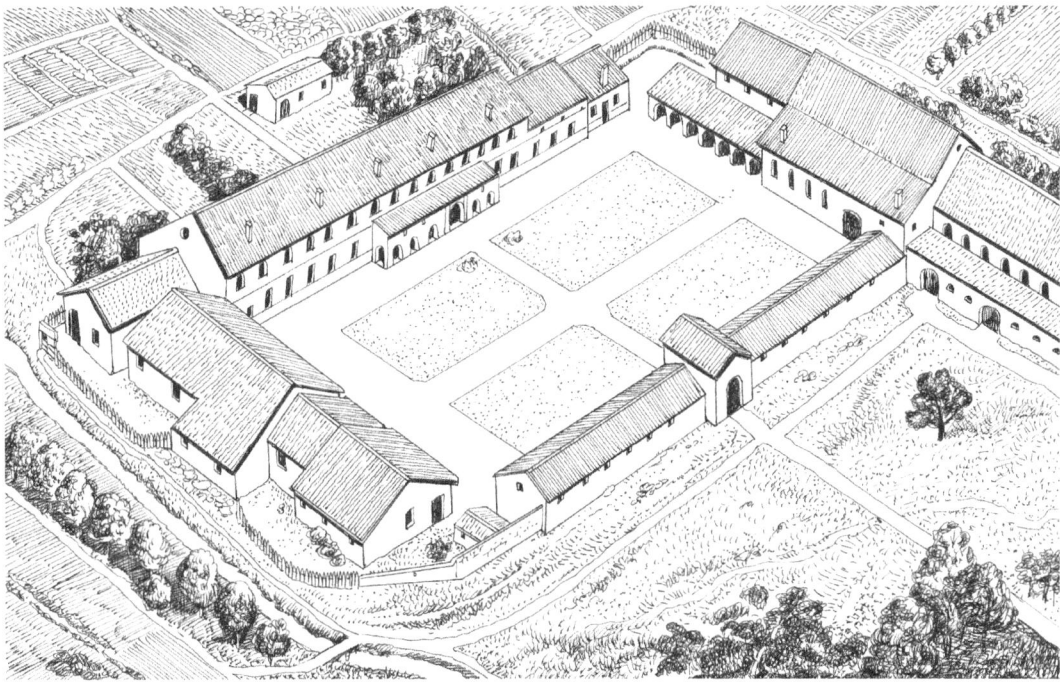

Roman villa. The illustration (based on Chedworth, England) shows how a villa might have looked around A.D. 350. A villa was a self-contained agricultural community, the focal point in many rural areas of the Roman Empire. A villa could have included hundreds of people living there, surrounded by hundreds and even thousands of hectares of fields. Located in or near the villa were orchards, herb gardens, flower gardens and vineyards. Animals kept here included horses, sheep, goats and pigs. The villa was often built around a central yard with buildings made of stones or bricks covered with a tile roof. Buildings included many different farm structures and workshops, such as a blacksmith, bake ovens, stables and so on. The owner and his family could either live at the villa in a residence or in a nearby town, in which case he had his estate managed by a foreman or overseer who conducted the work of gardeners, maids, nannies and other household servants, most of them being slaves. Some peasants would live at the villa, but most would live in small huts with their families in the fields surrounding the villa. Some would be slaves, others would be free farmers renting land from the land owner. A number of villas survived the collapse of the Roman Empire and grew into permanent settlements that eventually came to be called villages.

administrated the native population in the countryside. Many coloniae and municipiae were at first army camps and the Latin word for fortified camp, *castrum*, has remained part of many town names, indicated by the suffixes -chester, -caster or -cester; for example Gloucester, Doncaster, Winchester and many others. Soldiers and officials did their best to reconstruct the backgrounds of sunny Italy in this misty and wet climate. The newly created towns were built with stone as well as wood, and their streets intersected at right angles, forming regular blocks occupied by dwellings, markets and shops, a forum, baths, temples and a basilica. Towns were connected

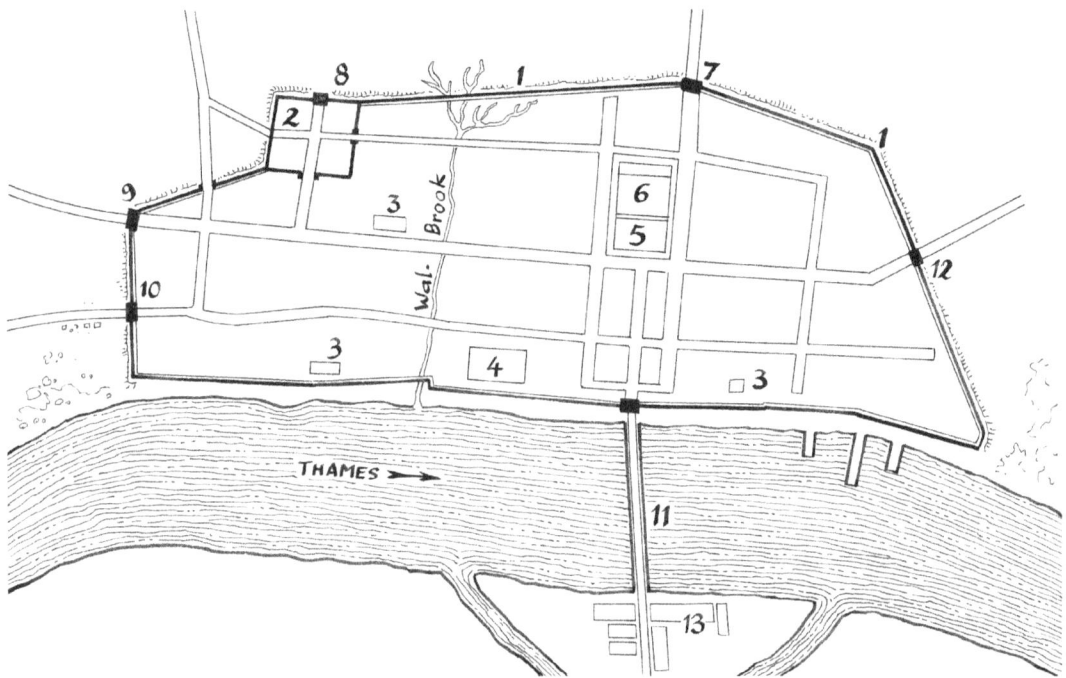

Roman London. Londinium was founded by the Romans in A.D. 50, at the point where the Thames was narrow enough to build a bridge, but deep enough to take seagoing vessels. Some ten years after its foundation, the town was sacked by the Iceni, led by their queen Boudica. Londinium was rebuilt, expanded rapidly, and soon became Britannia's largest city, and an important commercial and trading center. By the end of the 1st century, Londinium had replaced Colchester as the capital of Roman Britannia. In the early 2nd century a large part of the city was destroyed by fire. London appears to have recovered, however, and by about A.D. 140 Londinium had reached a population estimated at 50,000. By the middle of the century Londinium included the following fortifications and major public buildings.

1: The wall, built about A.D. 200, enclosed an area of about 330 acres (130 hectares), was 6 to 9 feet (2 to 3 m) wide and about 18 feet (5 m) high, with a ditch (or fossa) measuring some 6 feet (2 m) deep by between 9 and 15 feet (3 to 5 m) wide. It included a number of walltowers (at least 20) spaced about 70 yards (64 m) apart; 2: Arx (built in c. A.D. 120, a citadel for the city garrison); 3: Public bath; 4: Praetorium (administrative palace); 5: Forum; 6: Basilica; 7: Bishopsgate; 8: Cripplegate; 9: Newgate; 10: Ludgate; 11: London bridge; 12: Aldgate; 13: Southwark suburb. In the second half of the second century Londinium appears to have shrunk in both size and population; the cause was possibly a plague epidemic and economic recession. The Romans abandoned London in A.D. 410.

by a road network, and six of them met in Londinium (London). Here the Romans chose a place on the north bank of the Thames where ships could lie in safety, and they built a walled trading city, which became later the capital city of about 20,000. The former capital of Britannia was, however, Camulodunum (Colchester).

Outside the towns, the most significant change during the Roman era was the growth of large agricultural demesnes named villas. These self-contained productive units included the master's house, laborers' dwellings, farm buildings, livestock, fields, meadows, orchards and vineyards. Villas belonged to some discharged Roman veterans, and to the local wealthy Briton chieftains, who, like most city dwellers, were more Roman than Celt in their manners and way of life. Admittedly the accommodations of the villas' masters were lightly fortified. Some had a vallum (wall) and a fossa (ditch) of military appearance. Not that Britannia was particularly lawless, but it is easy to imagine that a retired Roman legate or centurion could not escape the need to continue his civilian life according to his army background, and that wherever he lived, there had to be a ditch and a wall around his dwelling, and his villa would not be an exception to that rule. The villas were generally close to towns so that their products could be sold easily.

At first Roman towns had no defensive walls, but that changed after the revolt led by the queen of the Iceni tribe, Boadicea (or Boudica) in A.D. 61 in what later became East Anglia. The Britons at first had great successes. They captured the hated Roman settlement of Camulodunum (Colchester). The warrior queen Boudica and

Aldgate, London, c. A.D. 200. The reconstructed gate shown here is seen from within the town.

Gatehouse Chester (reconstruction).

her allies gave no quarter in their victories and when Londinium and Verulamium (St. Albans) were stormed, the defenders fled and the towns were sacked and burned. Finally the Romans assembled an army of 10,000 regulars and auxiliaries, the backbone of which was made up from the XIVth Legion. The Roman historian Tacitus in his *Annals of Rome* gives a very vivid account of the final battle, which was fought in A.D. 61 in the Midlands of England, possibly at a place called Mancetter near Nuneaton. The rebellion was crushed, but important damage had been done to a number of towns deprived of defenses. Soon most veterans' coloniae — the most reliable towns — became semi-militarized fortified centers. Then, from the end of the 2nd century to the end of the 3rd century A.D., almost every town in Britain, as well as many villas in the countryside, were fitted with fortifications, suggesting a policy decision taken at the imperial level. At first many of these were no more than palisades and earthworks, but by A.D. 300 many towns had stone walls with towers and gatehouses. Colchester, for example, was hemmed with a wall 3 km in perimeter (of which over 900 m can still be seen today), fronted by a 6-meter-deep and 3-meter-wide ditch. The wall, fitted with walltowers, was made of rubble and mortar with inner and outer revetments of bricks alternating with layers of squared stone. The wall was about 3.7 m high, and featured a 1.8 m crenelated parapet. The city had seven gates.

As long as the Pax Romana (Roman Peace) reigned, urban fortifications apparently had, however, more a symbolic function than a real military significance. The gate generally had more the appearance of a triumphal arch than that of a fortified point, a fact particularly noticeable at the Balkerne Gate in Colchester. As for the

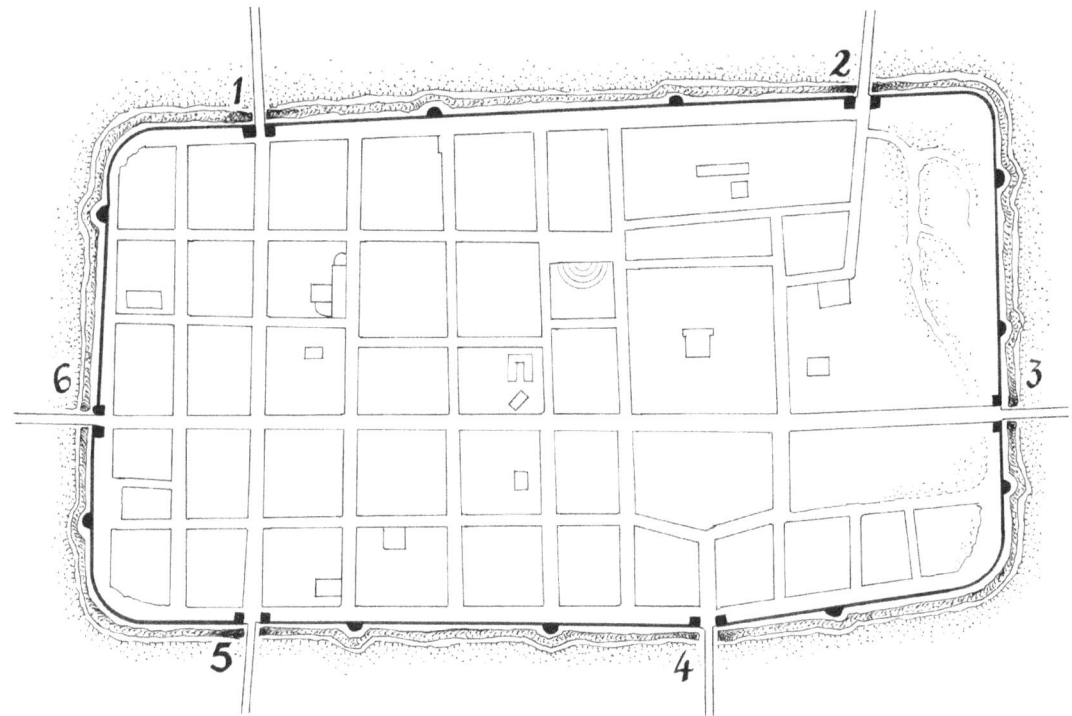

Roman Colchester. Colchester in Essex was one of the most important Iron Age settlements in Britain. It was the capital of the major pre–Roman power, King Cunobelin of the Catuvellauni and the Trinovante tribes. After the Roman invasion, it was established as a colonia named Camulodunum for retired Roman military officers and soldiers, and the city retained this high status throughout the four centuries of Roman rule. The map shows the town in the 2nd to 4th centuries. 1: North Gate; 2: Duncan's Gate; 3: East Gate; 4: South Gate; 5: Head Gate; 6: Balkerne Gate.

towers, they were often constructed against the rear of the wall, which means that they did not protrude in the ditch, and therefore could not provide flanking fire along the outer curtain. Besides some important and large buildings such as arenas, theaters and amphitheaters were often built outside the defended perimeter.

In A.D. 367 the Picts, Scots and Saxons joined forces in a well coordinated revolt, which seems to have taken the Roman authorities by surprise. The fortified towns seem to have formed islands of refuge in an otherwise turbulent and unsafe countryside. This suggests that the reorganization of urban defenses had been carried out by that time. Already in A.D. 343 there had been trouble on the northern frontier, and forts and towns had been sacked beyond Hadrian's Wall. There was evidence of destruction as far south as Great Casterton in Leicestershire in the Midlands, and the Emperor Flavius Julius Constans I (reign 337–350) visited Britain in person. The realization that raiders and possibly invaders from the north of Hadrian's Wall could penetrate so far south may have impelled Constans to order a complete reorganization of urban defenses along more military lines. This was in keeping with the general pattern on the continent and reflected the growing defensive attitude of the 3rd

Top: *The Balkerne Gate (Colchester) is one of the most impressive surviving gateways to a Roman town in Britain. It was built in the 1st century A.D., around A.D. 55. It began as a dual archway over the road to London. Ten years later, when the town walls were built, the gateway was adapted into these new defenses. In the 4th century A.D., most of the gateway was blocked with rubble, leaving only an arched footway open for pedestrian traffic. This was done to strengthen the defenses of the town when it was threatened by Saxon raiders.*

Bottom: *Close-up of a Roman masonry wall. Towards the end of the 3rd century, offense was no longer possible, and this change in mentality was clearly reflected in stronger fortification designs, and heavy stone walls which represented a departure from simple earthworks of the preceding centuries. The close-up shows courses of large stone blocks forming the plinth, above which was the exposed rubble core of chalk, flint and septaria (beetle stone). Between them, brick bonding courses provided horizontal stability by running from the facing into the center of the core. Square holes were spared to hold the scaffolding.*

Cross-section of a Roman wall. The foundations (1) consisted of large blocks, flint cobbles, and vertical wooden piles. The external revetment (2) was made of stone and brick bonding courses. The offset stone internal revetment (3) was larger at the base than at the top for increased stability. The core of the wall (4) was made of rubble and mortar.

and 4th centuries in the western Roman Empire as a whole. In the first two centuries confidence and aggression were the hallmarks of Roman policy along its huge borders. In the 3rd and 4th centuries, however, due to the ever-increasing pressure of the barbarian tribes beyond the frontiers, and due to the enormous burden of maintaining large military forces, the forts, fortresses, and fortified towns were no longer springboards for attack and conquest, but purely defensive strongholds which might survive in a sea of aggression.

During their occupation of Britain the Romans founded a number of important settlements, many of which still survive. The main cities and towns which have Roman origins, or were extensively developed by them, include the following: Alcester (Aluana); Bath (Aquae Sulis); Caerleon (Isca Augusta); Caernarfon (Segontium); Caerwent (Venta Silurum); Canterbury (Durovernum Cantiacorum); Carlisle (Luguvalium); Carmarthen (Moridunum); Colchester (Camulodunum); Corbridge (Coria); Chichester (Noviomagus Regnorum); Chester (Deva Victrix); Cirencester (Corinium); Dover (Portus Dubris); Dorchester (Durnovaria); Exeter (Isca Dum-noniorum); Gloucester (Glevum); Leicester (Ratae Corieltauvorum); London (Londinium); Lincoln (Lindum Colonia); Manchester (Mamucium); Newcastle-upon-Tyne (Pons Aelius); Northwich (Condate); St Albans (Verulamium); Towcester (Lactodorum); Whitchurch (Mediolanum); Winchester (Venta Belgarum); and York (Eboracum).

Silchester
0 400
Feet
N
1
2
3
4
5
6
7
8
9
10
11
12

Roman Carlisle

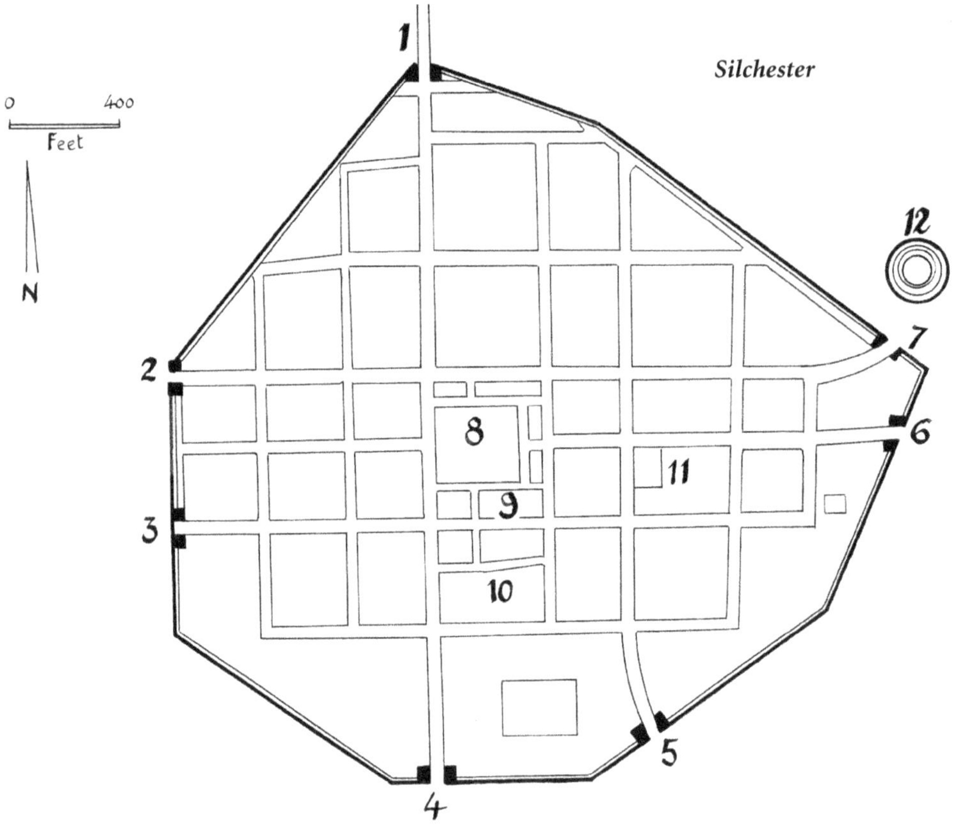

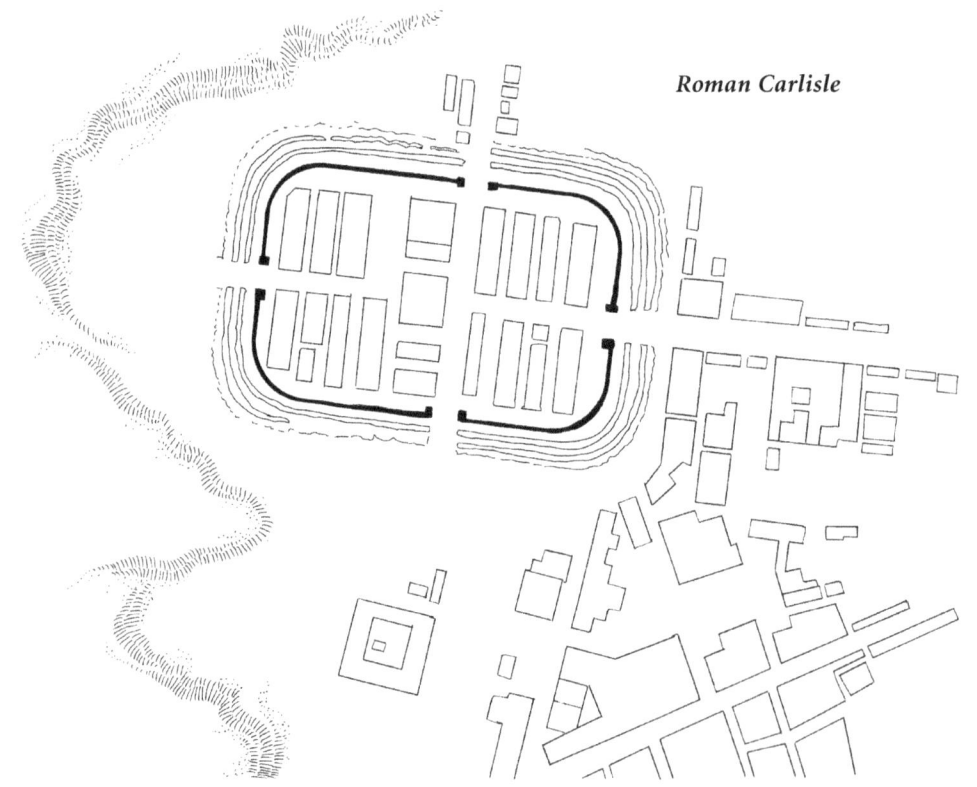

Opposite top: Silchester, located southwest of Reading in Hampshire, is best known for the adjacent archaeological site and Roman town of Calleva Atrebatum, which was first occupied by the Romans in about A.D. 45 and includes what is thought to be the best-preserved Roman wall in Great Britain.

1: North gate; 2: West gate; 3: West postern; 4: South gate; 5: Water gate; 6: East gate; 7: Postern to amphitheater; 8: Forum; 9: Church; 10: Temple; 11: Bathhouse; 12: Amphitheater.

Opposite bottom: Roman Carlisle. After the Roman invasion in A.D. 43, governor Agricola built a wooden fort on the site of Carlisle in Cumbria about A.D. 78. Called Luguvalium, the fort attracted civilians and soon a settlement grew up nearby with a market and probably a forum with public buildings around it, including baths. By the 4th century Roman civilization had declined, troops were withdrawn from Hadrian's Wall in A.D. 399 and the last Roman soldiers left Britain in about 407. Soon afterwards the Roman way of life broke down and most Roman towns were abandoned. Carlisle may not have been deserted completely. There may have been some peasants living inside the walls and farming the land outside. However, it seems certain that Carlisle ceased to be a town and all its Roman buildings fell into ruins. Carlisle was part of a Celtic kingdom until the 7th century, when it fell to the Saxons. The Celts gave Carlisle its name. They called it Caer Luel, the fortified place belonging to Luel. In 876 the Vikings captured Carlisle and sacked it. They occupied the town until the 10th century, when the Saxons once again captured it. Carlisle was rebuilt and revived by King William Rufus in 1092. He built a wooden castle, which was rebuilt in stone in the 12th century.

PART 3

Early Medieval Fortifications
A.D. 409–1066

Anglo-Saxon Invasion

Roman control of Britain came to an end as the empire started to collapse. Significant signs were the attacks by Scottish Celtic Picts from Caledonia in A.D. 367. Despite their elaborate fortifications, the Roman legions found it more and more difficult to repulse raiders from crossing Hadrian's Wall. The same was occurring on the European continent as Germanic groups, Goths, Franks, Alamans and other tribes began to attack the empire. Around A.D. 409, Rome withdrew her last soldiers out of Britain and the Romanized and Christianized Romano-British Celts were left to fight alone against the Scottish and the Irish raiders from the north, and against the Angle, Jute, and Saxon invaders coming by sea from Denmark and north Germany in the mid–5th century. These invaders were more or less identified with each other, forming people of mixed stock but with a number of common characteristics, and therefore termed by historians Anglo-Saxons for convenience. At first gangs of Germanic warriors came as mercenaries to help Britain against attacks from Scotland and Ireland. They soon sent word to their homelands of the easy pickings and larger groups combined to raid Britain, and after the Romans' withdrawal whole tribes began to occupy the country. The Jutes settled mainly in Cantium (Kent), the Isle of Wight, and part of Hampshire; the Saxons and the Angles controlled the east and the north Midlands, and the Angles gave the larger part of Britannia its new name, England, "the land of the Angles." The Christianized Celtic Britons fought the invaders in the early 6th century, with such brave leaders as a certain King Arthur—a legendary warlord who, according to medieval histories and romances, led the defense of Britain against the Saxons. Whether or not there was a historical individual on whom the Arthurian legends are based we do not know, and may never know. What is for sure is that the Saxons were steadily pushed westward by the advancing Germanic invaders in the 5th and 6th centuries. Some fled into the mountains of Wales and Scotland, as well as across to Ireland, where their Celtic languages—Welsh, Gaellic

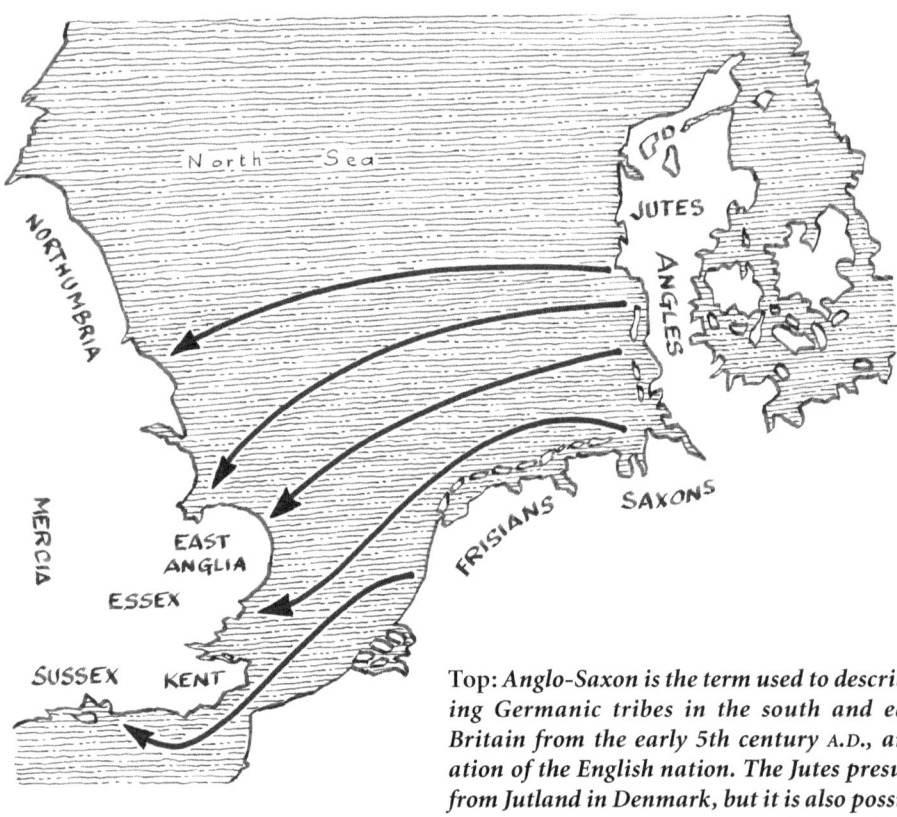

Top: *Anglo-Saxon is the term used to describe the invading Germanic tribes in the south and east of Great Britain from the early 5th century* A.D., *and their creation of the English nation. The Jutes presumably came from Jutland in Denmark, but it is also possible that they originated from what today is Belgium. The Angles came from Denmark, and the Saxons from Lower Saxony in northern Germany. Other possible invaders were Frisians, who came from present day Netherlands, as well as some Flemings and perhaps a number of Franks from Belgium and some German Swabians.*

Left: *Anglo-Saxon kingdoms c.* A.D. *886. The thick dashed lines indicate the Danelaw (Scandinavian sphere of influence).*

and Erse — are still spoken today. Some Brytonic Celts (or Bretons from south Wales and Cornwall) went into exile in Armoricae in Gaul, giving the French western province the name Britanny (Breizh in Breton).

The Romano-British were almost wholly unable to make use of Roman fortifications and fared better when they fell back on the traditional hill forts of their ancestors. There is evidence that many of these came back into use after the Romans had departed, at least in the southwest, for example at South Cadbury in Somerset and at Castle Dore in Cornwall. In a few cases new hill forts were erected, such as the large earthworks of Dinas Emrys in Gwynedd.

By the beginning of the 7th century, the Romano-British were defeated and reduced to subjugation. Hardly anything was left of Roman language and culture, and England, at least until the Norman conquest of 1066, became a culturally oriented Scandinavian/Germanic land. By then Roman urban centers were partly abandoned or completely deserted, and buildings, towers and walls in many cases became stone quarries.

The Angles, Saxons and other invaders took possession of all the land and divided it into a number of small kingdoms, e.g., Essex, Sussex, Wessex, Mercia, East Anglia, Kent. One of the strange ironies of history is that having established a reputation as fearsome sailors and conquerors, the Anglo-Saxons rapidly settled down and became farming landlubbers. Or perhaps that is another of the myths of history. Perhaps only a few were ever adventurous sea raiders, the arrival of their families abruptly curbing their roving habits.

Romano-Briton warrior c. A.D. 400. The depicted man wears a Roman helmet without a crest, and is armed with a spear and a gladius.

Although they had a Witan (council summoned by Anglo-Saxon kings, composed of aldermen, thanes and bishops discussing royal grants of land, church matters, charters, taxation, customary law, defense and foreign policy, and the succession of a king), and although they were religiously united, the Anglo-Saxon realms were politically divided and could make no organized resistance to the next wave of northern invaders, the Vikings (Norwegians and Danes), who eventually attacked the rocky coasts of Scotland and northern England.

Danish Invasions

The Vikings were not a single people but a recognizable cultural group. Indeed, Viking is a blanket term used to refer to many related Norwegian, Swedish and Danish clans who all engaged in raiding, conquering and settling in Britain and Europe. Scandinavian people had traded in Britain and Europe prior to the 8th century A.D., and their move into violent plunder and conquest is not well understood. Early raids may have been caused by trade disputes, and perhaps partly as a response to population pressures in their homeland, so they wanted new lands to settle, not merely easy plunder. The "Viking Age" began with the attack on Lindisfarne in A.D. 793 and ended with the Norman invasion of Britain in 1066. The complex history and culture of the Vikings served as an important part of the formation of the European continent, and had a tremendous impact on the history of Great Britain.

The Vikings were in fact superior to the forces brought against them, alike in tactics, in armament, in training and in mobility. They made good use of fortified settlements as bases to expand, and their use of helmets, shields, chain mail, and particularly the long-handled battle axe meant they were often better armed than most of their foes. Ships used by Viking Scandinavian warriors and traders from the 5th to 12th centuries were long (up to 150 feet), and were powered by both oar and sail. This allowed them to ride on the vicious North Sea and North Atlantic waves, and to go up inland waterways.

Evidence of Viking raids and settlements has been found throughout the British Isles, all along the coastline of the English Channel, the North Sea and even the Baltic Sea as far west as Russia. Some evidence of Viking visitation has even been found in Greenland and possibly in North America in Newfoundland (Canada).

In the 9th century, the Viking challenge grew to serious proportions. At the last moment the Saxons were saved by the courage and determination of King Alfred of Wessex (born 849, reigned 871–901). Alfred, popularly nicknamed "the Great," strengthened and reorganized Wessex defenses and armed forces, established friendly diplomatic relations with other English kingdoms and the Welsh, issued laws limiting the practice of blood feuds, promoted learning and literature, invited scholars from neighboring nations and Europe to his court, encouraged his subjects to learn to read English, learned Latin and translated some important works into English himself, fostered an atmosphere of literary endeavor, and may have been responsible for the creation of the Anglo-Saxon Chronicle (a list of significant events in British history from the year A.D. 1 to 891 compiled by unknown chroniclers). Alfred was not only a promoter of learning and an administrator of talent, he was also a skillful military leader who is popularly credited as being the founder of the British Royal Navy. He did build a fleet of improved ships manned by Frisians and on several occasions successfully challenged the Danes at sea. On land Alfred resisted and defeated the Danes in a series of battles. In 878, he re-captured London, brought intermittent peace, and forced the Danes to accept the Christian faith, but as they had gained a solid foothold in England, he could not prevent them from settling in what became known as Danelaw (eastern, northern and central England, comprising the Kingdom of Northumbria and Kingdom of East Anglia, and the lands of the Five Boroughs of Leicester, Nottingham, Derby, Stamford and Lincoln, roughly the area to the north of a line drawn between London and Chester). The Danes did not settle the whole of this wide area intensively, but their powerful military aristocracy dominated for a sufficient period to leave its imprint on local custom. The unification of England, and the strong defenses and organized army prevented the Danes from capturing more English lands. Gradually the English took back control of the Danelaw lands. By 954, when Edward the Elder and his son Eadred defeated and forced the king of Norway, Eric Bloodaxe, out of Northumbria, Danelaw was no more.

Near the end of the 10th century, however, there was renewed Scandinavian interest in England, with the conquests of Sweyn of Denmark and his son Cnut (955–1035), and a Danish dynasty ruled over England until 1042. At first Cnut used harsh measures: he had some prominent English rulers outlawed or killed, and he engineered the death of rivals. But within a few years he evolved a more even-handed policy, and allowed more Englishmen into positions of power. His reign proved stable, peaceful and prosperous, and the power base he developed in England helped him pursue claims in Denmark and Norway. However, after his death in November of 1035, the empire he had built rapidly disintegrated into its various components. Cnut's direct heirs ruled for only a handful of years before the lands he had conquered reverted to the old royal lines. Besides, the union of Saxon Britain and Scandinavian Denmark and Norway was artificial. Cnut's empire was so large that he was compelled to delegate authority to the increasingly powerful local Saxon earls who ruled their own regions without much royal interference — an early version of feudalism. Cnut's successors lacked their father's authority and in 1042 the independence of England and the House of Wessex were restored in the person of one of Ethelred's sons, Edward (c. 1000–1066). However, the day of Saxon England were numbered. Indeed, by 1066 there were three lords with claims to the English throne, resulting in two invasions and the battles of Stamford Bridge and Hastings, the results of which established French Norman rule in England.

Dikes

In contrast to the wide range of fortifications in the preceding Roman and succeeding medieval periods, not a lot is known of fortifications in Britain during the centuries of the Early Middle Ages (c. A.D. 410–1066, roughly from the departure of the Romans until the Norman conquest), a period sometimes designated by the rather negative term of Dark Ages. In order to investigate Dark Age fortifications in Britain we are stepping into a region of doubt and obscurity. Historical sources available for this period are rather scanty. But for the Anglo-Saxon Chronicle, there is little written evidence from this time and much of what we know from the early written sources was actually transcribed much later. The Venerable Bede's *Historica Ecclesiastica* writings, for example, which provide us with the most complete account of the history of this period, date from the mid–7th century. These writings are by monks who had no interest in military matters and no comprehension of strategy, tactics or fortifications. Thus the topics of military architecture in Dark Age Britain remains somewhat unclear, and no precise conclusions may be drawn with certainty. It is fortunate, however, that the general characteristics of the period render its military architecture comparatively simple. Of sophisticated strategy there could be little in an age when men strove to win their ends by hard fighting rather than by skillful operations or the use of extraneous advantages.

The centuries of the Dark Ages, however, saw the gradual evolution of new forms of warlike efficiency whose result was—out of necessity—the establishment of a mounted military class as the chief factor in warfare. In the absence of any centrally organized resistance, the defense fell into the hands of the local nobility, whose members became semi-independent sovereigns. To these petty rulers the landholders of each district now commended themselves, in order to obtain protection in an age of insecurity and anarchy. At the same time, and for the same reason, the poorer freemen were commending themselves to the landholders. Thus the feudal hierarchy was established, and a new military system appeared, when counts, dukes and earls led out to battle their vassals and their mounted retainers.

It seems that the Angles, Saxons and Jutes had their own military fortifications, which fall into two main categories: linear works, known as dikes, and burhs (fortified towns). Burhs, described separately below, actually belong to the last two centuries before the Norman conquest of 1066, leaving only dikes to fill the four centuries between A.D. 410 and c. A.D. 800.

While fortifications were not unknown to the Anglo-Saxons, battles tended to be in the open. Many of the conflicts in Dark Age Britain were followed by some sort of treaty or oral agreement, whereby one side or the other promised to keep within its own territories. This is probably the origin of linear earthworks, emphatic and remarkable expressions of territoriality, some still featuring in the British landscape.

Wansdike

Wansdike is a rather enigmatic and unknown Dark Age dike, consisting of two main linear earthworks; the piece that is believed to have connected the two pieces is now known to be a Roman road, which is 15 miles (22 km) long. The western half extends nine miles from Dundry Hill southeast of Bristol to just south of Bath. The eastern half runs ten miles from south of Calne to Great Bedwyn on the edge of Savernake Forest. Presumably built at different times from the 5th to the 7th century A.D., the line includes a ditch and rampart some 25 meters in total width and 7.5 meters from the bottom of the trench to the top of the bank. Two Iron Age hill forts along the western part of the Wansdike have been incorporated into its structure (Stantonbury and Maes Knoll) and some scholars have concluded that the builders used the hill forts to save on labor. But as the builders did not refortify the forts, garisson them or patrol the dike (apparently a walkway on top of the ramparts was not built), it is now believed that the Wansdike was simply an expression of territoriality, a kind of border marker. Both sections run along an east/west line, with the ditch facing north, and scholars disagree not only about its precise location but also as to whether the dike was built by the Romano-British Celts as a defense against Saxons encroaching from the upper Thames valley westward into what is now the West Country, or, if later constructed, by the Saxons of Wessex against their rival Saxons in the Midlands.

Offa's Dike

Of greater renown and more precise dating is Offa's Dike, a massive linear earthwork, roughly following some of the current border between England and Wales. The origins of the Dike are, however, shrouded in mystery, so many of its aspects are speculated upon rather than being fully understood. It has been claimed that it was built by the Emperor Septimus Severus about A.D. 200, but this is probably incorrect as the sources of the story of Severus building a turf wall in Britain are probably confused references to him rebuilding the Antonine Wall. Severus fought against the Picts in the north, and refurbished the Antonine Wall, and he would have had no reason for building a barrier in the western part of Britannia. It was Asser, King Alfred's friend and biographer, in the 9th century who first ascribed the dike to Offa. It is now generally accepted that much of the earthwork can indeed be attributed to Offa, king of Mercia from A.D. 757 to 796. By that time Mercia was the dominant power in England south of the River Humber, and Offa was recognized in Europe as virtually king of the whole country as he had influence in international affairs, links with the Papacy, and diplomatic contacts on more or less equal terms with the Carolingian Frankish Emperor Charlemagne, the most powerful continental European ruler. Offa influenced the setting up of a third archbishopric in England at the cathedral at Lichfield and near his principal residence at Tamworth. He established the use of the penny as the standard monetary unit in England, with the same silver content as coins in circulation in the European Carolingian Empire, thereby assisting both national and international trading. Offa's kingdom covered the area between the Trent/Mersey Rivers in the north to the Thames valley in the south, and from the Welch border in the west to the Fens in the east. At the height of his power Offa also controlled Kent, East Anglia, and Lindsay (Lincoln). He also had alliances with Northumbria and Wessex, sealed by the marriage of two of his daughters to their kings, Aethelred and Beorhtric, respectively. Offa was, therefore, effectively an early king of England.

The earthwork that bears his name ran from Prestatyn on the northern Wales coast to Cheptow on the River Severn in the south, a length of about 120 miles. The "dike," today a mere raised hedgerow and small earth mounds, then consisted of a continuous bank fronted by a ditch about 50 feet wide, in places, up to 65 feet (20 m) wide (including its surrounding ditch) and 8 feet (2.5 m) high. In certain sections the Severn and the Wye Rivers were use instead of a wall. How Offa's dike (and other linear earthworks) functioned as military structures (or even if they were military structures at all) is open to debate. Some sections may have been garrisoned and patrolled in some unknown periods, but the dike was probably a purely symbolic border between places where the movement of goods was controlled (like the Salt Tax Hedge in India, a purely economic border between two areas, both under British control, showing that a barrier does not have necessarily a military purpose). The fact is that Offa's Dike could not possibly have been permanently manned, as the Mercian realm could hardly afford to maintain a permanent army. Besides, there is no evidence of fortified accommodation such as milecastles, interval towers and forts for a supporting garrison as on the Roman Hadrian's Wall. Obviously this thin line would not have prevented infiltration; it would never have repulsed or slowed down a gang of raiders, let alone an army. So it was not a proper line of fortification, but presumably the result of negotiation rather than conquest. However, the construction of such a work was clearly a considerable undertaking and an impressive tribute to Offa's prestige. In the 8th century the dike expressed Offa's power, and formed a physical frontier delineating the Anglian kingdom of Mercia and the Celtic Welsh kingdoms of Gwynedd, Powys and Gwent. The provision of a visible frontier secured the stability of disputed territory, and Offa's Dike marked a border and constituted a clear warning for Welsh intruders that beyond that line they were risking retribution from the Mercians.

The upper hand enjoyed by the Mercians did not long survive Offa's death. In the 820s a series of victories by Egbert, king of Wessex, broke Mercian control in the southeast. The 9th century may well have turned into a struggle for the upper hand between Mercia and Wessex if not for one thing: England was once again the subject of recurring raids from across the seas. This time it was the Danes and Norwegians, as said above. The Danes attacked the east coast of England, and the Norwegians attacked the north by way of Ireland and Scotland.

WAT'S DIKE

Another much less famous linear work was so-called Wat's Dike, an earth wall and ditch running more or less parallel to, and to the east of, the northern part of

Offa's Dike through the northern Welsh Marches from Basingwerk Abbey on the River Dee estuary, passing to the east of Oswestry and onto Maesbury in Shropshire, a distance of approximately 40 miles (64 km). The dating of the earth wall has been disputed. Some scholars dated it to between A.D. 411 and 561 (centered around A.D. 446), placing the building in the post–Roman era. Others think the dike formed part of the late Roman attempts to counter "barbarian" attacks (i.e., Pictish and Irish) in

Wansdyke today (near Spye Park).

Offa's Dike today (near Spring Hill, Shropshire).

the region of modern North Wales. The consensus view now places the date of construction in the early 8th century by Aethelbald, king of Mercia, who reigned from 716 to 757. Aethelbald was the predecessor of King Offa of Mercia, and his (uncompleted) work was intended to perform the same function as his successor's: a physical mark of the frontier of his realm. For centuries, both dikes had a cultural significance, symbolizing the separation between the English and the Welsh, similar to the symbolism of Hadrian's Wall between England and Scotland. Crossing these lines with drawn sword corresponded to handing over an official declaration of war in more literate eras.

There are several other notable linear earthworks in Britain, notably the Bokerly Dike on the Dorset/Hampshire border. The Devil's Dike in Cambridgeshire, with a length of 9 miles and a well-preserved section between Swaffham Prior and Stetchworth, is thought to have been built between A.D. 500–600 by the East Anglian Saxons to block attacks from Mercians to the west.

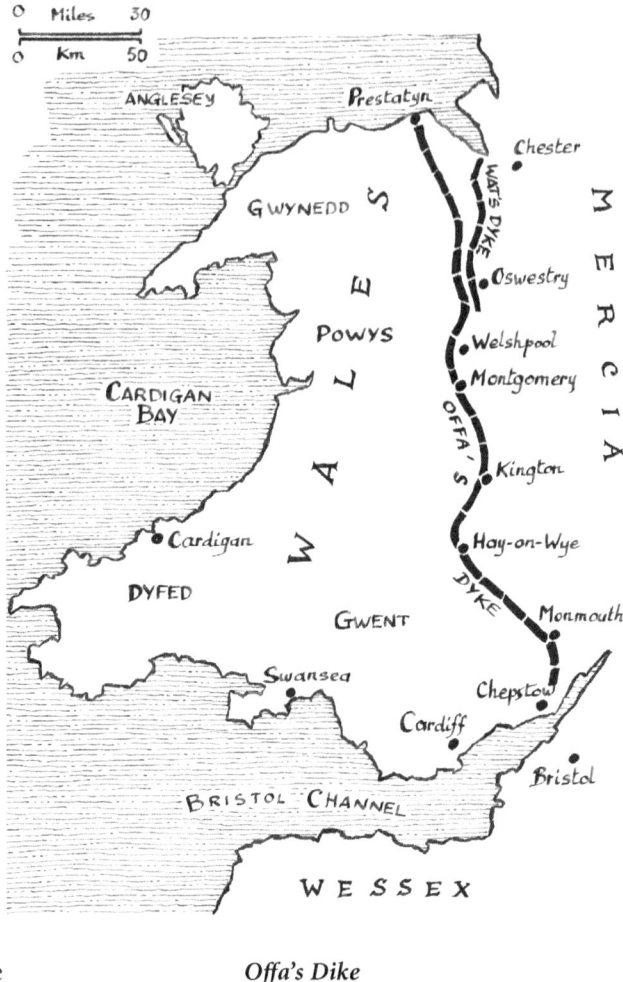

Offa's Dike

The rash of dike building in Britain in the early part of the Dark Ages may have been initially inspired by the Roman practice of building physical border limes, as Hadrian's Wall. But these enigmatic linear structures have not yet revealed all their secrets about this period of British history.

Burhs

A tenet of history — that the Anglo-Saxons shunned all cities as haunted, and therefore preferred to live in isolated farmsteads — has been shown to be more mythical than real. After the Anglo-Saxon conquest, many Roman sites lost their importance. Some cities did indeed fall into disuse, but their decay had already set in under Roman rule. A number of stone-built Roman towns (e.g., London and Colchester) survived and had their defenses rebuilt and maintained until the Middle Ages and even later. The Anglo-Saxon kings of England laid importance upon defended sites. The long and numerous wars between the Anglo-Saxons and the Danes saw the appearance of the so-called *burhs*, the origin of the modern word borough. The term seems to have come from the Latin word *burgus* (watchtower), many of which had been erected along the German boundary of the Roman Empire. While Devil's Dike, Offa's Dike and Wat's Dike were mere boundary markers, burhs were fortifications in the true sense of the word. In England the establishment of a defensive system of burhs is associated with the reign of King Alfred the Great (871–899). Owing to the *Burghal Hidage* (a unique Anglo-Saxon document compiled under Edward the Elder between 910 and 914, providing a descriptive list of 33 fortified burhs in Wessex and elsewhere in southern England), these fortified towns built as defenses against the Vikings are comparatively well documented. The scale and organization of Alfred's burh system represents much more than simple ad hoc defensive arrangements, as had been the case previously. They were much more than a local and communal defense, the *Burghal Hidage* indicating a much clearer centralized national effort, and there was a considerable attention given to organization and detail. Alfred's burhs represented a new, positive approach to defense, incorporating centralized planning and local communal effort. That they were successful militarily is obvious, but that the burhs were also economically and socially successful is demonstrated by the number which survived the wars and became thriving towns. Alfred's burhs were a necessity partly because of the nature of warfare and weapons. Indeed, a highly mobile enemy such as the Vikings could not be met simply with a field army, because whenever the army arrived the Scandinavian raiders had gone. It was necessary to build fortified points for protection, and local bases from which warriors could look out for the Vikings and sally out to meet them in the field when they appeared. Oval or rectangular in shape, burhs were indeed intended to protect persons and goods, and to provide a base from which cavalry (and on the coast, ships) could operate against marauders, raiders, and Viking invaders. Burhs also provided for the control of the economy and promotion of trade, and constituted administrative centers as well as religious and spiritual centers, as the protection and defense of the Church was a responsibility of the king. They had official status recognized by grants such as the right to mint coinage. In Wessex, these fortified communities were geographically distributed so that everyone lived within a day's march of such a place of refuge, where frightened people could hide while the tide of Viking fury washed around them and hopefully abated. Forming strongholds located in strategic positions primarily along the coast and the borders of Alfred's lands, a number of burhs were connected by a military road called the Herepath. This ran up from Combwich, Cannington and over Stowey, along the present course of the Stowey road, across Dead Woman's Ditch to Crowcombe Park Gate, south along the main ridge of the Quantocks to Triscombe Stone, then west across the valley to the Brendon Hills and Exmoor. The road connected a

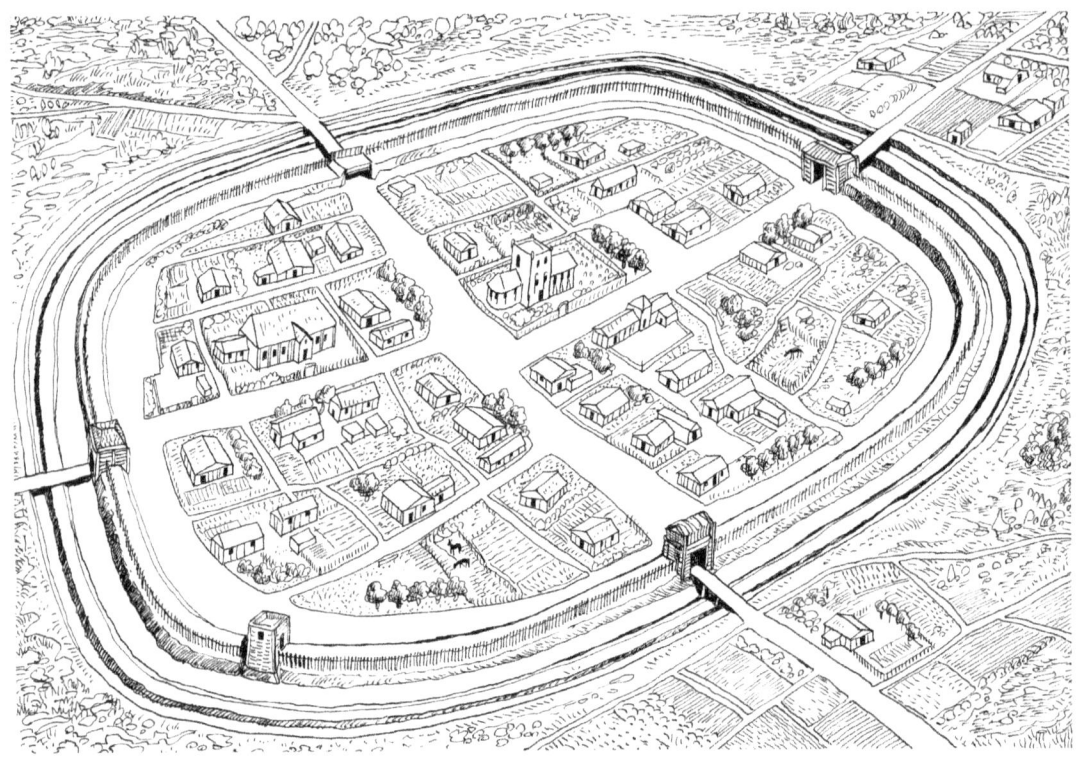

Anglo-Saxon burh (conjectured reconstruction). The fortifications consisted of a timber-revetted bank with one or more ditches.

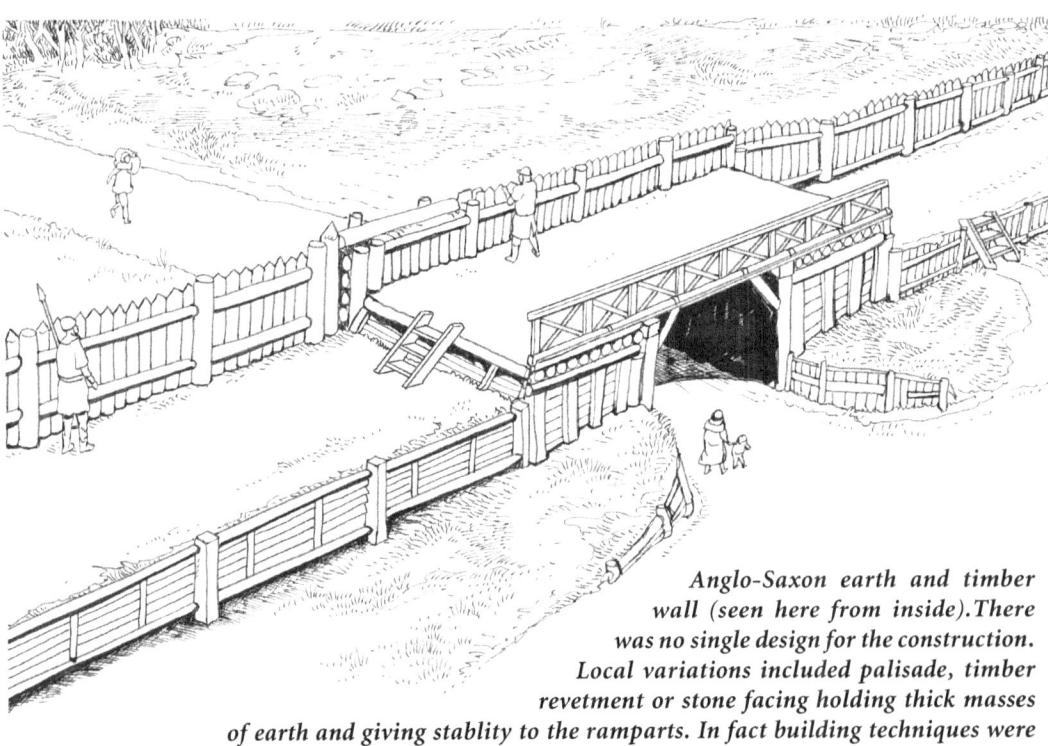

Anglo-Saxon earth and timber wall (seen here from inside). There was no single design for the construction. Local variations included palisade, timber revetment or stone facing holding thick masses of earth and giving stablity to the ramparts. In fact building techniques were rather similar to ancient Iron Age practices.

series of forts and lookout posts, which allowed Alfred's armies to move along the coast to cover Viking movements at sea and forestall any raids ashore. This shows how thoroughly Alfred protected his remaining kingdom of Wessex, once the Danish Vikings had captured parts of England.

Burhs were not built to a rigid pattern, but as local conditions permitted. Tech-

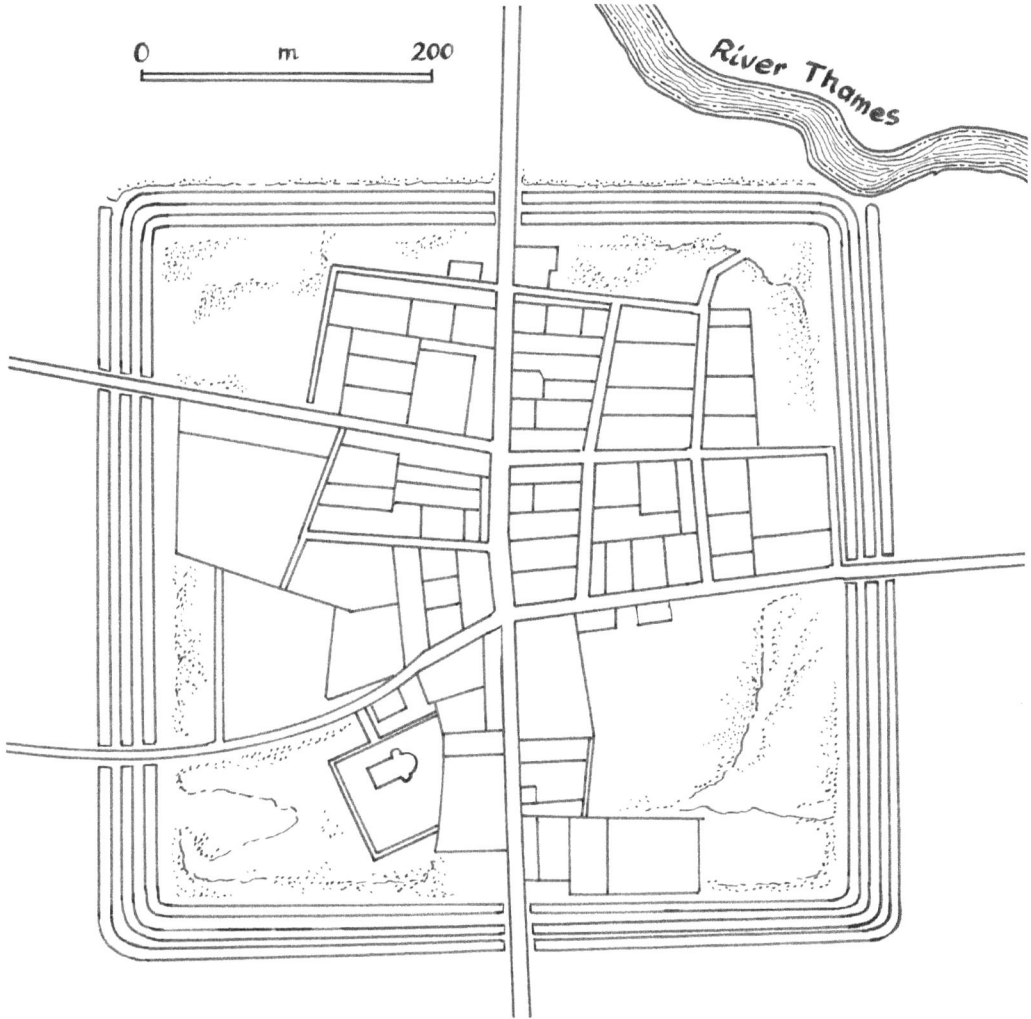

The town of Cricklade in north Wiltshire, on the River Thames, situated midway between Swindon and Cirencester, is one of the most regular examples of the Saxon burh, created as part of a fort system in the late 9th century. Built in the short period of 878–879 both to defend Wessex against the Vikings under Guthrum, and to act as an offensive to the Viking presence in Mercia, its earthwork defenses are relatively well preserved, and show particularly good evidence of rectilinear planning, being roughly 1,350 feet square. The regular layout and grid pattern of streets reveal a reuse of a pre-existing Roman settlement. The enceinte consisted of a 6-meter-wide clay bank surrounded by a triple ditch arrangement. The banks formed a rough square with sides 510–550 m long. A narrow walkway of laid stones ran along their inner face.

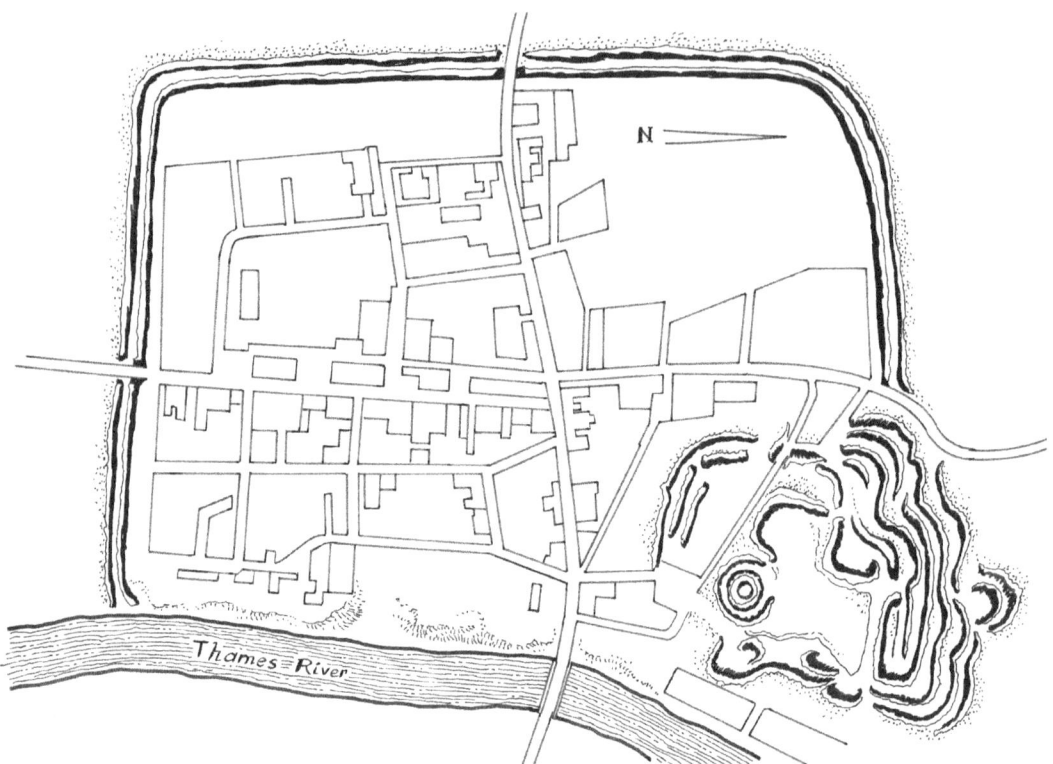

The settlement of Wallingford in Oxfordshire grew on an important crossing point in the upper Thames valley. It was first mentioned by name in a charter dated around A.D. 895. However, Wallingford had, in fact, probably been a focus of both road and water-borne communications since late Roman times. It was around this small settlement that King Alfred had a massive earthern rampart (approx. 2,500 by 1,800 feet) erected in a rectangle enclosing some 41 hectares of land. Its layout was expanded over a formal street-grid system in the southern half, the most important route being the wallstreet, which allowed troops to move quickly along the ramparts. Wallingford burh seemed to have had accommodation for 2,400 men, and its first occupation may have been completely military in nature, but the population soon grew with the development of associated specialist craft industries.

nically speaking, a typical Alfredian burh might have been a small- to medium-sized fortified town, defended by an earth wall topped with a palisade and fronted by one or more ditches filled with water when available, obviously a copy or inheritance of earlier Roman practice. Some burhs were entirely fresh Saxon creations such as Cricklade, others were the result of following the line of earlier intact Roman defenses on the same site, e.g., Winchester, Exeter, and Gloucester (revived as a royal and ecclesiastical center in the 7th century, and as a fortified burh and planned town in the 9th. Situated at the lowest bridgeable point on the Severn River, Gloucester was for a long time an important inland port). In a few cases, even Iron Age hill forts were reused (e.g., Daw's Castle in Somerset).

Though Alfred began the refortification of England, many sites were built by his successors in the early 10th century. Alfred's son, Edward the Elder (reign

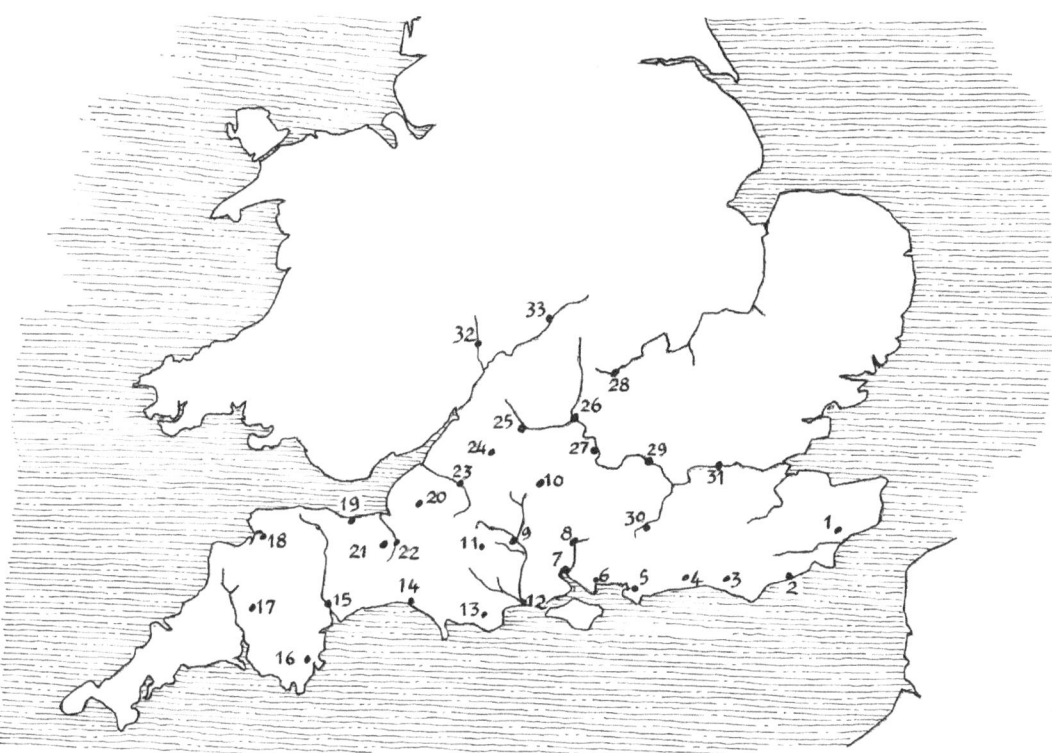

Alfredian burhs (from the Burghal Hidage). 1: Eorpeburnan; 2: Hastings; 3: Lewes; 4: Burpham; 5: Chichester; 6: Portchester; 7: Southampton; 8: Winchester; 9: Wilton; 10: Chisbury; 11: Shaftesbury; 12: Twynam; 13: Wareham; 14: Bridport; 15: Exeter; 16: Halwell; 17: Lydford; 18: Pilton; 19: Watchet; 20: Axbridge; 21: Lyng; 22: Langport; 23: Bath; 24: Malmesbury; 25: Cricklade; 26: Oxford; 27: Wallingford; 28: Buckingham; 29: Sashes; 30: Eashing; 31: Southwark; 32: Worcester; 33: Warwick.

901–925), continued his father's policy of establishing fortified towns, and he and his sister, Lady Aethelflaed of Mercia, built a new double row of burhs along the old Roman road of Watling Street, which marked the border of the Danelaw as it ran from the Mersey to Essex. Unfortunately for posterity, most Saxon buildings were constructed of earth, wood, and wattle and daub. The depredations of time and of the Danes left very few of these vulnerable buildings standing. Of the burhs that have survived as modern towns, little remains of the Saxon settlements, and only a few surviving examples have been found. Although ramparts have become gentler over the centuries and ditches shallower and overgrown with brambles, a few interesting remnants can be seen notably at Wareham, located eight miles (13 km) southwest of Poole in Dorset, southwest England. Wareham was a strategic dry point between the River Frome and the River Piddle at the head of the Wareham Channel. Founded by the Saxons, the burh, built by order of King Alfred the Great in the 9th century, was more or less rectangular in plan (c. 2,300 by 2,000 feet) with earth ramparts and timber facing rising up to 15 feet, later replaced by a stone wall. The town was a Saxon royal burial place, notably that of King Beorhtric (king of Wessex from 786 to 802). The River Frome served as a small harbor and the town was a port in centuries when boats were smaller and before the river silted up. It is interesting to note that in 1940 the ditches of Wareham were reshaped and reinforced with pillboxes to serve as anti-tank obstacles should Nazi Germany have carried out Operation Sealion, the invasion of Britain. Other remnants of Anglo-Saxon burhs can be seen at Cricklade in Wiltshire, and Wallingford in Oxfordshire.

Below: Anglo-Saxon ceorl. The Anglo-Saxon army was known as the fyrd, made up of all fit free men between the ages of 15 and 60. The depicted ceorl (peasant) wears daily life civilian clothes, and is armed with an axe and a spear. On the left: various forms of Anglo-Saxon socket spearheads.

Opposite left: Anglo-Saxon thegn. A thegn (or thane), originally the sworn comrade of the king or war leader, was a lord who held his land directly from the king in return for military service in time of war. Thegns could earn their titles and lands or inherit them. Under the pressure of constant warfare the more important free landholders were absorbed into the thegnly class, while the lesser ones sank into serfdom. The depicted thegn is armed with a scramasax (a single-edged sword) and a dagger. He wears a conical metal helmet and a byrnie (a hip-length, thick leather padded tunic with short sleeves), and carries a round shield.

Opposite right: Anglo-Saxon huscarl. The huscarls were the elite of the Anglo-Saxon warriors. They were originally the professional soldiers who made up the personal bodyguards of the kings and earls. The name huscarl literally means household man. Indeed, as well as being warriors, some huscarls performed administrative and legal functions similar to those of a modern magistrate. They were important and trusted servants of their masters. The depicted horseman, who was rather similar to the cavalryman of the Continent, is armed with a heavy battle-axe on a long shaft. His sword is of the spatha style (with a broad two-edged blade about 75 cm long). He wears a conical helmet with nasal, known as Spangenhelm, and a chain mail hauberk (a body armor tunic made of interlinked small metal rings).

Siege Warfare

Due to a lack of reliable written sources, the ways in which Anglo-Saxon burhs were attacked and defended remain largely conjectural. Siege warfare was more than probably quite primitive and rudimentary, particularly compared to the sophisticated Roman use of siege machines and siege fortifications. It probably differed very little from tactics developed in the Iron Age. Attackers would, as ever, use treachery, surprise, intrigue, and negotiation under pressure. In the case of a direct military attack, they would simply attempt to smash the gate with a ram (often no more than a tree trunk), archers would shoot arrows at the defenders and, given the relatively small height of earthwalls and palisades, would directly assault these defenses using scaling ladders, or try to destroy the palisades by fire. Defenders would shoot arrows, throw javelins and spears, drop rocks and stones upon the attackers, or would sally on horse or on foot for hand-to-hand combat outside their walls. Although warfare in the British Dark Ages was the preserve of the thegns (well-armed armored nobility), if need be, poorly armed local peasants and townsmen of the burh might be engaged in the defense of the ramparts. Besides, all Anglo-Saxon fortifications, like Roman ones, were essentially communal and royal. All able-bodied Saxons were obliged by customary law to take part personally or contribute money to the building and maintenance of defense works.

Aftermath

The Norman conquest closes what is called the Saxon period of English history, during which the English nation may be said to have taken form. As a conclusion it can be said that, on the whole, Anglo-Saxon fortifications in the period circa A.D. 410–1066 looked back rather than forward, utilizing earlier structures and techniques little different from the Iron Age hill forts or, when building anew, doing so on lines deriving from ancient Celtic and Roman practices. It is for this reason that the succeeding Norman fortifications provide a clear contrast to what had been done before, clearly marking the beginning of a new era.

Part 4

Norman Castles 1066–1154

The Normans and England

THE NORMANS

While the Viking Danes attacked and established themselves in parts of Britain, other groups of Scandinavian raiders harassed what is now France. They were known as Normans (from "Northmen" or "Norsemen," after the Vikings from Scandinavia), and as a result of repeated harrying of the French kingdom, they were eventually able to settle down permanently in France too. The last Carolingian kings who ruled France were powerless, and in 911 at Saint-Clair-sur-Epte, king Charles III the Simple (879–929) agreed under strong pressure to yield the northwestern coastal Channel region around the mouth of the Seine River to a Northman chief. This warlord, named Rollo, became a feudal vassal who payed homage to the king of France and swore to defend the territory entrusted to him. In this way Charles III ensured a buffer land between his vulnerable kingdom and further raiding Vikings. From being landless sea rovers and freebooters, Rollo and his men became settled landowners. They adopted the Christian faith, married local women, and mingled freely with the native Frankish inhabitants. The wild and ferocious plunderers turned from adventurers into farming rulers, and little by little Germanic Scandinavian and Latin French societies blended together into a Norman breed. The Anglo-Saxons and Danes in Britain had encountered a Latin civilization, which was still very feebly rooted, and they left a strong Germanic mark upon it. But the Normans confronted by Rome in the form of latinized France were swallowed up by the Latin spirit with surprising speed. After less than a century the Norman Vikings spoke nothing but old French, had adopted French customs and behaved more or less like good Christians. Under the firm leadership of strong dukes succeeding Rollo, the territory prospered, the fief was enlarged and developed into the dukedom of the Northmen, better known as Normandy, with a political capital, Rouen, and a religious center, Bayeux. The Duchy of Normandy was one of the great large fiefs of early medieval France, and when the Normans invaded England in 1066, they were more French than Scandinavian. The Normans adopted the ceremony and hierarchy of continental chivalry and feudalism much sooner than did the English. After the fall of the Carolingian Empire and due to the insecurity caused by the Viking incursions, feudalism had developed as a result of the need for local defense, but by the 11th century it was regulated with more precision, and social classes were controlled by strict rules. Under the Duke of Normandy stood the barons who ruled territories, and who in turn had power over smaller lords and knights, owners of land the tenure of which involved military service. At the Duke's summons, the barons had to present themselves with their knights armed and mounted, ready to remain in the field for forty days. This was a short time but suited to short campaigns in the summer.

For half a century before 1066 England and Normandy had been drawing closer together. The king of England, himself Edward the Confessor, was more Norman than English and French/Norman speech, habits and customs were prevalent at his court. But how came it that a Duke of Normandy, in the 11th century, conceived the idea of making himself king of England?

The Conquest

Guillaume le Bâtard (William the Bastard) was born in 1027, the illegitimate son of Duke of Normandy, Robert the Magnificent, and a tanner's daughter from Falaise, named Arletta. He was acknowledged by his father and succeeded him in July 1035. He inherited the duchy when only a boy, and the desperate struggle for survival that preoccupied his early years reinforced his natural tendency towards ruthlessness and resolution. He married Matilda, the daughter of Count Baldwin of Flanders, who transferred a vague descent in the female line from the Anglo-Saxon House of Wessex. He was also second cousin of the childless Edward the Confessor but, genealogically, being a bastard, he had no rightful claims to the English crown. But William of Normandy was a hard man in every sense, a ferocious warrior, and a harsh, stubborn, ambitious, ruthless and cunning ruler who claimed, after Edward's death in early 1066, that he was entitled to become king of England. The Normans still had the Viking taste for adventure. A day's sail could carry them to England. It was a temptation. We are, however, somewhat in the dark as to the basis of his claim. To achieve his goal, William and his counselor Bishop Lanfranc engineered a diplomatic machination against the only possible rival, Harold Godwinson, Edward's brother-in-law and earl of Wessex. There is a story that William had visited the court of Edward the Confessor in 1051 and had become his vassal on the condition that, should Edward die childless, he was to designate William as his successor. In fact Edward was not allowed to offer the crown, which was dependent, not on himself, but on the choice of the Witan (the traditional Anglo-Saxon council of influential nobles and bishops who elected the king of England). In 1064 William extorted under unclear circumstances a promise along the same lines when the unfortunate Harold was shipwrecked in Normandy and taken prisoner. But Harold did not regard himself bound by an oath given under duress, and again the choice of a king of England was not in his hands but in the Witan's. When Edward died, there was no question at all of William of Normandy. The Witan showed no hesitation and elected the bold and well-beloved Harold Godwinson. Everything in Harold's career suggests that he would have made a ruler in the best Saxon-Dane tradition — brave, vigorous, honorable and generous. However, his position on the throne was challenged by two rivals and by two nearly simultaneous invasions.

Immediately after Harold's coronation, William of Normandy, who always subtly lent a moral covering to his desires, presented himself as a victim and instigated a well-staged propagandist campaign against Harold, who was accused of felony for having violated both feudal law and a solemn oath. William's bad faith is beyond doubt, but the facts as presented seemed to press strongly against Harold. As was usual in those times, the quarrel was solved by force. Pope Alexander II knew how the oath had been obtained and what William's claims were really worth, but he wished to reform the Church of England, and therefore favored William's claim. The

Norman knight. The Normans developed a strong, heavily armored cavalry. The use of stirrups (introduced in the 9th century) and a well-designed saddle gave the horseman a stable balance on his mount, making it possible to couch a long spear tightly resting under his arm. The additional force of the horse's impetus could be brought behind the spear, delivering a formidable blow.

papacy condemned Harold and blessed in advance any expedition that William might undertake to assert his rights. The conquest of England — in fact an act of pure international brigandage and aggression — therefore took on the character of a sort of holy war. For so difficult a campaign the ordinary 40-days' feudal military service would not have sufficed, but as the expedition had been well advertised, many knights and adventurers not only from Normandy but also from France, Anjou, Britanny and Flanders, flocked to William's standard. All these adventurers were promised profits in the form of money, plunder and land in England. While William's half-brother, Odo Bishop of Bayeux, recruited men throughout Western Europe, a fleet was built. These important events in the history of England are depicted in a remarkable work of art known as the Bayeux Tapestry. On September 28, 1066, a fleet transporting some 12,000 soldiers, of whom 5,000 were horsemen, landed unopposed on the shore of Pevensey, East Sussex.

William of Normandy was not the sole invader of England in 1066. The death of King Edward the Confessor in January 1066 had triggered a succession struggle in which a variety of contenders from across northwestern Europe fought for the English throne. Another claimant was the king of Norway, Harald Hardrada. Aided by Tostig, Harold's own brother, Hardrada landed with 15,000 troops in Northern England. Harold dashed north, defeated the invaders at the battle of Stamford Bridge, near York, on September 25, then rushed back south to fight William. The main battle of the conquest was fought on

Norman weapons and armor. The principal weapons used were the heavy two-handed axe (1), spear and javelin (2), bow and arrow (3), sword (4), dagger (5), and wooden mace (6). Body armor was an indication of social rank and wealth. The main armor garment was a hauberk of chain mail (made of small metal rings linked together in a pattern to form a protective mesh). A conical metal helmet with nasal (nose piece) was worn in battle. The legs were protected with mail coverings laced up the back, or puttee-like hose. Further protection was provided by a wooden shield very often kite-shaped. Some shields were painted and decorated but genuine heraldic designs didn't appear until later. For the sake of mobility, the horse went into battle unarmored.

October 14, 1066, at Senlac Hill, approximately 6 miles northwest of Hastings. Harold was killed in the fight and his army defeated. The superiority of cavalry (supported by archers), already well established in Europe, was confirmed by the memorable battle of Senlac. The defeat was so conclusive that Saxon England disintegrated.

Within a few weeks the Witan had no other choice than to accept William as their king. London opened its gates to him, and William was crowned on Christmas Day, 1066, at Westminster. Guillaume the Bastard had become William I the Conqueror, "lawful" sovereign of England.

Norman England

Defeating an army in battle is one thing, but imposing one's rule over a whole country is another matter. The transition from an invading army to lawful rulers was difficult and painstaking, and the period right after the invasion saw the fruits of the victory at Hastings hang in the balance. The Norman conquest of England was not completed until about 1072, by which time several regional revolts in the north, in East Anglia and at Exeter, had been suppressed with extreme ruthlessness. William, then both Duke of Normandy and King of England, was able to turn his full attention to the governing of his new kingdom. William's policy in regard to England exhibited profound statesmanship. He introduced the Norman feudalism to which he was accustomed, but took good care that it should not weaken his personal power. William ensured the supremacy of the crown without interfering with English customs, and declared that he did not propose to change the English customs but to govern as Edward the Confessor, the last Saxon king whom he acknowledged, had done. The English who had refused to join him before the battle of Senlac were declared traitors, but were permitted to keep their lands upon condition of receiving them from the king as his vassals. The lands of those who actually bore arms against him at Senlac, or in later rebellions, including the great estates of Harold's family, were confiscated and distributed among his faithful followers, both Norman and English, though naturally the Normans among them far outnumbered the English. William avoided giving to any one person a great many estates in a single region, so that no one should become inconveniently powerful. Instead he granted several pieces in different parts of the country. The only exceptions were the great lords of Hereford, Shrewsbury, Chester and Durham, who had to be strong in order to guard the Welsh and Scottish borders. In 1085 the famous Domesday Book, a detailed description and record of all the wealth in England, was begun in order that taxes could be collected. Lanfranc, William's new archbishop, reorganized the English Church. Finally, in order to secure the support of the smaller landholders and to prevent combinations against him among the greater ones, he required every landholder, vassal and sub-vassal in England to take an oath of fidelity directly to him.

It is clear that the Norman conquest was not a simple change of dynasty. William was ruthless, it is true, but he was a great administrator who gave England the first foundations of a stable and effective form of government. Had the conquest never happened England would probably have become part of the Scandinavian world. For all its cruelty the conquest opened the floodgates of European culture and institutions; it brought England closer to Western latinized Europe and created strong links (later rivalry) with Normandy and France. Although the Normans transmitted large parts of the Saxon heritage, a new element was added to the English people. We cannot tell precisely how many Normans actually emigrated across the Channel (perhaps between 6,000 and 10,000 of a total population of one million?), but their influence upon the English court and government was significant. A century after William's arrival the whole body of the privileged nobility, the bishops, abbots, and government officials, were practically all Normans. For a short time these newcomers remained a separate people, but before the twelfth century was over they had become for the most part indistinguishable from the great mass of English people amongst whom they now lived. They had made the Anglo-Saxon people stronger, more vigorous, more active-minded, and more varied in their occupations and interests.

An important point resulting from the conquest of England by the Normans was that William I and his successors were, as Dukes of Normandy, tenants and subjects of the king of France, and at the same time independent kings of England. As they were more powerful than their suzerains and sovereigns, the weak French Capetians from Paris, the result was protracted rivalry and practically constant conflicts and wars with France until the 15th century. Conflicts had already started during William's lifetime. The Duke of Normandy and King of England was mortally wounded at the siege of Mantes in France whilst fighting against his feudal overlord, the king of France. William I died on September 9, 1087, aged 60, and was buried in St. Stephen Church in Caen, Normandy. Another important change was introduced: the crown was no longer elective but hereditary. Before his death William left Normandy to his eldest son, Robert, and England to his second son, William Rufus. Henry, the youngest son, was given cash. The period of 1087–1106 is best viewed as a three-way struggle between the brothers as they attempted to reunite the two territories, a conflict into which England was occasionally dragged through the intrigues of the cross-Channel aristocracy, who found themselves in the uncomfortable position of having bonds of loyalty to warring lords.

Norman Military Architecture

The war of conquest waged by the Normans on their new subjects between 1067 and 1072 changed the face of the English landscape. Castles were the main Norman devices for stamping their authority on a hostile population. Regarding the castles built by the Normans, we can only make a few general remarks. The Normans brought nothing really new to military architecture. In fact many features of the so-called motte-and-bailey castle (basically the combination of ditch, earth rampart, and wooden palisade) had already been used in Celtic hill forts, Roman forts, and the

Anglo-Saxon burhs. Some of the Norman early stone constructions were inferior in design to those of the Romans. In fact the Normans had no organized engineering corps and their castle designers were civilian architects and master-builders who constructed indifferently military, civilian and religious buildings. The Anglo-Saxons, as we have seen, had burhs erected before 1066, but the castle was, however, definitely a Norman import. To William I fortifications were an essential part of his strategy for keeping England in subjugation once he had conquered it. It was indeed the strategic and tactical concepts which the Normans most contributed and innovated. They saw strongholds not just as simple refuge places or temporary overnight camps, nor as barracks for the soldiery, but as integral units in the administration of their realm, and as solid bases for a mobile form of warfare mainly using armored cavalry. Nonetheless the new types of fortification they introduced, notably the massive stone keep, were more ambitious and greater in size and scope than anything the Celts and Saxons had been able to achieve before them. The Celtic hill fort was a collective tribal undertaking, while the Roman fort was a public work, part of a state system defense, as was the Saxon burh. By contrast, the Norman castle, although it was a major part of their governance, was a private stronghold built, financed and occupied by a feudal landlord. The difference is radical, and must be grasped at the outset by all who wish to understand the significance of castles in British history. This point is indeed essential. There were royal castles, but nationwide these were only a small minority. They were built in nearly every instance to overawe the towns and cities, and so left the countryside, where the bulk of the population lived, virtually in the hands of local feudal magnates, great or small, good or bad.

The Normans devoted tireless enthusiasm to the task of fortress construction and they brought a measure of standardization. That is not to say that all Norman castles were exactly the same. Each was a unique example specifically intended to meet the requirements of that particular geographical and political situation, but the Normans introduced a number of typical models. When we think of a Norman castle, there rises before our mind the image of a mighty square stone tower, like the keeps at Dover, Porchester, or Rochester or the White Tower in London. Yet the huge square stone keep was the exception rather than the rule, and the great majority of Norman castles were not made of stone but of timbered earthwork.

There is no doubt that the earliest Norman castles were built as temporary overnight camps protecting Duke William, his knights and his soldiers when campaigning to complete the invasion after the victory of Hastings. They had prefabricated camps with them, a series of stout wooden panels fixed to posts, which could be hammered into the ground. Such a temporary camp was not impregnable, but strong enough to keep out disgruntled Anglo-Saxon peasants. The next morning the prefabricated elements were dismantled and stowed in wagons before the column set off again. When the expedition became a permanent conquest, the occupation of large territories and the control of hostile populations demanded more elaborate fortifications. William I's first task was to make the country secure. To do so, he granted his barons lands and permission to build strongholds (what became the license or the "right to crenellate") to overawe the defeated Saxons by their magnitude and to serve as military bases in case of rebellion.

Motte-and-Bailey Castles

In the 12th century, most Norman castles in Britain consisted of the motte-and-bailey castle made of earthwork and wood. They were also built in Denmark, Norway, the Low Countries, the Rhineland and South Italy, all regions which came under Viking influence, and it has therefore been suggested that the motte-and-bailey castle was perhaps a Norman invention, or if not, one which the Vikings took up and exported. At that time England was a densely forested land and large parts of the low-lying districts were covered with oak trees. Oak was the traditional building material.

There was, of course, no standard design, as each motte-and-bailey was built by a private owner. Dimensions could vary a lot, but basically a typical motte-and-bailey castle, as the name implies, comprised two main parts.

THE MOTTE

First there was the motte, a site which at once was both elevated and difficult to access, as the Normans were no less willing than the Celts before them to take advantage of height provided by natural features. If there was a suitable hill in the area it could be adapted by scarping, steepening the sides by cutting away the lower slopes in order to make a flat-topped cone. If no escarpment was provided by nature, an artificial mount (10 to 15 m) was erected. Part of the material for the motte derived from the ditch that surrounded it, but additional earth was required to bring the mound up to any appreciable size. The motte was more than a simple dump of earth. In many cases it was composed of several alternating horizontal layers of material, including stone, peat, chalk rubble and rammed or beaten-down earth, and a final coating of clay in order to resist erosion. The top of the motte was flattened and surrounded by a palisade. In the middle of this enclosed platform there was a building, usually a squat rectangular or square timber tower (often called the domus) topped off with a pitched or sloping roof. The domus was sometimes on stilts to allow for free movement of the garrison, or it rested on heavy timber posts, forming a strong foundation anchored in the motte. The domus had two or three floors. The lower level was a storehouse for supply and provisions. The upper floor, whose door was accessible to the ground by means of a strong removable ladder or a light timber bridge, served as a permanent dwelling place for the lord of the castle. It could also be reserved mainly for use in time of siege as a place of withdrawal from which, when the bailey had been taken, the defense could be continued. Direct assault up the steep slopes under a hail of missiles would have been daunting to the attackers, but starvation was also a potent instrument of war and the tower on the motte could have been little less than a trap unless outside help was certain and speedy. Besides, it was vulnerable to fire. The motte was often surrounded by a deep ditch, which could be filled with water. The timber tower on the motte was reached from the lower bailey either by a bridge carried over the ditch or by steps climbing the mound. Of course all the actual work—chopping down trees, digging ditches and throwing up earth, for example—was done with very primitive tools by the Anglo-Saxon villeins and serfs who were right at the bottom of the feudal social system. It should be noted that the French term *motte* (mound) has been transferred and limited in English to the ditch and transcribed as moat.

THE BAILEY

Second there was the attached bailey, placed at the foot of the motte. The bailey, in fact the largest part of the castle, was a subordinate courtyard sheltering the wooden subsidiary buildings of the lord's household: hall, chapel, stables, byre, granary, service buildings, and accommodation, huts and workshops for retainers, servants and craftsmen, as well as corrals for animals, training ground for the soldiers, and gardens and orchards. The number, size and arrangement of baileys were infinitely variable and as can be imagined no two sites were exactly the same. The simplest type of bailey was usually oval-, D- or U-shaped. A motte could also have two baileys (as in Windsor Castle). In Old Sarum in Wiltshire, the bailey was an ancient Iron Age Celtic hill fort, which had been reused. The motte could be built on one side of the bailey or in the middle of it. The bailey formed a sort of small village enclosed by a ditch, another earth wall and another palisade, which formed a complete circuit around the whole site. This outer embankment served as the first line of defense, and the bailey was used as a refuge by the peasants of the neighborhood and their cattle in case of attack.

The motte-and-bailey castle could withstand the type of attack that could be mounted in the 11th century, except for the danger of fire.

FUNCTION OF THE MOTTE-AND-BAILEY CASTLE

The motte-and-bailey castle was a fortified residence, a stronghold to deter or repulse aggression from external foes, and a base from which the lord could launch raids and attacks on his enemies. The motte-and-bailey castle was designed with defense firmly in mind. At first it was merely a castle of subjugation, but it soon became a small political, economical, juridical, administrative and tax and toll collecting center, the very image of collective security, but also the symbol of oppression and seat of power for the military command through all the surrounding villages. It was the visible form of feudal social relations. A castle could not function for long without its locality. The peasants of the vicinity were burdened with a multitude of tasks. For example they were required to work on buildings and earthworks, and to find wood for the fireplace.

The appearance of a motte-and-bailey castle must have been strikingly impressive and picturesque, particularly as all the woodwork was brightly painted and the tower undoubtedly decorated. As it was rather small, cheap and quickly built, the motte-and-bailey castle was within the means of most junior lords, but it could not withstand a long siege. It was too small to hold a large volume of supplies or to

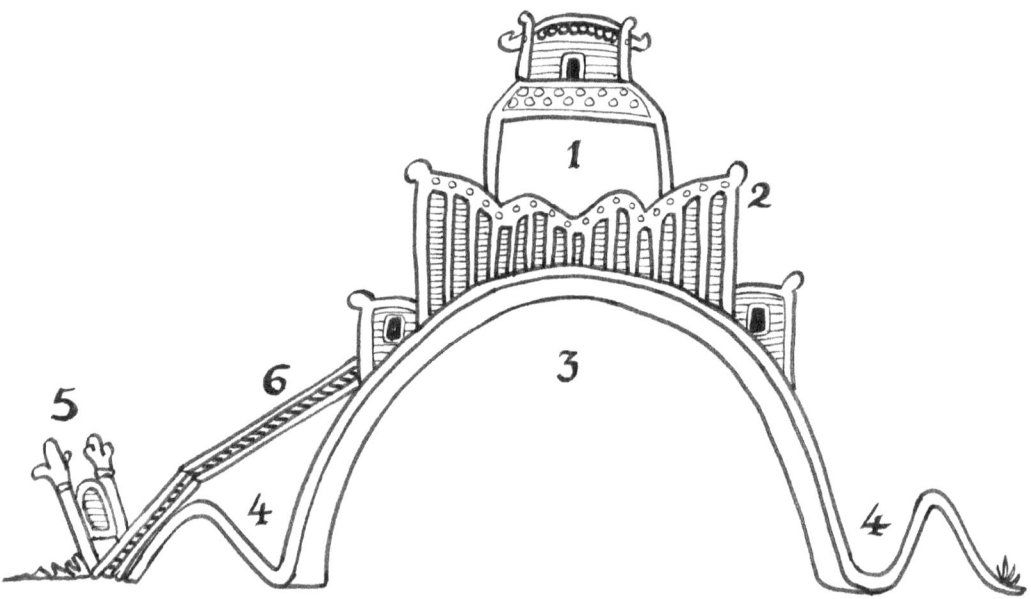

Top: *If we are to trust the Bayeux Tapestry—whose accuracy is in other matters thoroughly borne out by all contemporary evidence—the motte-and-bailey castle of the Dinan, Normandy, France, included the following: the tower (1), and the palisade (2) on top of the motte or mount (3), the ditch (4), the gate (5) and the bridge (6) connecting the tower to the lower bailey.*

Bottom: *The early medieval motte-and-bailey castle, in its simplest form (here based on Dinan motte-and-bailey castle as shown on the Bayeux Tapestry), consisted of a timber tower (1) on an earth mound or motte (2) with a palisade on top. The bailey (3) was a protected space featuring various service buildings. It was surrounded by a palisaded outer wall and a ditch (4).*

accommodate a significant garrison and the wooden defenses could be set on fire or chopped up relatively easily. Sadly, like the Alfredian Saxon burhs, none of these structures have survived. Timbered earthwork being highly vulnerable to the attrition of time, no motte-and-bailey castle has come down to us in complete preserved form, but we can see pictures of them on the Bayeux Tapestry.

In the landscape, only a few remnants of motte-and-bailey castles have been preserved in the parts of Britain into which the Normans penetrated. Several thousand were built during the century and a half following the conquest in 1066. In terms of distribution, motte-and-bailey castles are spread widely over England, Wales, Lowland and eastern Scotland, and the eastern half of Ireland — as a result of the invasion in 1167. A very large number of motte-and-bailey timber castles were built in

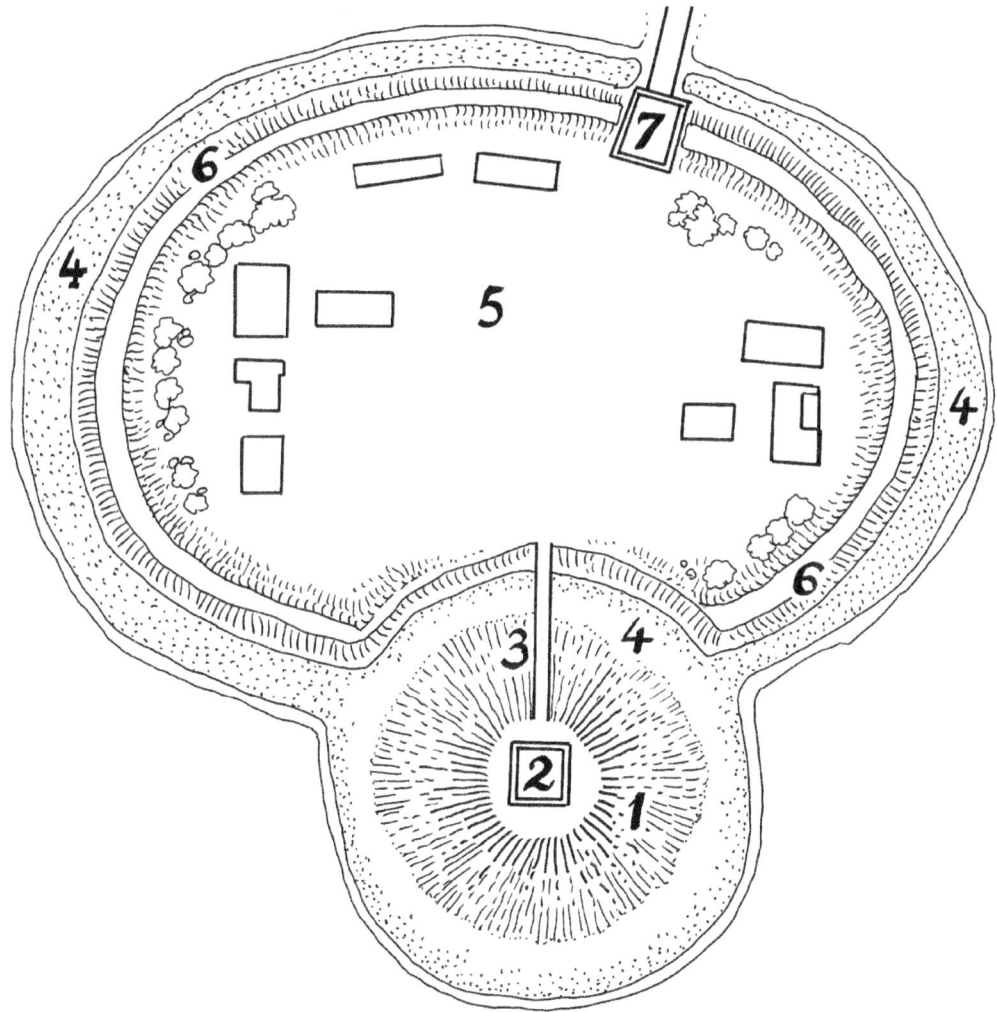

Laughton-en-le-Morthen is located to the south of Rotherham, South Yorkshire, England. 1: Motte; 2: Tower; 3: Bridge; 4: Ditch; 5: Bailey; 6: Earth wall with palisade; 7: Gatehouse and entrance.

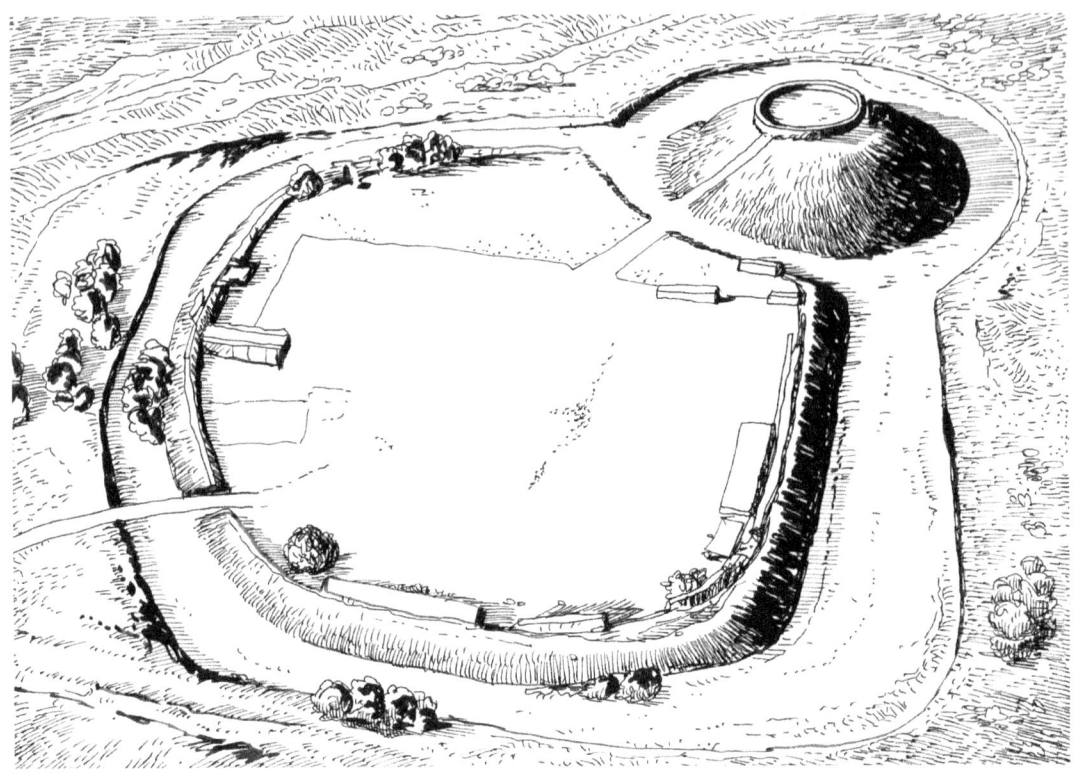

The motte-and-bailey castle of Berkhamsted in Hertfordshire gives a good example of a Norman stronghold. The motte is 13.7 meters high and 55 meters in diameter while the bailey measures 137 meters by 91 meters.

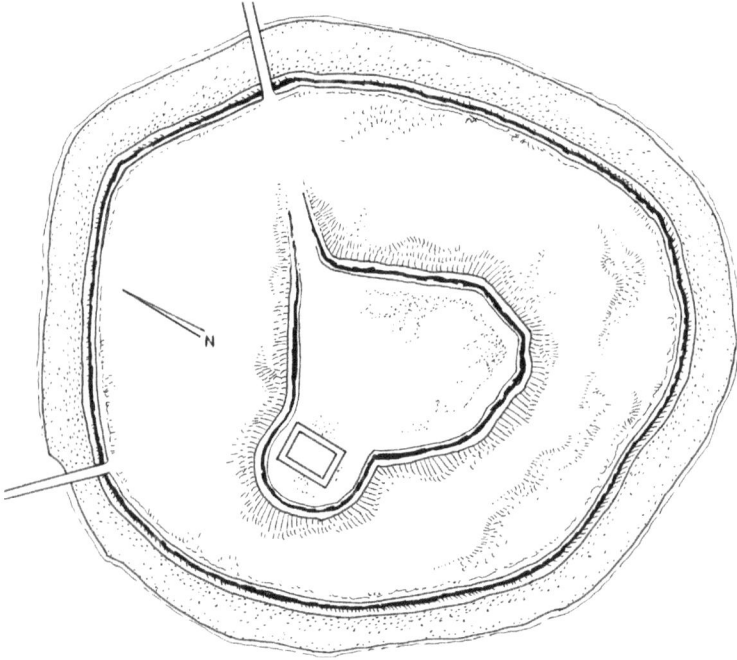

Duffus Castle, near Elgin, Moray, Scotland, was a motte-and-bailey castle built by a certain Freskin (probably a mercenary from Flemish origin) in c. 1140. The motte was a large man-made mound with steeply sloping sides hemmed by a wide and deep ditch. Over time the original earth and timber motte-and-bailey castle underwent many alterations, notably the replacement of palisades with stone walls, and the construction of stone buildings. The castle was occupied until 1705.

the early days of the conquest when the Norman lords established themselves in alien and hostile territory. There was another outburst of building during the civil wars known as the Anarchy during the reign of King Stephen (1135–1154) when many timber castles were constructed as temporary expedients, only to be abandoned and destroyed when order was re-established.

There is no point here to listing all British timber castles, but in England the more impressive sites are Rayleigh Mount in Essex, Pickering and Tickhill in Yorkshire, Berkhamstead in Hertfordshire, Thetford in Norfolk, and Tonbridge in Kent. In Scotland remnants of such fortifications may be seen at the Mote of Urr in Galloway, the Peel of Lumphanan and the Doune of Invertnochty in Aberdeen, and Duffus Castle in Moray.

Shell-Keeps

It can be easily imagined that the motte-and-bailey castle was a rather primitive dwelling place and a rather weak and rudimentary fortification. Militarily its main inconvenience was that it was made of wood, the material most accessible and most easily worked, but also the most flammable. Obviously buildings, obstacles and fortifications made of earthwork and wood were perishable. When intended to be permanent works, they could not be left unattended for years, and therefore had to be constantly reviewed, maintained and renewed. For these reasons, in the 12th century some powerful and wealthy lords had all or parts of the timber work (the domus, the palisade cresting the motte, and the palisade enclosing the bailey) replaced with a stone wall known as a curtain, enceinte or chemise (French for shirt). The result was an improved version of the motte-and-bailey castle known as motte-and-stone-wall or shell-keep. This was characterized by a circular, oval or polygonal stone wall, generally with the accommodations built against its inner face, leaving an open and commodious courtyard in the center, which was accessed by a porch-like entrance. Access to the wallwalk and battlement was by means of staircases. A shell-keep was an enclosure rather than a building, and as such, its height was usually relatively low in comparison with its diameter. Shell-keeps were comparatively small, their walls being on average 2.5–3 meters thick and rising at the most to a height of 7 or 8 meters.

However, not all shell-keeps were later replacements of earlier timber works. Some of them were built not on an earlier motte but on level ground. Some at least appear to have been built within a few decades of the conquest, and shell-keeps should not be seen as a transitional form between the motte-and-bailey castle and the stone keep but rather as a part of the repertoire of Norman fortification techniques, showing their capacity for adapting themselves to all kinds of circumstances. Shell-keeps show wide variations of a common type, and form the nucleus of a high proportion of British castles, even if it is sometimes difficult to recognize them due to later additions. The Round Tower of Windsor Castle in Berkshire is an exam-

Top: *Shell-keep.*
Bottom: *Bramber Castle, located on a steep hill above the wide, once marshy valley of the Adur River in West Sussex, is a shell-keep originating from a motte-and-bailey castle. Originally a timber castle was built on a motte (in a central position in the bailey) by a certain William De Braose in c. 1070. This was modified in c. 1100 when a gatehouse of flint and stone construction (measuring about 38 × 40 feet), an outer curtain with wallwalk and battlement, and domestic buildings and a church were built. The conjectured illustration shows how the castle might have looked in the 12th century.*

4. Norman Castles 1066–1154   131

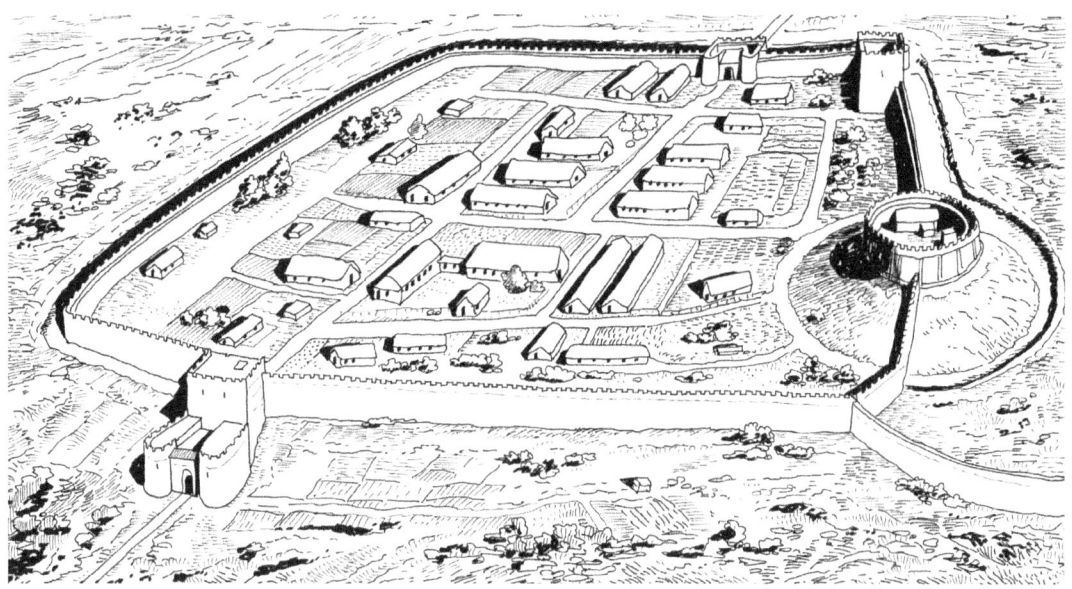

Lincoln. In 1068 William the Conqueror built a wooden motte castle (replaced with a stone shell-keep castle in the 12th century) to control the townspeople.

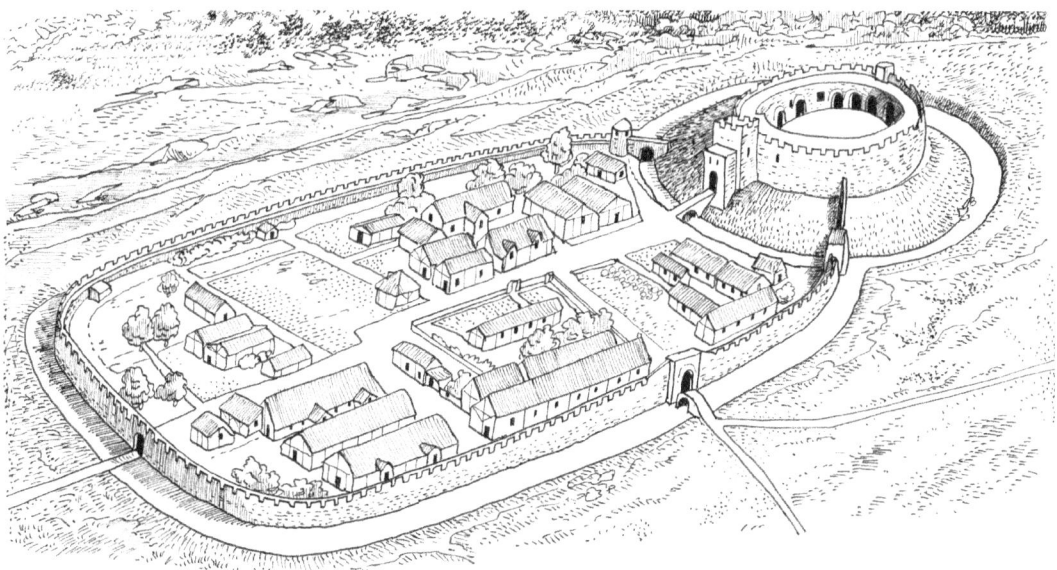

Restormel Castle (conjectured reconstruction), located on a spur of high ground dominating the River Fowey near Lostwithiel in Cornwall, was one of the four Norman castles of Cornwall, the others being Launceston, Tintagel and Trematon. The castle of Restormel was built in c. 1100 in the typical shell-keep style by the sheriff of Cornwall, Baldwin Fitz Turcin, as replacement of an older original timber defense. The oval castle enceinte (approx. 30 feet high, 8 feet thick and 125 feet in diameter) was built on top of a 17-meter-high artificial motte. A gatehouse with drawbridge gave access to a large (now disappeared) quadrangular bailey enclosed with a stone wall, which extended on gently sloping land southwest from the motte. The impressive ruins of Restormel Castle are now administrated by English Heritage and are open to the public.

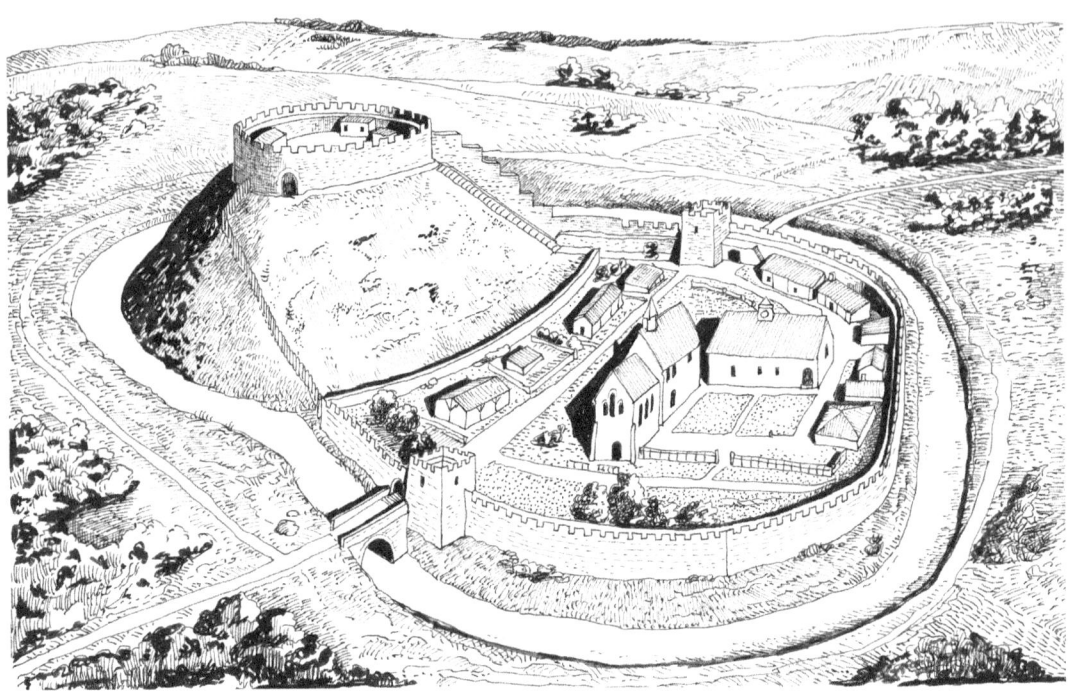

Totnes Castle, a fine example of a Norman shell-keep, was one of the first three castles to be built in Devon, in a clear attempt to tighten William's hold over this potentially rebellious shire. The shell-keep of Totnes Castle was built in the 11th century, probably about 1100, and reconstructed in the 14th century. The castle was almost circular in plan and there were lean-to sheds and houses lining the wall, as well as a crenellated wallwalk that was 15 feet above courtyard level. The shell-keep stands on top of a large nearly circular motte nearly surrounded by a 70-feet-wide ditch. The motte is made of layers of earth, rock and clay packed down onto a natural rock mound, and it would originally have been topped by a wooden tower. The adjacent D-shaped bailey was originally enclosed by a palisade and later by a crenellated stone wall as well as by a large ditch. In the bailey there were the usual domestic buildings and a church. A stair placed along the east wall led from the bailey to the summit of the motte. The conjectured reconstruction shows Totnes Castle as it might have appeared in the 14th century. The site, now amputated of its bailey, stands in the middle of the city of Totnes. It is owned by English Heritage and is open to the public.

ple of such a transformation. The original structure was a massive retaining wall 12 feet thick and 130 feet in diameter. Within this wall King Henry II erected another work, and in 1826 came the final neo–Gothic addition, giving the tower the appearance it has today.

There was a great concentration of motte-and-bailey castles along the Welsh border, in Pembroque and in the Midlands, whilst a high proportion of shell-keeps are to be found in the southern half of England. Good examples of shell-keeps (often with later additions) are Restormel Castle and Launceston, both in Cornwall; Totnes in Devon; Arundel and Lewes, both in Sussex; Tonbridge in Kent; Caldicot in Monmouthshire; Carisbrooke on the Isle of Wight; Bramber Castle in West Sussex; and Rothesay in Scotland.

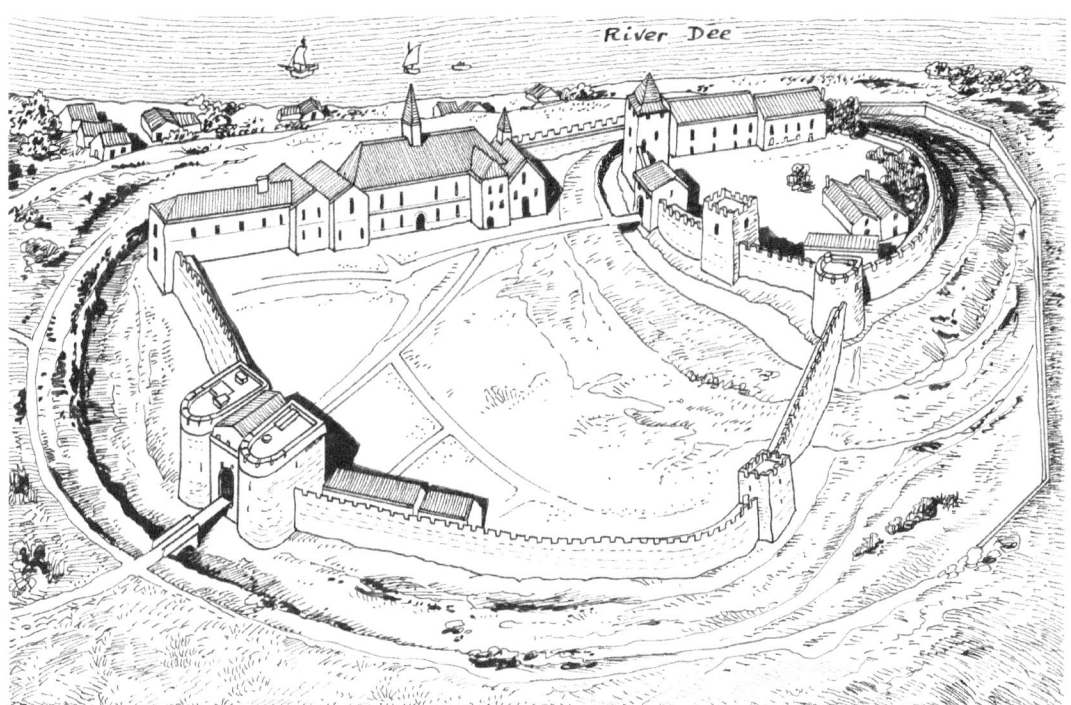

Chester Castle is located in the city center, off Castle Square in Cheshire. Chester provides a good example of a simple Norman timber castle developed into a large stone fortress. The structure originates from a Norman motte-and-bailey castle, founded by Hugh Lupus of Avranches, first earl of Chester. Standing on an eminence, it was intended to command a bridge over the River Dee. In the 12th century the wooden tower was replaced by a square stone tower, called the Flag Tower. During the same century the stone gateway to the inner bailey was built. In the 13th century, during the reign of King Henry III, the castle was enlarged. Later in the century, during the reign of Edward I, a new gateway to the outer bailey was built. This was flanked by two half-drum towers and had a drawbridge over a moat 26 feet (8 meters) deep. Further additions to the castle at this time included individual chambers for the king and queen, a new chapel and stables. Sadly all that is left of this large and important castle are fragments of the 12th-century inner bailey curtain wall, the Flag Tower and the original inner bailey gateway called the Agricola Tower. In the 18th century the remaining medieval buildings and towers were levelled to make way for a new barrack block and the Assize County Courts. The castle neoclassical buildings designed by Thomas Harrison, built between 1788 and 1813, are used today as Crown Courts and as a military museum. The site is now managed by Chester City Council and the Agricola Tower is open to the public. The illustration shows how Chester Castle might have appeared in the 13th century.

Stone Keeps

GENERALITIES

The Normans were by no means confined to timber motte-and-bailey works and stone shell-keeps. Rather than a single type, they brought with them a comprehensive range of fortification techniques which they used as need, funds, and material dictated in each particular case.

The donjon or stone keep already existed in Normandy and elsewhere in Europe, so there is no question of it having developed in Britain from the timber type. That stage of development, if ever there was one, had already taken place elsewhere. Although the square stone tower became associated with Norman architecture, the Normans were not the first to use it. That honor is accredited to the French count of Anjou, Foulque Nerra (Fulk the Black), who about 995 created the castle of Langeais, west of Tours in France. Langeais was a simple rectangular donjon 16 by 7 meters in plan with roughly hewn masoned walls, wooden floors, and entrance by means of a small projecting turret with a stone staircase leading to the proper entrance on the first floor. As the dukes of Normandy shared a common frontier with Anjou it was inevitable that in time they, too, would erect castles of stone for practical military purposes as well as to symbolize their own pride, wealth and strength.

The choice between a timber castle and one of stone by the Normans in Britain depended on the conditions obtaining in a particular place at a particular time. Where speed was essential then a timber building would be constructed, perhaps to be replaced at a later stage, often during the 12th century, by one of stone. Where time allowed, and other conditions made it desirable and affordable, a stone keep would be erected from the start. There was no hard and fast rule, but the power and wealth of the owner stood central. While lesser local lords had to content themselves with timber motte-and-bailey castles, the king and the more powerful barons had large stone buildings built. When earth and timber motte-and-bailey castles were numerous, stone keeps were much less common. Obviously the gigantic costs involved meant that only the king and extremely wealthy noblemen could afford them. Indeed, in the long term, large stone towers contributed to, reinforced and maintained a hierarchy within the privileged feudal military nobility. Because of its cost, a stone castle necessarily conferred more status on its owner and reflected more authority than an earth and timber castle. Because of their wealth, and thus their military power, kings, counts, earls and dukes subjugated many smaller vassals, barons and marquis who in turn dominated, poor noblemen and landowners as well as impecunious knights and squires. Masoned fortification marked the first step of the evolution permitting kings and dukes to impose their will on their vassals. Eventually the time would come when only they could finance, build, confiscate or dismantle castles according to their own interest and strategy. Although many wooden castles from shortly after the conquest were later strengthened or rebuilt in stone, the process was slow, and timber structures did not disappear overnight. Until the middle of the 13th century many local and modest landlords could not afford or were not allowed by their suzerains to build masoned castles. After all, timber castles were much cheaper, easier to build and, in many cases, more convenient and comfortable for daily life than the huge, vertical, and gloomy stone towers. For example the motte-and-bailey castle of Rayleigh Mount in Essex, built by a certain Swein in the 11th century shortly after the Norman conquest, was extended by Henry of Essex in c. 1180 and further developed in c. 1290, surviving for nearly 300 years into the reign of King Edward I (from 1272 to 1307), the builder of the greatest and most sophisticated British castles.

Loches Castle. Built in the early 11th century, Loches is situated near Tours in the Loire Valley in France, a good example of an early stone keep.

The building of stone castles in Britain began within a decade or so of 1066, but many of them actually belong to the 12th century and later. Although designated as belonging to what is usually termed the Norman style of architecture, many of them belong not to the Norman but to the Plantagenet-Angevin period.

Stone castles are the most visible legacy of the Norman period. They were centers of aristocratic power, projecting political might and military strength over the surrounding regions, and this the Normans did not only in the British Isles but also in Normandy (e.g., Caen, Chambois, Ivry-la-Bataille), and in southern Italy and Sicily, where Norman adventurers and mercenaries conquered territories from the Arabs in the 11th century (e.g., Melfi, Caccamo, Adrano, Palermo).

Function and Description

The more elaborate high stone keeps and more resilient and durable masoned great-towers fulfilled the same function as moat-and-bailey castles as previously discussed. They constituted the residence of a lord, his family, his warriors and his retainers and servants, and were self-supporting military strongholds reflecting power and authority. However one should not be too theoretical, and some Norman donjons are quite puzzling regarding their function. In some instances the lack of obvious accommodation is so noticeable that the only conclusion to be drawn is that some keeps were designed as impressive statements of power, only as a stately public building used for banquets and the reception of important guests.

Donjons share many features, though not all display every characteristic.

A Norman keep was a formidable fortress, which could vary considerably in size, from very large ones such as Colchester (approx. 150 by 150 feet in area), to very small ones such as Clitheroe (only approx. 32 square feet). On the whole typical Norman keeps were characterized by an imposing verticality and height. They had a square or rectangular plan (allowing a convenient internal layout), thick walls (reinforced with pilaster-butresses), and small square corner turrets (for observation and which generally contain the staircases). The main part of the walls also rose above the (wooden) roof level of the top story in order to protect it from attack by fire.

The inner volume was divided into various stories whose functions are not always clearly defined. In a large number of cases we simply do not know, but we can make educated and cautious guesses. The donjon often included a blind vaulted ground level used as storeroom. For safety reasons, the entrance was placed on the first floor and was only accessible by means of a removable timber stair (capable of being quickly dismantled or destroyed in case of danger), or a permanent staircase housed in a structure built against the side of the keep, known as a forebuilding. The door was usually intended to let only one pedestrian through at a time, it was made of thick oak planks reinforced with heavy nails and metal plates; it was closed and blocked from inside by means of strong transversal beams. Large loads could not be transported through the narrow entrance, and therefore were hoisted by a crane and a winch placed on top of the building. The vertically arranged rooms included an aula or hall — a kind of large multi-purpose living room — sleeping rooms for the lord and his family, accommodation for servants and a few guards, and a chapel, as well as various domestic facilities such as fireplaces, latrines, aumbries (mural cupboards), and food-stores. A well or a cistern for drinking water was, of course, of vital importance. Access between the various levels was done via narrow staircases spared in the thick walls or spiraling in the corner turrets. The summit of the building was fitted with a roof and a platform for observation of the surrounding countryside and active defense. The platftorm included a solid man-high parapet fitted with crenels— hollow spaces between two standing merlons. In time of war the platform would be fitted with hoarding, removable wooden scaffolding balcony, a kind of roofed timber gallery jutting out from the external surface of a wall. The imposing mass of the great-tower could be seen for miles around, and would have seemed like a skyscraper to a local population mainly used to low wooden buildings with thatched roofs. The keep thus played a deterrent role and reflected with ostentation the presence, the power and the authority of the lord.

At the foot of and around the stone keep, just like in an earth and timber castle, was the usual bailey packed with the previously discussed service buildings: hall, chapel, sheds, workshops, stables, houses and huts. The bailey was defended by a comprehensive range of fortification, including thorny hedges, earth entrenchments, palisaded walls, ditches, and eventually a masoned enclosure (called enceinte, chemise, shirt, curtain or mantle).

Huge Norman keeps were heavily concentrated in the southeast (e.g., Colchester, Hedingham, London, Rochester, Canterbury, Dover, Pevensey). Another group is to be found in the north (e.g., Carlisle, Newcastle, Bamburgh, Scarborough, Appleby, Brough, Bolsover, Bowes and Richmond). A smaller group is located on the Welsh border and along the line of the Severn River. The remainder are sparsely sprinkled over the rest of the country, so it is difficult to theorize and draw conclusions about their distribution. One thing is for sure: Stone keeps were not only very strong, but, to friend and foe alike, were extremely impressive symbols of dominating power, and it may well be that they were erected where such emphasis was most needed.

Construction

Norman building has become synonymous with solidity. What is more rock-like and enduring than the Norman keep? The main characteristic of all Norman construction (known as Romanesque architecture) was its massiveness and its roundness: round arches, massive cylindrical columns, barrel vaults, and thick flat walls. To the Norman designers the square and the circle were the most important shapes. They stressed compactness, bluntness, and overwhelming strength to convey a feeling of certainty and stability, and they had disdain for embellishment.

As can be easily imagined, the construction of a large stone donjon was a formidable undertaking costing a lot of money, involving many people and lasting quite some time. First architects and master-builders, most of whom remain unknown, made a design. The names of these men did not count in the anonymity of the early medieval centuries. These engineers were apparently content to be craftsmen working for a cause much greater than their own personal fame, and it was only in the 13th century that the self-confidence of the individual grew, and personality came to be appreciated. Master-builders surely lacked the technical training and knowledge of the modern architect, but they were men of great experience, having started their careers as young apprentices. They often took a hand in the actual construction work, particularly in the supervising role, for example controlling the quality of materials and checking alignment and verticality with the use of levels and plumblines. No actual plans or sketches or models have come down to us. Either they never existed or they were not preserved. Then or simultaneously a suitable site was selected and the building was marked out on the ground. For obvious tactical and strategical reasons, keeps were preferably constructed in places with a difficult access, such as on a crag, on a hill or on a pre-existing motte, or within an old Roman or Anglo-Saxon work. However, the classic fairy-tale castle perched on an inaccessible crag would be an impregnable fortress, but it would also make a poor administrative and economic center. So a successfully sited castle had to have a two-way relationship with its surroundings. If it was built on a plain or in a lowland, the keep included a ditch. In some cases, it seems that keeps were built on mottes. In fact a closer inspection reveals that the base was "emmotted," which means that a huge mass of earth was heaped up around the substructures to add stability, resist battering rams and make mining impossible or at least very difficult. When building in a town, the Normans chose the best site without regard for existing buildings. In Lincoln some 166 houses were demolished to make way for the keep, in Cambridge, 27, and in York and many other towns varying numbers. Once the site had been chosen there was undoubtedly some kind of (religious) ceremony to announce and bless the project. Then the construction started. The preferred foundations were solid rocks in order to withstand the enormous weight of the future building and also to prevent mining in time of war. When this was not possible foundations consisted of a large trench dug in the ground, filled with rammed stone rubble or oak piles driven into the soil. The tower could also stand on a splayed-out plinth or foundation made of solid stone slabs, which not only helped distribute the enormous weight of the tower, and thus provide very solid support for the building above, but also made undermining by attackers very difficult. The walls were usually made by building a facing of ashlar (neatly trimmed blocks of smooth stone of uniform shape and size), and filling the gaps with rougher stone, binding the whole together with mortar. Ties of metal could also be added to help bond the structure together. As the walls rose, putlog holes were left in them, enabling beams to be inserted for support scaffolding. The outer walls were reinforced with flat pilasters, mere thickenings of the wall, relying on the dead weight and solidity of the construction to take the sideways thrusts. The Normans had good building stone, notably the famous white stone of Caen, which was imported at great cost from Normandy, but of course, used only for important royal buildings. Hard granite from the west and north, and flint and chalk from East Anglia were also employed. Jurassic limestone, which is durable and hard, and stands up well to exposure, was readily available, very popular and widely quarried and used. Towards the end of the 12th century the famous Purbeck marble from Dorset and Sussex came into use for building and decorative purposes. Once the walls were built, the internal flooring, waterpipes, drainpipes, gutterings, doors, gates and windows were added. The roof was a timber framework on which was laid a waterproof covering, shingles (tiles of wood), lead or tiles. The lower floors were made of vaulted chambers and higher levels of heavy planks held by strong beams resting on corbelled stones.

All these works involved both specialist craftsmen and unskilled laborers. There were various kinds of masons. The rough hewers quarried the stone, the superior masons worked it for ashlar, and junior masons actually laid the stone. Until the end of the 12th century, the decorative carving was part of the mason's work. Later with the development of a sculpture independent of the building, new artists of stone appeared, known as imagers. Subsidiary to the masons were the mortarmen, barrowmen, and all non-skilled (impressed) laborers who, for example, did the digging and the transporting of bulky materials and heavy loads. Carpenters also played an important role, e.g., making scaffolding as well as cutting trees and putting in place palisades and beams for floors and roofs. The timber was of oak where possible, but owing to the cost of transport the tendency was to cut down the nearest trees and quite often use them immediately. Being unseasoned, the wood was liable to warp. The Normans brought with them experienced carpenters and masons, but since they had to use local Saxon labor, semi-skilled by their standards, their buildings were at first very rough in finish. As time passed building techniques became more and more elaborate until a degree of technical ability in both carpentry and masonry was reached.

Daily Life

From literary sources and manuscript illustrations we can eke out a picture of the mode of life in such a keep-and-bailey castle. Although it is unwise to draw strict conclusions, it seems that the essentials of modern comfort were badly lacking, and stench, cold and draft dominated. Norman keeps were fortified dwellings and if they suggest little comfort by today's standards they, however, must have offered well above that of the average 11th-century peasants' life. The great hall was an all-purpose room. Its walls were probably plastered or whitewashed; some might have been decorated. The fire burned on a central hearth, and the smoke eddied round the hall and escaped as best it might through a louver in the roof. Window glass was unknown. Openings were few, narrow and placed rather high. They were intended to let fresh air and light come in but in case of a siege they were used as combat emplacements to shoot down arrows. They usually widen out on the inside in order to form small niches with side benches. At night openings were shuttered and the only light was provided by smoky torches, lanterns, guttering candles supported on candlesticks, or a cheaper (and smelly) light made from peeled rushes soaked in animal fat. Tresle tables were erected for mealtimes and removed to provide sleeping accommodation at night. The benches might remain as beds for a few lucky ones. Generally the floor was of trodden earth covered with rushes or straw. Eating habits, in which fingers took the place of modern cutlery, made handwashing before and after meals most desirable. Privies were usually placed within the thickness of the walls, sometimes in pairs, side by side or back to back with small windows for ventilation and chutes leading to the foot of the walls or corbelled out. Modern people are often shocked by the lack of privacy. Privacy in the Middle Ages was indeed a luxury enjoyed only by persons of status—kings, dukes, counts, lords and ladies who could retire when they wished to their personal camera (sleeping room) or to a solar, a room where the head of the household, and especially the senior women of the household could be sole (alone or with a small company of intimates) and away from the hustle, bustle, noise and smells of the hall. The lord kept his money, jewels and his clothes in his own bedroom or in a small adjoining chamber, which came to be known as the wardrobe. All Norman castles included a place of worship, if not a sort of oratory or chapel in the donjon itself then a separate church placed in the bailey. The chaplain, a priest or clerk, was an important figure in the community. He was in charge of liturgy, provided Christian teaching, heard confession, shrove the dying, and, often being the only literate person, read and wrote the lord's letters, as well as kept written archives and records.

Without doubt access to the keep was restricted to those having legitimate business within, so the essentials of daily life were concentrated in the bailey. Today baileys look empty and bare but then they were often very packed. The walled enclosure included all buildings and facilities necessary for keeping the castle in working order. Each castle had to be as much as possible self-sufficient, living in a kind of autarky with the countryside it possessed. Of course, the number of residents in a castle varied a lot. Some could run on a skeleton staff, others would have an important garrison of knights with numerous assistants, servants, washerwomen, and serving girls. Whatever the size of the population, there were food-stores matching the importance of the garrison, one or more mills, a bakehouse, a brewery, one or more kitchens, and, where space was available, gardens and orchards. For horses and pack animals there were stables, stalls, and foraging-stores. Water supply was essential for both humans and animals. It was either supplied directly came from a stream, or came from a well or cisterns with piping system. Hunting was an obsession for many Norman lords, so they possessed kennels for a pack of hunting dogs and a mews for keeping hunting birds (falcons). There were barns for cattle, cattle-sheds, poultry-houses, dovecotes, rabbit-hutches, and a butchery as well as sheds for vehicles, and farm equipment such as ploughs or harrows. As wood and timber were so important, there was always a carpenter's workshop. A blacksmith's workshop provided nails, hinges and metal implements of all sorts, as well as weapons and pieces of armor, although this later became the job of specialist professional armorers. The bailey was thus a place of great activity, strongly smelling of farm, and the castle inhabitants' daily life followed the slow rhythm of seasons, closely related and dependant on agriculture and the cycles of nature. It was punctuated by harvests and vintages, daily worries, death and mourning but also by petty pleasures, religious feasts, births and marriages. The routine was only occasionally broken when the community was visited by a traveling friend or a relative, a party of pilgrims, a political ally, a religious dignitary, or the suzerain or the king himself, which gave the residents the opportunity to organize a banquet and a feast with rejoicing, entertainment, music and dance, and to get news and gossip from the outside world. The lady of the castle nominally ran the castle when the lord was absent, and this might well include organizing the defense during a siege. The routine could indeed be gravely disturbed when a conflict broke out.

KEEP AND BAILEY AT WAR

Until the end of the 12th century, the high keep and its walled bailey offered a reasonable solution to military security problems because of the simplicity and inadequacy of siege methods.

The bailey was a place of refuge for the villagers of the countryside around the

Opposite bottom: *Front view and cross-section of hoarding. Hoarding (sometimes called propugnacla) was a temporary covered wooden balcony-like construction placed on top of the exterior of ramparts and towers of a castle or a town threatened by a siege. The purpose of hoarding was to allow the defenders to improve their field of fire along the length of walls and towers, and most particularly, directly downwards to the wall base. In peacetime, hoardings were stored as prefabricated elements. The installation of hoarding was facilitated by putlog holes that were placed in at appropriate positions in the masonry of the wall. Hoardings were quite useful. They offered protection, constituted a second parapet overhanging the wall and gave archers greater mobility and a wider field of fire in times of siege. They were fitted with openings in the floor, which facilitated firing and dropping projectiles directly onto the enemy's heads, without the need to expose the defenders to danger. During a siege, these wooden covered walkways were, however, vulnerable to fire, and often they were covered with wet hides to protect them. Later, permanent structures with similar functions (known as machicolation) were built of stone.*

Combat platform. Placed on top of the keep, the battlement enabled the defenders to throw missiles and shoot arrows on attackers down below. 1: Roof of the keep; 2: Merlon (solid); 3: Crenel (void).

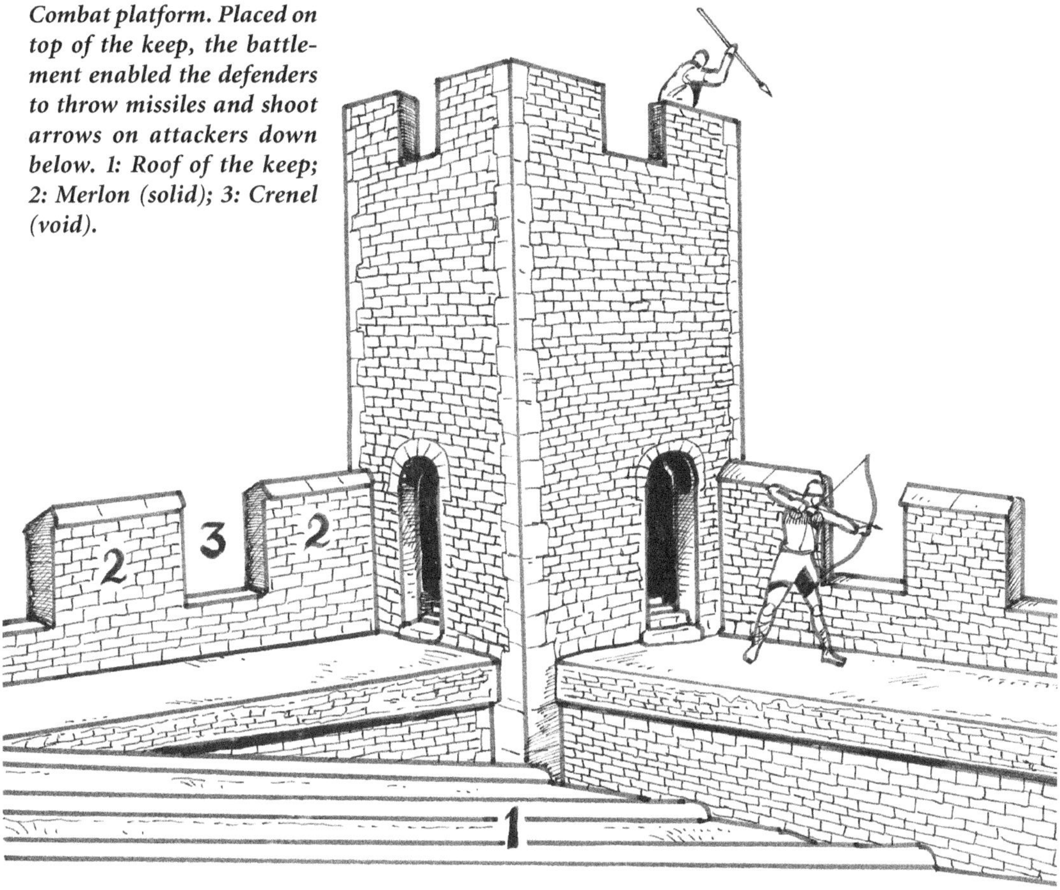

Top: *Also called a loop-hole or arrow slit, this was a vertical void arranged through a solid wall for use by archers who remained under cover. In its simplest form the loop-hole was a long narrow vertical slit, perhaps 2 m long, but many forms were experimented with so as to provide a broader view and a wider field of fire. There was usually a plunging opening to the outside to allow the archer to shoot down towards ground level. At the base or top or middle of an arrow slit, there could be a small round opening, called an oilette, allowing a broader view and field of fire. Later, for the use of crossbows, arrow slits (then called crosslets) were given a cruciform shape with one or more horizontal splits, which enabled the crossbowman to aim and shoot his weapon with efficiency.*

Left: *Arrow loop. There was often a splay on the inside of the wall so that the outer opening was narrower than the inner one. This provided room for the soldier and his equipment, as well as watch-banks, as the loophole could also be used as an observation post. The loophole also served to provide ventilation and enabled the small amount of light to fan out inside, and illuminate a greater area.*

castle, so in time of war it was often overcrowded. It was the garrison's duty to bear the brunt of the fighting, but all hands might be called upon to assist in the defense.

First there was the deep ditch forming an effective obstacle, particularly when it was filled with water, revetted with wooden beams to make it slippery to climb, or fitted with spiky vegetation. Then there was the mantle or skirt confronting the attackers before they could reach the bailey. The mantle consisted of walls, whose tops were fitted with a wallwalk and a crenellated parapet, and jutting walltowers with a top combat platform and arrow loops. The entrance to the walled bailey was defended

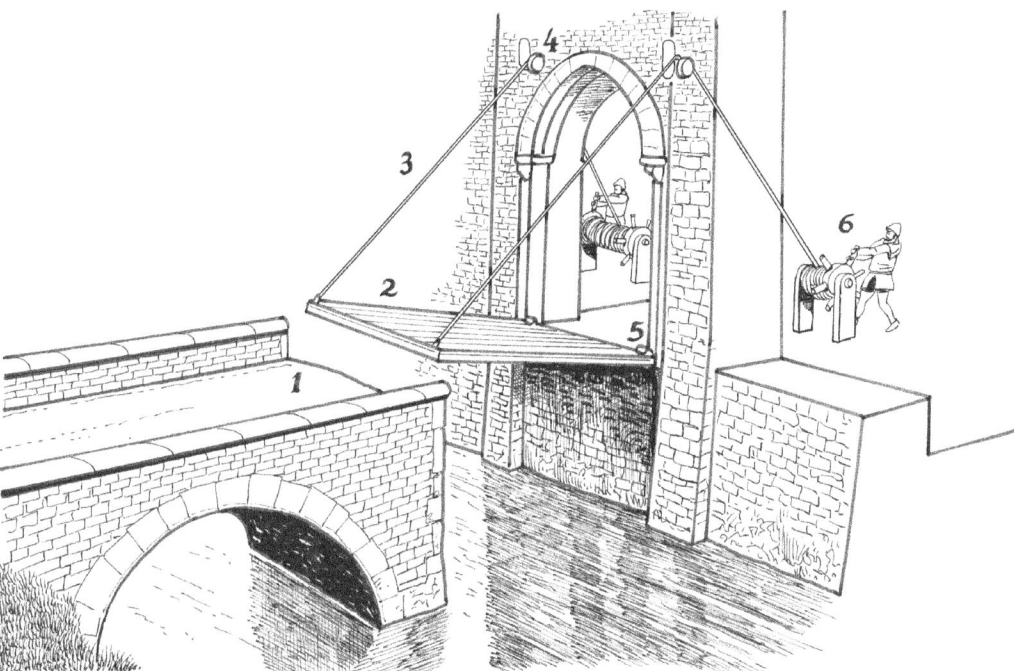

Drawbridge. Many castles featured a ditch, a fundamental element of fortification forming a passive and extremely effective obstacle, the more so when filled with water. When the ditch was wide, there was a non-movable section made of wood resting on stone-piles—eventually composed of masoned arches. At about 4.5 meters from the gate, this permanent part was interrupted by a drawbridge, which would be raised in moments of crisis. Removable bridges existed in many variations. A typical arrangement would have the drawbridge immediately outside a gatehouse, consisting of a wooden deck with one edge hinged or pivoting at the gatehouse threshold, so that in the raised position the bridge would be flush against the gate, forming an additional barrier to entry. The bridge was raised or lowered using ropes or chains attached to a windlass in a chamber in the gatehouse above the gate-passage. Only a very light bridge could be raised in this way without any form of counterweight, so some type of bascule arrangement was normally found. The bridge could extend into the gate-passage beyond the pivot point, either over a pit into which the internal portion could swing (providing a further obstacle to attack), or in the form of counterweighted beams that drop into slots in the floor. The raising chains could themselves be attached to counterweights; in some cases a portcullis provided the weight, as at Alnwick Castle. These clumsy arrangements were eventually replaced with more advanced drawbridges using counterweights in order to ease the manouver. 1: Bridge; 2: Movable wooden roadway; 3: Chain; 4: Pulley; 5: Pivot; 6: Winch.

by a drawbridge and a gatehouse, very often in the form of a tower with a vaulted passage through it. The gate was closed with thick doors and the tower (fitted with a crenellated platform and arrow loops) accommodated guards. The active defense consisted of repulsing assault ladders, shooting arrows and throwing javelins through the crenels and by dropping missiles (pieces of rock and stones) from the hoarding — removable wooden scaffolding balcony, a kind of roofed timber gallery jutting out from the external surface of a wall. Finally if the skirt and the bailey were taken some of the defenders could retreat into the keep. The height and massive, thick walls of the keep were intended to create a strength ratio favorable to the defenders. Height increased the dominating situation of the defenders and worsened the inferior position of the attackers. Although the masoned mastodon gave only a passive defense, enabled a handful of defenders to resist numerous besiegers. Such a massive great-tower could only be taken by treason, surprise or attrition, but the development of elaborate siege weapons such as the trebuchet, mangonel and catapult, as well as the siege assault tower towards the end of the 12th century, showed the limit of usefulness of these blind carapaces. True arrow loops were rare, so most of the defense was concentrated on the top platform for shooting arrows, throwing javelins and dropping stones. Square and rectangular keeps were convenient internally for the disposition of rooms, but externally they had certain disadvantages. The corners were relatively vulnerable to undermining by an attacker because they could be tackled from two sides. It was also difficult for a defender on top of the keep to see exactly what was happening down below around the base of the corners, unless he leaned out and by doing so dangerously exposed himself. Defenders could find themselves trapped in the keep and have to rely on their supplies (stockpiled in the basement) to hold on until external help comes. Since not all donjons possessed internal kitchens there would be little hot food if the defenders were forced inside the keep, other than that which could be cooked over the fireplaces or

Opposite: *White Tower in London. The first Norman fortification on the site of the White Tower in London was a prefabricated timber fort (using a section of the old Roman wall) built in December 1066, in which William the Conqueror dwelt while waiting for the preparation of his coronation. This temporary timber castle was replaced with a stone one, erected between 1078 and 1097. The White Tower (so called because of a plastered whitewash) was the king's residence in London, but it was also an arsenal and a fortress intended to impress and subdue the local population. Built under the supervision of master-builder Guillaume Le Roux and Gandulf, bishop of Rochester, who was known to be very competent at stone construction, the tower is a large rectangle 35.9 m long by 32.6 m wide, with four corner turrets. The walls, of Kentish ragstone and Caen ashlar, are divided into bays by wide pilaster butresses and are 31 m high, 4.6 m thick at the base and 3.3 m at the summit. The main structure stands on a high sloping plinth or base, and is made of rubble with open joints, characteristic of early Norman work. Originally the castle consisted of the keep and a bailey running down to the Thames in the southeast corner of the old Roman city wall. During the following centuries many additions were made to the original keep and bailey, transforming the structure into the large complex we know today, including a concentric arrangement of keep, inner bailey, middle bailey and outer bailey partly blurred by a cluster of residential and administrative buildings. Never in its long history has the Tower been invaded or assaulted and a legend of invulnerability has come into being.*

braziers. If relief was not expected or supplies were running out, they either had to negotiate surrender or try to defeat the attackers by making a sortie and fighting them outside the donjon. Obviously when the keep became no more than a refuge, this meant that its lord had lost control of the surrounding territory and was probably about to become an ex-lord.

(Continued on page 158.)

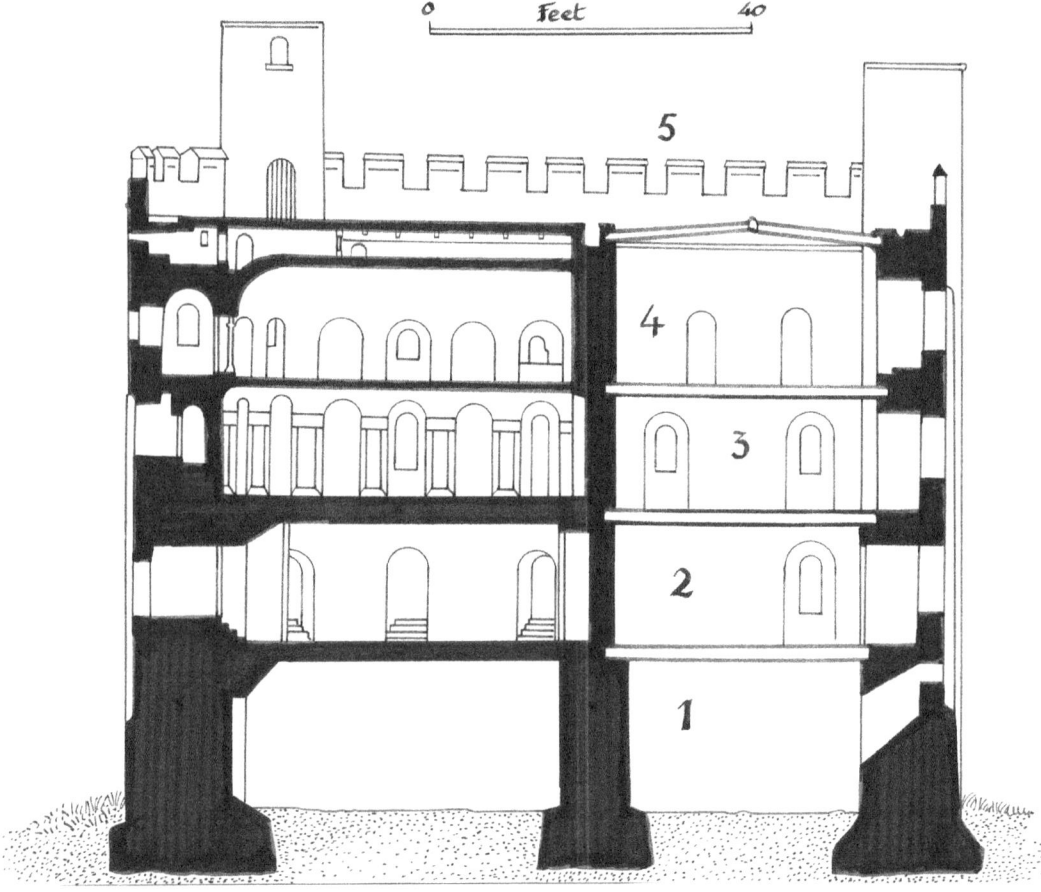

Cross-section of the Tower of London. The London royal fortress is so pre-eminent that it is habitually referred to as the Tower. It had four stories. The groundfloor/basement (1) had no window, no access from outside and was used as stores for food and supplies. The first level (2) included the entrance through a forebuilding, which has since disappeared. The first and the second floor (3) probably included a great hall, chamber and chapel and other smaller chambers in a mural gallery. The royal apartments were perhaps on the third floor (4). Perhaps the rooms were designed for a sort of theatrical pageantry, whereby visitors were deliberately led through the impressive building before they could reach the king. The top of the building is covered by a roof with an open crenellated wallwalk (5) for the guards. The Tower of London is of the type sometimes referred to as "hall keep" in which each main floor is divided internally by a cross wall to produce two large rooms of unequal size. The cross wall also helps to reduce the span required for timber floor beams.

Colchester was one of the most important Iron Age settlements in Britain, and the capital of the major pre-Roman power, King Cunobelin of the Catuvellauni and the Trinovantes. After the Roman invasion, it was established as a colonia (named Camulodunum) for retired military officers and the city retained this high status throughout the four centuries of Roman rule. The building of Colchester castle in Essex was started in 1074, the site having always been regarded since Roman times as important because of its strategic location on the roads from East Anglia to London and from the Thames estuary northwards. Probably designed by the same architect, Colchester keep and the White Tower in London present many similarities. Although larger in area (c. 153 by 115 feet), Colchester's remains are less impressive because it appears to be unfinished and needs to be envision as about twice its present height with the corner turrets higher still. It is not known if it ever had additional upper floors. Its internal arrangement included a blind basement, entrance floor and main floor with the traditional distribution into a great hall, chambers, chapel, etc. But whilst the Tower of London developed into a great concentric fortress, Colchester remained incomplete, without any substantial outworks, and in fact now looks like a church. For most of its subsequent history, Colchester castle was a prison. Its cellars were used as an armory for the Colchester Volunteers during the Napoleonic Wars, and as an air raid shelter during the Second World War. Today the castle is a museum.

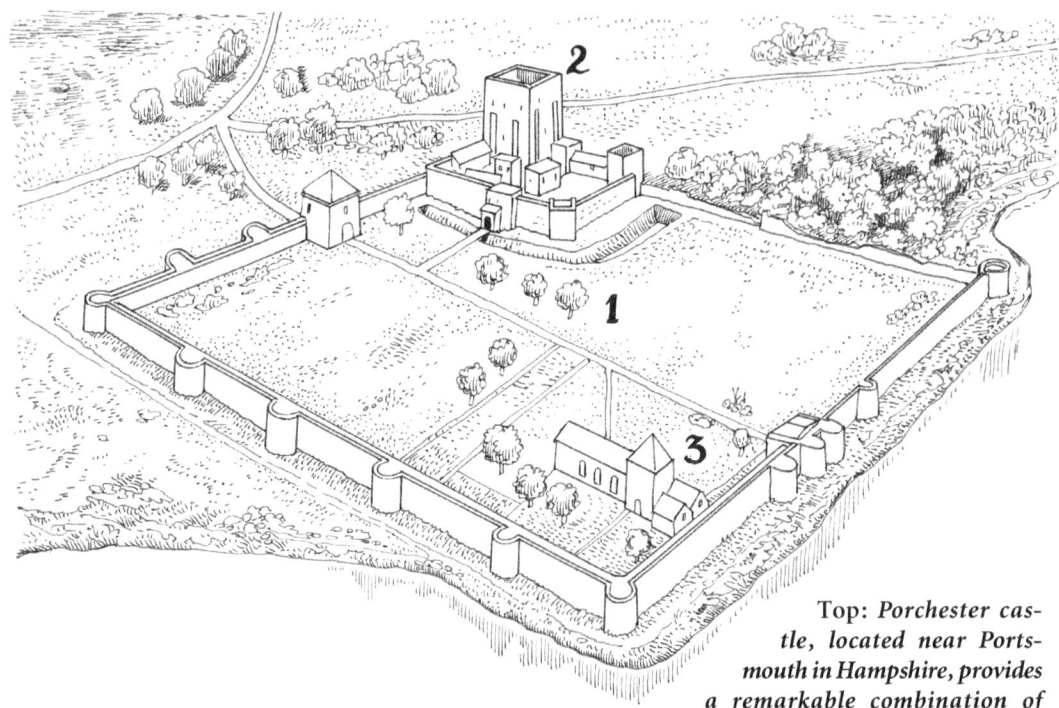

Top: *Porchester castle, located near Portsmouth in Hampshire, provides a remarkable combination of Roman and Norman military architecture. The Roman Saxon shore fort (1) - then named Portus Adurni, has ready been described in Part 2. At the northwest angle of the Roman enclosure a mighty Norman keep (2) was erected during King Henry I's reign (1154–1189), and this 100-feet-high structure forms the citadel of the whole castle. By placing the donjon in the corner the Normans acquired two ready-made walls and only needed to construct the other two to create a square bailey. In the diagonally opposite corner of the latter stands a beautiful Norman church (3), all that remains of a priory of Augustinian canons-regulars founded by Henry I in 1133. After Henry had constructed the keep, the canons probably found the proximity of its garrison uncomfortable and then moved to Southwick.*

Left: *The well-preserved keep at Porchester measures approx. 58 by 56 feet, and has an elaborate forebuilding to the east.*

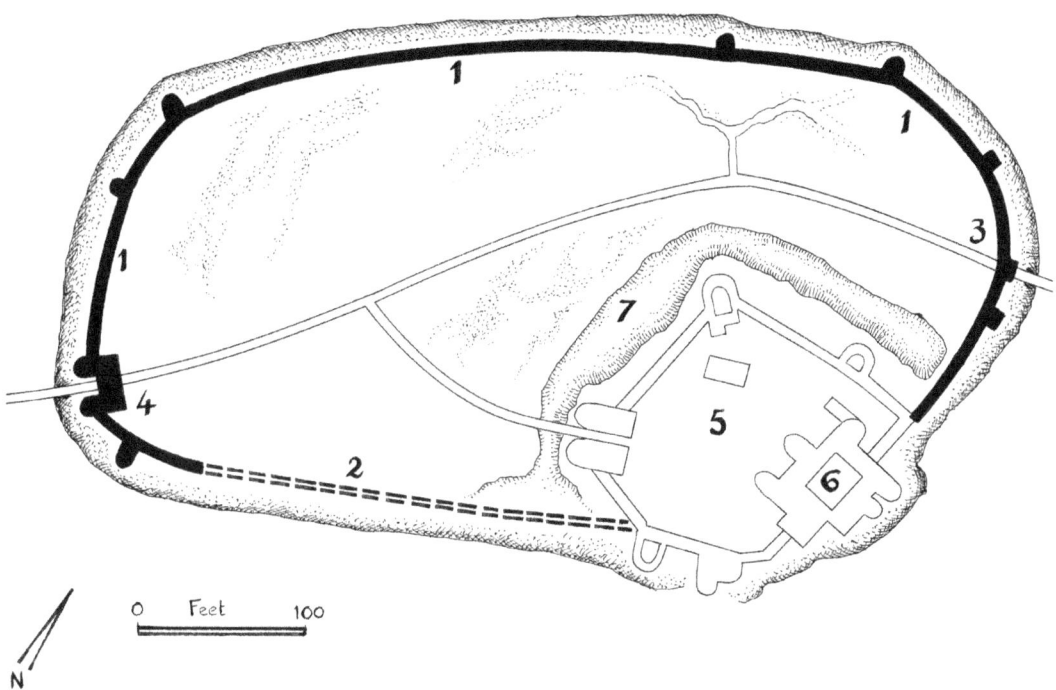

The roughly oval plan of Pevensey Castle in East Sussex dates from Roman times, and evidence of this period can still be seen in the remains of the rectangular gatehouse and a small postern in the northwest wall. Remarkably, the walls of Pevensey Castle have remained in a relatively good state of preservation, providing a good indication of the layout and structure of the castle buildings. Although some of the early earthwork defenses were subsequently replaced by structural fortifications, the old Roman ditches and mounds around the site are still visible. Much of the Norman fort remaining on the castle site is due largely to the work of Robert of Mortain (half brother to William the Conqueror), who was granted Pevensey Castle shortly after the Norman conquest. De Mortain used the existing Roman fort, which had lain derelict for over 600 years, as the base for building his castle, carrying out only minor repairs to the walls forming the outer bailey, and building a new inner bailey at the eastern end and a stone keep in c. 1130. The plan shows 1: Roman wall with towers and ditch; 2: Part of Roman wall missing today; 3: East gate; 4: West gate; 5: Norman castle; 6: Norman keep; and 7: Ditch.

Hedingham Castle is located in Essex, England. The keep was built in c. 1140 by the Norman baron Aubrey de Vere. The building, 110 feet (35 m) high, had two corner turrets, and a forebuilding (today badly damaged) giving access at the second story level. Internally it is divided into four floors, including a magnificent banqueting hall spanned by a remarkable 28-feet arch, one of the largest Norman arches in England. The walls of beautiful and regular ashlar are 12 feet thick and furnished with an outspreading plinth or apron which served the double purpose of thickening the base of the building and causing projectiles and materials cast down from the wall top to ricochet among attackers down below. A large ditch was cut through a natural spur into the Colne Valley in order to form a ringwork and inner bailey, whilst an outer bailey extended south, further into the valley and into what is now the modern village of Castle Hedingham. The keep is the only medieval element of the castle to have survived. The hall, drawbridge and outbuildings were all replaced during the Tudor period by modern structures. The castle was held by the de Vere family until the late 16th century.

Arundel Castle is located in West Sussex and is built on the site of an existing Saxon fortification. Arundel Castle was the work of the Norman Roger de Montgomery, who was granted the land by William the Conqueror. Roger had the task of defending the southern coast from attack and this castle's lofty location was perfect for keeping watch over the river Arun. The castle remained with the family of Roger until 1102, when forces under Henry I forced the surrender of Robert de Belleme, the owner at the time. The original Norman fortification consisted of two baileys and a mound, all of which can be seen today. The circular keep was possibly begun by Robert de Belleme and finished by Henry I when he took control of the castle. In the dispute between Matilda and King Stephen, William de Albini, the castle's owner, gave refuge to Matilda and was besieged by the king. Among all the great British castles in private hands and still inhabited there is perhaps none which exceeds Arundel in grandeur. Despite much building and rebuilding over the centuries, the Norman keep on its motte, rebuilt during the reign of Henry II, still stands on a commanding height overlooking the town.

Located 42 miles north of Newcastle-Upon-Tyne (Northumberland), Bamburgh Castle straddles the top of a natural defensive site, a massive rock outcrop 150 feet above a sandy beach, with almost vertical cliffs on three sides. Evidence indicates that this natural fortress was occupied for centuries by Iron Age warriors, Romans, and Anglo-Saxons, before the Normans arrived. The present castle began as a Saxon stronghold, and was later developed by the Normans to become one of the most powerful castles of the North Country, playing a vital role in combating the ever present Scottish menace.

The original Norman stronghold was built by Roger de Mowbray, Earl of Northumberland, in the late 11th century. Bamburgh remained a royal castle for much of its life but its history is very sketchy. The great keep was most probably completed by Henry II along with the castle's three baileys, and further work was carried out by King John and Henry III. In the 14th century the castle was massively fortified by the Plantagenets and turned into one of the strongest castles in the north.

The remarkable vaulted King's Hall is a major feature, as are the distictive round-headed Norman arches of the keep. The keep has sturdy walls, 12 feet thick in places, and with its crenellated battlements, huge towers and mighty curtain wall, Bamburgh Castle, perched dramatically on its high coastal crag, is one of the finest looking castles in England.

4. Norman Castles 1066–1154   153

There may have been a previous Roman fort on the site of Cardiff in Wales, probably built about A.D. 55 during the conquest of the Celtic Silures tribe. The Norman keep was built in c. 1091 by Robert Consul, Earl of Gloucester, replacing the timber defenses of Robert Fitzhamon, Norman Lord of Glamorgan. The artificial motte on which the keep is built is 10.67 m high with a summit 33 meters in diameter. Additions made in the 13th and 14th centuries included a gatehouse with a stone staircase leading to the stone bridge which replaced the timber drawbridge across the moat. The gatehouse was removed during landscaping in the 18th century, and in the early 19th century the castle was enlarged and refashioned by the architect Henry Holland into a Victorian mansion in Gothic Revival style.

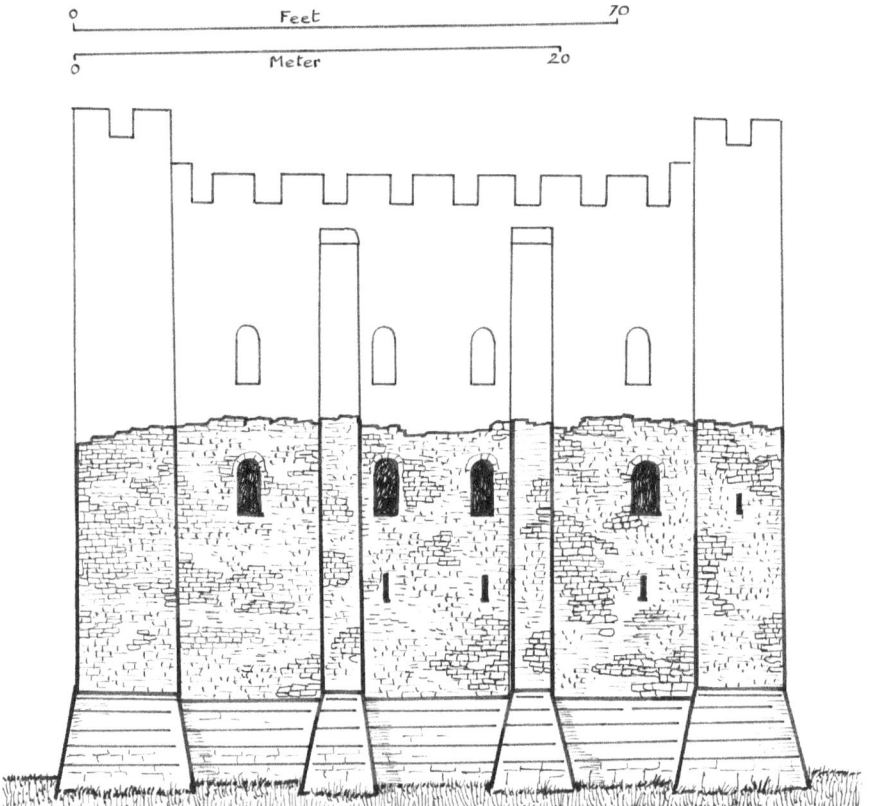

Canterbury Castle was one of the three original royal castles of Kent (the other two were at Rochester and Dover), all built very soon after the Battle of Hastings. They were all on the main Roman road from Dover to London, the route taken by William the Conqueror in October 1066, and it is more than likely that they were all built originally as motte-and-bailey castles in the winter of 1066–1067 to guard this important route. In Canterbury this original castle was almost certainly in the southern angle of the third-century Roman city walls in the area of the present public gardens. The great mound known as the Dane John, which was landscaped to its present form in 1790, would have been the motte. Dane John is a corruption of the Norman word for "keep"—"donjon." The outer bailey extended northward. Early in the twelfth century, during the reign of Henry I, the great stone keep was built. This massive structure, which measures about 98 by 85 feet externally at the base, was originally probably at least 80 feet high. It is mainly made of flint and sandstone rubble (the walls are 14.5 feet thick at the base), but had quoins and a plinth of Caen and Quarr stone (from Normandy and the Isle of Wight, respectively). On its northwest side was the original entrance at first-floor level, accessible by a great external staircase (only the foundations of which now exist). The keep originally had no entrances at ground level. At the first-floor level were the great hall, a principal chamber and the kitchen (in the southwest corner); two very fine fireplaces still survive in the walls. Above this was a second floor which was sadly mostly demolished in 1817.

From at least the twelfth century the Castle's main use was as a prison for the County of Kent and it was under the control of the Sheriffs. Apart from the keep, there was an outer bailey (of about 4 ½ acres) which was enclosed by a wall and ditch and had a main gate with two drum towers facing up Castle Street into the City. Sadly, the 18th and 19th centuries saw important demolition and the end of the castle. The sketch shows the east elevation with the upper part of the turrets and walls reconstructed.

4. Norman Castles 1066–1154   155

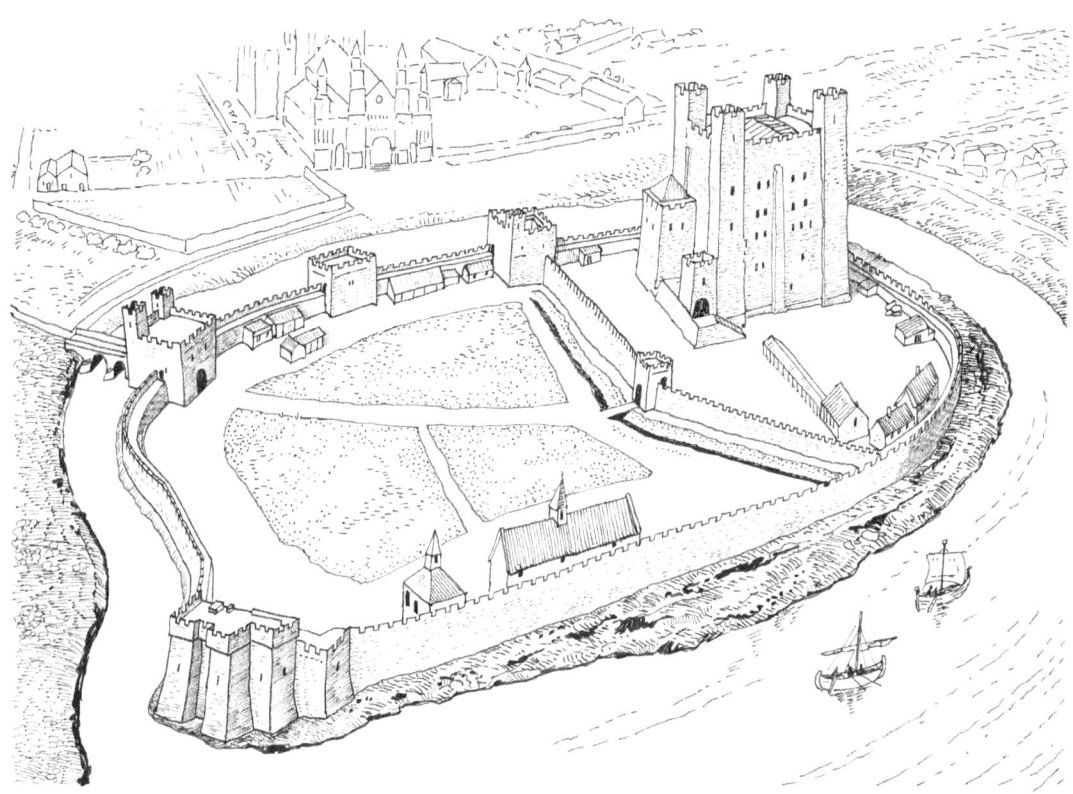

Rochester in Kent is a good example of the development of an earlier site by the Normans. The city (then called Durobrivae) was already surrounded by walls from Roman origin. After the conquest the Normans built a timber motte-and-bailey castle on Boley Hill, and both city and castle were held for the king by Bishop Odo, William I's turbulent half-brother. By 1089 a new stone castle was built as replacement of the timber work under the supervision of Gandulf, Bishop of London, who was also responsible for the construction of the White Tower in London, which explains the great similarities between both keeps. The construction was continued by William of Corbeil, archbishop of Canterbury between 1127 and 1142. Completed in 1142, Rochester keep is 70 feet (21 meters) square and 113 feet (34 meters) high with four corner turrets adding an extra 12 feet (3.7 m). It has four stories with a great forebuilding giving entry at the second-floor level. Although featuring military defenses such as turrets, crenels and holes for hoarding, the number of largish windows indicates that the keep was intended primarily as a residence and administrative center. The keep was enclosed by a pear-shaped walled bailey and a broad ditch filled with water, over which a drawbridge (incorporated into a strong gatehouse) led to the city of Rochester.

The well-preserved Rochester tower is the highest and the most impressive of all the Norman stone keeps in the British Isles.

The keep at Richmond, located in the valley of the Swaledale river in North Yorkshire, was built in c. 1071 by the Norman baron Alain le Rouge (Alan the Red). Erected over an original gateway, which was eventually blocked, the entrance was at first-floor level from the wall-walk of the adjoining wall. The keep is about 52 by 45 feet and still stands to its full height of 30 m.

Above: *Castle Rising is located four miles northeast of Lynn in Norfolk. The Norman castle stands on slightly elevated grounds overlooking, to the west, the low marshy coast of the Wash. Work on the keep began around 1140. Modeled on the castle at Norwich, the keep is square and massive (99 by 69 feet) with 9-feet-thick outer walls at ground level, and still in good condition. The walls were probably whitewashed, and would have been seen from the sea, thus creating a formidable first impression for travelers. Although Castle Rising is now a mere hamlet, in the early Middle Ages it was a harbor town. In the 14th century the castle was a royal demesne, and it became famous as the prison, or rather the place of honorable confinement, of Edward II's guilty Queen Isabella, the "She-wolf of France." By the 1540s the castle was increasingly derelict. Neglected, it fell into disrepair, and Rising's importance dwindled into insignificance. Today it is looked after by English Heritage and open to the public.*

Bottom: *Castle Rising: Plan of first floor. 1: Vestibule; 2: Entrance; 3: Hall; 4: Gallery; 5: Kitchen; 6: Ante-chapel; 7: Chapel.*

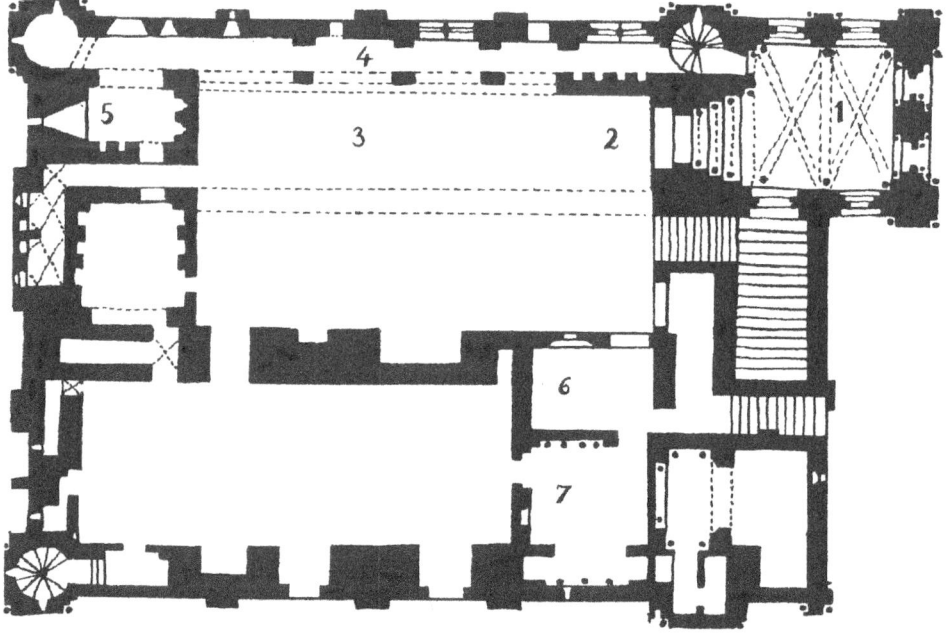

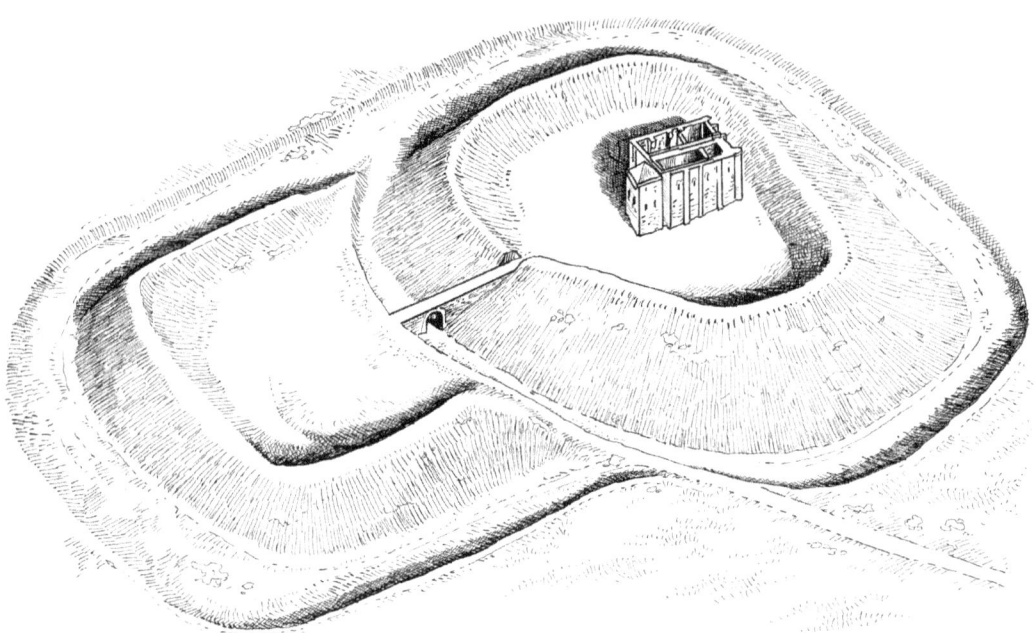

Above: The keep site is enclosed by large artificial ramparts of earth (which probably were reinforced by a stone wall, square towers and a gatehouse) and an outer bailey which is crossed by an ancient bridge. The bank covering some 12 acres is one of the largest earthworks at any castle in England.

Opposite: The castle situated in the town of Taunton in Somerset originated from a timbered burh erected by King Ine of Wessex, in about 710. Taunton is found in Domesday Book as a moderate-sized borough belonging to the Bishop of Winchester. The castle, originally a manor-house from c. 1107, was rebuilt as a mighty castle between 1129 and 1138, during the civil war that raged during the chaotic reign of King Stephen. Taunton is a typical Norman keep of the first half of the twelfth century, but squarely built, 50 feet long by 40 wide, in three stories, with walls some 13 feet thick. This was let into the walls of an inner ward with a stone enceinte and there was an outer bailey represented by the modern "Castle Green." Wet ditches around it were probably supplied from the Potwater Stream. In 1158 the castle was expanded, but its present aspect is Edwardian, rather than Norman, and it also displays Tudor traces of the work of Bishop Walter Langton, a great builder in the time of King Henry VII.

Aftermath

The Norman invasion had dramatic and far-reaching consequences for the British monarchy, ruling elite, social system, language of government, architecture and landscape. It also brought a dramatic shift in England's position in Europe. Instead of remaining within the orbit of a greater Germanic-oriented Scandinavian empire, England was dragged into continental politics, with new enemies to fear, mainly the French.

The Norman castles were at first a necessity for the conquest, and later an expression, however harsh and unwelcome, of disciplined power and administrative order under the firm leadership of William I. William I was succeeded by his son, William II Rufus (reign 1087–1100), who kept peace and suppressed two baronial rebellions

4. Norman Castles 1066–1154   159

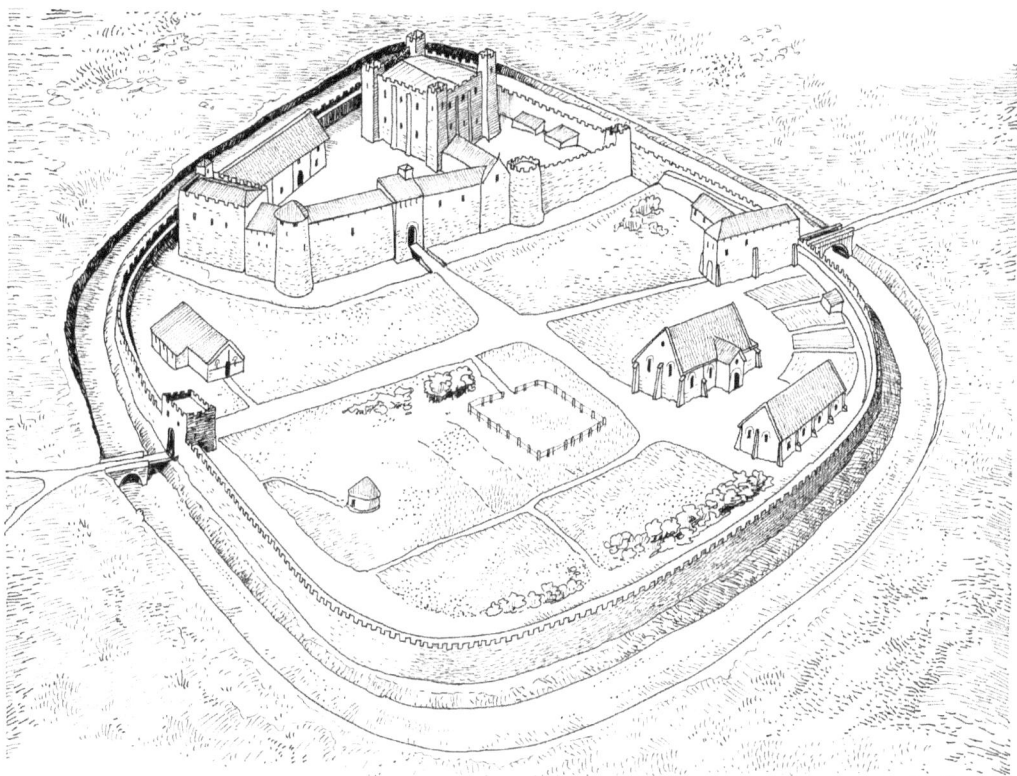

with success. Rufus also regained Cumbria (northwest England) from the Scots and mastered much of South Wales. He was killed accidentally by an arrow while hunting and was succeeded by his young brother, who became King Henry I (reign 1100–1135). Henry I, nicknamed Bauclerk, proved an able diplomat as well as an energetic general. He reigned for the most part in peace but in 1106 he made war upon and defeated his older brother, the duke of Normandy Robert, after which he seized the duchy. Upon the death of Henry I in 1135, the Norman realm of England went through a terrible period of civil war, for some of the nobility supported the Conqueror's grandson Stephen of Blois, and some his granddaughter Matilda. The baronage broke every bond, delighted in civil war, established themselves as independent rulers, and openly defied the weak and unreliable monarchy. Mercenaries had been called in from the continent by the rivals for the throne, and had become a national plague. During this period, known as the Anarchy, castles proliferated into a swarming curse. They were built everywhere, serving as instruments of terror, as, according to the Anglo-Saxon Chronicle (which finally came to an end at this time), *every castle was filled with devils and evil men.*" This state of anarchy has been, however, exaggerated and was not as widespread as the Chronicle would have us believe. The Anarchy and the struggle for the English throne were resolved by a compromise. When Stephen's son died in 1153, it was agreed that Stephen would retain the crown until his death (which occurred a year later in 1154) and that Henry of Anjou should subsequently become king as Henry II.

Regarding fortification, the development of the high and thick-walled donjon has been regarded by some historians as critical in the development of medieval warfare, for (they argued) as a result warfare became based around sieges rather than pitched battles in the open field. Whether this is true or not is still open to debate, but one thing is for sure. With the Norman fortification began the great period of British medieval castle building. This was to last until the advent of gunpowder and siege artillery, which rendered them useless and obsolete, some four centuries later.

PART 5

Early Plantagenet Fortifications 1154–1327

Historical Background

THE PLANTAGENET DYNASTY

The Plantagenet or Angevin kings were a long line of fourteen monarchs whose reigns, stretched from the accession of Henry II in 1154 to the death of Richard III in 1485. They originated from the French county of Anjou centered on the city of Angers in the lower Loire Valley. Anjou corresponds largely to the present-day département of Maine-et-Loire. From the 10th century, the Angevin counts pursued a policy of expansion, leading to the conquest of neighboring territories including Saumur, Touraine, Maine, and Normandy in 1145.

The name Plantagenet was originally the nickname given to Count Geoffrey of Anjou (1113–1151), father of Henry II, because of the gay yellow broom flower which he wore on his helmet. In time this emblem was embodied in the family heraldic arms. The Plantagenet period stretched over the whole Middle Ages, and obviously British castle design gradually evolved from the 12th to the 15th century in order to meet administrative, cultural and, of course, military requirements.

HENRY II

Few kings of England have done such lasting work as Henry II. He found a land in a state of chaos and confusion, and left it with a system of government and a habit of relative obedience that were able to keep the peace long after his death. On his accession to the English throne in 1154, the masterful young King Henry II restored the royal power, which had been greatly harmed during Stephen's reign. He ordered the wholesale destruction of all unlicensed, illegal or "adulterine" castles, sent off the mercenaries, and deprived many earls who had been created by Stephen and Matilda of their titles. Henry II's task was a difficult one, but the new king had a strong will, a fierce temper, indefatigable energy and quickness of mind. He restored order in

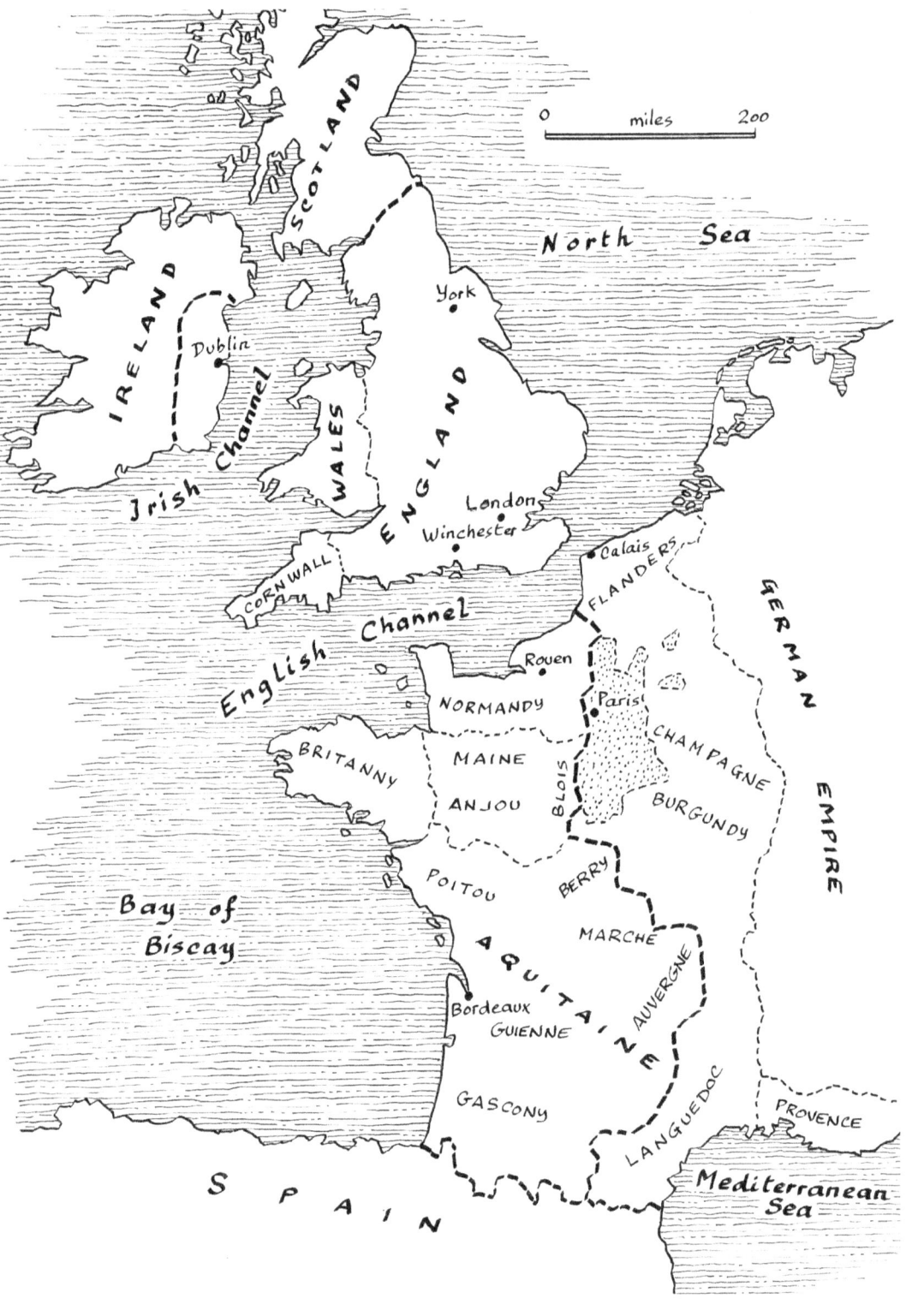

Above: *Dover Keep. Strategically located in the Strait of Dover facing Calais in France, Dover has always been regarded as the key access from the Continent to Britain. This is clearly demonstrated by an outstanding series of fortifications which go back over 2,000 years. Archaeogical evidence shows that Dover was a maritime center as early as 1300 B.C. in the Bronze Age. Traces of a Celtic Iron Age hill fort have also been found in the actual castle. The port, called Dubris, was founded by the Romans in A.D. 43 and was a base for the Roman fleet operating in the English Channel. By the mid–10th century, Dover had its own mint and was a flourishing harbor trading with northern France. The keep of Dover, today the central feature of a whole complex of fortifications, was built between 1181 and 1188 at the time of Henry II's reign (1154–1189) by the master-builder Maurice l'Ingénieur. The massive keep clearly shows the continuity of the traditional Norman keep. It is the latest and largest of the 12th-century keeps. It is virtually a cube in shape: 98 by 97 feet (approx. 30 m) in plan, and 95 feet (28 m) high. Its walls are unusually thick, varying from 17 to 21 feet (approx. 6 m), allowing many mural chambers, galleries and staircases. The internal arrangement includes a basement, middle storey and main floor. Entry was at the main level through an elaborate forebuilding. The keep was hemmed with a curtain wall with a square tower enclosing an inner bailey.*

Opposite: *The Plantagenet Empire. The Angevin Empire at its peak stretched from south Scotland to the Pyrenees. Henry II had inherited Anjou, Touraine and Maine from his father Geoffrey, and Normandy, England, the southern part of Wales and the western coast of Ireland from his mother, Queen Matilda of England. The large territories in southwest France (including Poitou, Berry, Marche, Auvergne, Aquitaine and Gascony) he had acquired by his marriage to Eleanor of Aquitaine in 1152. Brittany was gained by his son Geoffrey's marriage to Duchess Constance of Brittany. Only the lands around Paris (known as Ile-de-France) belonged to and were directly ruled by the French Capetian kings. Flanders, Champagne, Burgundy, Toulouse, and Languedoc were large independant principalities recognizing the Capetians as overlords.*

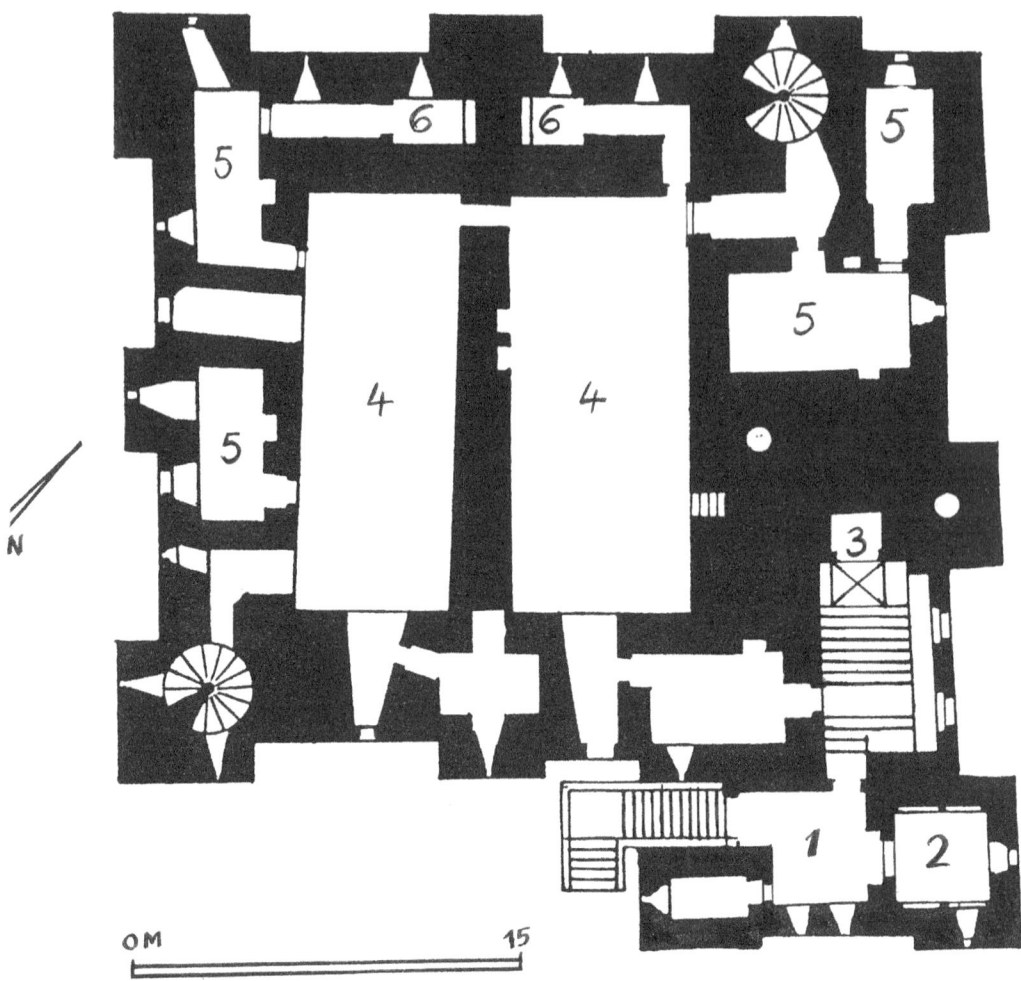

Above: *Groundplan of Dover keep. The plan shows the second story of the keep. 1: Entrance; 2: Chapel; 3: Drawbridge; 4: Halls; 5: Chambers; 6: Galleries and latrines.*

Opposite top: *Dover Castle c. 1300. During the reigns of King John (1199–1216) and his successor Henry III (1216–1272), much additional work was done on the outer defenses, and by 1256 Dover Castle had reached most of its present day extent and appearance. Although Norman and conservative in design, the general concept of Dover castle is advanced, being that of a concentric castle, which uses a system of defense consisting of two independant walls. Although the medieval town walls no longer survive, Dover Castle continued in use beyond the Middle Ages and later additions (seaforts, redoubts, linear entrenchments, coastal batteries, and concrete bunkers and shelters) from the 16th to the 20th centuries display an impressive history of British military architecture.*

Opposite bottom: *Plan of Dover inner bailey. 1: Keep; 2: King's Gate; 3: Northern Barbican; 4: Service buildings; 5: Hall; 6: Palace's Gate.*

5. Early Plantagenet Fortifications 1154–1327

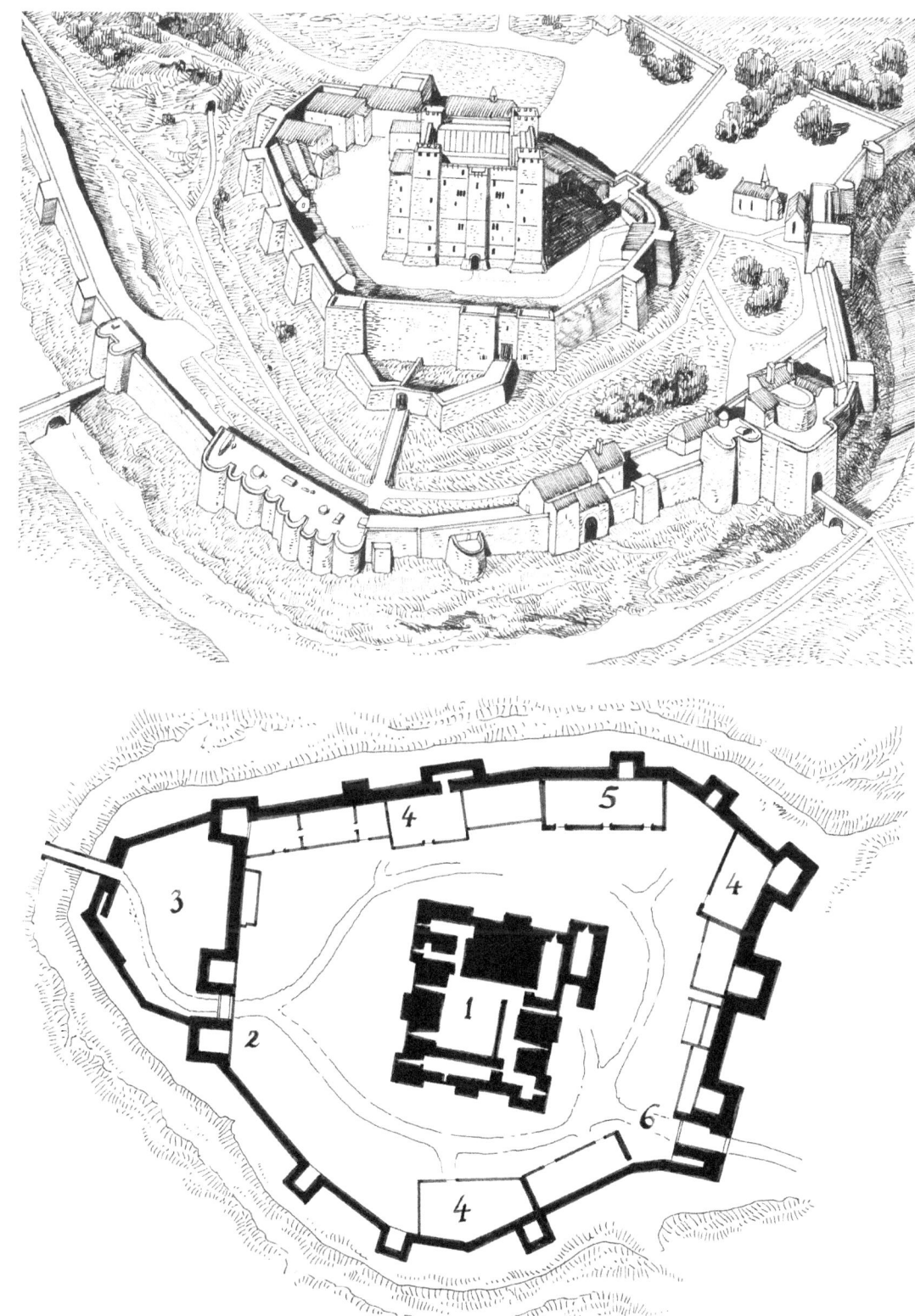

England and reconstructed the English legal system, and at the same time ruled the wide realms on the continent which he had either inherited or gained through his marriage with Eleanor, heiress of the dukes of Aquitaine. Henry II was indeed one of the most powerful kings in Europe, ruling all the lands between Scotland and Spain. He received all of northwest France from his father and all of southwest France from his wife. Ruling an empire greater than that of any English king before him, he was a figure of European stature, comparable in prestige to the German Emperor Barbarossa. Although he spent the greater part of his reign across the Channel, he still

Chambois Donjon. The keep of Chambois, located near Trun in Orne, Normandy, was built in the second half of the 12th century. Its construction is probably the work of Guillaume de Mandeville, who was loyal to the English King Henry II. After 1204, the castle was given by Philippe-Auguste to his marshal Henri Clément. This rectangular keep (21.4 m by 15.4 m from the exterior) is the best preserved in Normandy. Its walls are intact and rise to 25.7 m; their summit was given a gallery of machicolations and crenellations in the 14th century. The castle was originally surrounded by a wall, which was destroyed in 1750.

Crusading knight. Warriors of the First Crusade in 1099 differed little from William the Conqueror's knight in 1066. Gradually some changes appeared, though, including a close helmet and a cloak or surcoat worn over the chainmail hauberk.

found time to be one of the greatest of all England's rulers. Henry II triumphed brilliantly over the nobility, but he was in turn worsted by the Catholic Church, and his reign was embittered by the famous struggle and clash with his chancellor, archbishop of Canterbury, Thomas Becket. Henry II's sons, Richard and John, continued their father's policy but with much less success, and the uneasy and unresolved relationship between France and England led to generations of conflict.

RICHARD I

Henry II was succeeded by his son Richard I. Handsome, gay, frank, open and generous, a patron of poets, Richard was a complete cosmopolitan military adventurer, a chivalrous knight, a restless wanderer, an able general, and a tough crusader. Richard I, nicknamed Coeur de Lion (the Lionheart), however, played a very small part in the internal affairs of England, spending only ten months in the realm during his ten-year reign from 1189 to 1199. Otherwise, he was campaigning in France, Sicily and Palestine. Richard was also a castle builder who ordered the construction of the formidable Château Gaillard in Normandy and made additions to the Tower of London. Though his prowess in the field aroused wonder, Richard was no statesman. Despite his excellent reputation, as King of England he was a disaster, a thoroughly bad king. War was his delight and he drained the country to near bankruptcy because he regarded his kingdom only as a source of revenue. His subjects paid for his extravagant and chivalric exploits—notably they had to finance a huge ransom when the wandering king was captured by the duke of Austria in 1192 on his way back from

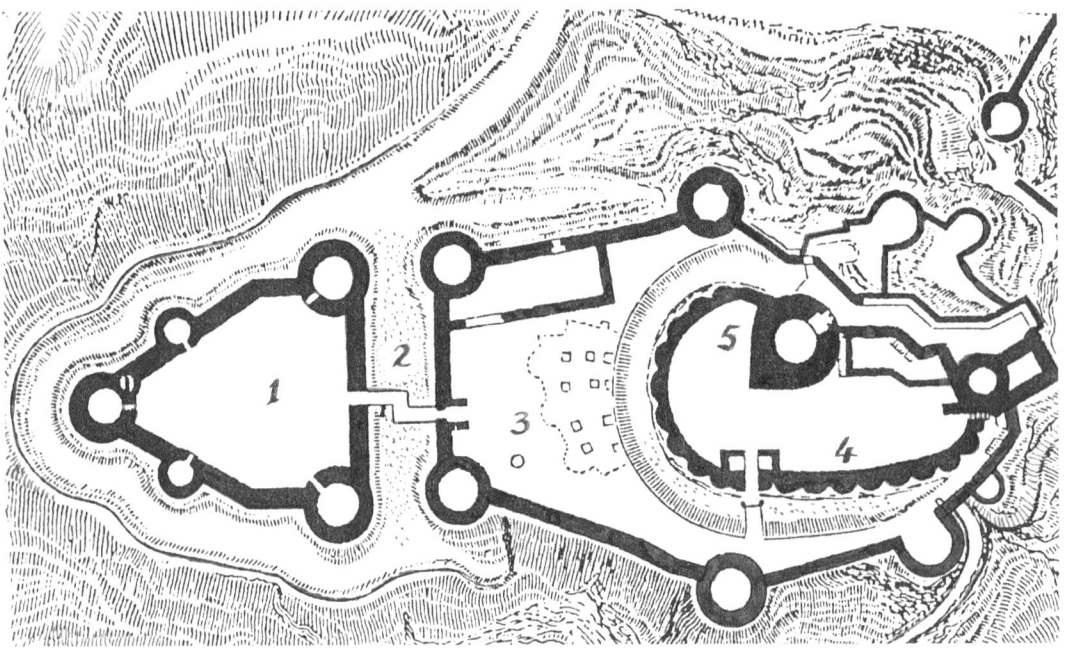

Palestine. Although the government of the realm was fortunately in the hands of capable deputies who successfully combated the ambitions of his brother John and the intrigues of the nobility, Richard's absentee rule ushered in a weakening of the royal power. The careless and glamorous Richard died childless in 1199, aged 42, and was buried at Fontevrault in Anjou, France.

JOHN

It fell to Richard's brother, John, to meet the series of internal upheavals and external assaults, which inevitably assailed the unmanageably vast Angevin empire. Tradition has exalted the memory of Richard I and denigrated that of John. A striking contrast to his brother, John was a thoroughly unpleasant man, cruel, lustful and debauched, unreliable, treacherous, avaricious and lacking prestige. John, nicknamed "Lackland," has often been regarded as the archetype of the wicked and bad king. During his 17-year reign, from 1199 to 1216, he worked hard at the business of government, but his ventures were complete failures. The articulate elements of society, both clerical and lay, united against John clashed with Rome, causing England to be placed under papal interdict from 1209 to 1213. Unsuccessful as a general, outmaneuvered by King Philippe of France, he burdened his people with taxes. English barons, dissatisfied with his erratic rule, forced him to concede a list of privileges—

Opposite top: *Château-Gaillard (conjectured reconstruction), located along the Seine River on a steep cliff extending above the towns of Grand and Petit Andelys in the Eure département in Normandy, was built in an amazingly short time in 1196–1198 by order of Richard I. It was an imposing castle intended to deter King Philip Augustus of France from invading Richard's Norman territories, and to act as a base from which Richard could launch his campaign against the French. Richard was particularly proud of the fortress and boasted when it approached completion in 1198: "Behold, how fair is this year-old daughter of mine!" The castle became Richard's favorite residence, but the king of England did not enjoy the benefits of his "daughter" for long, however, as he died in Normandy on April 6, 1199, from an infected arrow wound to his shoulder, sustained while besieging the castle of Châlus. In 1203, Philip II Augustus laid siege to the stronghold of Château-Gaillard and took it. With the castle under French control, the main obstacle to the French entering the Seine valley was removed. They were able to attack and take Normandy. The city of Rouen surrendered to Philip II in June 1204. After that, the rest of Normandy was easily conquered by the French. Thus, for the first time since it had been granted as a duchy to the Viking Rollo in 911, Normandy was directly ruled by the French king. Much later, in 1599, Henri IV of France ordered the demolition of Château-Gaillard. Although it was already in ruins at the time, it was felt to be a threat to the security of the French realm. Today the castle ruins are listed as a Monument Historique by the French Ministry of Culture and are open to the public.*

Opposite bottom: *Plan of Château-Gaillard. The castle was a remarkable fortress with features well ahead of its time. In building it, Richard put into practice ideas which he had brought home from the Crusades. It consisted of three wards. The triangular outer ward (1) served essentially as a barbican, for to gain access to the castle, attackers had to go through the outer ward first. A dry rock-cut ditch (2) separated the middle and outer ward, the two connected by a fixed bridge. The middle ward (3) included the entrance, a large chapel, latrines, stables, workshops, and storage facilities. The inner ward (4), laid out at the end of the spur near the cliffs, housed the living quarters and the almond-shaped keep (5).*

the famous Magna Carta of June 1215, the "cornerstone of English liberties," which limited the monarch's power. John's greatest problem was the disloyalty of his barons, particularly the vassals of his French possessions, who were bound to develop French rather than English allegiances, and after the fall of Château Gaillard, Normandy was reunited with the French throne in 1204. The universally hated John died in 1216 and was succeeded by his nine-year-old son, Henry.

Henry III

After a regency by capable deputies, the young Henry III (born in 1207) started to rule in 1227. Henry was a weak man, who under the pressure of the English nobility

Standing on a steeply sloping hill above the village of the same name in the county of Dorset, the strategically sited Corfe Castle commanded a gap in the Purbeck Hills on the route between Wareham and Swanage. The oldest surviving structure on the castle site dates to the 11th century, although evidence exists of some form of stronghold predating the Norman conquest. Construction of a stone hall and inner bailey wall occurred in the 11th century and extensive construction of other towers, halls and walls happened during the reigns of Henry I, John and Henry III. By the 13th century the castle was being used as a royal treasure storehouse and prison. Refortified in 1202–1204, the castle remained a royal fortress until it was sold in the 16th century by Elizabeth I to her lord chancellor, Sir Christopher Hatton. The castle was besieged in 1646 by Oliver Cromwell's force and destroyed by explosives and undermining to ensure that it could never stand again as a Royalist stronghold. In the centuries that followed, the local populace took advantage of this easy source of building material and masonry. Today the skeletal ruins of the castle dominate the village skyline and are open to public. The illustration, based on a 17th-century engraving, shows how the castle might have appeared before the siege of 1646.

was forced to accept the principle of consultation, concessions and compromises instead of absolute royal power. A series of crises strengthened the position of the baronage. In 1258 Henry was forced to accept a settlement known as the Provisions of Oxford, which effectively established a baronial council to regulate the king's government. Under his weak rule, the Angevin Empire collapsed. It was formally buried by agreement with Louis IX of France (Saint Louis) in 1259, leaving only Gascony in English hands. Henry III loved splendor and display but lacked judgment and asserted himself more obstinately than shrewdly. He greatly admired Edward the Confessor, whom he somewhat resembled. He was a failure as a king, but he was a great patron of medieval architecture. Notably, Henry III transformed the Tower of London into a major royal residence and had palatial buildings constructed within the Inner Bailey to the south of the Norman keep. During Henry III's long reign from 1216 to 1272, the plain, massive style of the Normans gradually gave way to the elegant Gothic style. Henry III died in 1272 and was succeeded by his son Edward I. With Edward began an important period in the evolution of British castles, and it

Liverpool castle, which occupied a prominent site overlooking the Mersey, was probably erected under the orders of William de Ferrers, earl of Derby, between 1232 and 1237. The most detailed medieval account was made in 1347, which described the castle as having "four towers, a hall, chamber, chapel, brewhouse and bakehouse, with a well therein, a certain orchard and a dovecot." It was surrounded by a dry moat. Owing to the development of the city, the castle was dismantled and the last vestiges had disappeared by 1726.

Lanthorn Tower in the Tower of London was constructed between 1238 and 1272 by order of King Henry III. Its name comes from its use as a marker by nearby ships along the Thames via a lantern that was lit each night in the top turret. Lanthorn Tower was destroyed by a fire in 1774 and reconstructed in 1851.

may be useful, before dealing with the formidable Edwardian castles, to take a break and see what progress siege warfare had made, and what evolution had taken place regarding castle design.

Siege Warfare

GENERALITIES

The development of fortifications has always been dictated by the type of siege tactics and equipment used against them. The strength of the Norman keep lay in the extraordinary solidity of the construction of its high and thick walls. This structure, solid and tall, with no woodwork to be set on fire and no openings near the ground to be battered in, had an almost endless capacity for passive resistance. Even a weak and small garrison could hold on, of course, as long as its supplies lasted. However, the basic techniques of siegecraft established in the ancient world, notably by the Roman army, were rediscovered during the Crusades, and dominated siege warfare until the introduction of the cannon. The knowledge and experience acquired by the Crusaders heralded a new era in siege warfare. In the whole medieval military history the most striking features are undoubtedly the importance of fortified places and the ascendancy assumed by the defensive. If battles were few, sieges were numerous and often quite lengthy. Sieges were the main ingredient of any campaign in the Middle Ages, and, like a kind of chessboard tactic, the real object of military maneuvers was to deprive the enemy of his strongholds and hence of control of the countryside. The medieval fortress owed its strength not only to its construction, but also to the rather feeble nature of the attacking methods of the period. Overcoming a fortress was slow, difficult and costly. A military siege was a large-scale undertaking demanding time, comprehensive logistics and considerable organization. Besides, armies of the feudal age were very slow to move and mobilizable only for short periods (usually forty days a year). The success of a siege was largely due to the skills of specialists in siegecraft and the use of mercenaries who were prepared to sit out a long siege, unlike the feudal levies (vassals and peasants/soldiers mobilized by the suzerain) who became impatient and were liable to go home at the end of their allotted time, regardless of the state of the campaign. As can be easily imagined, the length of time that a siege could last varied enormously. When facing impregnable defenses, and unless pressed for time, many medieval commanders would prefer to starve out a garrison, as no castle could hold out forever, and any stronghold would eventually succumb to starvation. But time itself was a cost. The besieging army could do nothing else and decisive victory could prove elusive. The disproportionate resources needed to take a castle in comparison to those needed to defending it was one of the key reasons for the constant rebellions of the nobility that characterized the medieval period. The nobles could often defy their monarch with impunity, at least in the short term, behind the walls of their castles. The purpose of a siege was not necessarily the destruction of the besieged. The aim could be to bring a rebellious vassal back to submission or to obtain political and economic compromise.

Retreating behind walls might also imply that a cost of reliance on castles was the sacrificing of offensive strategy. This was, however, not always quite true. Castle spending inevitably meant less money for the field troops, but defending a castle was not quite the same as defensive warfare. A castle could have both offensive and defensive purposes, and very few castle builders thought solely in terms of defense, as a stronghold also served as a base for attack. Castle strategy also included action and offense. First, sallies might be made against the immediate besiegers. Second, raids from the castle could threaten areas within a day's round-trip or so. And third, the castle's troops could be launched on a major operation against a neighboring principality. Siege warfare became the operational center of medieval warfare, not just to overcome the defense but also to prevent the fortified enemy from engaging in offense. In civil wars the focus on castles was even greater than normal because there was more emphasis on establishing and maintaining control of territory. Sieges, while difficult and expensive, were inevitable, but the business of laying siege to a castle was a highly complex and costly affair that was not undertaken lightly. The number and strength of the fortified places of medieval Western Europe demonstrate the apparent futility of many campaigns of the period. A land could not be conquered with rapidity when every district was guarded by several castles and walled towns, which would each need several months' siege before they could be reduced. Campaigns tended either to become plundering raids, which left the strongholds alone, or to be occupied in the prolonged blockade of a single fortified place.

Entrenched behind high, thick and strong stone-walls and towers, defenders were — in theory — in an advantageous position, but high walls were not always sufficient to stop enemies. The outcome of a siege depended for a great deal on factors such as physical courage, individual bravery, logistical preparation, morale, determination and pugnacity on both sides. Throughout history there are many examples of both attacking and defending troops cracking when things went wrong. Weather conditions also played an important role; if it rained, camps and roads became quagmires, bows and hurling machines were useless, and morale could collapse. Medieval wars only took place in spring and summer. The best the defenders could hope for was to raise the price of victory to the point at which the besiegers would be unwilling to pay it.

The besiegers had several means to achieve by force the capture of a stronghold.

INTIMIDATION AND TREASON

Attackers could force the defenders to surrender only by displaying their strength, and threatening terrible retaliation (pillage, fire, rape and general massacre). They might intrigue and profit of internal quarrels among the defenders and negotiate various advantages with one against the others. They could use guile and treachery by infiltrating parties disguised as merchants, pilgrims, traders or travelers in need of assistance. Once inside the friendly-posing party would open the gate to admit hidden armed comrades waiting outside. Traitors could be paid to do the same. The besiegers could also launch a surprise attack at the end of the night when guards were tired after a long watch. Sometimes the Church intervened in wartime activities. The knights defending Bedford in 1224 were excommunicated by the archbishop of Canterbury on behalf of the king. The same spiritual weapon was used at the siege of Kenilworth in 1266. So owing to intimidation, menace, negotiation, ruse, treachery, corruption, surprise, threat of eternal damnation, and often a great deal of luck, the operation could be quickly concluded.

BLOCKADE

One way to obtain the surrender of a fortress was by using of attrition. Attackers would establish a hermetical blockade intended to isolate the place and cut all communication and supply lines. The besiegers then waited until the besieged were worn out and exhausted by hunger, isolation, sickness and discouragement. It was consequently important for the encircled garrison to have sufficient supplies and to have reliable allies coming to their rescue. Clearly, allies were of crucial importance to the beleaguered. The attrition siege was based on patience, watchfulness, logistics and time. A besieging army, however, often suffered more than the besieged from lack of shelter, periodic food shortages, and the threat of a relief force appearing in the rear. The besiegers were accommodated in one or more temporary camps, providing living quarters and some sort of military base, but there was always the danger of running short of food, and camp conditions could become unsanitary. Unhealthy food and poor sanitation could result in outbreak of devastating deceases. Besides, it was difficult to sustain the morale and discipline of idle and bored troops. The result was an endurance contest that often ended without a decisive fight. Indeed, many successful sieges were the result of negotiation, not attacking and storming.

SIEGE ARTILLERY

The pressure on the besieged was increased by archers and crossbowmen deployed behind mantlets (wooden protective screens) shooting arrows and bolts, some incendiary. Fire constituted a real hazard to wooden and thatched-roof buildings inside the castle or in a town. Even more devastating were the bombardments effected by siege artillery machines. The ballista or springal was effectively a giant crossbow; it had an arm which was forced by tension and, when released, shot a missile, generally in the form of a dart or a spear. The catapult was an ancient hurling machine, a nevrobalistic or torsion weapon relying for propellent-power on twisting and releasing an elastic material like twisted rope or horsehair or sinew. The trebuchet (also called magonel)—probably introduced during the Crusade—was another hurling machine whose propellent energy was provided by a heavy counterweight. Projectiles launched by catapults and trebuchets were mainly stones or rocks, which killed men, crushed brattices, staggered merlons, punched and weakened walls and towers, and destroyed houses and huts. Occasionally incendiary substances were also hurled, including pots of tar, quicklime, powdered sulphur and Greek fire (an evil mix of oil, pitch, quicklime and sulphur), which could cause significant ravages to wooden, thached-roof buildings.

Breaching the Wall

Blockade and bombardment were preparing actions, they proceeded the most important and most dangerous phase of the siege: the making of a breach and the assault. This phase of the siege was highly hazardous, the attackers were in a disadvantageous position, so repeated calls for negotiation and surrender were made. If they were refused the siege continued. The decisive assault could be done in two main ways: either by assaulting the top of the wall or by making a breach.

Assaulting the top of the wall could be achieved by throwing grab-dredgers fitted with rope or by using scale-ladders. An armored man climbing an unsteady 10-meter-high ladder holding a sword and a shield under a hail of arrows, stones, darts and spears was obviously vulnerable, so a much safer method of assaulting the top of the wall was by means of a beffroy or belfrey. This was a mobile wooden assault tower as high as the wall to be attacked. The tower was a strong timber frame mounted on wheels or on large wooden rolls. It was moved by means of capstans, pulleys and ropes maneuvered and winched (or simply pushed) by a party of men. The tower was rolled close to the wall; it was fitted with ladders permitting the assaulting party to climb in safety. The summit included a platform where a group of archers could shoot at the defenders; the platform also included a sort of drawbridge, which when dropped allowed attackers to set foot on the parapet for a hand-to-hand combat with the defenders. At the siege of Bothwell in September 1301, King Edward I had built a giant wooden belfrey several stories high, constructed in Glasgow, which was dragged along the rough track to Bothwell, about ten miles (16 km) away, in two days. A bridge was built over the Clyde River and finally a corduroy path was made in order to wheel the monster tower right up to the castle wall.

The attackers could also decide to destroy a section of the defensive wall by mining. Special units of experienced miners and engineers would dig an underground gallery under the wall and hollow out a space by removing masonry. As the tunnel progressed, its sides and roof were supported with wooden timbers to prevent the entire operation from prematurely crashing down on the unfortunate tunnellers. Once the required length of tunnel had been achieved, the excavation was packed with combustible material—cotton, straw brushwood and others, together with animal fat or petroleum. That was then fired after the men had scrambled to safety. The wooden props, now the only means of support for the undermined section of the defenses, would burn away and the wall above, bereft of support, would collapse. Undermining was a long, arduous and dangerous operation. It was not always successful and not always possible, obviously, if the castle was built on marshy or wet ground or on solid rock, or if its foundations were particularly strong. Only when other means had failed would recourse to the dangerous practice of mining be contemplated. In Britain, mining appeared early on with the Norman conquest, notably at William I's siege of Exeter in 1067. The anarchy during the reign of Stephen 1135–1154 involved considerable siege activity, notably Exeter again in 1136, and Lincoln in 1143. Henry II used mining at the siege of Bungay Castle in Suffolk in 1174. The siege at Rochester Castle, Kent, directed by King John in 1215, is one of the best-known instances of the use of mining in siege warfare.

Another means to make a breach was sapping. Stones at the base of the wall were individually picked off, dislodged and torn out until collapse of the wall. Another ancient method of making a breach was using a battering ram. The ram was maneuvered by a party of men giving a backwards and forwards movement against a gate or a masoned wall. The violent shocks worked by direct percussion but also by causing vibrations, which loosened the stones. Sapping and battering were very dangerous operations because the defenders dropped stones, threw down incendiary materials and spears and shot down arrows on the exposed attackers. In reaction a cat was constructed; a cat (also called penthouse, rat, chasteil or tortoise from the Roman testudo) was a stout, strong, movable (often wheeled) timber gallery covered with a solid sloping roof intended to protect sappers, rammers, miners, or men attempting to fill the ditch.

Assaulting

When a breach was practical the attack was launched. For the ordinary soldier, the assault was extremely hazardous, and it was not always easy to get troops to assault. Very often it required knights, leading nobles and rulers to lead from the front. As seen above, King Richard I found his death on April 6, 1199, from an infected arrow wound to his shoulder while leading the assault on the castle of Châlus in Normandy. The frontal assault in the breach was thus often led by knights who regarded it as a great honor to be among the first into a beleaguered fortress and many volunteered for this honor. At the siege of Saint-Jean-d'Acre (Palestine) in 1189, King Richard I Lionheart, him again, offered a gold piece to any man who would bring him back a stone from the walls of the city. The assault in the breach was a confused and bloody hand-to-hand battle. It was a crucial confrontation for both parties and the turning point of the siege. Individual factors, such as physical fitness and bravery, played a central role, but pugnacity was not enough against sheer numbers. A repulsed assault generally cost a lot of casualties, it could become a harrowing defeat loosening all the bonds of discipline and generating fear, panic and rabbling retreat.

Of course the tactics discussed above could be combined. At the siege of Dover Castle, Kent, in 1216 Prince Louis of France used stone-throwing machines, a battering ram and mining. Henry III did the same at the siege of Bedford in June–August 1224. Overall, the advances in offensive siegecraft were countered by subsequent advances in defensive military architecture, and the reverse.

Evolution of Castles in the 12th and 13th Centuries

Round Keeps

About the turn of the 12th and during the 13th centuries important developments took place in British castle design. This was largely due to the experience gained in the Crusades by western military architects, who for the first time not only made close acquaintance with the mighty fortifications of the Byzantine Empire and the Muslim civilization, but also were confronted with sophisticated siege methods. The single keep with surrounding protective walled bailey reinforced with mural towers continued as a basic design, but gradually changes and improvements were introduced. The sitting and design of castles reflected concerns about advances in siege warfare, and military architects were anxious to devise works that eliminated these threats. Buildings prominently located on elevated solid rock outcrops were considered to be very secure, and the provision of a broad ditch was regarded as the best deterrent to siege tactics, the more so when the ditch was filled with water. Another noticeable change was the discarding of the Norman rectangular or square plan, replaced with a polygonal, circular or cylindrical plan. Over a square keep a

Conisbrough today. Located in Doncaster, South Yorkshire, the keep was built by Hamelin Plantagenet, Earl of Warenne, a half-brother of King Henry II in the 12th century. The tower is entirely built with beautiful magnesian limestone ashlar. It measures 50 feet in diameter and 90 feet in height. It is supported throughout its entire height by six massive butresses. The tower has five stories, including, from the top downwards, a top fighting platform (today destroyed), the lord's private room (with a chapel built in the thickness of the buttress), a hall, and two tiers of cellarage and a well. Communication between the stories was obtained by separate flights curving round the building and arranged in the thickness of the wall. The tower, leaving no doubt about its military character, also had rich architectural details (chapel, fireplaces, latrines and other domestic fitments) clearly indicating that it was the regular dwelling for a powerful magnate. By the end of the 1400s, Conisbrough had been abandoned as a residence and, ironically, it was its very state of disrepair that saved it from total destruction during the English Civil War. The castle is now owned by English Heritage and is open to the public.

round tower presented several advantages. It limited the dangerous dead angles or dead grounds (spots which could not be seen and shot at from the top). It lent itself readily to dome-vaulting on all, or at least on the principal floors, and thus could be made virtually fireproof. Space for space, a round building is volumetrically more economical in masonry than is a square one, and it has no corners (weak points exposed to the battering ram or the miner's pick). That a rectangular or square keep was vulnerable

Right: *Conisbrough keep (conjectured reconstruction). Note the use of plinth (also called talus, or batter), referring to the base of a wall being provided with a thick, compact and widening slope. This mass of large stones added stability to the construction, strengthened the bottom of the wall against undermining and sapping, and provided a ricochet surface for projectiles such as rocks being dropped down that would splinter and bounce off horizontally, creating a crushing shrapnel effect on enemies below.*

Bottom: *Plan of Conisbrough Castle. 1: Outer bailey; 2: Motte; 3: Inner bailey; 4: Cylindrical keep.*

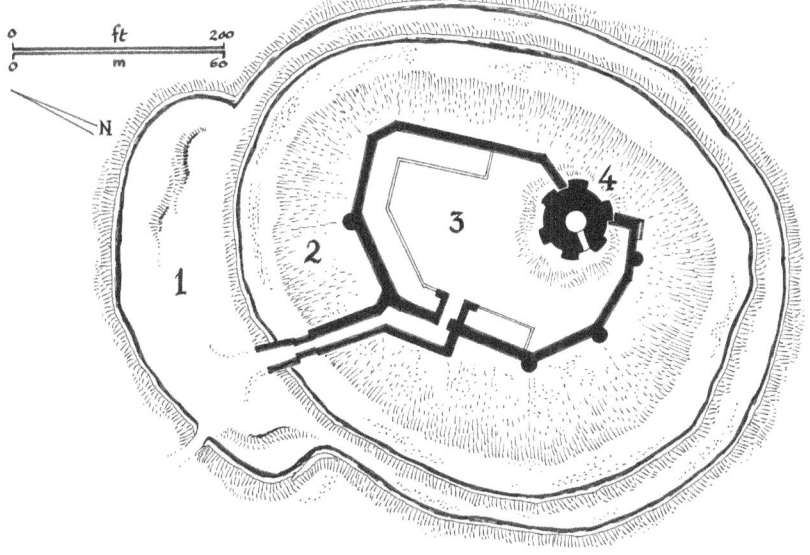

Conisbrough Castle (Conjectured reconstruction)

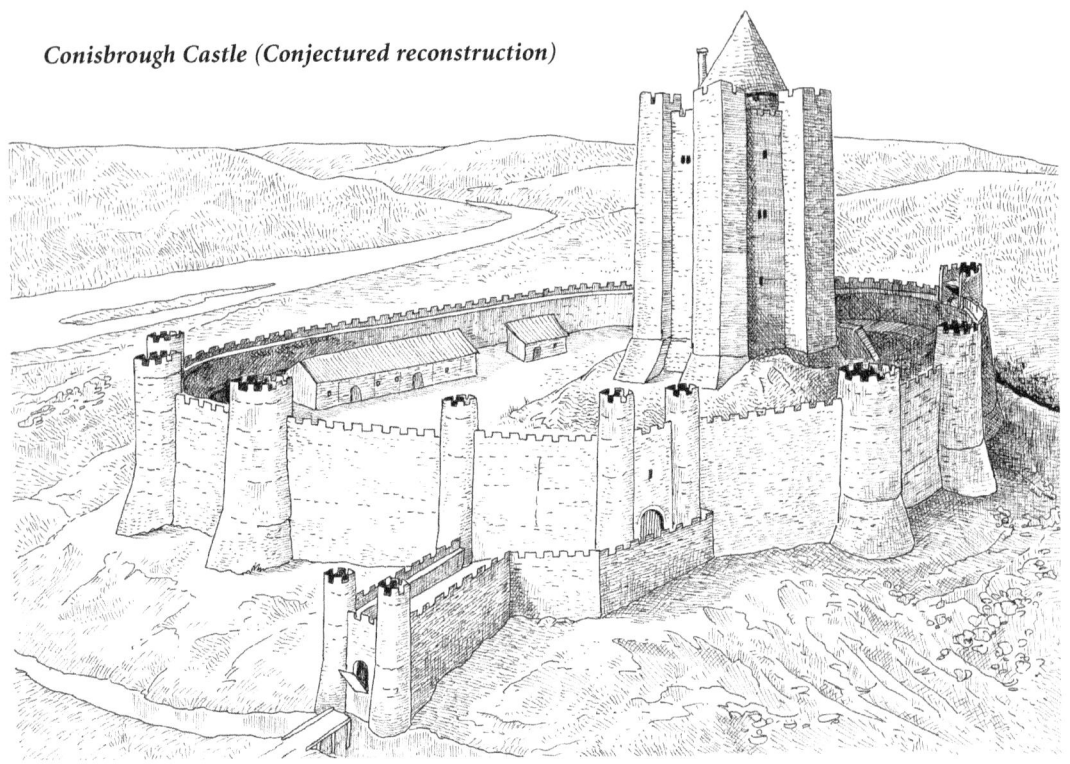

Orford Castle, located 12 miles (20 km) northeast of Ipswich in Suffolk, was built by order of King Henry II between 1165 and 1173. Its purpose was to overlook Orford harbor. Technically speaking, Orford was a link between the Norman square keep and the Angevin round tower. Its core is circular but it has a multi-angular external outline broken by three large rectangular projections, not mere buttresses like Conisbrough, but wings devised to supply additional accommodation, with two kitchens, a chapel and a variety of rooms opening off the central structure. One of the wings has an additional forework with a defensive entrance. The keep was placed in the center of a bailey enclosed by walls and towers. Today, the outer curtain wall has largely disappeared, leaving only traces of the outer defenses and a deep trench surrounding the central keep. The well-preserved tower of Orford is now managed and maintained by English Heritage.

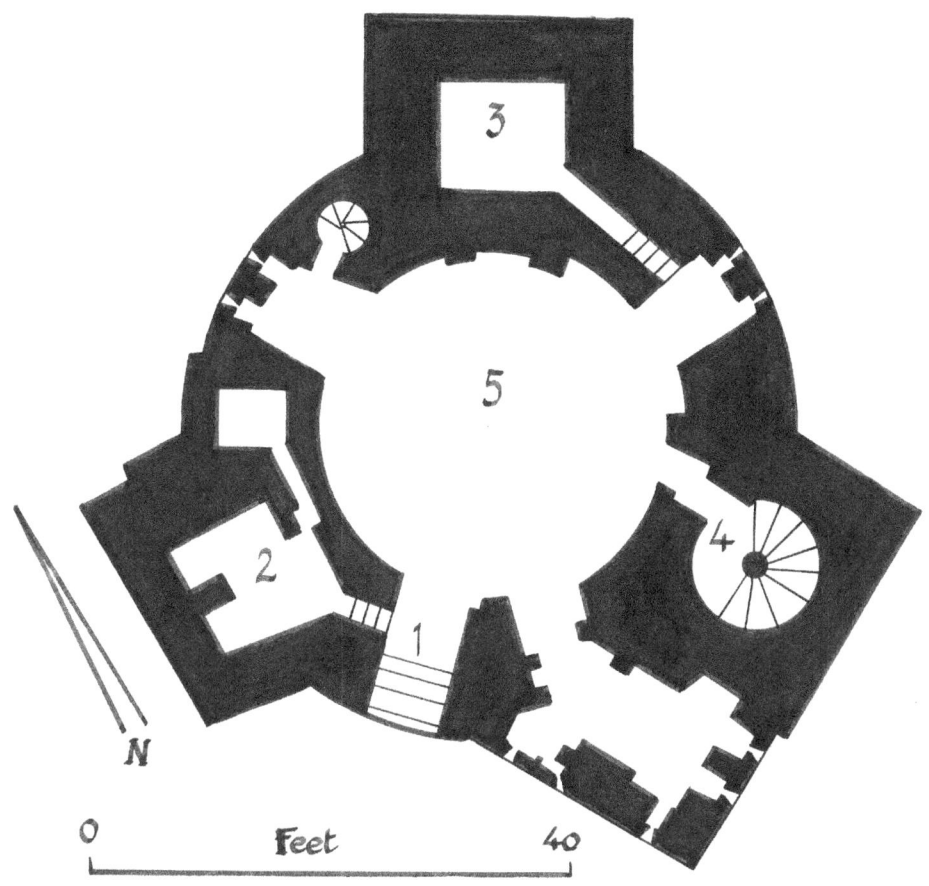

Plan of Orford Castle. The plan of the second floor shows the circular core and the three rectangular projections. 1: Main entrance; 2: Kitchen; 3: Sleeping chamber; 4: Staircase; 5: Guard room.

to mining was demonstrated in 1215 when parts of the keep of Rochester were destroyed by a mine, which did nullify all the keep's ponderous strength and brought its massive walls tumbling down in ruin. That siege of Rochester proved the point and paved the way to the round tower and the development of the concentric castle. However, even before 1215, everywhere in Western Europe round keeps were erected. In Britain, one of the first and best instances of this new fashion is the keep of Conisbrough in Yorkshire, celebrated in Sir Walter Scott's historical novel, *Ivanhoe*. Other remarkable keeps based on a cylindrical design include Orford in Sussex and Pembroke in Wales. More sophisticated forms were also experimented with, such as the quatrefoil (or quadrilobe, consisting of four intersecting vertical cylinders), as can be seen at Clifford's Tower in the royal castle of York, and at the donjons of Pontefract in Yorkshire. In the 13th century the fashion of cylindrical keeps was continued and spread northward into Scotland, and the donjon of Bothwell Castle provides a remarkable example.

(Continued on page 188).

Above: *Pembroke, located on a strategic steep rocky promontory dominating the Pembroke River in West Wales, is one of the outstanding examples of a cylindrical keep. Around 1093 the Norman Arnulf de Montgomery built a small motte-and-bailey castle at the end of the promontory. In the late 12th century, c. 1189, the castle was acquired by Earl William Marshall, who turned it into an impressive stone castle with a cylindrical donjon. The massive donjon, forming the central feature of the castle, was built in 1200. Made of limestone ashlar, it stands on a massive plinth and its walls, approximately 19 feet (6 m) thick, rise to a height of 80 feet. The keep has a diameter of 53 feet, and was divided into four stories, the uppermost roofed with a stone dome 30 feet high at the center. Externally there were two fighting terraces, the uppermost around the top of the dome. Below and outside this was a second terrace or rampart walk on top of the main wall. Another remarkable feature of the castle is the gatehouse, which defended the outer ward and which had a complex barbican and no fewer than three portcullises. Historically, Pembroke is important not only for its architecture but also for the fact that Henry VII, who inaugurated the Tudor line of monarchs, was born there in 1457, reputedly in the tower now known as the Henry VII Tower. Today, Pembroke Castle is owned and managed by a private charitable trust. The imposing ruined castle is open to the public all year. The illustration shows how the donjon and the inner ward might have appeared in the early 13th century.*

Opposite top: *Plan of Pembroke Castle. 1: Circular keep; 2: Chapel and Western Hall; 3: Inner ward; 4: North Tower; 5: Court; 6: Norman Hall; 7: Northern Hall; 8: Prison Tower; 9: Inner gatehouse; 10: Monkton Tower; 11: West Gate Tower; 12: Town walls; 13: Henry VII Tower; 14: Barbican; 15: Great Gatehouse; 16: Barbican Tower; 17: North Gate Tower; 18: St. Ann's Bastion; 19: Outer ward; 20: Moat.*

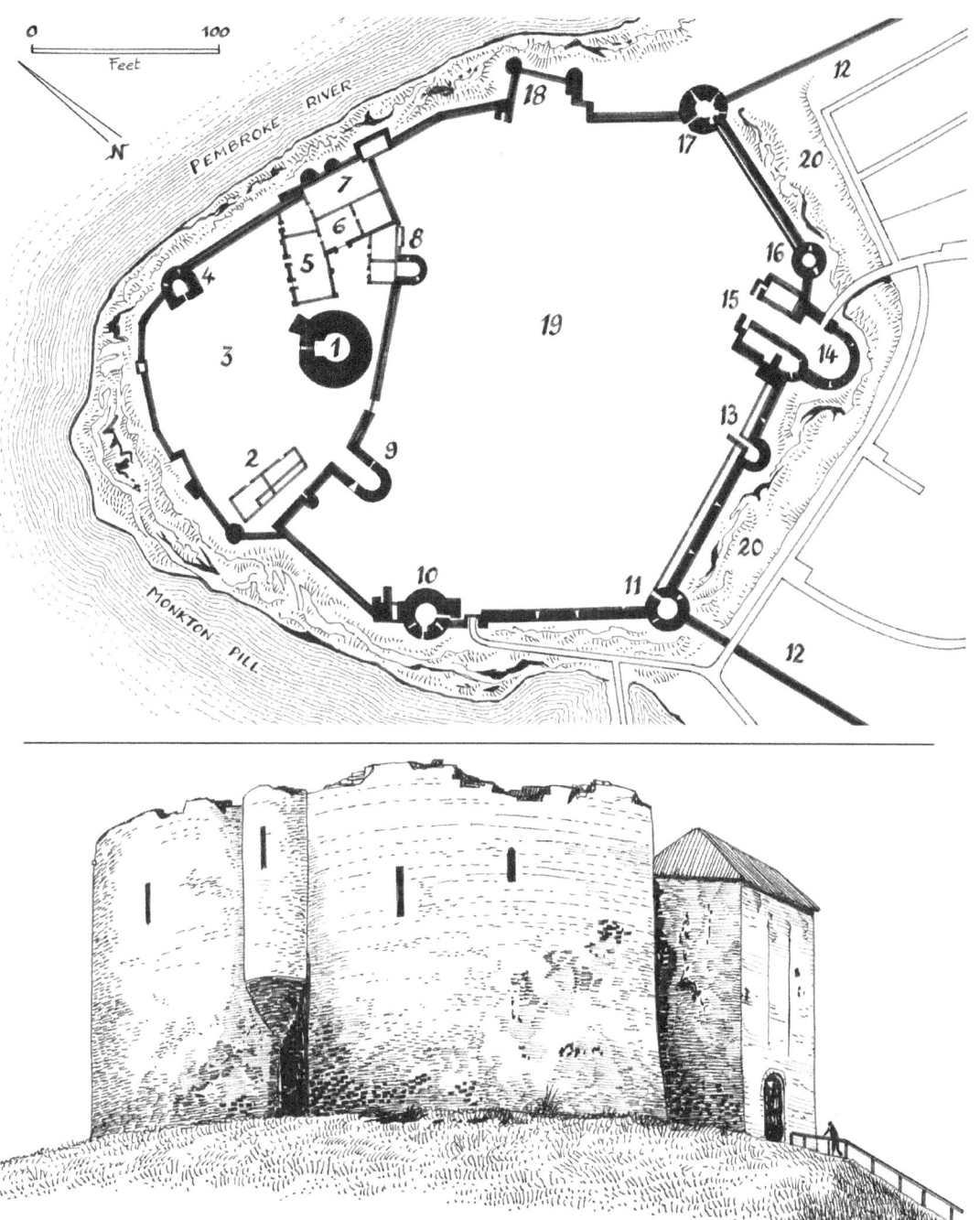

Clifford's Tower (originally known as King's Tower) in York originated from a typical Norman timber motte castle erected in 1068–1069 by order of King William I the Conqueror right after the conquest. Rebuilt by order of King Henry II, Clifford embodied the new concept that round walls were harder to destroy than sharp corners. The still-existing stone tower of quatrefoil plan stands on top of a large motte approximately 100 feet in diameter. The tower is about 49 feet high with only two stories. Entry was at ground level through a forebuilding with porch. The building derived its present name after Edward II's victory at the battle of Boroughbridge in 1322. Sir Roger Clifford, being on the losing Lancastrian side, was executed in the castle.

Above: *The illustration shows how the King's Tower (later renamed Clifford's Tower) might have appeared in the 12th century.*

Opposite top: *Chepstow, on its rock above the swirling waters of the River Wye, stands guard over a strategic crossing point into Wales. Started not long after the Battle of Hastings in 1066 by William Fitz Osbern, a companion of William the Conqueror created Earl of Hereford, it was a landmark in many ways. Chepstow, built to secure Fitz Osbern's new territories in the Welsh borders, was amongst the first of Britain's stone-built strongholds. The mellow-walled (soft, toned-down by time) Chepstow we see today is an intriguing amalgam of different periods. Started during the infancy of castle building, it was improved throughout the centuries right up to the Civil War and beyond. Beautifully preserved Chepstow Castle is a history lesson in stone, which brings to life the way a castle can grow from rudimentary keep to sophisticated fortress. At its core remains the Norman stone keep. In later centuries, towers, walls, gatehouses and barbicans were added, until the long, narrow castle occupied the entire cliff backed ridge above the Wye. As a final complement to its strength and siting, Chepstow was adapted for cannon and musketry after a long siege in the Civil War, and continued in use until 1690. The map shows 1: Barbican; 2: Southwest Tower; 3: Upper bailey; 4: Great Tower; 5: Middle Bailey; 6: Lower bailey; 7 and 8: Domestic buildings, hall and kitchen; 9: Outer gatehouse; 10: Marten's Tower.*

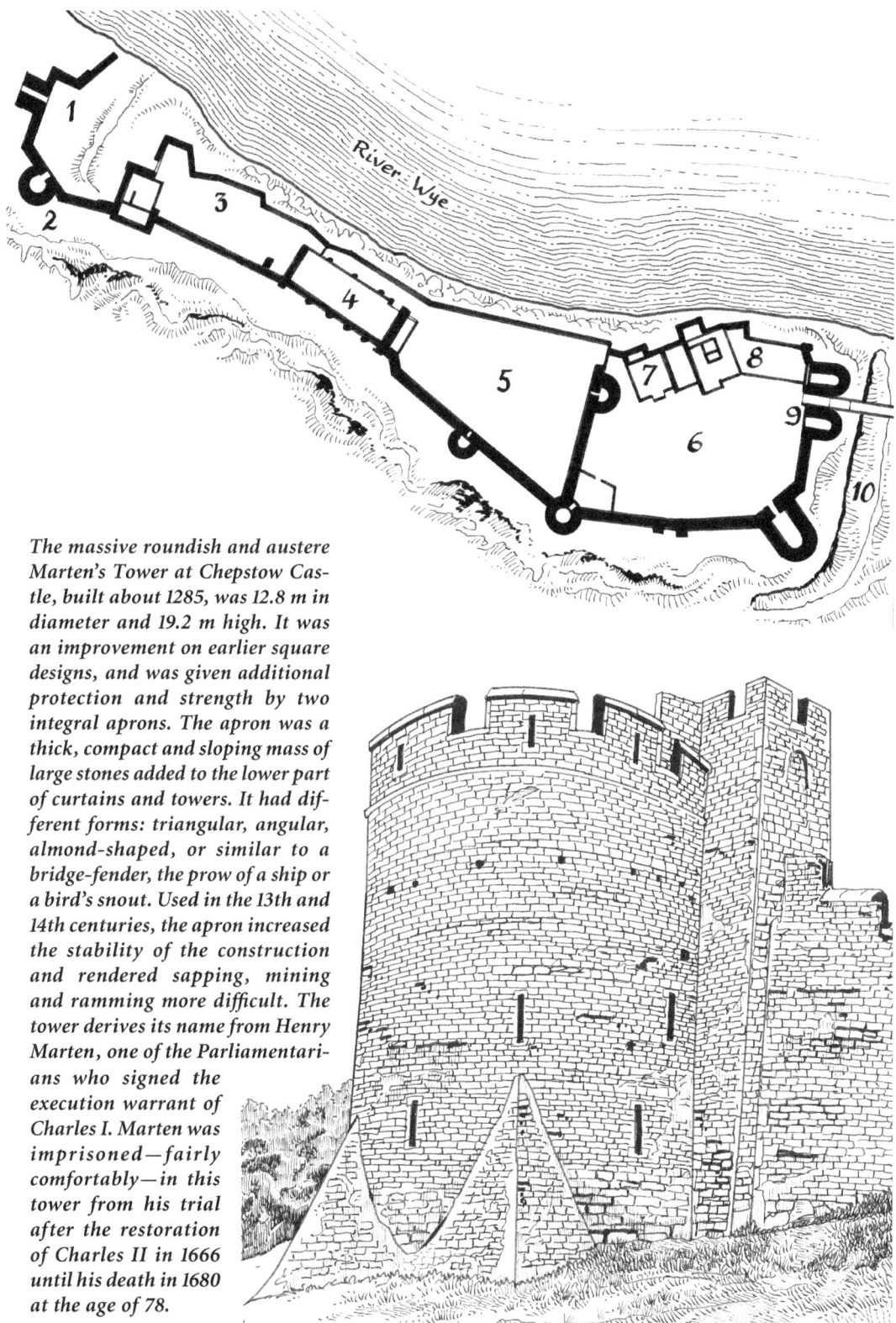

The massive roundish and austere Marten's Tower at Chepstow Castle, built about 1285, was 12.8 m in diameter and 19.2 m high. It was an improvement on earlier square designs, and was given additional protection and strength by two integral aprons. The apron was a thick, compact and sloping mass of large stones added to the lower part of curtains and towers. It had different forms: triangular, angular, almond-shaped, or similar to a bridge-fender, the prow of a ship or a bird's snout. Used in the 13th and 14th centuries, the apron increased the stability of the construction and rendered sapping, mining and ramming more difficult. The tower derives its name from Henry Marten, one of the Parliamentarians who signed the execution warrant of Charles I. Marten was imprisoned—fairly comfortably—in this tower from his trial after the restoration of Charles II in 1666 until his death in 1680 at the age of 78.

Left: *Nenagh Castle in the county of North Tipperary, Ireland, was built by Theobald Walter around 1200. The castle boasts the finest cylindrical keep in Ireland, named "Nenagh Round." Built of limestone rubble, irregularly coursed, and measuring about 55 feet in external diameter at the base, it rises now to a height of about a hundred feet. The topmost quarter, however, is modern (c. 1860), the original height to the wallwalk being about 75 feet. Above this, there was the crenellated parapet. The keep included four stories, with a basement, which was accessible, originally, only from the entrance story above. At the base, the walls are 16 feet thick, and at the top, just 11 feet. The architecture is gracefully decorative, and it includes a series of clerestory windows beneath a corbelled parapet wall ornamented with stepped merlons.*

Below: *Nenagh Castle plan. Like most keeps, Nenagh Round formed part of the perimeter of the fortress, being incorporated into the curtain walls surrounding a rather small, five-sided courtyard. These walls have now almost disappeared (dashed line on the illustration), but fragments (in bold) remain. There were originally four flanking towers, one on each side of the entrance gateway to the south, the others at the east and west angles of the pentagon; the great keep occupied the northern angle.*

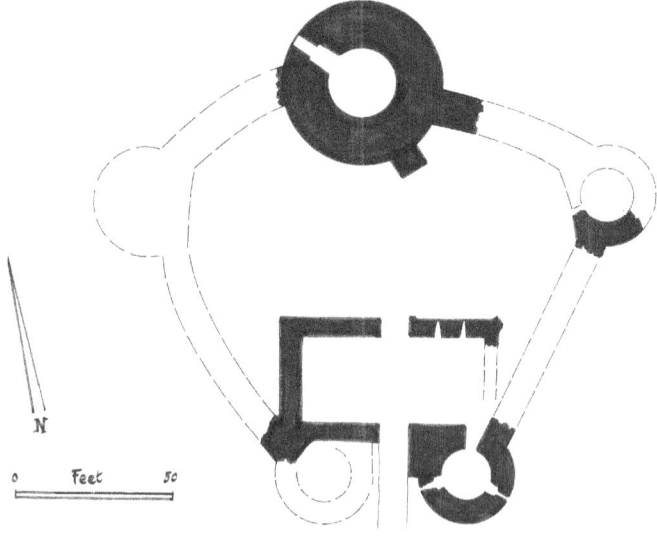

Dirleton Castle (Conjectured reconstruction), located in the village of Dirleton about 2 miles (3.2 km) west of North Berwick, and around 19 miles (31 km) east of Edinburgh in East Lothian, Scotland, was built by John De Vaux around 1240. Dirleton Castle stands on a rocky outcrop, at the heart of the rich agricultural lands of the former barony of Dirleton, and guards the coastal approach to Edinburgh from England, via the port of North Berwick. Basically the plan is an obtusely angled L-shape, with four part-round towers ranged along the two arms of the curtain wall, raised on the almost vertical crag completing the fortified area. Two small corbelled, snuffer-roofed turrets flanked the entrance. The ruins comprise a 13th-century keep and a 16th-century house which the Ruthven family built adjacent. Only the basement levels survive of the 14th- and 15th-century additions built by the Haliburton family, notably a large hall and tower house along the east range. Other buildings within the courtyard have also been demolished. Surrounding the castle are gardens, which may have been first laid out in the 16th century, although the present planting is largely of the 20th century. The ruins of sternly romantic appearance and gardens are now maintained by Historic Scotland.

Above: *Bothwell Castle (conjectured reconstruction), located on a steep ridge above a bend of the River Clyde in South Lanarkshire southeast of Glasgow in Scotland, strongly recalls Coucy and Najac castles in France, of which built in 1277, it was the exact contemporary. The castle of Bothwell is composed of an oblong walled inner bailey with walls reaching 60 feet high, with jutting towers, and at its western end an enormous round donjon. To the north there are substantial foundations of a gatehouse, towers and curtains to enclose a roughly triangular outer bailey. These were never completed. Bothwell is a very grand but rather unfortunate castle with a confusing history made of construction, incompleteness, sieges, captures, partial demolition and rebuilding, and final abandonment in the 18th century. Bothwell Castle is now managed by Historic Scotland and is open to the public.*

Opposite: *Bothwell donjon. The Bothwell keep is nearly 70 feet in diameter and still survives today to a height of 90 feet. The polished ashlar reveals a possible French involvement. The donjon had four stories, with the lord's private apartment on top.*

Towered Curtain

At the same time that the fortress designers were experimenting with round, multi-angular or even quadrilobed keeps, they were devoting more and more attention to the curtain walls. By the 13th century the bailey was more often enclosed by increasingly massive curtain walls, flanked by wall- and corner-towers either of the older rectangular or newer cylindrical pattern. Bartizans, also called échauguettes or pepper-pot towers—small corbelled watchtowers or turrets projecting from the corner or flank of a tower or wall, overhanging at the top—were also introduced. They had the same flanking combat and observation function as normal towers, but they were much cheaper to build.

The bailey still screened the usual domestic buildings, but the hall and the chapel, now built in stone, had grown in importance.

The hall was the main room in a castle, often of great dimensions, in which all parts of the household of the castle community would eat and live, with those of highest status being at the end, often on a raised dais, and those of lesser status.

It was a room of relative comfort and status, which usually included a fireplace (with additional braziers and charcoal-pans in winter) and decorative woodwork, trophies, tapestries, and wall hangings. The hall was used as place for entertainment, banquets, feasts, and celebrations, but also as a room to gather a meeting, a council, or a court of justice. At night it could be used as a dormitory for servants. As seen before, in the early Middle Ages it was a large room in the keep, but increasingly it became a separate building in its own right, a hall-house placed in the bailey. By far the noblest medieval hall in Britain is Westminster Hall, built by King Rufus and remodeled by King Richard II. This astounding structure measures internally 239 by 67 feet, but it is rather an independent building in its own right rather than a castle hall. Another remarkable hall is that of Winchester Castle, built by King Henry III between 1220 and 1236. This splendid stateroom measures 110 by 56 feet and is constructed like a church with a nave and aisles separated by arcades. Another noticeable great hall was that of Grosmont Castle in Monmouthshire, built by Hubert de Burgh. Grosmont Castle stands within a D-shaped moat and includes a walled enclosure with two round towers and a simple gatehouse. Along the straight or rearward side stands a hall-house measuring 96 by 32 feet. This

Murder-holes (1) were voids spared in the ceiling of a gateway or above a passageway—generally in the gatehouse—through which the defenders could drop down projectiles at attackers. Invented by the Romans in c. 200 B.C., the portcullis (2) was a vertical wooden grille often shod with iron, placed above the doorway of a gatehouse. It could be raised open using to a winching system (3) of counterweights, pulleys, ropes or chains and a windlass placed on the first floor of the gatehouse (seen here in profile). In time of crisis the portcullis could be instantly lowered by releasing a latch, and the heavy grilled door slid down along side-grooves or guides owing to its own weight. These elements, together with the drawbridge (4), were standard parts of the defense of the entrance of a castle.

is massively constructed and strongly buttressed, almost in a Norman fashion, yet clearly dated to the early 13th century.

Next in importance to the hall came the chapel. Norman keeps, as we have already discussed, had a room arranged as an oratory or a chapel, but in the new castles of the 13th century it became an independent church placed in the bailey. It often had outstanding features such as a circular nave, vaulted rectangular chancel, sanctuaries and rich decorations in the so-called Gothic style. Some remarkable castle chapels in Britain may be seen, amongst many other examples, at Ludlow Castle in Shropshire, Kildrummy in Aberdeenshire, and Dunstaffnage near Oban in Scotland.

In some instances the keep lost its importance both as dwelling and military structure, and the bailey and its fortified enceinte tended to become essentially the castle. The donjon was sometimes reduced to the position of just one tower on the line of the curtain, larger and stronger than the others, often vaulted on one or more

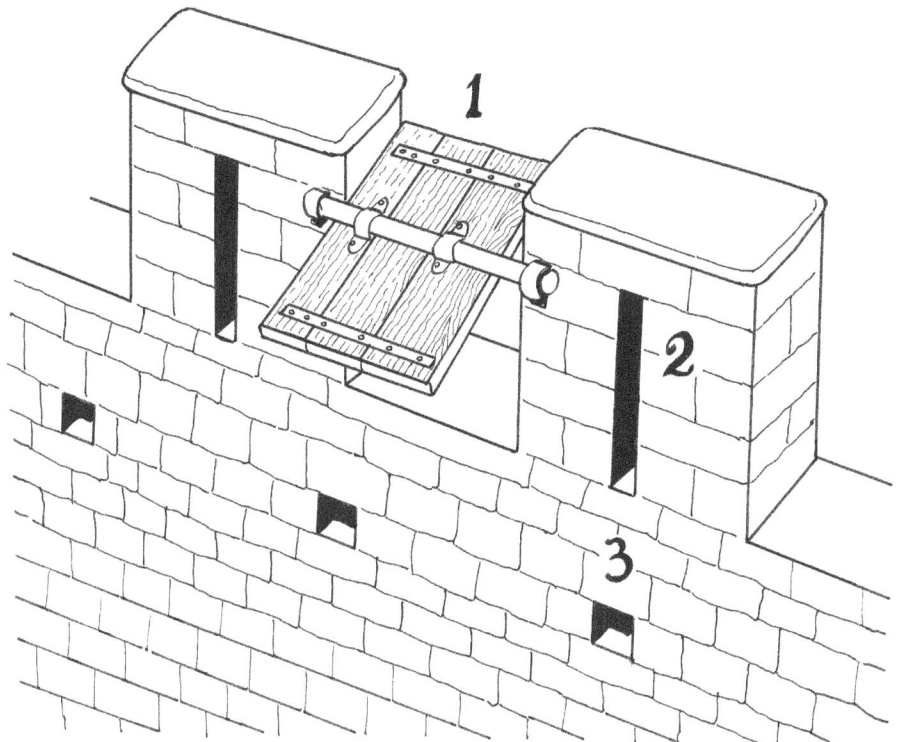

Above: *Shutter.* The crenel (void between two solid merlons) could be fitted with a wooden shutter (or huchette) hanging upon swivels in the merlon on either side. The shutter (1) could be pushed far open when required in order to enable an archer or a crossbowman to shoot his weapon through the crenel while the sloping shelter offered him overhead protection from enemy projectiles. The merlons could be pierced with observation slits (2), and below the battlements there was often a row of weepers (3) for carrying off the rainwater from the wallwalk.

Right: *A brattice* (also called a bretèche or bretasche or moucharabieh) was a small masoned or timber projecting balcony resting on corbels introduced in the 12th century. Often placed above an entrance, it was a variation of the murder-holes, as its floor was fitted with one or more machicoulis—openings through which missiles could be thrown downwards upon assailants. It was a cheap substitute, allowing vertical flanking. Its summit was either roofed or open and furnished with one or two crenels. The brattice, originating from the Middle East, was introduced in the western military architecture by the Crusaders.

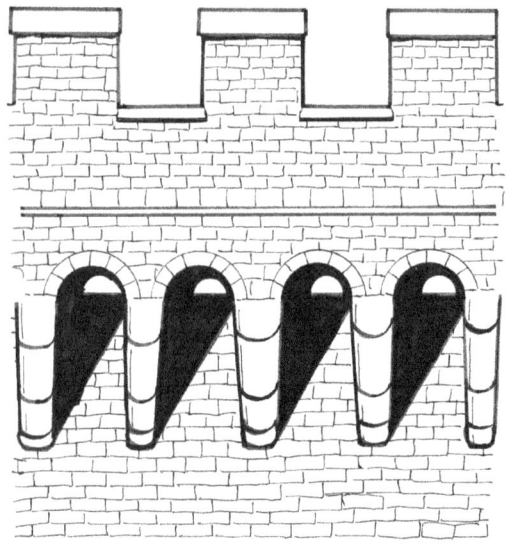 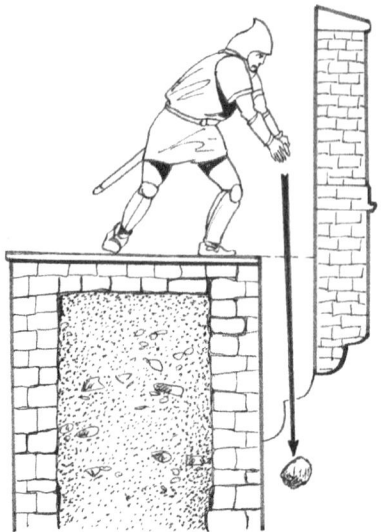

Above: *Machicolation (or machicoulis),* introduced in the late 13th century, is an opening made in the floor of the wallwalk on top of a wall, between supporting corbels, through which rocks or other projectiles could be dropped down on attackers at the base of a defensive wall.

Bottom: *Skenfrith Castle.* An early and interesting example of a transitional disposition may be seen at Skenfrith Castle in Monmouthshire, Wales. Skenfrith originated from an 11th-century earth and timber ringwork and bailey fortress, founded by William Fitz Osborn. In the late 12th century, King Henry II founded the stone castle, encasing the platform with a curtain wall flanked by a small square keep. In the early 13th century, Hubert de Burgh, Earl of Kent, demolished the earlier fortress and founded the stone keep and courtyard castle on the levelled site. The great circular three-story keep is placed in an archaic position in the center of the bailey, and stands on a sub-rectangular platform, which was encased by a wide stone revetted motte. The enceinte enclosing the bailey is trapezoidal with a wall approximately 8 feet thick. It was reinforced with a round projecting tower at each corner, a fifth on the west flank, and a gatehouse now destroyed. The castle was surrounded by a wet moat fed from the River Monnow.

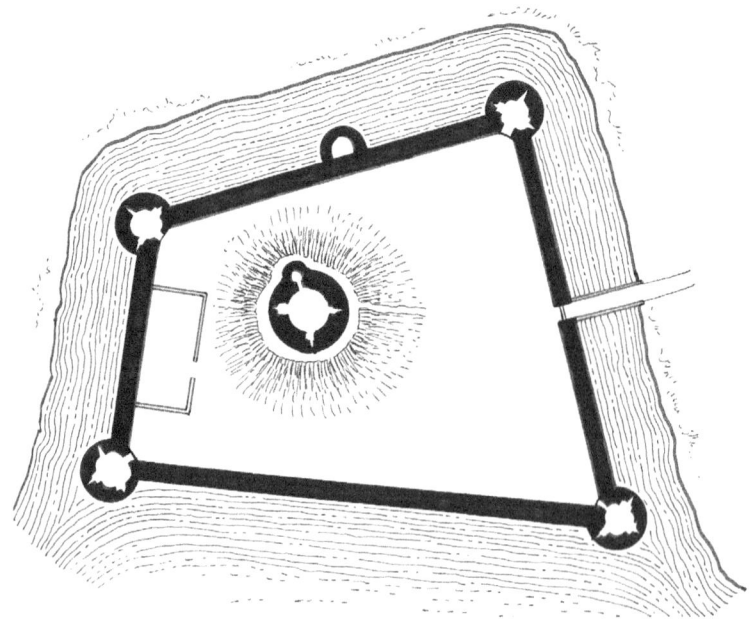

Skenfrith Castle Keep. The illustration shows the keep in its actual state.

floors and provided with its own well so that it could serve as the last defensive place if the castle were invaded and captured. In such castles, the donjon was generally sited as remotely as possible from the entrance, always the weak point in the defense. Therefore great attention was now devoted to the strengthening of the entrance, which began to take the form of a regular and powerful gatehouse. Basically the gatehouse included a wide arched portal—large enough to let a cart through. The portal could of course be closed by heavy stout wooden folding doors reinforced with nails and metal parts. The portal was arranged either into a rectangular building, or a mural tower through which the entryway passed, or, very commonly, was deeply recessed between a pair of strong flanking towers. This large and complex gatehouse was increasingly heavily fortified and defended with a drawbridge, one or more portcullises, arrow loops, and murder-holes in the vault or ceiling of the entrance passage.

In addition the defense of the gatehouse was often reinforced with a barbican—an advanced or exterior work protecting the gatehouse of a city or castle. The barbican, originating from the Middle East and brought back to Europe by returning

Gatehouse of Carisbrooke Castle, situated near Newport on the Isle of Wight, originated from a Roman fort, then an Anglo-Saxon settlement and a Norman motte-and-bailey castle. Re-built in the 13th, 14th and 16th centuries, the castle was the strongest point on the island. The depicted gateway was erected by Lord Scales, who was owner of the castle in 1464.

Crusaders, could be a simple palisade or an earth wall with stockade, but these were often replaced with a thick masonry work. It could have various forms, for example a large round tower or a strong rectangular building, or an oval or horseshoe shape, or an advanced walled enclosure, or even an outer ward with towers and turrets. Erected on the far side of the ditch, at the exterior end of the bridge, it concealed the gatehouse, worked as a filter, and provided an additional external line of defense as it was fitted with combat emplacements, its own ditch and its own drawbridge. The entrance to the barbican was not placed in line with the main portal but on a flank, so as to check a direct rush upon the latter. The provision of successive lines of defense had long been a well-understood device in the designing of castles. The barbican also enabled the assemblage of a party to prepare for a sortie or to protect a retreat.

Enceinte Castle

In some examples the keep was discarded altogether, and the castle became a fortified enclosure with walls, towers and gatehouse, but now without donjon or main tower. The bailey then provided protection, and the defense focused on the gatehouse, corner- and wall-towers, and curtains. Towers and walls were amply fitted with arrow-loops and often furnished with hoardings—timber oversailing galleries enabling the defenders to command the bases of their walls. This arrangement was also a great improvement regarding the daily life and organization of the community living in the castle. The bailey (sometimes covering several acres) offered more space and easier communication between service buildings and living quarters, which had previously been included in the crowded vertical keep. All elements could then be placed commodiously at ground level in separate buildings in the courtyard. Castles of this type are thus often termed enceinte-castles.

Again it must be stressed that not every baron in the 13th century lived within strong castles as just described. Many of the smaller landlords continued to dwell in homesteads made of timbered earthwork, or in mansions and manors which hardly deserved the term of castle. They were forced to do so either because they were not

Ludlow Castle (conjectured reconstruction), situated in the Marches of Wales in south Shropshire, probably originates from a Norman castle built soon after William I's conquest. Construction was extended over the centuries, and the castle was a border stronghold and a fortified royal palace. It occupies a strong defensive position on a steep cliff above the rivers Teme and Corve. Ludlow Castle stands prominently on high ground, able to resist attack from would-be invaders from over the Welsh border. For the first 200 years, Ludlow Castle was owned by the De Lacy family, and then came into the possession of the Mortimers until 1461, when it became Crown property. During the next 350 years it remained largely a royal castle, but had fallen into a state of decay by the mid–18th century, becoming the lovely romantic ruin seen today.

rich enough to afford elaborate fortifications or because they had not received a royal license to "crenallate." In medieval parlance to crenellate was to embattle, which meant to fortify his residence. In theory at least, no lord was allowed to do so without the king's permission. It need hardly be said that such a regulation was apt to be more honored in the breach than in the observance, particularly when the central royal power was weak.

It is still unclear where the initiative for new castle designs lay. While skilled

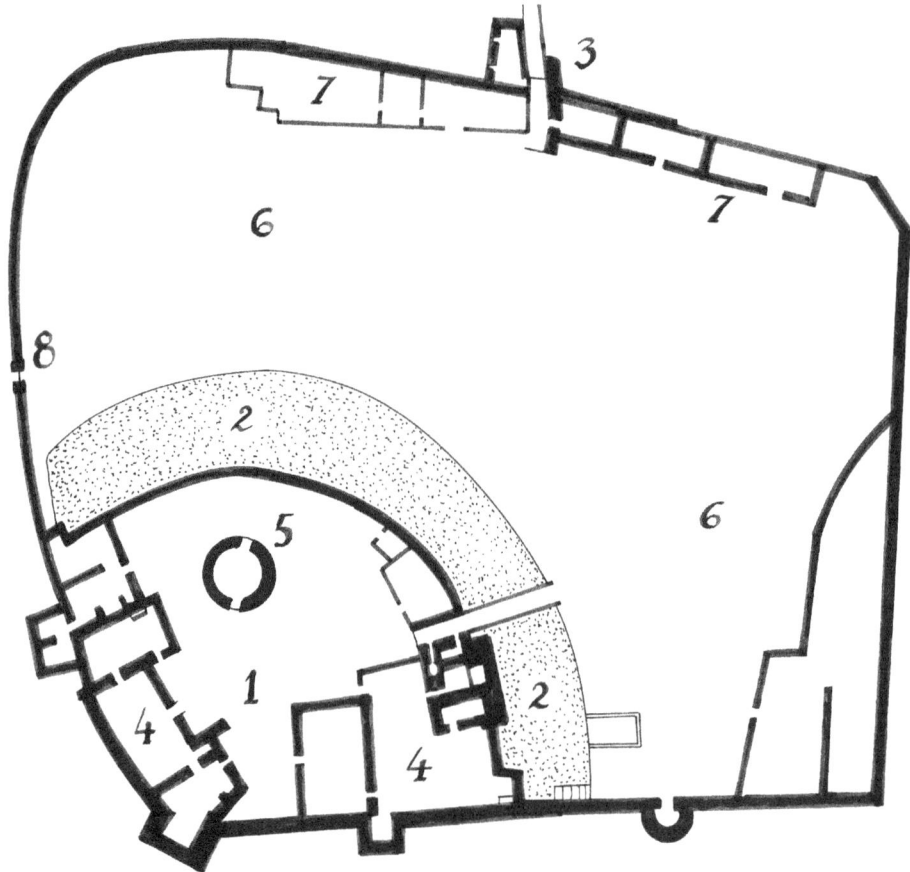

Plan of Ludlow Castle. Situated at the northwest extremity of the town of Ludlow, the castle forms a large rectangular enceinte, with the town and principal entry on the east side, and the west side overlooking the river. The northwest corner is enclosed by another enceinte wall (1) and a moat (2) forming the inner ward and the heart of the castle. In the early 12th century, the gatehouse was extended and converted to a four-story rectangular keep (3), containing a living hall and private solar, and to which entry was gained by a bridge. The inner ward contains the residential buildings (4) that formed the castle's principal accommodations. These buildings feature large windows that overlook the courtyard. The most important structure in this range was the Great Hall, a huge room measuring some 60 feet (18 m) by 30 feet (9 m), with an undercroft beneath. In addition, the inner ward features the remains of the Chapel of St. Mary Magdalene (5) with an unsual circular chancel reminiscent of that of Temple Church in London. The outer ward (6) contained service buildings (7), and a sallyport (8).

master-builders would presumably bring their own experience to bear on the most suitable solution for a defensive building, the commissioning lords were also innovative soldiers who had been besieged and who had besieged themselves. These professional warriors undoubtedly had their own views on how to construct and attack a castle. Castle-designers, kings, barons and lords traveled around Europe; some went on pilgrimages or crusades in the Holy Land. They would certainly have taken note of any fortresses they saw, remembering and eventually copying impressive and useful features.

Concentric Castle

From the mid–12th century a new development appeared, called the concentric castle. This had no keep where the defenders could retreat, but a series of enclosing walls punctuated by towers, one inside the other, in fact two castles in one. The early motte-and-bailey castle was highly vulnerable because the various parts of the defense

Caerphilly Castle, located in south Wales, is one of the great medieval castles of Western Europe. Several factors give it this pre-eminence: its immense size (1.2 hectares), making it the largest in Britain after Windsor; its large-scale use of water for defense; and the fact that it is the first truly concentric castle in Britain. At the time of its building in the late 13th century, it was a revolutionary masterpiece of military planning. The castle was built by one of Henry III's most powerful and ambitious barons, Gilbert de Clare, lord of Glamorgan. His purpose was to secure the area and prevent lowland south Wales from falling into the hands of the Welsh leader Llywelyn the Last, who controlled most of mid- and north Wales. De Clare built other castles on the northern fringes of his territory for the same purpose, such as Castell Coch. He had seized the upland district of Senghenydd, in which Caerphilly lies, from the Welsh in 1266 to act as a buffer against Llywelyn's southward ambitions. Apart from the remodelling of the great hall and other domestic works in 1322–26 for Hugh le Despenser, no more alterations were carried out, making it a very pure example of late 13th-century military architecture.

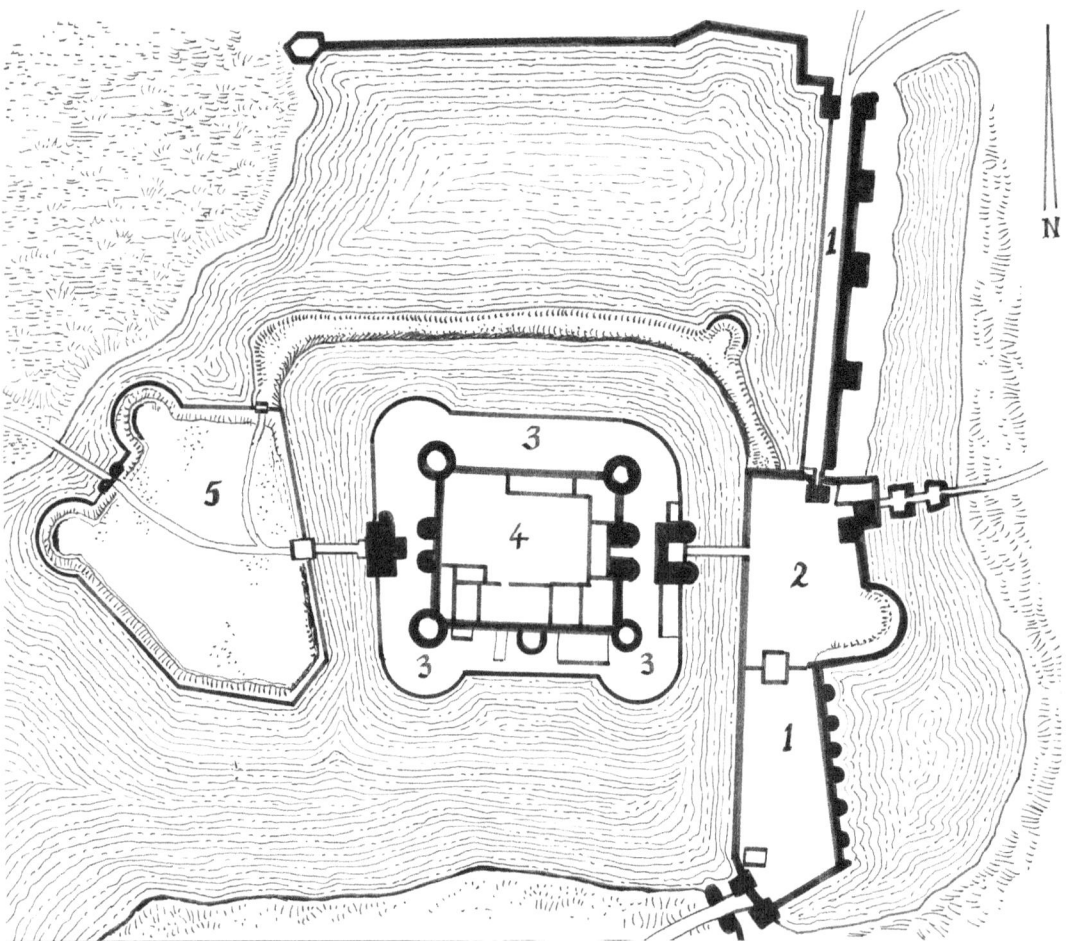

Plan of Caerphilly Castle. Walls and towers are not the only elements in fortification, and water defenses, both natural and artificial, have always been important. The castle standing in the loop of a river is a commonplace, but there are two supreme instances where the elaborate flooding of shallow valleys are transformed into lakes by damming: Kenilworth and Caerphilly. The central part of Caerphilly Castle is a concentric arrangement, quite similar to Harlech and Beaumaris, standing originally on an island in a lake held on one side by a dam called Grand Front (1), nearly 1,000 feet long, protecting the approach from the east. There are gateways on to the dam at either end and at the center, a barbican (2) and a drawbridge giving access to the castle proper, on the island. There was an outer bailey (3), whose lower curtain wall follows closely the plan of the inner; it is plain, without towers, except for those of the two gatehouses, on the eastern and western sides opposite the inner gatehouse. The inner bailey (4) is of the usual rectangular form (c. 200 by 150 feet) with boldly projecting corner-towers and two twin-towered gatehouses in the east and west wall. In front of the western entrance is another large outwork in the form of an island called Hornwork (5), with a curtain wall, covering the western approach. All in all Caerphilly, with its concentric inner castle, its two great outworks and its water defense, is a formidable fortress.

could not support each other. That was solved by the introduction of flanking towers and concentric walls. The inner enclosure had the highest walls, dominating the outer lower walls around it. This enabled the inner, higher defenders to command, or fire over the heads of their comrades deployed on the outer lower enceinte, so creating sophisticated killing-grounds for the attackers. Thus both enceintes could be simultaneously in action, and a combined instead of successive defense faced assailants. The concentric castle was invented in the Middle East, and brought back to Western Europe by returning crusaders. One of the earliest examples of this new concentric design was Belvoir Castle, built north of Jerusalem in Galilee in the Jordan Valley in Palestine about 1168, and rebuilt in the 1170s by the Knights of the Hospital. It has been argued that the concentric design originated from the military/religious lifestyle; the interior courtyard (a sort of religious sanctuary) would have been restricted to the warrior-monks, and the outer courtyard would have been left for use by secular knights and mercenaries employed and hired by the brethrens. Alternatively it has been argued that the concentric design evolved in order to meet new developments in siege techniques used by the Muslims in Palestine. Other historians point out that the crusaders simply took on Byzantine military architecture, hence the similarities between the concentric castle and the fortifications of Constantinople, for example. Anyway, as we have just seen, the concentric design presented obvious military advantages.

One of the earliest concentric castles in Britain was Caerphilly, built in the 1270s by order of Gilbert de Clare, Earl of Gloucester.

Appearance

A castle had to be militarily strong, of course, but by the 13th century, attention was also paid to its appearance. Kings and lords of that period stressed that castles not only had to look impressive, but had to be beautiful as well. Walls, towers, and gatehouses had to be strong, thick and high, but buildings, particularly the great hall offered a degree of comfort that made a striking contrast with the gloomy early Norman keeps. Refinements became elaborate, with, for example, magnificent stairways rising up to the main doorway, tall and delicately carved chimneys rising above roofs and battlements, beautiful painting and decorations on the interior walls, tapestries and stands of arms adorning the stateroom, and banners hanging from finely carved windows. Towards the end of the 12th century leaded glass for windows became available, giving the builders opportunities to allow more light and air inside the building and create refined decorations. Engineering skill had greatly increased and builders had come to a proper understanding of the thrusts set up inside a structure based on arches, resulting in elegant vaulting in the inner chambers. Stonecutting was by then improved beyond all recognition, and alternating courses of stone, smooth ashlar and brick produced a striped effect and decorative patterns, which enhanced the beauty of the walls. Sculpture, too, had made enormous advances and capitals on top of elegant columns became deeply undercut with beautiful

Above: *Gothic decorations. Left: Window; Right: Capital on column.*

Opposite left: *Crossbow man.* The crossbow or arbalest, although known since antiquity, appeared as a weapon of war in Western Europe only in the late 11th century. It consisted of a short but strong bow mounted on a stock, with a groove cut along it to guide the quarrel or bolt (short arrow). A pivoting nut held by a trigger-catch kept the drawn string back. Various systems were invented to span it. The illustration shows the man using the leverage exerted with an iron crow's foot, which helped pull back the string of the powerful stave. The crossbow was slow to bend (a skilled arbalestier could shoot two bolts per minute) and thus had a slow rate of fire, but it was a powerful weapon capable of piercing a knight's body armor at a range between 150 and 200 yards. Held up and aimed very much like a rifle, the crossbow's compactness enabled it to be fired easily from behind defensive walls. The Church considered it too deadly a weapon and so repeatedly banned its use (in 1097, 1099 and 1139), but to no avail. Mercenary crossbowmen, usually from Gascony, France, were employed by the Plantagenet kings in most of the Welsh and Scottish campaigns. The crossbow continued to be employed as a weapon of war until the 16th century, when it was replaced with the matchlock musket.

Opposite right: *Gothic chimney.* This tall octagonal chimney still to be seen on the great hall of Grosmont Castle (Monmouthshire) rises from a delicately molded base and terminates in a truncated spirelet sumounted by a crown. The base of the spirelet is surrounded by a series of gablets, one for each side of the octagon, and beneath these are trefoiled lancet openings to allow the smoke to escape.

representations and elaborate stone patterns. Builders and artists were no longer, as the Normans were, so interested in mass and thickness, but liked to create a feeling of spaciousness by allowing the eye to travel past objects in the immediate foreground and glimpse possibilities of further spaces beyond. Inside the castle the internal layout was designed to emphasize the prestige, power and authority of the lord, to impress, ravish and subdue visitors. These remarkable achievements were eventually derisively termed "Gothic" by the classicists of the 18th century, implying barbarity. It is difficult to imagine a more inappropriate word with which to describe the great engineering feats of the Middle Ages, but the name has stuck, and, having lost all its original meaning, it is now used quite without any intention of disparagement.

Edwardian Castles

Edward I

The Romans, the Anglo-Saxons and the early Norman kings had never succeeded in submitting Wales and Scotland, but under the Plantagenets things went differently. The Norman conquest of 1066 had raised a double barrier of language and grievances between French Norman patricians and Saxon plebeians, between the rulers and the commoners, between the castle and the village. Gradually the Saxon peasants realized the worth of the Norman order and the Norman lords learned to respect the customs of the common Englishmen. On Edward I's accession the fusion of the two civilizations was almost complete and symbolized in the person of the king of England. The Plantagenet kings who preceded Edward I had ruled over large territories in France but only over a portion of the British island. To the north of England was the kingdom of Scotland, which was quite independent except for an occasional vague recognition on the part of its rulers of the English kings as their feudal superiors. To the west of the kingdom lay the mountainous district of Wales, inhabited by that remnant of the original native Britons whom no invaders had been able to conquer so far. For centuries border warfare had been carried on between the English and the Welsh. William the Conqueror had found it necessary to establish a chain of earldoms on the Welsh frontier, and Chester, Shrewsbury, and Monmouth became strong Norman outposts. While the raids of the Welsh constantly provoked the English kings to invade Wales, no permanent conquest was possible, for the enemy retreated into the mountains about Snowdon, a region unsuited for the use of cavalry. The long and successful resistance which the Welsh made against the English intruders must be attributed not only to their inaccessible retreats but also to their patriotic inspiration. The Welsh firmly believed that they would sometime reconquer the whole of England, which they had possessed before the coming of the Angles, Saxons and Normans.

Bearing the old Saxon name of the Confessor, Edward I (born 1239, reign from 1272 to 1307) was known in his lifetime as "Longshanks" because, at well over 6 feet tall (about 2 meters), he stood head and shoulders above most of his people. He was also known as "The Hammer of the Scots," a nickname he earned from his ruthless wars against William Wallace and Robert the Bruce. Edward was a pragmatic monarch and primarily a man of war who, before he came to the throne in 1272, had already gained a great experience of warfare, siege and fortification, both at home and abroad. Once he was king, Edward recovered the ground the Crown had lost during the troubles of his father's reign, and stopped the growth of the feudal hierarchy, hereby starting the slow decline of feudalism. Then he expounded English nationalism and was unashamedly expansionist in his outlooks. Edward I was determined to enforce English kings' claims to primacy in the British Isles, and his main objective was no longer to reconquer Normandy or rebuild the Angevin Empire, lost by John and Henry III, but to attempt to unify Britain by bringing first Wales and then Scotland to submission. Edward I succeeded in conquering Scotland temporarily and Wales permanently.

The turbulent princes of Wales, under their new leader Llywylyn, were defeated and brought to order in the first ten years of Edward's reign, but two campaigns were necessary before the Welsh finally succumbed. As a gesture of reconciliation the king's newborn son was proclaimed Prince of Wales, and the title has been held by successive heirs to the English throne ever since. By the Statute of Wales in 1284 English laws and customs were introduced into the principality, but Wales remained outside the kingdom proper. It was finally annexed to the English Crown in 1536 under the reign of Henry VIII.

The conquest of Scotland proved a far more difficult matter than that of Wales. The early history of the kingdom of Scotland is a complicated one. When the Angles and Saxons landed in Britain, a great part of the mountainous region north of the Firth of Forth was inhabited by a Celtic tribe, the Picts. There was, however, on the west coast a little kingdom of the Irish Celts, who were then called Scots. By the opening of the tenth century the Picts had accepted the king of the Scots as their ruler. As time went on the English kings found it to their advantage to grant to the Scottish rulers certain border districts, including the Lowlands, between the river Tweed and the Firth of Forth. This region was English in custom and speech, while the Celts in the Highlands spoke, and still speak, Gaelic.

The death of the last representative of the old line of Scot kings in 1290 was followed by the appearance of a number of claimants to the crown. In order to avoid civil war, Edward I was asked to decide who should be king. He agreed to make the decision on the condition that the one whom he selected should hold Scotland as a fief from the English king. This arrangement was adopted, and the crown was given to Robert Balliol. But Edward unwisely made demands upon the Scots, which aroused their anger, and their king renounced his homage to the king of England. The Scots, moreover, formed an alliance with Edward's enemy, Philip the Fair of France. Henceforth, in all the difficulties between England and France, the English kings always had to reckon with the disaffected Scots, who were glad to aid England's enemies. Edward marched in person against them and speedily put down what he regarded as

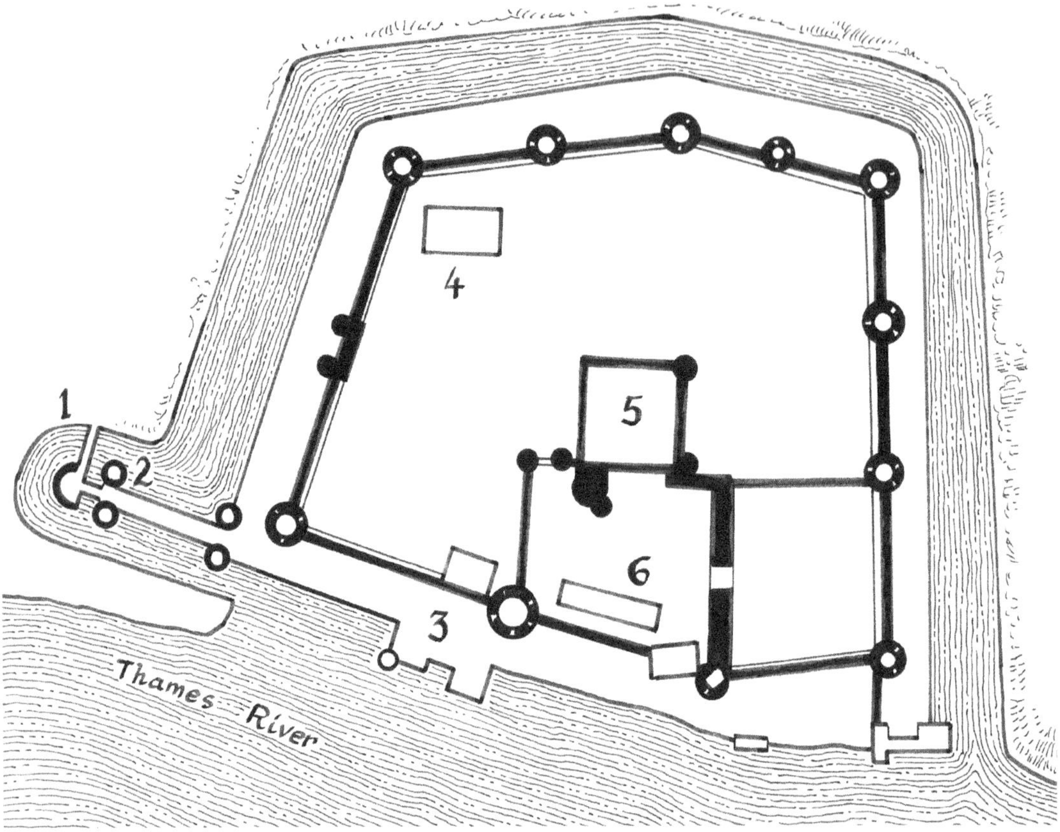

a rebellion. In spite of considerable success in 1296 and 1298, Edward I's attempt to assert his overlordship of the Scots was a failure and Scottish resistance continued under the leadership of Robert Bruce. Edward I died, old and worn out, in 1307, while on his way north to put down a rising under Bruce, and left the task of dealing with the Scots to his incompetent son, Edward II. The Scots acknowledged Bruce as their king and decisively defeated Edward II in the great battle of Bannockburn in June 1314, the most famous victory in Scottish history. Nevertheless, the English refused to acknowledge the independence of Scotland until forced to do so in 1328. It was much later, in 1707, that the kingdoms of England and Scotland were joined by the Acts of Union to form the Kingdom of Great Britain.

Apart from his achievements in strengthening the unity of what became Great Britain, Edward I was a powerful and effective lawgiver, a formidable administrator, and a remarkable castle-builder. It is hardly surprising that in later years his reign came to take on almost the quality of a golden age for British military architecture.

EDWARDIAN STRONGHOLDS IN WALES

Before becoming king, Edward had been a crusader, and without doubt he had learnt a lot about castle design during his campaigning in Palestine. Edward was a man of rapid action and decision, and during the Welsh campaign and right after having defeated the Welsh, he embarked on a very ambitious program of major projects in North Wales. In fact Edward, a genuine expert in fortification, inaugurated the largest scheme of castle building in the whole history of the English Crown. The program stretched over more than a quarter of a century, but it was concentrated in three main stages, corresponding with the campaigns of 1277, 1282–1283 and 1294–1295. Basically there were four groups of castles. The first were the existing royal border fortresses of Chester, Shrewsbury, Montgomery and St. Briavels, all of which were remodeled and strengthened. Second came three captured native castles,

Opposite top: *Plan of the Tower of London c. 1300. Edward I completed the defensive works begun by Henry III. Between 1275 and 1285 the king created England's largest and strongest castle, with multiple lines of defense. The work included building the existing Beauchamp Tower, but the main effort was concentrated on filling in Henry III's moat and creating an additional curtain wall on the western, northern and eastern sides, and surrounding it with a new moat. This new wall provided two new entrances, one from the land on the west, passing through the Middle and Byward Towers, and another from the river under St. Thomas's Tower. New royal lodgings were included in the upper part of St. Thomas's Tower. The plan shows the following. 1: Lion Tower; 2: Middle Tower; 3: Water Gate; 4: St. Peter ad Vincula Chapel; 5: Norman keep; 6: Great Hall.*

Opposite bottom: *The Loch Leven Castle, located on an island in Loch Leven in the Perth and Kinross region in Scotland, was built about 1275. It saw military action during the Wars of Scottish Independence (1296–1357). In the later 14th century the castle was granted to William Douglas, First Earl of Douglas, and remained in Douglas hands for the next 300 years. The castle was composed of a curtain wall, with service buildings, a four-story tower house, or keep, measuring 36.5 feet (11.1 m) by 31.5 feet (9.6 m), at one corner, and the projecting round Glassin Tower added to the southeast corner of the ancient curtain wall in the 16th century.*

Flint Castle, situated near Chester in Flintshire, on a small rocky platform dominating a strategically important ford across the River Dee, was the first castle built by Edward during his conquest of Wales. The site of Flint Castle was selected because it was about a day's march along the ancient Roman road from Chester, and because of its accessibility to seagoing ships. Beyond Flint, another day's journey away, lay Rhuddlan Castle. Like all the other new towns and castles built for Edward I in Wales during subsequent years, the accessibility of Flint by sea as well as land reduced the chances of a successful siege in time of war. Work started in July 1277. The castle took approximately eight years to complete, costing around six thousand pounds, but the donjon roof was not completed until 1302. In plan the castle is rectangular with one corner cut off. The inner ward measures 160 by 145 feet and is about half an acre in area. The castle has three three-quarters engaged towers and one separate tower at the corners. Flint Castle is indeed unique among other Edwardian castles. Although it reflected the changing pattern of 13th-century fortification, it also had, somewhat strangely for its date of 1277, a huge circular keep or donjon, which resembles the Tour de Constance at Aigues Mortes in Provence (France). During his journeying to the Crusades' and his sojourn in France before his accession to the throne, Edward had become acquainted with the deliberately planned towns and bastides of southern France and the Crusaders castles, and he resolved to adopt features of these fortifications in the plans for his fortresses to secure the suppression of Wales. The idea for the dungeon may have come from Master James of St. George. While forming part of the constructive scheme of the castle, the southeastern donjon is not fitted into the structure of the fortress, as are the towers at the other three corners of the quadrangle. It stands at the southeast corner, but a little outside it, the southern and eastern curtains avoiding it by a sweeping inward curve. The donjon tower was used as the residence for the constable of the castle. The tower was also used as the last means of defense should the castle come under siege. Entry to the castle was through a square tower (today in ruins) certainly completed before 1281, with a gateway and portcullis by way of a drawbridge across a ditch. This was originally about 20 feet deep, separated the south curtain wall and the southwest tower from the outer bailey, and would have also been filled by the tidal waters of the Dee. The gatehouse leads directly into an enclosure, the inner bailey. Within this enclosure were the domestic buildings, which included a hall, stables, a chapel, a kitchen, a well, latrines, a bake-house, a granary, a brew-house and the garrison quarters. At Flint Edward was founding not only a castle, but also a totally new town. English traders were encouraged to settle in the town, with at least at first this privilege denied the Welsh. Burgage plots in the town for new English settlers were being granted in February 1278, and by 1292, there were 74 such settlers or burgesses in Flint wealthy enough to be taxed. Both the castle and town at Flint went on to become a permanent fortified base. In 1301, Flint Castle passed to Edward of Caernarfon, Earl of Chester, who was later to become King Edward II. The illustration shows how the castle appears today.

Dolwyddelan, Criccieth and Bere, which were rebuilt. Third, there were new lordship castles built: Denbigh, Hawarden, Holt and Chirk. Finally, and most important, there were new royal castles constructed: Builth, Aberystwyth, Flint, Rhuddlan, Hope, Conwy, Harlech, Caernarvon and Beaumaris, which varied considerably in design and appearance.

An integral part of Edward's policy of control and pacification of the Welsh was the establishment of colonies of loyal citizens among his recalcitrant new subjects, and to this end several castles were provided with new fortified towns beside them. The reason for strong defensive walls becomes clear when one considers that Edward I not only imported builders and soldiers to construct and garrison his castles but also imported a whole population of English settlers to Wales. These new inhabitants were foreigners to the Welsh, and therefore had to be carefully protected from the

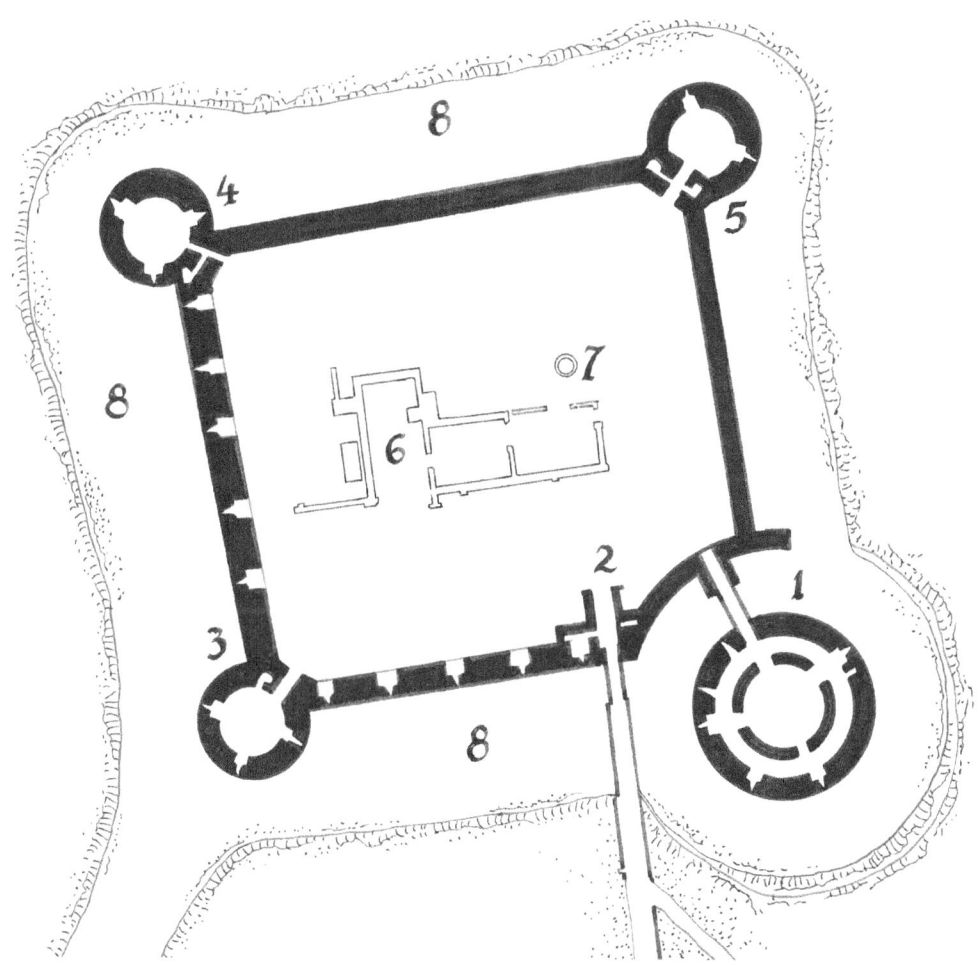

Plan of Flint Castle. 1: Southeast tower or donjon; 2: Gatehouse with drawbridge; 3: Southwest tower; 4: Northwest tower; 5: Northeast tower; 6: Bailey with (today ruined) service buildings; 7: Well; 8: Moat.

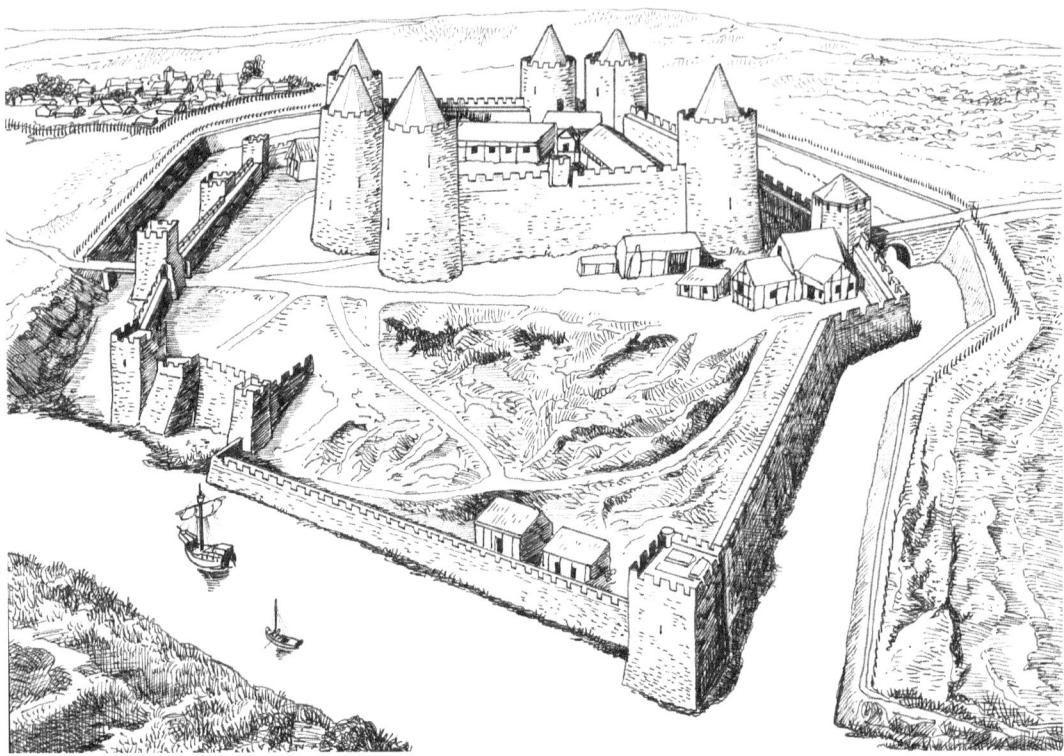

Rhuddlan. In 1277 Edward moved forward to Rhuddlan on the River Clwyd, where he brought about the surrender of the Welsh leader Llywelyn ap Gruffydd. There was already a timber motte-and-bailey castle there, and James of St. George was ordered to build a new fortress. Rhuddlan was of concentric plan with basically an inner curtain wall, surrounded by an outer enceinte, a ditch, and an outer palisade. However the relatively low and weak outer curtain was not really related to the core of the fortress, and one does not see here the complete integration of the defense which is so impressively evident in the later castles of this period. The inner ward or bailey (measuring approx. 150 by 130 feet) is diamond shaped, and accommodated timber service buildings. Its wall, about 9 feet thick and 35 feet high, had an uninterrupted wallwalk with crenelled parapet, and was reinforced with six circular towers, four of which form two twin-towered gatehouses at opposite corners. These towers are 40 feet in diameter and were about 50 feet high, divided into four stories. The curtain wall of the outer bailey was lower and reinforced with square towers. It also comprised two gatehouses and a small port on the canalized River Clwyd two miles distant from the sea. The ditch, nearly 50 feet wide and about 15 feet deep, was revetted in stone. On the counterscarp there was a palisade forming a sort of covered way. To the northwest of the new castle was a newly created town, defended by an earth-and-timber rampart and palisade, to which English settlers were attracted by low rentals and fiscal privileges. The town, surprisingly—for Edward had real plans for Rhuddlan—was never walled in stone. By 1283 Rhuddlan Castle and town were nearing completion. Today Rhuddlan Castle is in ruins because it was taken by Parliamentary forces after a siege in 1646 during the English Civil War (1642–1651). The fortress was then partially demolished to prevent any further use in 1648. It is now managed by Cadw.

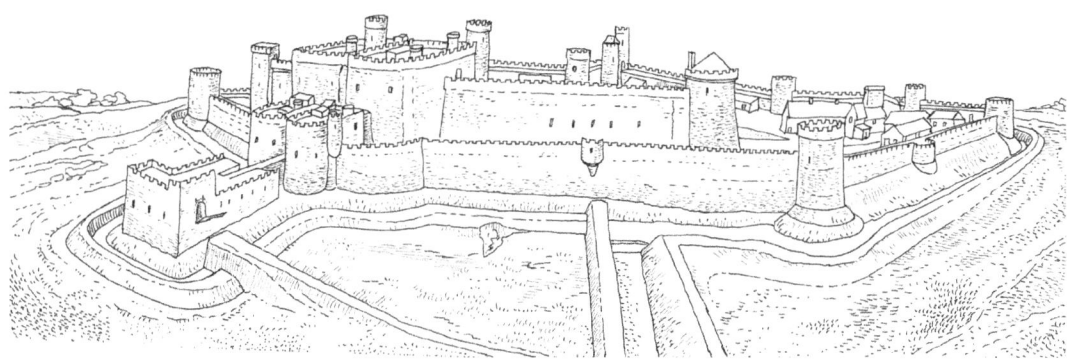

Aberystwyth Castle (conjectured reconstruction). Located in Aberystwyth, Ceredigion, Wales, this castle was begun in 1277 together with Flint and Rhuddlan. Aberystwyth Castle was a particularly taxing job. It still was not completed by 1282, when the Welsh briefly captured and burned it. Construction was finally completed in 1289 at great expense to the Crown. The castle was subjected to a lengthy siege during the revolt of Madog ap Llywelyn in 1294–1295. Aberystwyth Castle presented many similarities with Rhuddlan. It was built as a lozenge (diamond-shaped) concentric fortress, with strong gatehouses, mural and corner towers. Of the Edwarian strongholds established in Wales, Aberystwyth Castle has fared least favorably. Now little more than a few fragmented chunks of coursed rubble masonry (remains of the inner and middle walls) overlooking the Cardigan Bay are displayed in a well-kept public park. The current state of the castle is due to the order by Oliver Cromwell for it to be dismantled in 1649, combined with the use of it as a convenient supply of stone for the construction of other buildings in the town. The illustration shows how the castle might have looked in the 13th century.

local population by the castle and town walls. In a sense the Welsh boroughs were outposts of England within hostile enemy territory. The eventual result was a ring of castles around North Wales which hemmed it on three sides, and which could all be supplied and reinforced by sea, and were not, therefore, dependent on land communication through potentially hostile territory. Most of these settlements had a maritime trade–based economy. Some new boroughs in Wales like Flint and Caernarvon had a grid-plan of streets. Far removed from the sort of organic, meandering and chaotic street plans generally associated with medieval cities, the regular grid-plan allowed entire blocks of buildings to be dedicated to a specific use, but it also enabled troops to move quickly through the broad streets when sections of the urban walls were threatened with attack.

As ever, building castles and boroughs required vast resources of materials and manpower. Owing to impeccable bookkeeping and accounting we know a great deal about the day-to-day progress in building these royal fortresses. Every detail of materials and their cost is noted, as well as wages, carriage charges, methods of transport, ports of origin and the names of the men who designed, built, hewed and carved. Many trades were involved, including *cementarii* (bankers), *cubitores* (layers), *batrarii* (dressers), *fauconarii* (mortar makers and carriers), *hottarii* (sand throwers, water carriers, and hodmen), *portatores cuierum* (barrow men), *fossatores* (diggers), They also included smiths who sharpened tools and made nails, door hinges, latches and bolts; carpenters who provided and worked the huge amount of timber necessary for scaffolding, floorboards, beams, joists, ceilings, bridges, and doors; plumbers who inserted piping, made cisterns and placed lead on the roofs; as well as carters, and watchmen to control laborers. Edward's castles were for the most part designed by an architect named James of Saint George. In 1278, King Edward had brought over

Conwy Castle. Conwy along with Harlech is a masterpiece, and here one can only applaud in astonishment at the grandeur, power, and drama of this perfect harmony of disparate forms and textures, the smooth round towers and walls set against sharply pointed rocks with the flowing river nearby. Although 19th-century architects did their best in keeping with the adjacent medieval grandeur, the site has been disfigured by the construction of the Telford suspension bridge in 1826 and the tubular railway bridge in 1847. None-the-less Conwy Castle and walled town still survive magnificently, one of the most impressive of all the Welsh Edwardian realizations. Designed by Edward I's master castle builder James of St. George, Conwy was sited on a long narrow crag to command the important river crossing of the Conwy. Its catapult and trebuchet artillery could interdict hostile traffic on the river's estuary. Construction began in March 1283 and, at its height, occupied around 1,500 workmen. The walled town that was created at the foot of the castle formed a blunt triangle. Five years later, castle and town walls were complete. The castle has eight great towers (each 70 feet high), all of which are intact. These towers are connected by walls forming a rectangle, as opposed to the concentric layouts of other Edwardian castles in Wales. Conwy was intended to impress the Welsh and all exterior wall surfaces were originally rendered and whitened, creating an effect far more striking than can be seen today. The castle dominates the landscape, immediately conveying its sense of strength to the observer. Later the castle gradually deteriorated and was sold in 1624 to the Viscount of Conwy for just £100. Conwy Castle saw its last military action during the English Civil War. Cromwell's Parliamentary army besieged the castle for three months in 1646 before the defenders capitulated. After the restoration of the monarchy the Earl of Conwy took ownership of the castle. The Earl unfortunately used his position to strip the castle of iron, timber, and lead for building, leaving Conwy open to centuries of disintegration and neglect. The castle is, however, remarkably well preserved.

to England a team of master masons from Savoy, on the French border with Switzerland and Italy. Having carried out tours of inspection of other royal works in Wales, Master James appears at the head of the masons' payroll at Flint in November 1280. James of St. George was assisted by other Savoyard master-masons, notably Jean Francis, Jules de Chalons, Guillaume de Seyssel and Pierre de Boulogne. English architects included Richard of Chester, Roger of Cockersand, John of Sherwood, and Robert of Frankby. To these men who had developed their own style, the appearance of the Norman castle, with its irregular bailey and its keep on a mound in one corner, was haphazard and untidy. During the Crusades in Palestine the king and his

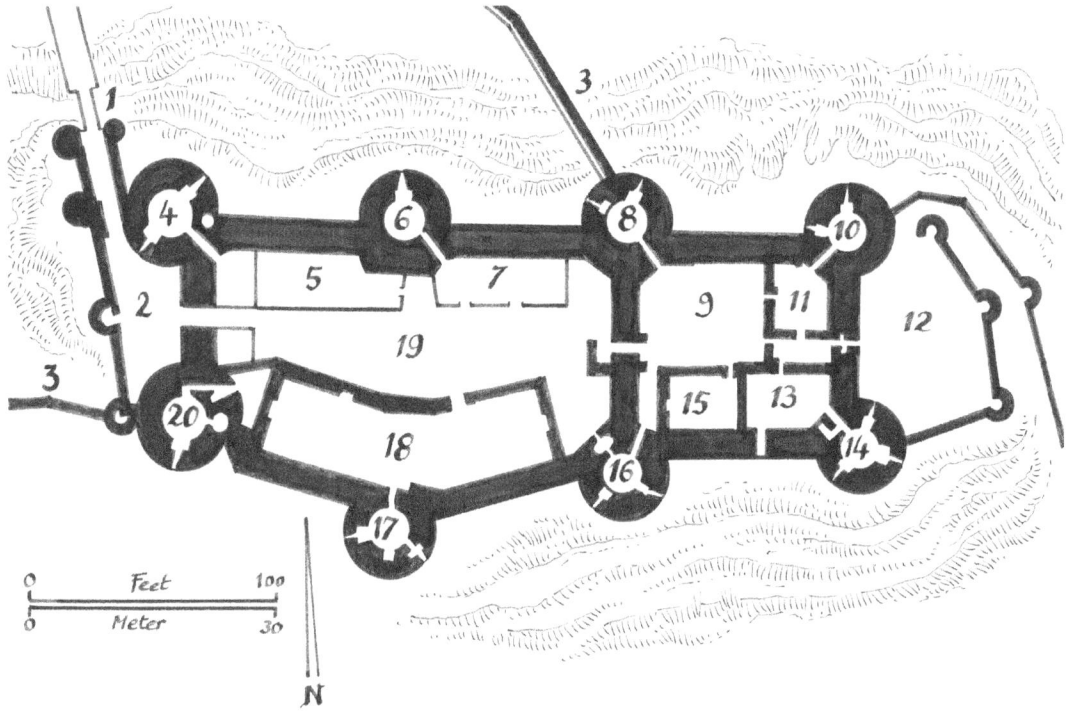

Plan of Conwy Castle. On the site of Conwy Master James of St. George had no option but to abandon the concentric layout. The long north side is straight, with four round towers, boldly projecting, each 40 feet in diameter and spaced at intervals of 55 feet. The southern side too has four similar towers, but the wall has a strong outward angle due to the natural crag. Each of the drum towers, were self-contained defensive work. The inner ward is a quadrilateral measuring 100 by 95 feet. Conwy (and Caernavon also) are sometimes described as "processional" castles in design since the visitor entering from the west gate, would travel up the ramp, over the drawbridge, through the west barbican, then through the outer ward, the inner ward, and the east barbican, effectively traversing all the castle. The inner ward contains the royal apartments built for Edward and Queen Eleanor in 1283. These apartments originally rose above heated basements, but the floors are no longer intact. The plan shows the following features. 1: Drawbridge and gateway; 2: West barbican; 3: Town walls; 4: Northwest tower; 5: Kitchen; 6: Kitchen tower; 7: Stables; 8: Stockhouse tower; 9: Inner ward; 10: Chapel tower; 11: Quarters; 12: East barbican; 13: King's apartment; 14: King's tower; 15: King's hall; 16: Bakehouse tower; 17: Prison tower; 18: Great hall; 19: Outer ward; 20: Southwest tower.

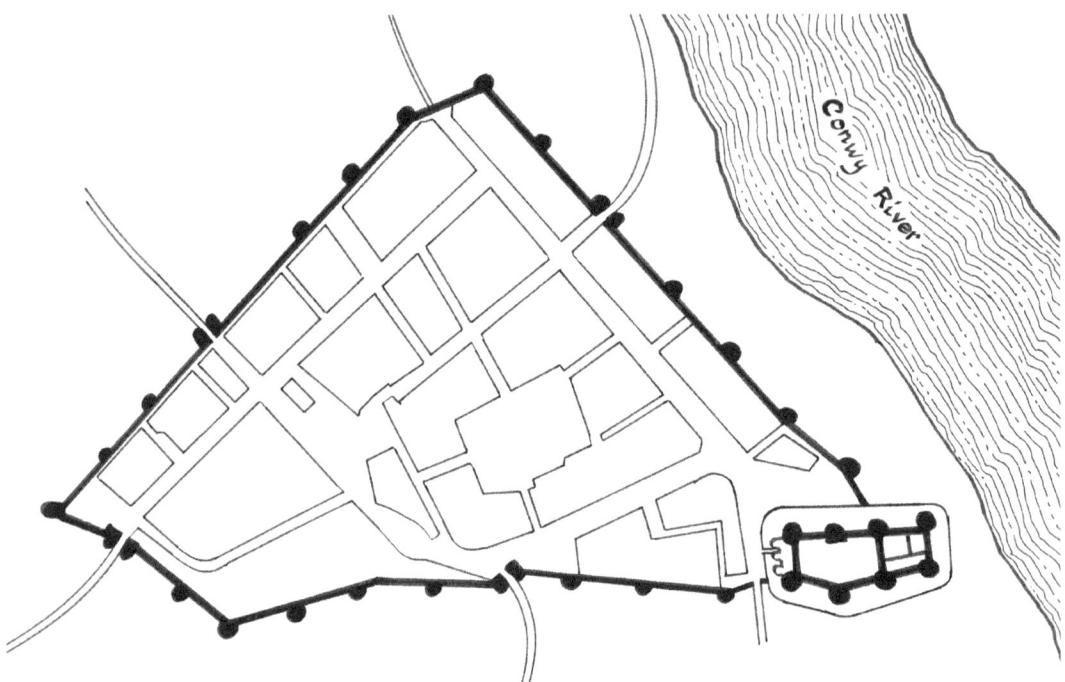

The town of Conwy is surrounded by a well-preserved wall lending an additional sense of strength to the site. Construction of Conwy began in 1283–1289. The circuit of the wall is three-quarters of a mile in length, with 21 towers at regular intervals of about 46 m. The wall is 1.68 m thick and 9 m high, with towers rising to 15 m. Externally it presented a continuous stone face, but the towers were open-backed, the wallwalk maintained across them by a series of removable wooden bridges. This ensured that each section, with its independent stair to ground level, could be isolated if it was attacked and scaled. At wallwalk level, each tower had a floor (set back from the bridge) which gave access to the lower arrowslits and to a stair to the battlements. Conwy city was the nearest equivalent to a North Welsh capital, notably because it contained a monastry which had the status of a national church like Westminster Abbey.

master-builders had gained valuable experience and rediscovered symmetry as a possible planning principle for castles— rediscovered, because Roman military architecture had known it long before them. They indeed ventured to make some castles (e.g., Harlech and Beaumaris) completely symmetrical concentric configurations. The effect of this daring of conception was one of overwhelming majesty, grandeur, and some of the most consummate masterpieces of European military architecture. In fact British Edwardian castles were probably the most forward, the most important and the most inspired in Europe. In spite of their size and cost Edward's castles were built with extreme rapidity. For example Flint was built in eight and a half years (1277–1286); Harlech took seven and a half years (1283–1290); Conwy five years (1283–1287); and Rhuddlan four and a half (1277–1282). There is, of course, no such thing as a typical or standardized Edwardian castle, Flint being totally different from Harlech, for example. In fact each Edwardian castle is unique and has its own specificity, which gives it its own beauty and distinctive charm. Some castles built in Wales, however, have certain common features that made them extremely powerful but also extremely expensive. Broadly speaking, these common features included: replacement of the keep with a rectangular or polygonal curtain; multiple walls; numerous towers; concentric circles of masonry to give strength to walls and towers; round, rather than square, towers; extensive interiors (as the castles were intended as royal residences as well); access to sea or waterway; single or multiple gatehouses always powerfully defended; and difficult locations, such as hilltops.

Edward I was keenly aware of the high cost involved — the later years of his reign were chilled by financial troubles — but he continued to build castles. Even when short of money, he went on with his plan, risking confrontation with vassals and taxpayers over the bill. To him, the benefit of permanent walls outweighed the cost. This was based on a very important consideration: the multiplicity of goals met by building castles. The castle was anything but a stone ring within which to hide from conflict. The castle dominated the landscape, figuratively and literally.

Postern at Conwy Castle. The importance of Conwy Castle from an architectural standpoint is borne out by the fact that it has been named a World Heritage listed site.

The Edwardian castles accommodated infantry and cavalry forces in order to enforce peace and crush any sedition. They were intended to serve as bases from which royal officers could collect taxes, gather intelligence about possible rebellion, and arrest suspects before they actually struck. Edward's castles were impressive symbols of the Plantagenet-Angevin domination; they reminded patriotic Welshmen of defeat and challenged them to overthrow it. For the English they were thus strongholds for the pacification of Wales, but for the Welsh they were citadels of oppression and occupation. Each castle was built no more than a day's march from its nearest neighbor, and they were also located where they could be easily supplied. The castles were indeed supply storeplaces, advanced headquarters, observation posts in troubled areas, and homes of loyal lords secure from attacks by enemies. Royal castles could in times of emergency act as havens for the king's field army, or supply the men to raise a new army if the field army was defeated. Castles were not only places of military power and refuge, but also centers of administration. This multiplicity of roles helps explain why castles were the main bones of contention and focal points of struggle. As a center of government and war in a warlike age, the castle was also a symbol. The great royal castles of Wales were more than Edward I's way of controlling the Welsh; they were a way of reminding the Welsh that he was there. Evidence suggests that Edward understood this perfectly well. External architecture was used as a means of impressing the people, such as at Caernarvon. Good locations were exploited without regard to expense, such as at Conwy, where the castle overlooks the town. In especially vulnerable locations, such as Beaumaris on remote

Caernarfon, located in Gwynedd, at the mouth of the Seiont River, was begun at the same time as Conwy in 1283. It was not completed for 50 years, indeed, it never was totally completed. It is ironic that this most ambitious of Edward's building conceptions should have suffered from the financial troubles which chilled the later years of his reign. Designed by the omnipresent James of St. George, it is very much the same sort of castle, including a high curtain wall reinforced by a series of massive polygonal towers and a twin-towered gatehouse, subdivided into inner and outer wards by a central building. Mighty Caernarfon, with its unique polygonal towers, intimidating battlements and color-banded masonry, is possibly the most famous of Wales's castles. Its sheer scale and commanding presence easily set it apart from the rest and, to this day, still trumpet in no uncertain terms the intention of Edward I, as it was constructed not only as a military stronghold but also as a seat of government, an administrative center and a royal residence. The castle's majestic persona, and grandiose ceremonial quality is no architectural accident. It was designed to echo the Theodosian walls of Constantinople, the imperial power of Rome, and Edward was not a man to miss an opportunity to tighten his grip even further on the native population. Caernarfon's symbolic status was emphasized when the king made sure that his son, the first English prince of Wales, was born here in 1284. In 1969 the investiture of the current Prince of Wales, HRH Prince Charles took place here. After all these years Caernarfon's immense strength remains unchanged and it still dominates the walled town also founded by Edward I. Caernarfon's position of pre-eminence is recognized in its status as a World Heritage inscribed site.

Anglesey, Edward's engineers incorporated every possible feature—double walls, moat, access to the sea, a profusion of towers—that could add to its strength. Edward's castles frequently included huge round towers that were doubly advantageous because they were harder to assault and gave the castle an especially imposing visage. This method of building was expensive because for structural reasons the walls consisted of multiple layers of materials, as erosion and age now reveal. The appearance of the castles was more than a matter of aesthetics or ego. As is shown by the elaborate and complicated interiors, these buildings were also the residences of high officials—and sometimes the monarch himself. The castle was wasted expense if it were mere vanity, but sensible expenditure if viewed from the perspective of occupation politics. For the expansion-minded magnate the castle was the best, perhaps only, means of laying permanent claim to disputed, threatened, or rebellious land.

Edward I took a personal interest in castle building, and did not disdain to make use of and repair and develop the Welsh castles captured in the campaign (e.g., Carreg Cennen, Criccieth, Castell-y-Bere). How much rebuilding, alteration and

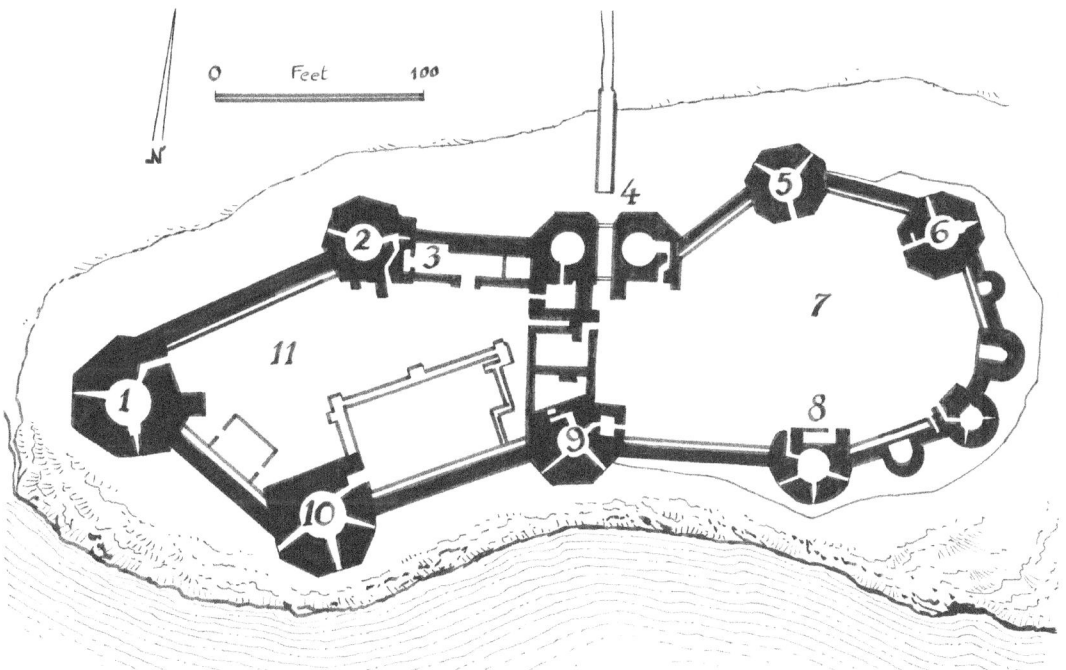

Plan of Caernarfon Castle. Not all Edwardian castles were concentric and symmetrical in plan. Caernarvon was a single vast enclosure of towered curtain wall, the outline of which was dictated by the rocky promontory on which it was built. Like Conwy, Caernarfon merged with the town walls constructed at the same time, and castle and town display what are clearly the most magnificent examples of medieval military architecture extant in Britain. The large enclosure measures 550 feet from east to west, and was protected by a moat on the north and east sides, and by the River Seiont on the south and west. The plan shows the following features. 1: Eagle Tower; 2: Well Tower; 3: Kitchen; 4: King's gate; 5: Granary Tower; 6: Northeast tower; 7: Inner ward; 8: Black Tower; 9: Chamberlain Tower; 10: Queen's Tower; 11: Outer ward.

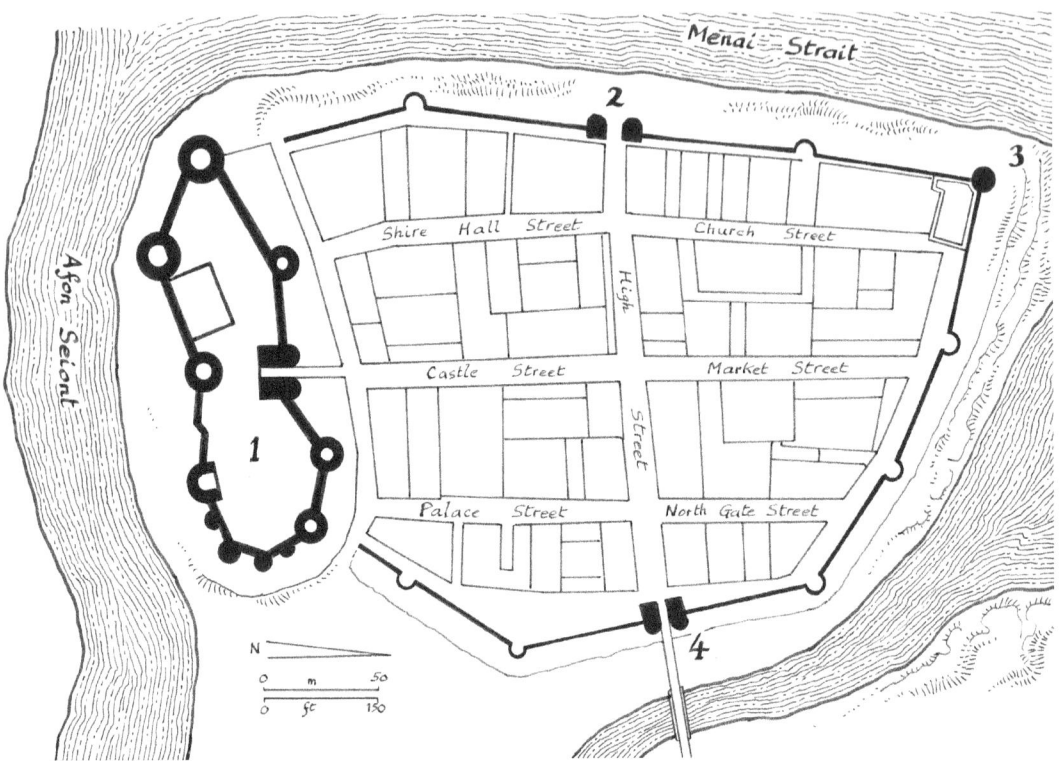

Caernarfon City and Castle. 1: Castle; 2: West Gate; 3: St. Mary's Chapel; 4: East Gate.

refurbishing on original Welsh castles was carried out by Edward's designers has been hotly debated. Castles of the native Welsh princes are amongst the least known and least appreciated of the castles of Wales. Yet they are every bit as significant as those of the Norman and Angevin periods, when monumental stone fortresses were erected to subdue and intimidate the Welsh populace. Welsh castles had both similarities to and distinct differences from their Norman/Plantagenet counterparts. They were often of irregular plan (e.g., Criccieth, Ewloe, Carndochan, Castell-y-Bere) in order to fit the terrain, curtain walls were rather low, and designers tended to flanking towers and elaborate gatehouses. However, their function was less one of aggrandizement of the lord and the result of subjugation of a people than as strongholds for an indigenous lord, inside which he protected his subjects in times of attack. Welsh castles tended to be simpler structures than the English ones, due primarily to the relative lack of funding available to a Welsh prince, particularly in comparison to the Norman-Plantagenet lords who could afford to hire the most skilled and experienced master masons from France. Welsh castles served their purpose, though, and valiantly defied the sovereignty of the English interlopers. Not all captured Welsh castles were reused and rebuilt though, since their strategical importance was often eclipsed by new modern English fortresses.

Eagle Tower, Caernarfon Castle. The Byzantine-looking Caernarfon castle presents us with a further peculiarity in that it possesses, alongside a keep-gatehouse in the most up-to-date style, an archaic survivor in the form of a donjon, the splendid Eagle Tower, which was crowned by three turrets, built at the extreme opposite end of the outer ward.

Harlech Castle. With Harlech and Beaumaris, the concentric symmetrical fortress appears in its perfected form. Harlech Castle, located in Gwynedd, is constructed atop a cliff close to the Irish Sea. It was built between 1283 and 1290, and like many of the castles in the area, it was designed by Master James of St. George, who was appointed constable of Harlech and held the post until 1293. At first sight Harlech Castle has a deceptive appearance of simplicity, but architecturally it is a highly sophisticated fortress. It is particularly notable for its massive gatehouse and concentric layout, with one line of defenses enclosed by another. The outer wall, defended by a 60-feet-wide rock-cut ditch, echoes the inner high wall outline and is set quite close to it. The outer wall was much lower than the mighty inner walls, and had no towers defending it besides the small gatehouse. The inner ward is rectangular (145 by 180 feet), with a large round tower at each corner. The domestic buildings, including the great hall, kitchen, buttery, bake-house, granary and others, are built against the inside of the inner walls. Since the surrounding cliffs made it practically impossible to attack the castle except from the east, this side is faced by the imposing gatehouse. The gateway is flanked by two massive D-shaped towers, and defended by a series of doors, portcullises and murder-holes. Harlech is also notable for its accessiblity from the sea. Edward's forces were often in danger from land-based attack, but the English enjoyed total supremacy on water. Many castles included sally ports which allowed resupply from the sea, but Harlech's is far more elaborate. Here, a fortified stairway hugs the rock and runs almost 200 feet (61 m) down to the foot of the cliffs, where (at the time of construction) the sea reached. Today, the sea has retreated several miles, making it more difficult to envisage the concept in its original setting. In addition there were two platforms established on the hillside where hurling machines could be placed to give cover to supply parties climbing the stairs. James of St. George's plan was a triumph; when the castle was besieged during Madoc ap Llywelyn's rebellion in 1294, this stairway helped the defenders survive until the siege was lifted. Like many of Edward's castles, Harlech was originally designed to be attached to a fortified town. In 1404, the castle fell to Owain Glyndŵr after a long siege in which starvation reduced the determined and fearful garrison to just 21 men. Even the strongest fortress is impotent in these circumstances, and mighty Harlech was no exception. Harlech became Owain's residence and military headquarters for four years. In 1409 Harlech Castle was retaken by Prince Henry (later Henry V) and a force of 1,000 men under John Talbot. In the Wars of the Roses in the first part of Edward IV's reign (1461–1470), Harlech was held by its Welsh constable Dafydd ap Ieuan as a Lancastrian stronghold. In 1468 it was the last Lancastrian fortress to surrender after a seven-year siege through its being provisioned from the sea. This was the longest known siege in the history of the British Isles.

5. Early Plantagenet Fortifications 1154–1327   219

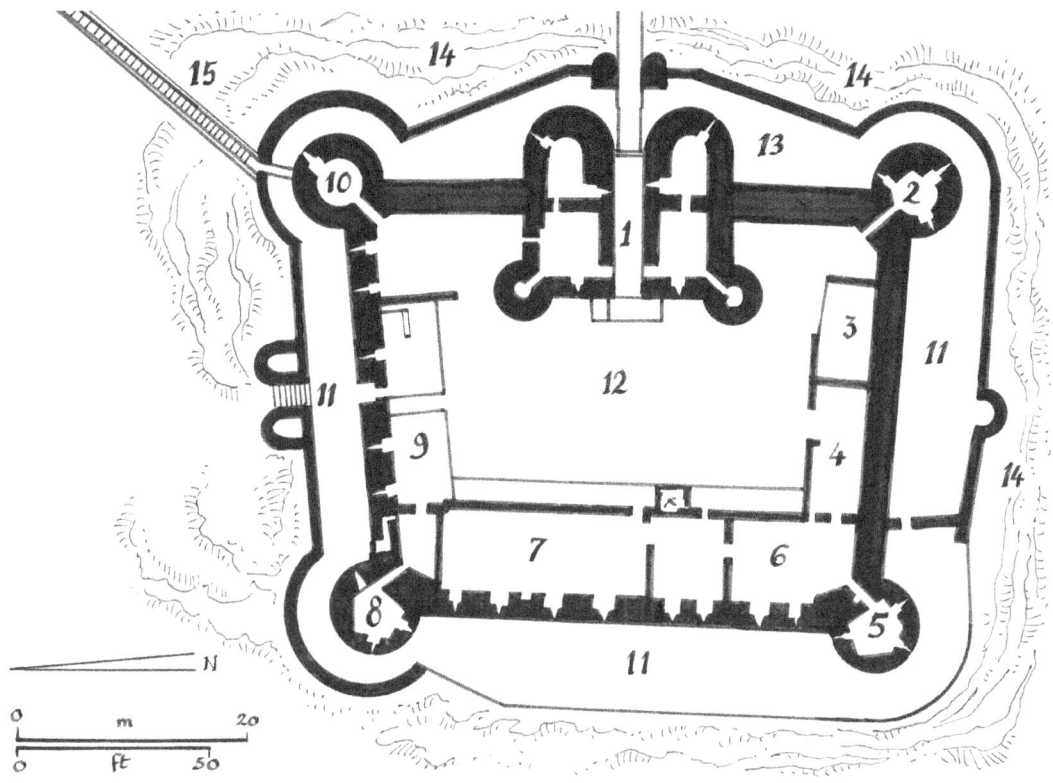

Above: *Plan of Harlech.* 1: Keep-Gatehouse; 2: Garden Tower (also named Southeast or Mortimer Tower); 3: Cellar and Granary; 4: Styngwerne Hall; 5: Westhercock Tower (Southwest or Bronwen Tower); 6: Kitchen, pantery and buteary; 7: Great Hall; 8: Chapel Tower or Northwest Tower; 9: Chapel; 10: Prison Tower (Northeast or Debtors' Tower); 11: Outer ward; 12: Inner ward; 13: Barbican; 14: Ditch; 15: Stairway to port.

Right: *Entrance to Harlech Castle.* The gatehouse was defended by a small barbican with two turrets. Today Harlech is in a remarkable state of preservation, in the care of Cadw and open to visitors.

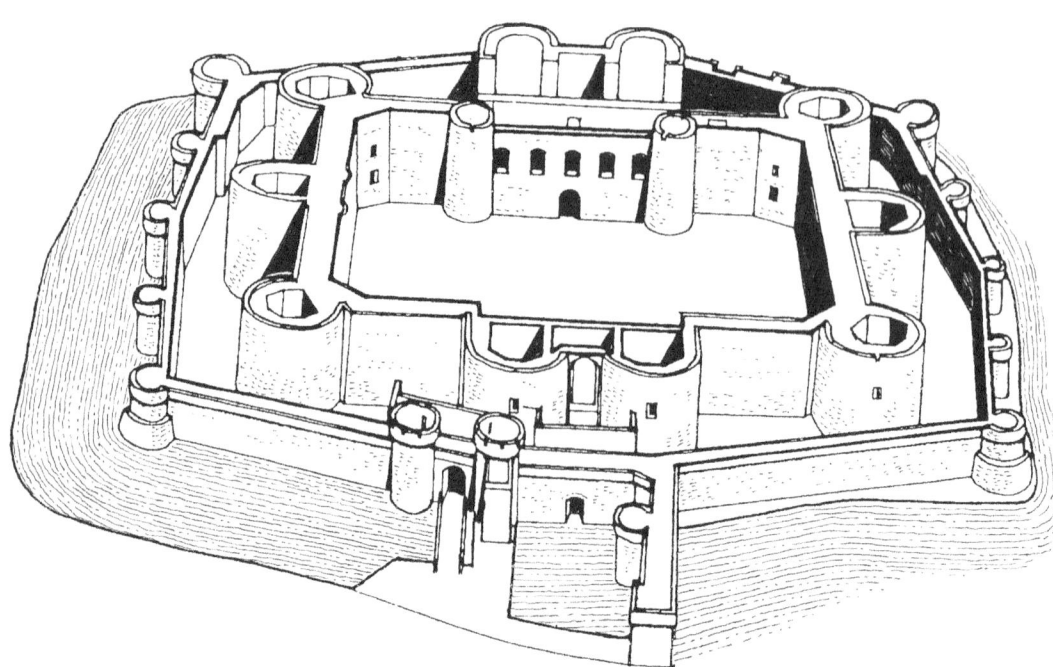

Beaumaris Castle on the Island of Anglesey is one of Edward's greatest masterpieces. It was built to palatial standards with five separate suites of noble lodgings, presumably for the king, the queen, the heir-apparent and his consort, and the constable (or viceroy), and its military function was to secure the northern end of the Menai Strait. Begun in 1295, it was also the last of Edward's castles. The castle was never finished, as money and supplies ran out before the fortifications reached their full height. The capture of the incomplete Caernarvon Castle at the southern end of the strait by the rebellious Welsh in 1294 must have enraged the English beyond measure, and the fact that the rebels were able to hold it for six months shows how serious the position must have been. Anglesey Island was overrun at that time and so when Edward had re-established his authority, the castle at Beaumaris was begun and an extraordinary concentration of laborers and materials went into it. Work started in 1295, came to a stop in 1300, was not resumed in a continuous way until 1306 and then went slowly on throughout the 1320s. Edward I died in 1307 and James of St. George in 1309, so the king and his architect did not live to see their masterpiece completed. In fact Beaumaris was never finished, gatehouses and towers were left incomplete and roofless and by 1341 the state of the castle was probably not very different from what it is today. Beaumaris is nonetheless an awesome sight, regarded by many as the finest of all the great Edwardian castles in Wales. The king's military architect, the brilliant James of St. George, brought all his experience and inspiration to bear when designing this castle—the biggest, most ambitious, and last venture he ever undertook. In pure architectural terms Beaumaris, the most technically perfect castle in Britain, has few equals. Its ingenious and perfectly symmetrical concentric "walls within walls" design was state of the art for the late 13th century. The castle was surrounded by a water-filled moat whose level was regulated by a sluice. Today Beaumaris is landlocked, but when it was constructed it was next to the sea and the gate next-the-sea entrance protected the tidal dock which allowed supply ships to sail right up to the castle. Beaumaris Castle stands at one end of Castle Street, inextricably linked with the history of the town. This was the "beau marais" (fair marsh) that Edward chose for a castle and garrison town. No wonder the fascinating and outstanding Beaumaris is now a World Heritage listed site.

Top: *Plan of Beaumaris Castle.* Beaumaris was remarkable for its symmetrical design, including a quadrangular inner ward (1) measuring 190 by 180 feet; walls 16 feet thick reinforced with round towers (2) at each corner, 42 feet in diameter and 60 feet apart; midway on the flanks two large D-shaped towers (3); two enormously compact keep-gatehouses (4) in the front and rear, which resemble those at Harlech but on a larger scale; and a low multiangular outer wall (5) garnished with no less than twelve small towers, two minor gatehouses (6) and a spur-work guarding the dock. The castle's overall symmetry of design did not mean that pedantry could obscure the facts of war. Indeed Beaumaris was also remarkable for its internal communication. There was free circulation to all combat sections not only via the wallwalk on top of the walls but also via a mural passage installed in the thickness of the walls that connected all the towers and both the keep-gatehouses. The designers obviously abandoned the theory of piecemeal defense in favor of flexibility allowing the garrison to move quickly from one point to another as all combat posts were closely related in the concentrated fortress.

Bottom: *Tower at Beaumaris Castle.*

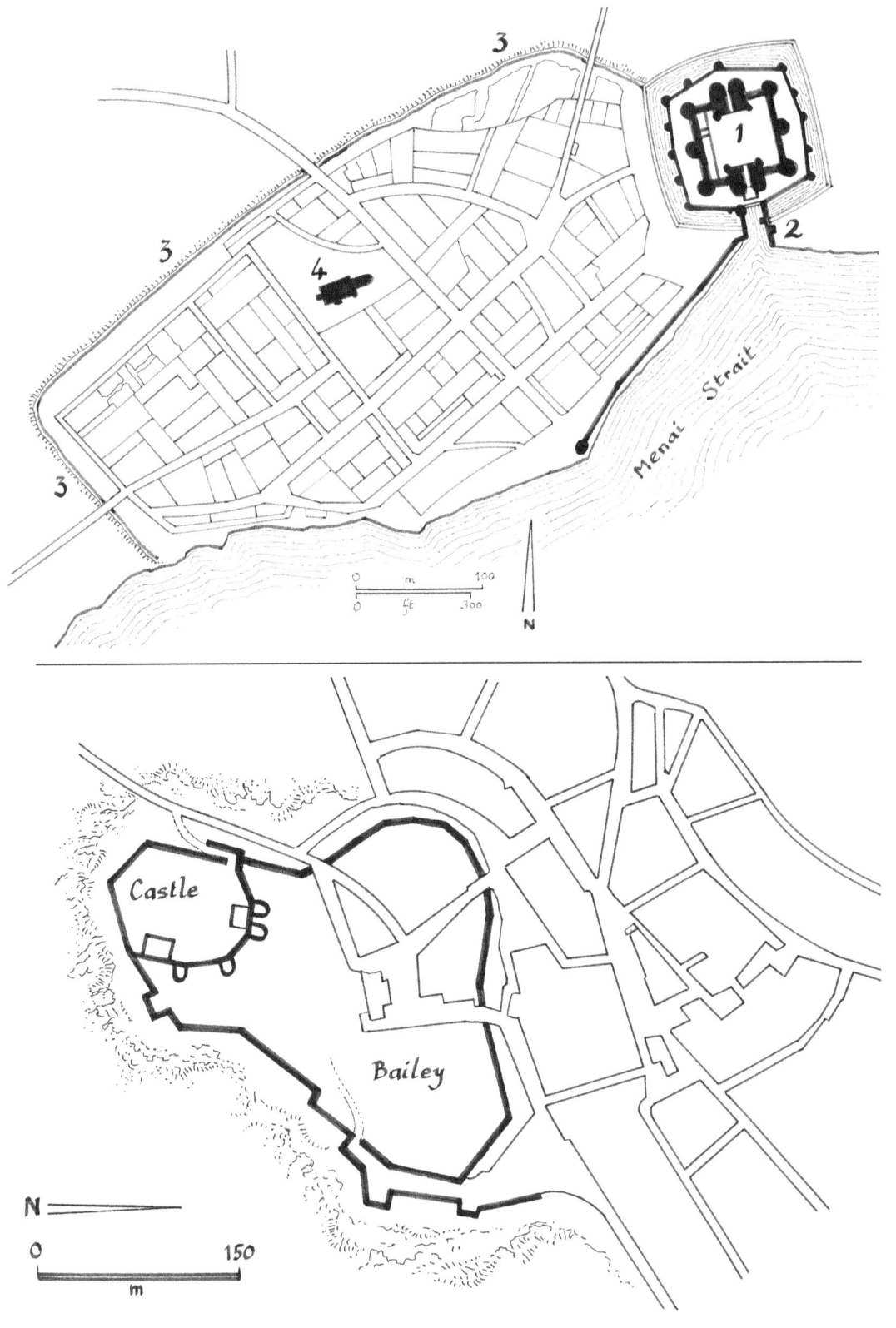

Above: *Denbigh gatehouse is now in ruins, but in the 13th century, as the conjectured reconstruction attempts to show, it was a powerful, self-contained fortress with a vaulted octagonal central hall, reminiscent of Caernavon in the excellent quality of its masonry and pentagonal shaping. It included a triangle of towers, an entrance passage with a drawbridge worked with counterweight, two sets of doors, arrow loops, murder-holes and two portculliess. Denbigh gatehouse, transformed into the equivalent of a keep, illustrates the characteristic of the period. At Denbigh it becomes apparent that the designing of castles had risen to a quasi-scientific level with prodigious strength and complexity.*

Opposite top: *Beaumaris Castle and Town. 1: Castle; 2: Port; 3: Ditch enclosing the town; 4: Church of St. Mary and St. Nicholas.*

Opposite bottom: *Denbigh. The king was not alone in building castles in Wales. Baronial fortifications were also constructed or repaired by powerful marcher lords, for example Denbigh. Although not an integral part of Edward's system for North Wales, Denbigh belongs to the period and displays interesting features, notably the octagonal towers and the gatehouse, which recall Caernarvon. Denbigh Castle (in Welsh Castell Dinbych) stands on a dramatic site, a rocky promontory rising high above the surrounding undulating landscape, and it dominates the Welsh market town of Denbigh, Denbighshire. Built upon an earlier Welsh stronghold, it was created by Henry de Lacy, a commander of the first Welsh expedition and Earl of Lincoln, with the active support of Edward I and under the supervision of Master James of St. George. Town and castle were treated as one unit, and constructed in two phases. First in 1280, the town walls and D-shaped mural towers were built but work was interrupted by the desperate Welsh revolt of 1294. After a short occupation by the insurgents, the English re-captured the site and work was resumed. In the second phase a great gatehouse was erected and the castle inner ward's curtain wall was refortified with thicker and higher walls. During the same period, the town walls were finished (about 1305) and the eastern section was defended by several large D-shaped towers. In the 1290s, Edward I had issued a Royal Charter as the market town of Denbigh had rapidly expanded beyond the town walls and its borough boundaries. After the Welsh attack in 1294, the town, originally confined to the castle's bailey, moved to a more spacious—also less protected—site outside. Improvement work continued well into the 14th century. In 1660 the castle was abandoned and left to fall into decay.*

Above: *Castell-y-Bere (conjectured reconstruction). One Welsh castle sometimes overlooked by visitors is Castell-y-Bere, once an impressive fortress built by Llywelyn ap Iorwerth, also known as Llywelyn the Great, Prince of Gwynedd, in the early 13th century. Embedded in the arms of the darkly foreboding, starkly greenish-gray landscape formed by rugged Cadair Idris and its mountainous cohorts near Abergynolwyn some 10 miles southwest of Dolgellau, the greatly ruined Castell-y-Bere now lies isolated from the major communication routes across Wales, atop a steep-sided, flat-topped rock, perfectly situated to stand guard over the surrounding valley floor. Captured and strengthened by Edward I, Castell-y-Bere's irregular elongated walls follow the contour of the hill, along with four main towers and two gatehouses. The illustration shows how Castell-y-Bere might have appeared at the end of the 13th century.*

Opposite: *The site of Carreg Cennen Castle (conjectured reconstruction), situated north of Swansea, one mile northeast of Trapp, just four miles from Llandeilo in Carmarthenshire, on the western fringe of Brecon Beacons National Park, South Wales, was occupied in the Iron Age and during Roman times. The first castle on the site, standing splendidly on a 300-feet-high-cliff-edge, was probably built by the Welsh Lord Rhys, Prince of Deheubarth, in the late 12th century. The original Welsh stronghold was demolished in the late 13th century and replaced with a new structure, the imposing ruin of which we see today. Built by John Giffard and his son, the castle has none of the symmetry and elegance of the royal Edwardian castles at Carreg Cennen. The core of the structure cuts into the outer ward in a crude and arbitrary way. All is square superimposed on square, which in its prime must have radiated an impression of brutal power. The most remarkable feature of the castle is the elaborate barbican in the form of a stepped ramp, which rises from the outer ward by a right-angled turn to the twin-towered gatehouse after passing over a series of pits crossed by drawbridges and under a lower and then a higher gatehouse. Rock-cut ditches protected the inner curtain and its towers and domestic buildings. This immense construction was far away from any center of population, and it fulfilled no important strategical purpose. Carreg Cennen seems to owe its existence only to its inaccessibility and natural strength. One feels that here was a kind of uncouth and sullen withdrawal from the world. Carreg Cennen is now considerably ruined, the result of demolition in 1462 after the Wars of the Roses. Today the impressive remnants of the castle are part of a private farm which can be visited. The illustration shows how the castle might have appeared in the 13th century.*

OTHER EDWARDIAN REALIZATIONS

Except in Wales few castles were built in Britain other than royal fortresses under the strong rule of Edward I. In Scotland, financial, political and military troubles prevented Edward from carrying out anything like the astonishing fortification program with which he secured his conquest of North Wales. Yet there is an Edwardian fortress (built in the French style, as at Bothwell Castle) at Kildrummy. Another important project carried out by Edward I was the reconstruction of the Tower of London, which became a large and excellent example of a concentric castle. Edward built the outer defenses including the rooms today known as the Medieval Palace. Edward I also built a number of bastides (fortified settlements) in southwest France, which will be further described in Part 6 (q.v.)

The disastrous outcome of Edward I's attempt to achieve by force the unity of Britain has left an indelible mark upon the domestic architecture of the northern shires, and no less upon that of Scotland. From the 14th century, warlike conditions persisted in the north for another two hundred years, and every small baron's house, lord's manor or quire's hall in the region north of Tees had perforce to be fortified. In many cases the obvious solution was found in the tower house. These massive rectangular buildings — turreted, crenallated, and often surrounded by a skirt wall and ditch in the ancient Norman fashion — were built as residences by the intermediate and minor landowners. The four northern English counties (Northumberland, Durham, Cumberland and Westmorland) as well as all Scotland became a "tower house land," with a profusion of small castles and fortified rural buildings.

(Continued on page 230.)

Above: *Caerlaverock Castle (conjectured reconstruction), located near Annan in the region Dumfries and Galloway in southwest Scotland, was built in c. 1277 by the Maxwell family with the support of the Scottish King John Balliol in order to control the Southwest entrance to Scotland, which in early times was the waterway across the Solway Firth. By 1300 it had been besieged and taken by Edward I during his war against the Scots. Possession of the castle was subsequently restored to Sir Eustace Maxwell, Sir Herbert's son, who at first embraced the cause of John Balliol, and in 1312 received from Edward I an allowance of £20 for the more secure keeping of the castle. He afterwards gave his adherence to Robert Bruce, and his castle, in consequence, underwent a second siege by the English, in which they were unsuccessful. Fearing that this important stronghold might ultimately fall into the hands of the enemy and enable them to make good their hold on the district, Sir Eustace disarmed the fortress, a service and sacrifice for which he was liberally rewarded by Robert Bruce. After a siege in 1640 that pitted the steadfast Catholic Maxwells against angry Protestant factions, the castle was permanently abandoned. During the battle the south wall and tower were demolished and remain so to this day. The romantic ruins took the fancy of Sir Walter Scott, who made Caerlaverock the centerpiece for his novel Guy Mannering, published anonymously in 1815. The ruined castle is now under the care of Historic Scotland and is open to the public. The illustration shows how the castle might have appeared in the 13th century.*

Opposite top: *Caerlaverock links the semi-circular plan of Kildrummy and the asymmetrical but pointed solution of Bothwell to form an equilateral triangle with a powerful twin-towered keep-gatehouse (1) at one apex with a wooden bridge and a drawbridge in the north, and two circular jutting towers in the southeast (2) and southwest (3) corners. The martial austerity and grandeur of the strong keep-gatehouse were tempered by picturesque decoration, including corbelled corner turrets, machicolated and battlemented parapets, chimneys, pointed roofs and gables. The castle was surrounded by a broad moat filled with water (4) and hundreds of acres of flat marshy willow woods (known in Scotland as a "moss"). The domestic and residential buildings (5) in the courtyard (6) were rebuilt in the 1600s by the first Earl of Nithsdale. They are a very fine example of the classical style introduced during the Renaissance, and are similar in conception to those at the Palace of Linlithgow between Edinburgh and Stirling. The visual harmony-by-contrast between the strong vertical silhouette and the long horizontals of the flat lands bordering the Solway and the sea show an intuitive sensitivity to shape and form, perhaps a French influence.*

5. Early Plantagenet Fortifications 1154–1327   227

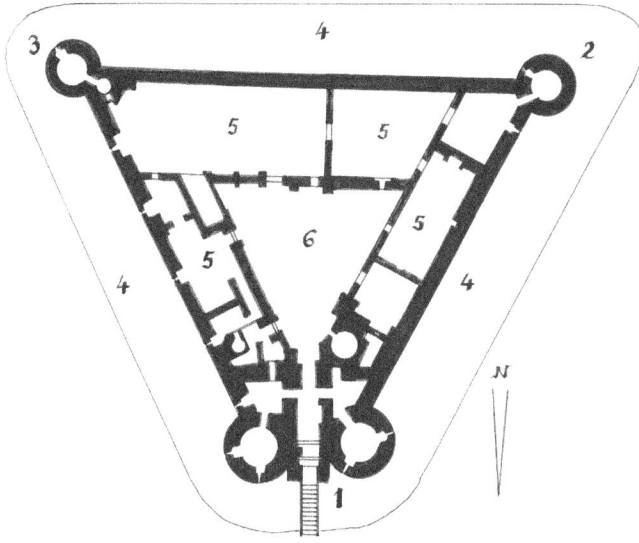

Bottom: *Kildrummy (conjectured reconstruction)*, located in Aberdeenshire, eastern Scotland, was built in the 13th century by Gilbert de Moravia, by order of Edward I. Kildrummy is a curtain-walled castle, shield-shaped in plan with independent towers. The flat side of the castle overlooks a steep ravine; moreover, on the opposite side of the castle the walls come to a point, which was once defended by a massive twin-towered gatehouse. The castle also had a keep, called the Snow Tower (collapsed in 1805), which was taller than the other towers and built in the French style, as at Bothwell Castle (both possibly based on the French Château de Coucy). The castle has a remarkable and elegant chapel forming a salient in the east front. Extensive earthworks protected the castle, including a dry moat and the ravine. The castle figured prominently during the Wars of Independence of the early 14th century and was occupied many times by both the English and Scots. "Bobbing John," the 11th Earl, used Kildrummy as the headquarters to organize the final details of the 1715 Jacobite Rising. After this failed, the castle was dismantled one last time and eventually used as a quarry. Only in 1898 were repairs and excavations undertaken by Colonel Ogston, owner of the estate. Today, the ruins of the castle are managed by Historic Scotland and open to the public. The illustration shows how the castle might have appeared in the 13th century.

Above: *Eilean Donan Castle (conjectured reconstruction) is situated in a superbly beautiful and romantic setting, on the small island of Loch Duich near Dornie about 8 miles from Kyle of Lochalsh on the west coast of Scotland. Although it was first fortified around the 6th century as a defense against the Vikings, the first fortified castle was built during Alexander II's reign (1214–1250), and stood guard over the lands of Kintail. Alexander III gave the castle to Colin Fitzgerald, the predecessor of Clan MacKenzie, and since then, at least four different versions of the castle have been built and rebuilt as the feudal history of Scotland unfolded through the centuries. Partially destroyed in a Jacobite uprising in 1719, Eilean Donan lay in ruins for the better part of 200 years until Lieutenant Colonel John MacRae-Gilstrap bought the island in 1911 and proceeded to restore the castle to its former glory. After 20 years of toil and labor the castle was re-opened in 1932. The castle is one of the most photographed monuments in Scotland and a popular venue for weddings and film productions.*

Opposite top: *Doune Castle is sited 5 miles (8 km) northwest of Stirling on the fringe of the Scottish Highlands. It was begun in the late 14th century by Robert Stewart, Duke of Albany (c. 1340–1420), the son of King Robert II of Scotland, and Regent of Scotland from 1388 until his death. The castle passed to the Crown in 1425, when Albany's son was executed, and it was used as a royal hunting lodge and dower house. The site is naturally defended on three sides by steeply sloping ground, and by two rivers to the east and west. The castle, made of coursed sandstone rubble, with dressings in lighter Ballengeich stone, forms an irregular pentagon in plan, with buildings along the north and northwest sides enclosing a courtyard. It is entered from the north via a passage beneath a tower containing the principal rooms of the castle. From the courtyard, three sets of external stone stairs, which may be later additions, lead up to the Lord's Hall in the tower, to the adjacent Great Hall, and to the kitchens in a second tower to the west. The main approach, from the north, is defended by earthworks, comprising three ditches, with an earthen rampart between them. The principal tower, which is also the gatehouse, is rectangular in plan: 59 feet (18 m) by 43 feet (13 m) and almost 95 feet (29 m) high, with a projecting round tower on the northeast corner, beside the entrance. It comprises the Lord's Hall, and three stories of chambers above, located over the entrance passage. The vaulted, cobbled passage, 46 feet (14 m) long, was formerly defended by two sets of timber doors, and today a yett (hinged iron grille) remains. In the later 16th century, Doune became the property of the Earls of Moray. The castle saw military action during the Wars of the Three Kingdoms and Glencairn's rising in the mid–17th*

century, and during the Jacobite Risings of the late 17th and 18th centuries. By 1800 the castle was ruined, but restoration works were carried out in the 1880s, prior to its passing into state care in the 20th century. The well-restored Doune Castle appears in the movie Monty Python and the Holy Grail from 1975, directed by Terry Gilliam and Terry Jones.

Right: *Smailholm Tower. This well-preserved peel tower, sited high on a rocky outcrop about 6 miles west of Kelso near Sandyknowe Farm in the Scottish Middle March, was probably built at the start of the 15th century as a fortified home for the Pringle family of Smailholm. Comprising three stories with a garret and parapet, the tower is nearly 60 feet high and its walls are 10 feet thick. It was originally surrounded by a barmkin wall enclosing the outhouses, chapel and kitchen. It was acquired early in the 17th century by the Scotts of Harden. Sir Walter Scott spent much of his childhood at nearby Sandyknowe, the farm of his grandfather. The tower was used as a setting by Scott both in Marmion and The Eve of St John. Since 1950 it has been in the care of Historic Scotland and open to the public.*

Aftermath

The system of fortification created by Edward I in North Wales crystallized the most modern developments of military architecture, and marked the culmination of castle building in the British Isles and Western Europe. The Edwardian castles bear witness to the new ideas on fortification that had been introduced during the 13th century. They form a substantial testimony to the determination of a great king, and to the architectural skills of a great designer. They also mark the transition from the austere fortresses of the Norman-Angevin age to the castle-palaces of the later Middle Ages. Edward's castles, however, soon fell into disrepair. Once the pacification of Wales was achieved, they were redundant, and became only costly burdens to garrison and maintain. Some of them (e.g., Caernavon and Beaumaris) were never totally completed. Already in the 14th century, with the exception of those which were royal residences, the ruinous castles had started to decay. Builth Castle in the Welsh county of Powys, for example, rebuilt in the late 1270s by order of Edward I, has totally disappeared. Stones from the castle were taken to construct new buildings in the nearby town. All that is left of Builth Castle are ruins, earthworks and the mound of the original former Norman motte-and-bailey castle. Some Edwardian castles provided useful strongholds during the Wars of the Roses, but it may be said that by the 14th century the great era of castellar construction in Britain had come to a gradual close.

Edward I died in 1307, and was succeeded by his son Edward II, who reigned from 1307 to 1327. The military triumph and remarkable castles of Edward I had been bought, however, at a heavy cost in taxes, and a new generation of baronial opposition had begun to make itself felt. Besides, Edward II lacked the military success of his forebear, and when victory in war was replaced by defeat (notably Bannockburn in 1314), discontent rose. Edward II's reign was marked by civil war and political confusion caused by his frivolous, lazy and extravagant behavior, as well as his favoring of personal friends (Piers Gaveston and Hugh Despencer), which alienated the barons. Edward II failed in the marriage department too, and his rule came to a grisly end when his wife, Isabella (the sister of Charles IV, king of France) and her lover, Roger Mortimer of Wigmore, had him deposed and viciously murdered in Berkeley Castle in 1327. Next in line was Edward III, and the simmering stew of dispute between England and France came to the boil.

Part 6

Late Plantagenet Fortifications 1327–1485

Historical Background

The Hundred Years' War (1338–1453)

Edward III, born in 1312, reigned from 1327 to 1377. Initially under the tutelage of his mother and her lover, Roger Mortimer of Wigmore, Edward III bided his time. In 1330 he struck, having Mortimer arrested and executed, and his mother imprisoned for life. With this, young Edward re-opened the war with Scotland and then against France, having realized that the defeat of Scotland was not possible whilst it constantly received French aid. Edward III had serious grievances against the French. Their ships were a constant threat in the Channel and were doing their best to spoil England's wool trade with Flanders. They were always supporting the Scots who stirred up troubles in the north. They held the Pope as a prisoner at Avignon and misused his influence on the English Catholic Church. They regularly broke their faith over English rights around the region of Bordeaux. Edward could not forget that all western France had belonged by right to his ancestor Henry II. Weak kings had lost most of the Plantagenet Empire, but a strong monarch could reconquer the lost territories in the same way. The English still retained, however, the extensive duchy of Guienne, for which the Kings of England did homage to the king of France. This arrangement produced constant difficulty, and the inevitable struggle between England and France was rendered the more serious by the claim made by Edward III that he was himself the rightful king of France. He based his pretensions upon the fact that his mother, Isabella, was the daughter of Philip the Fair. Philip, who died in 1314, had been followed by his three sons in succession, none of whom had left a male heir, so that the direct male line of the French Capetians was extinguished in 1328. The lawyers thereupon declared that it was a venerable law in France (the so-called Salic Frank Law, most probably created for the occasion) that no woman should succeed to the throne and transmit the crown to her son. Consequently Edward III

Above: *Queenborough Castle once stood on the isle of Sheppey in Kent. Built by order of Edward III in order to defend the Swale estuary, as well as the narrow passage between Sheppey and mainland Kent, which was then one of the chief sea-routes to the Thames and London, the castle was named after Edward's wife, Queen Philippa of Hainaut. The castle, designed by the architect John Box, featured a circular plan, which carried the principle of concentricity to its ultimate conclusion, and it would have been very difficult to storm. The outer bailey, hemmed with a moat, was concentric with the keep, but walled passages on each side connected the keep with the outer countryside and could still be defended even if the outer bailey was captured. The inner bailey featured six circular towers projecting from an inner curtain wall, and ranged around a circular courtyard. Queenborough was also one of the first English castles to be designed in order to withstand siege artillery fire and mount defensive cannons. Its novel design for its time anticipated the centrally planned artillery coastal forts of Henry VIII by nearly 200 years. For a while, Queenborough was a favored royal residence, but its importance declined with the decay of the River Swale as shipping route. The castle was declared obsolete in 1650 and demolished under the Commonwealth soon after. Today only a few mounds and Edward's church remain.*

Opposite top: *English archer. The English longbow (of Welsh origin) was a powerful weapon about 6 feet 6 inches (2.0 m) long used by the English, Scots and Welsh, both for hunting and as a weapon of war. The longbow proved its effectiveness against the French, particularly at the start of the Hundred Years' War in the battles of Crécy (1346) and Poitiers (1356), and most famously at the Battle of Agincourt (1415). The range of the bow is estimated to be 180 to 249 yards (165 to 228 m). Most of the longer-range shooting was not marksmanship, but rather archers would aim at an area and shoot a rain of arrows hitting indiscriminately anyone in the target zone, a decidedly unchivalrous but highly effective means of combat. The use of the longbow terminated the ascendancy in war of the mailed horseman of the feudal regime.*

6. *Late Plantagenet Fortifications 1327–1485* 233

Bottom: *The now ruined castle of Pontefract is located some 13 miles from Leeds in West Yorkshire. The history of Pontefract Castle begins with the Norman conquest as an earth and timber fortress built by Ilbert de Lacy in the 1080s. The castle was rebuilt in stone in the 12th century and other buildings were added as time went on. As the castle was strengthened so was the power of the de Lacy family. Following very successful marriages they became Earls of Lincoln and eventually estates were transferred to the powerful house of Lancaster. The castle played an important role in English medieval history. Thomas, Earl of Lancaster, was tried for treason at Pontefract Castle and executed on the hill adjacent to nearby St. John's Priory. There were other important prisoners—James I of Scotland and the French Charles of Valois and Duc d'Orleans (captured at the battle of Agincourt in October 1415 and held as a hostage for 24 years). But the most infamous event at Pontefract Castle was the incarceration and murder of King Richard II, immortalized in Shakespeare's play. The castle has been a ruin since 1644. Today, although a scheduled ancient monument in the care of Wakefield Council, it is still the property of Her Majesty the Queen as part of the Duchy of Lancaster. The illustration, based on a painting by Alexander Keirincx, shows how the castle might have looked before the English Civil War destruction. It included 1: Multilobed keep on motte (presenting similarities with Clifford Tower in York, and Etampes in France); 2: Piper Tower; 3: Gascoigne Tower; 4: Gatehouse; 5: Swillington Tower; 6: Constable Tower; 7: Queen's Tower; and 8: King's Tower.*

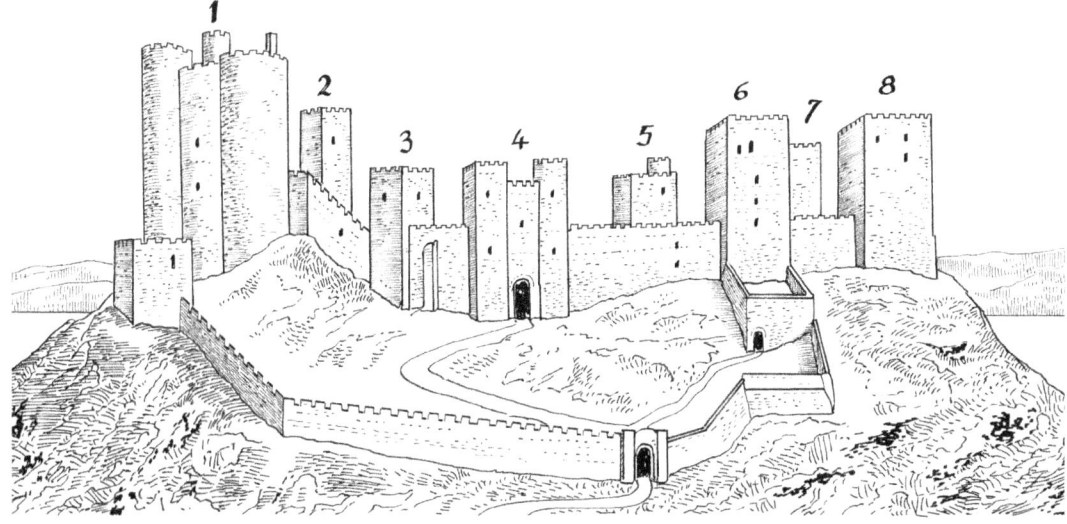

appeared to be definitely excluded, and Philip VI of Valois, a nephew of Philip the Fair, became king of France. At first Edward III appeared to recognize the propriety of this settlement and did qualified homage to Philip VI for Guienne. But when it became apparent later that Philip was encroaching upon Edward's prerogatives in Guienne, he publicly declared himself the rightful king of France. So started the so-called Hundred Years' War, a long but frequently interrupted series of conflicts between England and France. The struggle was carried on intermittently during the reigns of five English kings. From 1338 to 1360 the advantage lay with England owing to resounding victories at Sluys (1340), Crecy (1346), and Poitiers (1356), culminating in the Treaty of Bretigny (1360). In the 1370s the English lost command of the sea, at any rate from time to time, and England's coasts were exposed to attack by the French and their Spanish allies (e.g., Isle of Wight, Rye and Winchelsea). This was the first of the periodic invasion scares which, right up to the early 1940s, were to leave numerous fortification works on the southern coastline.

A deadly bubonic plague, known as the Black Death, appeared in Europe early in 1348, and spread over England one year later. It is impossible to tell what proportion of the population perished, but a careful estimate shows that in England toward one third of the population died.

With the death of the Black Prince in 1376, and the accession of Richard II (1377–1399), English fortunes reached their lowest ebb. Richard II also had to face in 1381 an important revolt of the peasants in Kent and Essex. There was a growing discontent among the English agricultural classes, which may be ascribed partly to the results of the great pestilence and partly to the new taxes, which were levied in order to prolong the disastrous, pointless and hopeless war with France, then being conducted by incapable soldiers and highly unpopular ministers. The reign of Henry IV (1399–1413) began a period of improvement, which was continued by Henry V (1413–1422), whose reign was marked by a victory at Agincourt (1415) and the Treaty of Troyes (1420). The accession of the nine-month-old Henry VI (1422–1461), and the appearance of Joan of Arc in 1428, saw the tide turn in favor of the French. By 1453, the Hundred Years' War was over, and although England still retained the port of Calais in northern France, the great question of whether she should extend her sway upon France was finally settled.

THE WARS OF THE ROSES (1455–1485)

The close of the Hundred Years' War was followed in England by the so-called Wars of the Roses, between the rival houses of Lancaster and York, which were struggling for the crown. The badge of the house of Lancaster, to which Henry VI belonged, was a red rose, and that of the duke of York, who proposed to push him off his throne, was a white one. Each party was supported by a group of the wealthy and powerful nobles—earls, dukes and barons whose rivalries, conspiracies, treasons, murders, and executions fill the annals of England during the period. The miserable Wars of the Roses lasted from 1455, when the duke of York set seriously to work to displace the weak-minded Lancastrian king, Henry VI, until the accession of Henry VII of the house of Tudor thirty years later. After several battles the Yorkist leader, Edward IV, assumed the crown in 1461 and was recognized by Parliament, which declared Henry VI and the two preceding Lancastrian kings usurpers. Edward IV was a vigorous monarch and maintained his own until his death in 1483. Edward IV's son, Edward V, was only a boy, so government fell into the hands of the young king's uncle, Richard, Duke of Gloucester. The temptation to make himself king was too great to be resisted, and Gloucester soon seized the crown, becoming King Richard III. Both the sons of Edward IV were killed in the Tower of London, with the knowledge of their uncle, it is commonly believed. A new aspirant to the throne organized a conspiracy. Richard III was defeated and slain in the battle of Bosworth Field in 1485, and the crown was placed upon the head of the first Tudor king, Henry VII. The latter had no particular right to it, although he was descended from Edward III through his mother. He hastened to procure the recognition of Parliament and married Edward IV's daughter, thus blending the red and white roses in the Tudor badge, and bringing an end to this bloody and pointless dynastic struggle.

Gunpowder and Artillery

During the Hundred Years' War appeared a small professional group of people who enjoyed no social status whatever, and who were barely accorded the humble status of soldiers: the artillerymen. The earliest instruction for using black powder was given by the English friar Roger Bacon in the 1240s but it was not until the battle of Crécy in 1346 that firearms seem to have made a first and timid appearance within the English armed forces. The origins of gunpowder are hidden away and who made the first firearm using black powder as propellent remains equally unknown. By the end of the Hundred Years' War, in the 1450s, cannons had been significantly improved, and they slowly but surely fundamentally changed the art of warfare. Gradually, the new weapons became more than a noisy and smoky curiosity, but their introduction did not bring a revolution in warfare overnight. A spectacular use of artillery occurred during the siege and fall of Constantinople in April and May 1453, when the Turks used enormous cannons that made breaches in the city walls. Artillery became established as an important and decisive weapon during King Charles VIII of France's Italian campaign in 1494. The introduction of firearms was thus a long, slow process that, however, could not be stopped. Gradually, as the new weapons had proved their worth on the battlefield and more particularly in siege warfare, artillery came to form a part of the military equipment of the armies of Western Europe. Carpenters had been the traditional engineers, siege experts and makers of war-machines, but now with the coming of gunpowder they began to yield place to the smiths. By the end of the 15th century, the more early exotic products had disappeared and the two fire weapons, which between them were to dominate the conduct of war, were emerging in clearly recognizable form: the crew-served cannon and the portable individual handgun. Gunpowder also allowed a new and more decisive employ of the

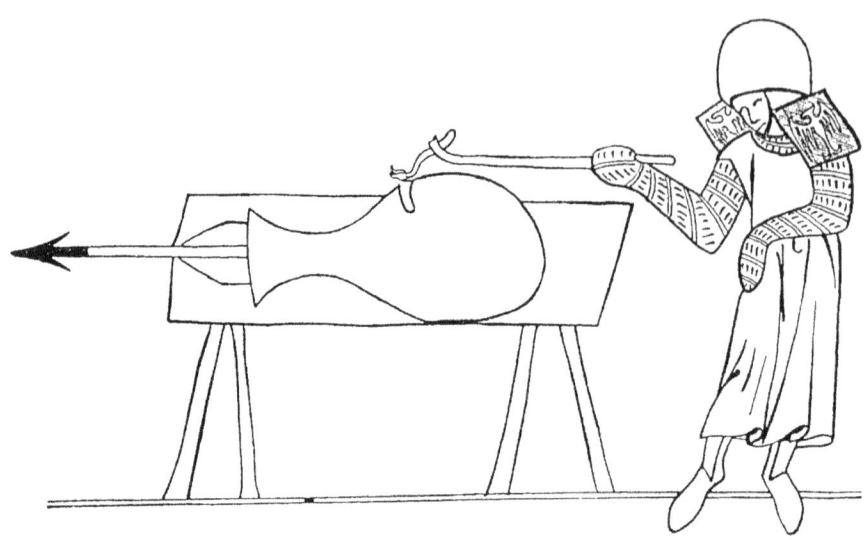

Above: *This illustration, based on a picture published in a book by Walter of Milimete in c. 1327, shows the first known representation of a gun. The barrel resembles a vase placed on a curious and rudimentary mounting which looks like a table-like surface. The gun is being ignited by a knight holding a taper to a hole in the base of the breech. The projectile is a kind of dart.*

Below: *The bombard was a ponderous early gun made of wrought-iron bars bound with hoops. Mounted on a rudimentary wooden frame, it was predominantly a siege weapon that shot stone balls with little accuracy, a limited range and a poor rate of fire.*

Left: *Mercenary billman. The English Wars of the Roses, with their constant shifting of loyalties, made the employment of mercenaries from the Continent an attractive proposition. German, Swiss, Burgundian, Flemish and French mercenaries were hired at one time or another during the struggle for England's throne. For example, by 1450 the Duke of Buckingham had a private army of 2,000 men. The illustrated man wears a salet helmet and a soft armored quilted jerkin. His weapons include a guisarme (bill), a "kidney" dagger, and a sword.*

Right: *Early small caliber arms (called fire stick, culverine, bombardelli, clopi, scopet, or petronel) appeared in the 1400s. They were awkward, slow and clumsy to use, actually cannons in reduction, comprising a simple iron tube eventually fixed to a wooden handle.*

mine in siege warfare methods. Henceforth, one of the standard techniques of breaching a fortress was to dig a tunnel under its wall, place kegs of gunpowder, and detonate them to let the explosion blast away the solid foundations. Gunpowder — packed in the form of an explosive charge known as a petard — could also be used to destroy barricades, obstacles, walls, posterns, doors and portals in gatehouses. Another significant development was the introduction in the early 16th century of a short and massive gun, called a mortar, which fired its projectiles up into the air in a high trajectory (called plunging fire) so as to lob and drop deadly charges over walls and other defenses, which the flat trajectory of the cannon could not reach. Improvement of gunpowder and artillery technology had political consequences. The development of really efficient cannons gave central authorities in all states of Western Europe an opportunity to establish their power over feudal lords, who tended to lack the resources to acquire them or to build fortresses capable of withstanding artillery.

Development of Castles in the 14th and 15th Centuries

THE LAST MILITARY CASTLES

Roughly speaking it may be said that, by the 14th century, the great period of castellar building in England was over. The country was by then amply furnished with castles and strong kings like the first and third Edwards did not encourage the construction of more. So following the brilliant Edwardian castle-building period there came a reaction that was something like somnolence. For the most part, castle building took the form of a few new creations and many additions and embellishments to existing structures. Except for the chronic state of intermittent warfare on the northern border with Scotland, there was a relative peace in England, though the mere fact that new fortresses were still being constructed demonstrates that security was far from being regarded as normality. The onset of the Hundred Years' War meant that the fighting men, the potentially troublesome barons and their knights, mercenaries and retainers waged war in France. When they came back, sated with rapine and slaughter, they brought with them the loot of France. Amenity and comfort then became important considerations in British castle building, though the fundamental military requirements were by no means neglected. Indeed the Hundred Years' War, with its accompanying danger of invasion upon the southern and eastern shores; the militarization of baronial life which resulted from the prolonged conflict with France; the increasing practice among the English nobility of maintaining mercenaries in their private service; and the failing vigor of the late Plantagenet and Lancastrian monarchies, culminating in the Wars of the Roses—all these circumstances led to renewed baronial gangsterism, and to a certain revival of castle building in the later 14th and 15th centuries. In these later castles, one can observe a strong tendency to reduce the size of the structure and to simplify its plan. Instead of large garrisons of half-trained feudal levies, the lords were relying more and more on small permanent troops of professional warriors and mercenaries. It was realized that the multiplication of defensive obstacles, which the designers had hitherto favored, hindered the rapid movement of soldiers around the walls in time of siege. The fact that mercenaries were loyal only so long as their pay was forthcoming also had its effect on castle architecture. In some cases the lord's residence was isolated from his soldiers' quarters and defended against mutinous or treacherous followers. A new fashion to emerged characterized by a single rectangular walled enclosure of moderate size, flanked by round or square towers, a less-complicated type of gatehouse, and domestic buildings in the courtyard drawn into a compact and well-articulated quadrangle.

Maxstoke Castle in North Warwickshire, built in 1345, is a fair example of the efficient and convenient square plan. This type of castle design is splendidly illustrated in the castle of Bodiam in Sussex built in 1385. Up in Yorkshire, Bolton Castle in Wensleydale, built at the same time, although more concentrated, displays very much the same design.

Maxstoke Castle plan. Situated to the north of Maxstoke, Warwickshire, this castle was built by Sir William de Clinton, 1st Earl of Huntingdon, in 1345 to a rectangular plan, with octagonal towers at each angle, a gatehouse on the east, and a residential range on the west, the whole surrounded by a broad moat. Additions were made by Humphrey Stafford, 1st Duke of Buckingham, who acquired it in 1437. Today the largely intact castle is privately owned and not opened to the public. The plan shows 1: Kitchen Tower; 2: Service buildings; 3: Great Hall; 4: Chapel; 5: Apartments; 6: Lady Tower; 7: Deadman's Tower; 8: Gatehouse; 9: Dairy Tower; 10: Wet ditch.

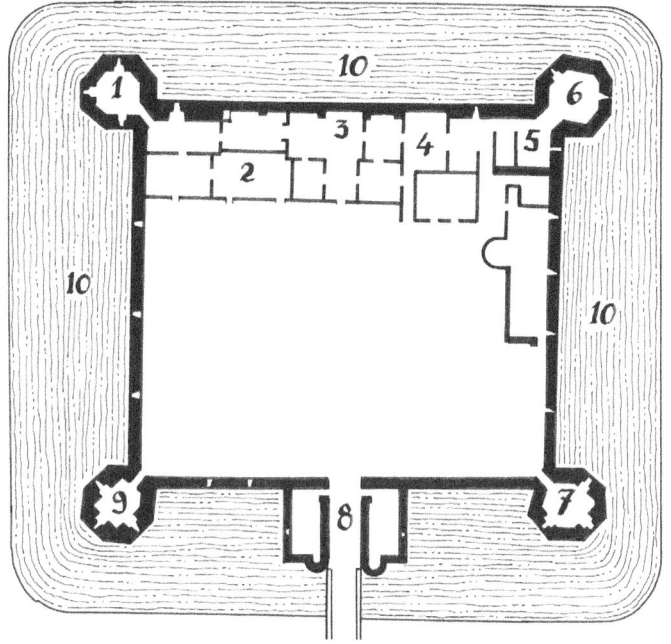

The Edwardian period was the climax of medieval castle building with predominantly military considerarions in mind. During the 14th and 15th centuries there was an increased interest in, and emphasis on, the more domestic aspects of the accommodation provided. Castles had always been domestic to some degree, but domestic considerations came a poor second to those of defense during the 12th and 13th centuries. In the 14th and subsequent centuries, however, the demand for more space and greater comfort was quite evident in the design of new castles and the additions made to existing ones. Although not universal, there was a movement from traditional medieval castle to comfortable manor house. In the new castles the appearance was still very much that of a military stronghold, but internally they tended to become pleasant dwelling places. The terms fortified manor and palace instead of castle became increasingly appropriate as time went by.

Adaptation to Firearms

The introduction of fire-weapons, of course, had consequences on fortifications. Military commanders and engineers were quick to realize that artillery, which so effectively attacked and reduced late medieval strongholds and walled cities, could equally well be used for defense. Gradually the problem of fortification versus firearm appeared to be twofold: how to protect one's self against enemy fire; and how to use guns from a permanent fortified position. Integrating guns into the defensive arrangement took several shapes. The first step was to adapt existing elements. The long, vertical and narrow loopholes, placed in medieval towers, gatehouses and barbicans, intended to allow shooting with bows and crossbows, were pierced with a round

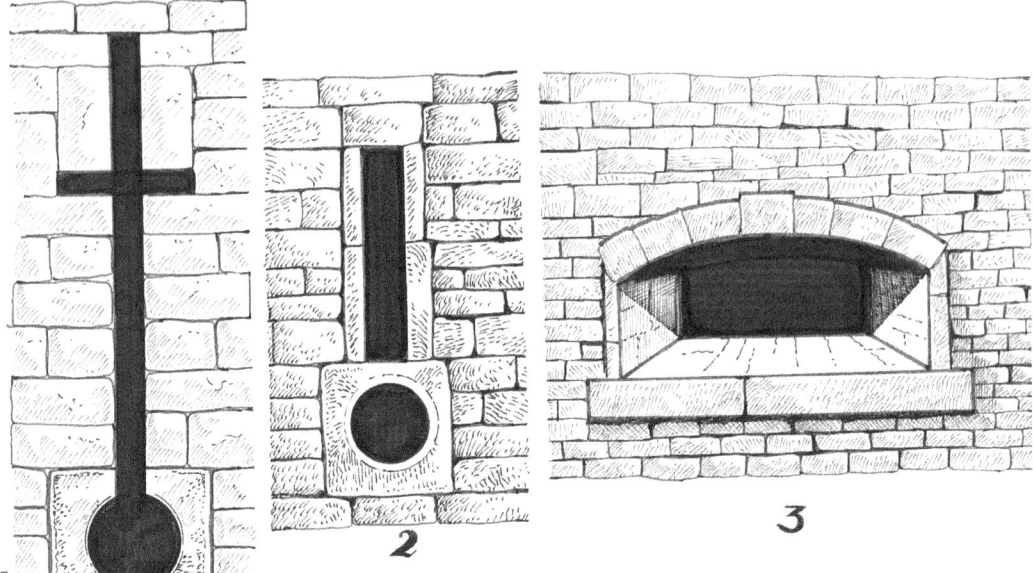

Gunports. 1: Cross-and-orb, a medieval arrowslit fitted with a hole; 2: Firing port; 3: Embrasure for cannon with inward part widened enabling gunners to aim their weapon.

hole enabling the passage of a long-barreled weapon. Eventually enlarged and widened, they became full-scale openings called firing ports, embrasures or portholes, permitting the discharge of firearms. Blocked with shutters when not in use, they were of various sizes depending on the weapons used (small for handguns, and large for cannons) and were often provided with vents and ventilation shafts for clearing choking fumes. In many cases, the new castles built in Britain were provided with gunports, thus revealing the reaction of the designers to the introduction of firearms.

The Last Medieval Castles

Another new feature, introduced from the Low Countries, was (for the first time since the Roman era) the use of brick instead of stone. Brick production proliferated along the English southeast coast due to an influx of Flemish weavers and a reduction in the amount of available stone, leading to a demand for an alternative building material. Splendid instances of brick castles in 15th-century Britain are Herstmonceux in Sussex, Caister-on-Sea in Norfolk, Tattershall in Lincolnshire, and Buckden in Huntingdonshire.

The influence exerted upon the latest phase of English castle-building by revived turmoil, culminating in the Wars of the Roses, was displayed in three notable instances: Raglan, Ashby-de-la-Zouch, and Kirby Muxloe. The castles built in this period were the last true castles to be built in England; they provided security and also separate suites of rooms for the lord and his guests, his domestic staff and servants, and garrison.

Bodiam Castle, situated beside the River Rother near Robertsbridge in East Sussex, was built in the late 14th century by Sir Edward Dalyngrygge (also spelled Dalyngrudge), a veteran of King Edward III's wars with France, originally as a coastal defense, a refuge affording temporary shelter for the local people. There was indeed need of strongholds along the shores. At that time French corsairs often ravaged the coast of Sussex, raiding towns, villages and manor houses (e.g., the devastating attack on Winchelsea). As raiders from the sea carried no siege equipment, every minute they were held at bay gained time for a relief force to come to the rescue. In 1385, Sir Edward Dalyngrygge was given permission to fortify his house against aggression and possible invasion from France, but then decided to build a new stone castle a short distance away from the house. The castle was completed in 1390. With an almost square construction, Bodiam Castle has a notable symmetry and is surrounded by a wide lily-decked moat. The moat was created from an artificial lake which, in turn, originated from allowing the river to flow into a rectangular area of marshy land. The moat was intended to prevent attackers from gaining access to the base of the castle's walls, but it also had the effect of making the castle appear larger and more impressive by isolating it in its landscape. At each corner of the curtain wall stands a 65-feet-high, four-story, cylindrical tower, and rectangular towers are located mid-way along each wall. The southern rectangular tower of the Postern Gate at one time carried the drawbridge across the moat. Symmetrically opposite stands the gatehouse, with its twin, rectangular towers consuming one third of the northern wall. A deep arch and parapet connect the towers of the gatehouse. The gunports on the towers were a later edition to the castle. Access to Bodiam Castle today remains via the moat on the north side, passing through the Octagon (an island outwork that had enough space for turning wagons), and the barbican before reaching the gatehouse. The barbican was originally constructed as a two-story gatehouse but only the lower part of the western wall survives. Bodiam Castle has no keep, thus employing the gatehouse as a defense to the bailey within the castle walls. The construction of Bodiam Castle appears to have been a good combination of medieval defense strategies and remarkably comfortable accommodation, thus creating a magnificent fortified dwelling place in an idyllic rural location. The fortifications were never tested to any degree, although during the English Civil War of 1642–46 the interior of the castle was virtually gutted. Bodiam Castle was then left to deteriorate until the early 20th century. In 1917, George Nathaniel, Earl Curzon of Kedleston, Viceroy of India, undertook a re-building program in order to restore Bodiam Castle to its former medieval appearance.

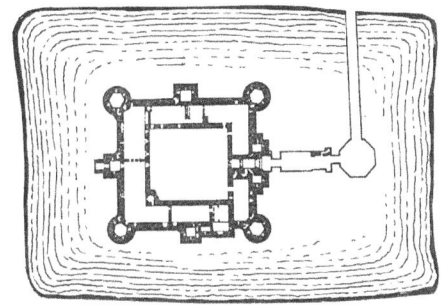

Bodiam's gateway is a large structure composed of two flanking towers defended by oiletts for arrows and gunports for light firearms, embattled parapets, and deep machicolations. A huge portcullis still frowns down upon us, and two others opposed the way. There was also a particularly ingenious barbican and outwork with wooden bridges and drawbridges at right angles to each other, contributing to a significant defensive potential.

The castles described below were partly or entirely new foundations of the 14th and 15th centuries, and as such reflected the current attitudes regarding to domestic comfort within fortified premises. Such new castles were, however, greatly outnumbered by existing structures which — for simple economic reasons — it made sense to modify rather than build entirely afresh. In such cases the demand for greater domestic space and comfort was met by additions to the existing structure, and this practice goes a long way to explaining the great variety in the British castles as we see them today. Frequently the additions took the form of an extension of the existing hall or the construction of new towers, which, with their many floor levels, added greatly to the amount of accommodation available. An excellent example of this is provided by the late-14th-century development at Warwick Castle.

6. Late Plantagenet Fortifications 1327–1485   243

Herstmonceux, built slightly later than Bodiam (in c. 1440) demonstrates another stage in the decline of the castle as a military fortification. Situated near Hailsham in Sussex, it was built by Sir Roger Fiennes, a veteran of Agincourt and treasurer of Henry VI. Although Herstmonceux has most of the formal requisites of a fortress (wall- and corner-towers, curtains with battlements and machicolation, a gatehouse and drawbridge, and a large moat), it is a play castle, built by a tired old soldier to remind him of battles long ago, but battles no longer dangerous or vicious. The result is not a defensive structure, but a palatial residence in a self-consciously archaic castle style. Herstmonceux—one of the earliest brick-built castles—is about 200 feet square. Internally, the arrangements were thoroughly domestic, clearly indicating that the builders of Herstmonceux Castle concentrated more on grandeur and comfort than on defense. The castle was dismantled in 1777, leaving the exterior walls standing, and remained a ruin until the early 20th century. Radical restoration work was undertaken by Colonel Claude Lowther in 1913 to transform the ruined building into a residence and it was completed for Sir Paul Latham in 1933 by the distinguished architect Walter Godfrey. In 1957 Herstmonceux Castle became the home of the Royal Greenwich Observatory and it remained so until 1988, when the observatory moved to Cambridge. Today the castle houses the Bader International Study Center. The castle is not open to the public except by tours, but the magnificent 550-acre Elizabethan gardens and the Science Center are open.

Beginning in the second half of the 14th century, the accent shifted to gaiety, grandeur and elaboration. The castle extended outwards in one or more inner and outer courtyards and rings of towered and embattled walls. Buildings were neatly and conviently ranged around the sides of the courtyard inside the castle. They became more specialized in function, profuse in decorations, better lit, and more lavish in their proportions. The keep had been largely abandoned as the living-place of the owner, and was replaced with large vaulted halls, elaborate suites of partitioned rooms and airy apartments. Glass had ceased to be a rarity and the simple narrow windows of preceding centuries became a riot of color and curved tracery. Highly decorative coats-of-arms, crests and blazons, finely carved in walls, staircases and above doors, expressed the nobility's pride and prosperity. In the 15th century the simplicity and economy of early English architecture gave place to a more highly decorated fashion, known as Perpendicular style. This late phase of Gothic architecture in England was characterized by rich visual effects through decoration, by a predominance of vertical lines in stone window tracery, the enlargement of windows to great proportions, upward curves and conversion of the interior stories into a single unified vertical expanse. Fan vaults, ornamental ribs springing from slender

Left: *Herstmonceux gatehouse. The substantial gatehouse was composed of two imposing towers rising to 84 feet on either side of the entrance and a drawbridge, whose rainures (5 lots in the gatehouse wall) for the gaffs (lifting arms) are still clearly visible. Along the walls of the castle and situated in each corner are a series of octagonal and semi-octagonal towers, each provided with defenses (crenels, machicolation, loopholes and gunports) suitable for firearm or crossbow. The castle never came under attack during its long history, which was a very good thing, because the brick walls were too thin to withstand any serious artillery bombardment for any length of time. Herstmonceux was constructed at a time when castles built as military fortifications were coming to an end. Instead it was designed along the lines of a grand mansion.*

Opposite top: *Drawbridge with counterweights and gaffs. By the 14th century a bascule arrangement was provided by lifting arms (called gaffs) above and parallel to the bridge deck, whose ends were linked by chains to the lifting end of the bridge; in the raised position the gaffs would fit into slots in the gatehouse wall (called rainures) which can still be seen in many castles. Inside the gatehouse the gaffs were extended to bear counterweights, or they might form the side-timbers of a stout gate, which would be against the roof of the gate-passage when the drawbridge was down, but would close against the gate-arch as the bridge was raised. The cross-section (right) shows how the bridge was operated. By pulling down the counterweight (1), the inner parts of the gaffs pivoted down (2), raising the drawbridge (3); the outer part of the gaffs pivoted up (4) and fitted into rainures or grooves (5) installed for this purpose in the façade of the gatehouse.*

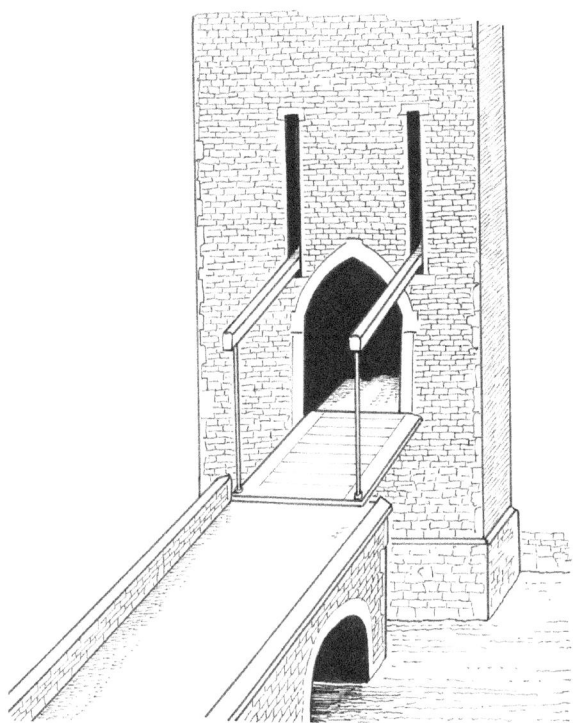
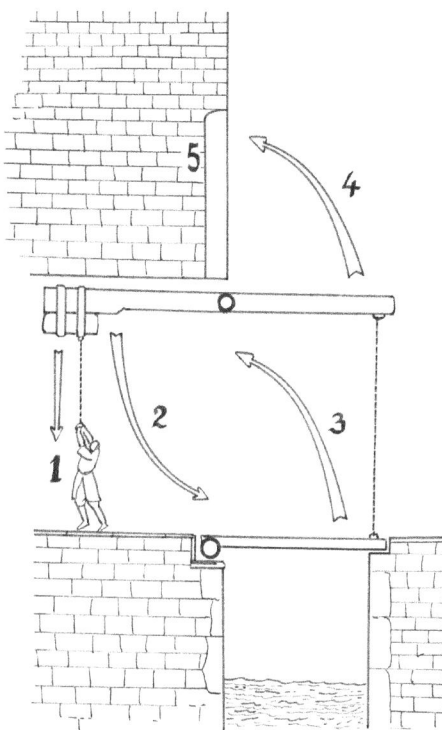

Right: *Caister-on-Sea, located some 3 miles (4.8 km) from Great Yarmouth in Norfolk, originates from a Romans vicus (settlement) established in the 1st century A.D. near a naval base associated with the Saxon shore. The medieval castle, built in 1432 on the site of an earlier fortified manor house and chapel, is an impressive moated fortress. It was founded by Sir John Falstolf, an immensely rich veteran of the Hundred Years' War, but also a patron of literature, and a writer on strategy. One of the first major brick buildings in England, Caister is rectangular in plan and included three wards. The remains of the hall and domestic buildings are still standing, flanked by round angle towers. In the inner ward there are three gunports in the lofty six-story northwest tower and several gunports in the high curtain wall. The outer ward is thought to be older, the curtain wall, which lacks strength, is flanked on the angles by open-backed round bastions, complete with arrow loops. The third ward, with its modified Barge House, wide arched water-gate and large round flanking tower was altered by the Paston family in the 15th century and is now known as Caister Hall, which was rebuilt in the 1830s. Today the castle holds the largest private collection of motor vehicles in the country, stretching from 1893 to the present day.*

Left: *Tattershall, situated northeast of Sleaford in Lincolnshire, was built between 1430 and 1450 by Ralph, third Lord Cromwell, who chose to use brick. About 700,000 bricks were used to build the castle, which has often been described as the finest piece of medieval brickwork in England. It was built as an addition to a 13th-century stone enclosure and a pre-existing hall. Despite its appearance and its martial garniture, Tattershall was not a kind of atavic reversion to the concept of a Norman keep. Like Herstmonceux Castle, it should rather be regarded as a private residence expressing barional pride and magnificence. The castle fell into neglect until 1911, when it was purchased and then restored until 1914 by Lord Curzon of Kedleston, who left it to the National Trust on his death in 1925. Today the castle is still in the care of the National Trust, and it is open to the public.*

Right: *Donnington Castle. This castle, which should not be confused with Castle Donington in the Northwest of Leicestershire, is sited at the top of a hill overlooking the River Lambourne, a mile north of Newbury in the small village of Donnington, in the county of Berkshire. It was built by its original owner, Richard Abberbury the Elder, under a license granted by King Richard II in 1386. The castle was a rectangular enclosure with a round tower at each corner and two square towers midway along the longest sides. The most impressive part of the castle, and indeed the only part now standing, was the depicted gatehouse. This is a three-story rectangular building with two round towers that flank the entrance and rise another story above the rest of the building.*

columns or pendants, became popular, and these fantastic schemes merged ribs and tracery patterns in a dazzling display of architectural pageantry. The oldest surviving example of this style is probably the choir of Gloucester Cathedral (begun c. 1335). Other major monuments include King's College Chapel, Cambridge (1446–1515), and the chapel of Henry VII at Westminster Abbey.

(Continued on page 252.)

Raglan Castle (conjectured reconstruction), located 7 miles southwest of Monmouth in the county of Monmouthshire, is one of the last true castles ever to be built in Wales. Construction of the castle began in the 1430s by Sir William ap Thomas, the Blue Knight of Gwent, and continued through 1525. William—a Welsh knight who had fought at the Battle of Agincourt with King Henry V in 1415—was responsible for building the Great Tower at Raglan, which became known as the Yellow Tower of Gwent. William ap Thomas died in 1445 and the castle passed to his son William Herbert, who continued in his father's footsteps by adding Raglan's gatehouse, stately apartments, and the machicolations to the top of the gatehouse and the Closet Tower. In 1589, during the time of William Somerset, third Earl of Worcester, the castle entered its last major building phase. Sir William Somerset added a new hammer-beam roof to the hall and a long gallery on the second floor overlooking the Fountain Court. Raglan Castle was besieged during the English Civil War in 1646. Following the siege, the castle was destroyed to the point that it would be indefensible; thus began its period of falling into disrepair. Raglan is now maintained by Cadw (Welsh Historic Monuments) on behalf of the Secretary of State for Wales, and its mighty and imposing ruins are open to the public. The illustration shows how Raglan Castle might have looked before the 1646 siege.

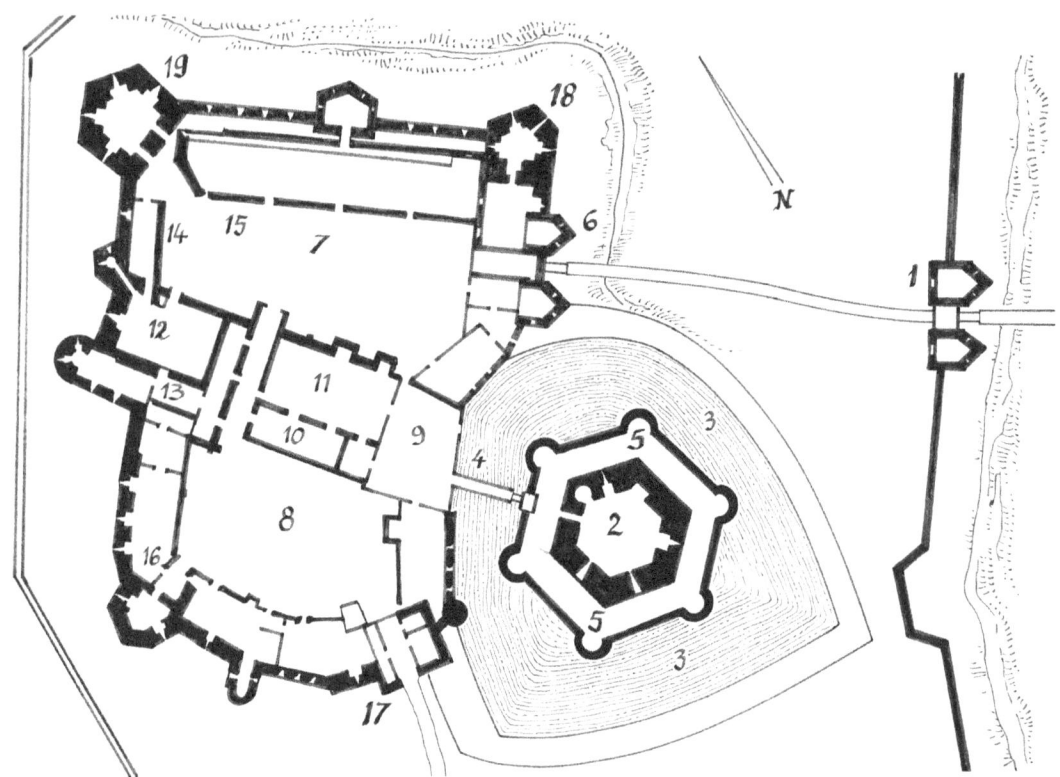

Raglan Castle can be seen for miles around the countryside, and its features (notably the association of the traditional crosslet loopholes and the new-fangled gunports) were designed for serious defense. There is no question here of a mere parade or pride display. There was a first low wall with an entrance known as the White Gate (1). The Great Tower, or the Yellow Tower of Gwent (2), the centerpiece of the castle, is a huge hexagonal donjon. It stands outside the enceinte and is surrounded by its own moat (3), which is crossable by a double drawbridge (4) from the main castle. The Great Tower also has a low enceinte apron-wall (5) at its base just above water level with six small corner towers. The massive gatehouse (6) was fitted with machicolations around the top of the towers and gargoyles on some of the tower corners. Raglan Castle includes two wards: the Pitch Stone Court (7) and the Fountain Court (8), with a series of large buildings of Tudor and Jacobean times including the parlour (9), chapel (10), hall (11), buttery (12), long gallery (13) and pantry (14). The Fountain Court includes the garden terraces (15), grand staircase (16), and a secondary entrance named the South Gate (17). The castle also has two other impressive towers, the Closet Tower (18) and the Kitchen Tower (19), which do not quite seem so large when compared to the Great Tower, but still very formidable to anyone trying to attack the castle. Raglan Castle was designed as a strong fortress with a pronounced military character, but it was also a stately residence that was richly furnished, decorated with luxurious taste, and enclosed in splendid grounds, including orchards and gardens.

This castle is located in the town of Ashby-de-la-Zouch, 18 miles northwest of Leicestershire. It originated as a Norman fortified manor house founded in 1160 by Alain de Parrhoët la Zouch. During the next three centuries it was extended. In 1474 it was granted by Edward IV to his chamberlain, William Lord Hastings, as a reward for his loyalty in the Wars of the Roses. William Lord Hastings was one of the principal actors on the Yorkist side in the tangled drama of the Wars of the Roses; he held numerous exalted posts and enjoyed enormous wealth. Like all the nobles of this turbulent period, he kept his own private armed force. William converted Ashby Castle into an impressive fortress. To the original walled courtyard, hall, kitchen and solar block, he added a dominating four-story machicolated square keep, with a seven-story rectangular extension, a chapel and a surrounding curtain wall. The keep, known as the Hastings Tower, was intended to provide William with a self-contained tower house to keep himself, his family and his personal household apart from the crowd of armed retainers whose services he bought with his ample purse. The tower was 90 feet (27 m) high. It was rectangular in shape, measuring about 47 feet (14 m) by 41 feet (12 m) with walls nearly 9 feet (3 m) thick on the ground floor. However, after the king's death in 1483, Hastings refused to support his successor, Richard III. The king had him beheaded, a scene that was included in Shakespeare's play Richard III. A Royalist stronghold during the Civil War, Ashby Castle finally fell to Parliament in 1646, and was then partially destroyed to make it unusable. Sir Walter Scott took Ashby-de-la Zouch Castle as the setting for the tournament in his novel Ivanhoe. The impressive ruined castle is now owned by English Heritage and open to the public.

Kirby Muxloe Castle is located in the center of the village of Kirby Muxloe, off Oakcroft Avenue, some 4 miles west of Leicester. Originally it was a fortified manor house founded by the Pakeman family in the 14th century. In 1480, William Lord Hastings founded a quadrangular castle when he was granted license to crenellate. Kirby Muxloe was one of the last quadrangular castles to be built in England. Despite the castle's having never been completed, the attractive site is an impressive tribute to its builder, William Lord Hastings, who for a time held a position of great power within the realm. The castle was left unfinished after Hastings's execution by Richard III in 1483. The rectangular platform, encased by a moat, supported a hall and chamber blocks, of which foundations remain. Kirby Muxloe was one of the first English castles to be systematically equipped with gunports and embrasures for the use of firearms. The picturesque moated site is now owned and conserved by English Heritage and open to the public.

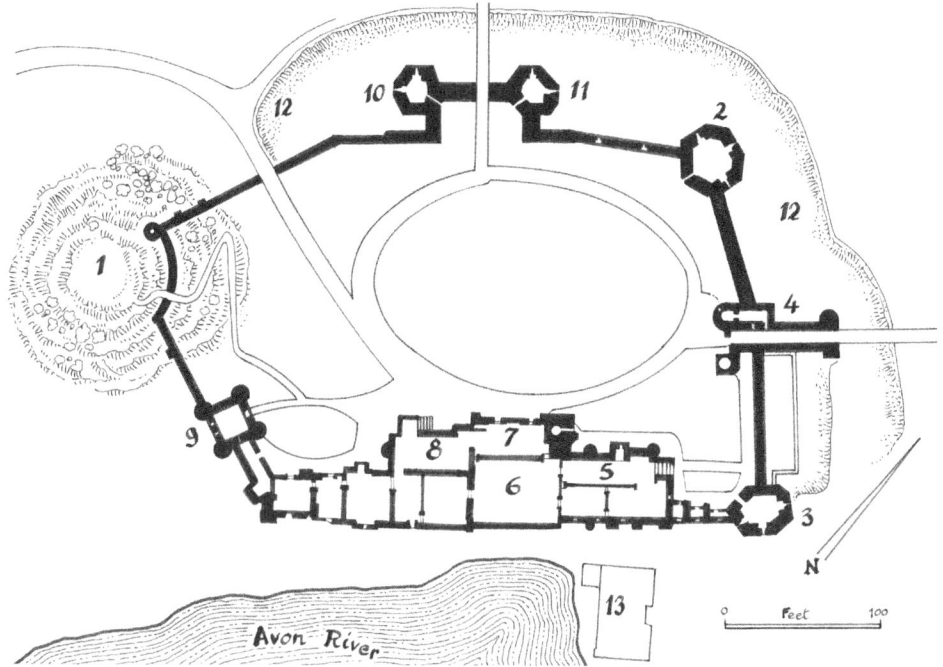

Above: *Warwick Castle consisted originally of a Norman motte with a shell-keep (1)—now planted with shrubbery—and a large bailey on its northeastern side built by William the Conqueror adjacent to the Anglo-Saxon burh of Warwick. In the later decades of the 14th century a new section of wall was built at the north-eastern end with two defensive points, Guy's Tower (2) and Caesar's Tower (3), at each end (providing both security and a considerable amount of accommodation) and a gatehouse (4) with a barbican in the middle. The fortified front represents one of the most recognizable examples of 14th-century military architecture. At the same time a large range of buildings was added to the northeast side of the bailey, including a library (5), great hall (6), dining room (7), chapel (8), as well as other domestic accommodations. Further additions, made in a later period, included the Watergate Tower (9), and another entrance, defended by two structures: Clarence Tower (10) and Bear Tower (11), and a dry ditch (12). Outside the castle, at the foot of Caesar's Tower, is the Mill Garden (13) created by the banker and horticulturist Arthur Bradley Measures. This is a charming waterside garden, with good views of the south front of the castle, the Old Bridge and the River Avon.*

Opposite bottom: *Guy's Tower, Warwick Castle is located some eight miles from Stratford-upon-Avon in Warwickshire. A fortified town (burh) was first established at Warwick by Aethelflaed, widow of King Ethelred, in 914–916. The town was fortified against the threat of Danish invasions. After the Norman conquest in 1066, William I moved northwards from London, to subdue resistance in the Midlands and Northern England. He founded castles at Warwick and Nottingham, run by his Norman barons. The castle at Warwick was founded in 1086 on a sandstone bluff at a bend of the River Avon. From 1088, the castle traditionally belonged to the Earl of Warwick, and it served as a symbol of his power. The castle was taken in 1153 by Henry of Anjou, later Henry II. It has been used to hold prisoners, notably King Edward IV. In the 17th century the grounds around the castle were turned into a garden, but the defenses were enhanced in the 1640s to prepare the castle for action in the English Civil War. Robert Greville, second Baron Brooke, was a Parliamentarian, and Royalist forces laid siege to the castle. Warwick Castle withstood the siege and was later used to hold prisoners taken by the Parliamentarians. The Tussauds Group purchased Warwick Castle in 1978 and opened it as a major tourist attraction. It is now protected as a scheduled ancient monument and a Grade I listed building. The depicted Guy's Tower (128 feet high) was named after Guy of Warwick, a legendary Anglo-Saxon mystic warrior. There is a reference to his story in Chaucer's Canterbury Tales.*

Urban Fortifications

Urban Revival

Until now we have considered only British castles but British cities and towns were fortified as well. The question of urban fortifications has been touched on already in dealing with the Roman towns, the Alfredian burhs and the Edwardian boroughs, but they require more attention. From the 5th to the 10th centuries, towns were reduced in size, limited in importance and greatly depopulated. Some had vanished, many were merely big villages, others were modest commercial or episcopal centers. After the year 1000, the stopping of invasions and the re-establishment of a relative security gradually favored demographic growth, trade and commercial activities. The instauration of money exchange, and the installation of markets and fairs made possible the rebirth of urban trade. Consequently urban population increased and transportation means became more rapid and less expensive owing to significant inventions and technical improvements, such as collars for horses and stern-rudders for boats. Throughout the 12th century there were many signs indicating that Europe was growing in strength and power.

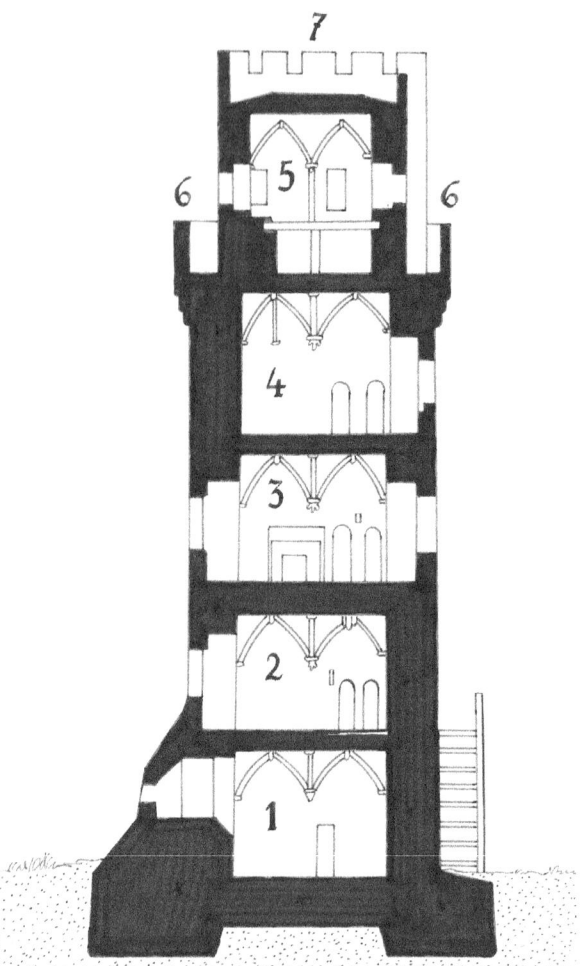

Cross-section of Caesar's Tower at Warwick Castle. Caesar's Tower (over 130 feet high) was divided into a basement prison (1), and three suites of rooms (2, 3 and 4), each on a separate floor, consisting of a main chamber (about 20 by 15 feet) with a fireplace and windows, a smaller mural chamber—perhaps arranged as a bedroom on one side—and a latrine on the other. The top of the tower housed a guardroom (5) with a corbelled wallwalk (6) and a combat platform on top of the tower (7).

But what was a medieval town? According to the historian M. W. Bresford, criteria helping to distinguish a small town from a large village were: borough charter; burgages (burgage tenure, or the presence of burgesses); reference to a burgus in the assize rolls (or separately represented by a jury before the judge of assize); taxation as a borough; and its members sent to any medieval parliament. To these legalistic definitions it may be added that a medieval town had: fortifications; a planned urban system; market(s); a mint; a role as a central place; a large or dense population; diversified economic activities; social differentiation; and complex religious organization.

The location of a town was of great importance, and successful organic towns prospered because they were situated at the right place for trade with regard to roads or navigable waterways. A town's success was thus a combination of its geographical position and the commercial acumen of its citizens. Some towns grew on the site of old Roman settlements, others enlarged on Anglo-Saxon burhs or Danish foundations, others grew or were made from existing villages, whilst still others were created ex-nihilo. The towns' layouts were extremely various. Many towns had a central open marketplace, grown outside the gates of a manor or abbey, that was triangular, rectangular or irregular (e.g., St. Alban, Bampton, Tauton, Richmond or Alnwick). Linear towns, growing along a road, were not uncommon (e.g., Henley-in-harden, Chipping, Campden). Many towns developed from the bailey of a timber motte castle, or grew or were established outside the gates of a castle, like the Edwardian boroughs in Wales, but also at Kilpeck, Whitecastle, Skenfrith, Bere, Kidwelly, Denbigh, and Windsor. Rectilinear street layouts and grid plans were often inherited from Roman castra or given to newly created settlements (e.g., Ludlow, Salisbury, New Winchelsea, Stratford-upon-Avon, Newport, Caernarvon, Flint and other Edwardian boroughs). Many British towns, however, have a composite plan simply because they have been subject to planned or unplanned growth occurring in different ways at different dates with piecemeal additional suburbs.

So cities were recovering ease and safety, and the revival continued in the 13th and 14th centuries. At the time of the Domesday Survey in 1086 there were probably only about fifty places with genuine urban features and functions. In the 13th century 65 new towns were established in England and 46 in Wales (coinciding with Edward's I military operations). By the early 14th century the number of towns in Britain had reached between five and six hundred, and most had grown considerably in size. Trade and industry made steady progress owing to many complex causes. The traditional feudal manors, principalities and kingdoms tended to be self-sufficient, but as the lords, earls, counts, dukes and kings grew richer they needed luxury products, manufactured articles and exotic goods that their own local craftsmen and peasants could not produce. To supply these wants, trade flourished again, particularly when the kings of France and England progressively re-established law and order in their kingdoms. Goods from the Far and Middle East reached Western Europe through the Italian cities (like Venice, Florence, and Genoa, which also greatly profited from the Crusades), over the Alps and down the Rhine to Germany (Cologne, Hamburg, and Nuremberg), and Flanders (Antwerp, Bruges and Ghent). The cities of Flanders became wealthy mercantile manufacturing (notably cloth) and distribution centers. The wool of England, on which Flemish industry was dependent, began to obtain its international renown. A constant stream of merchants from every corner of Europe found their way to fairs for the exchange of goods and the settlement of international debts. By then the outlines of the European economic system, as it persisted until the discovery of America, gradually came to existence. By about 1300,

254 British Fortifications

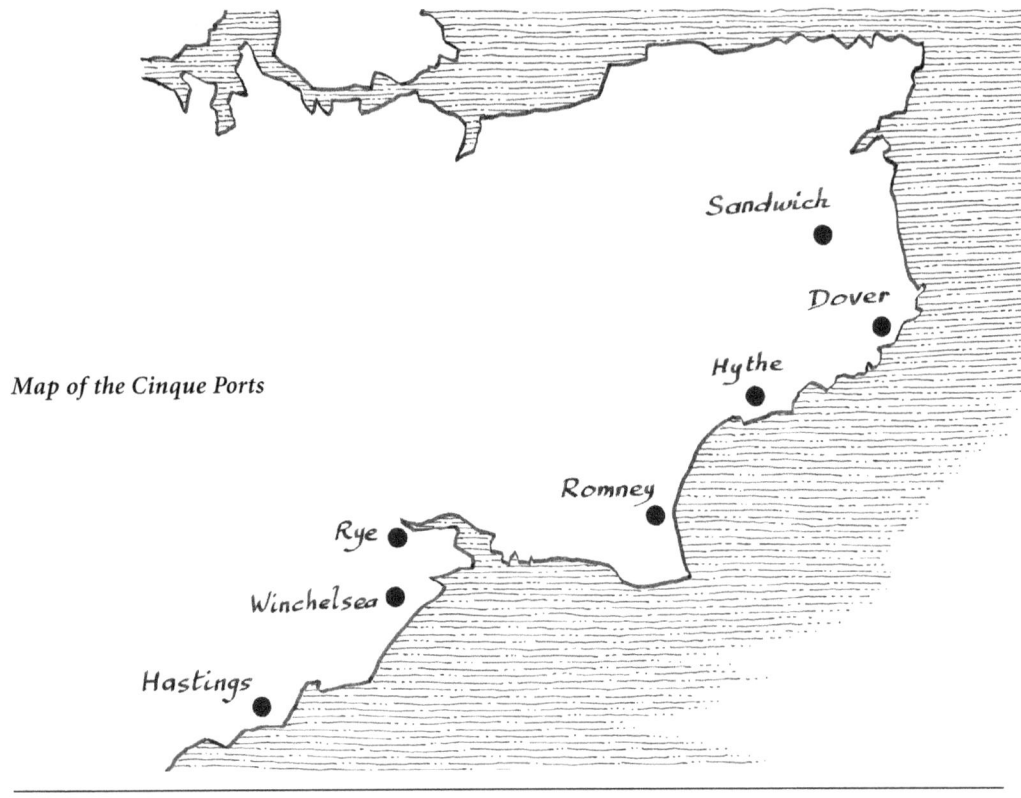

Map of the Cinque Ports

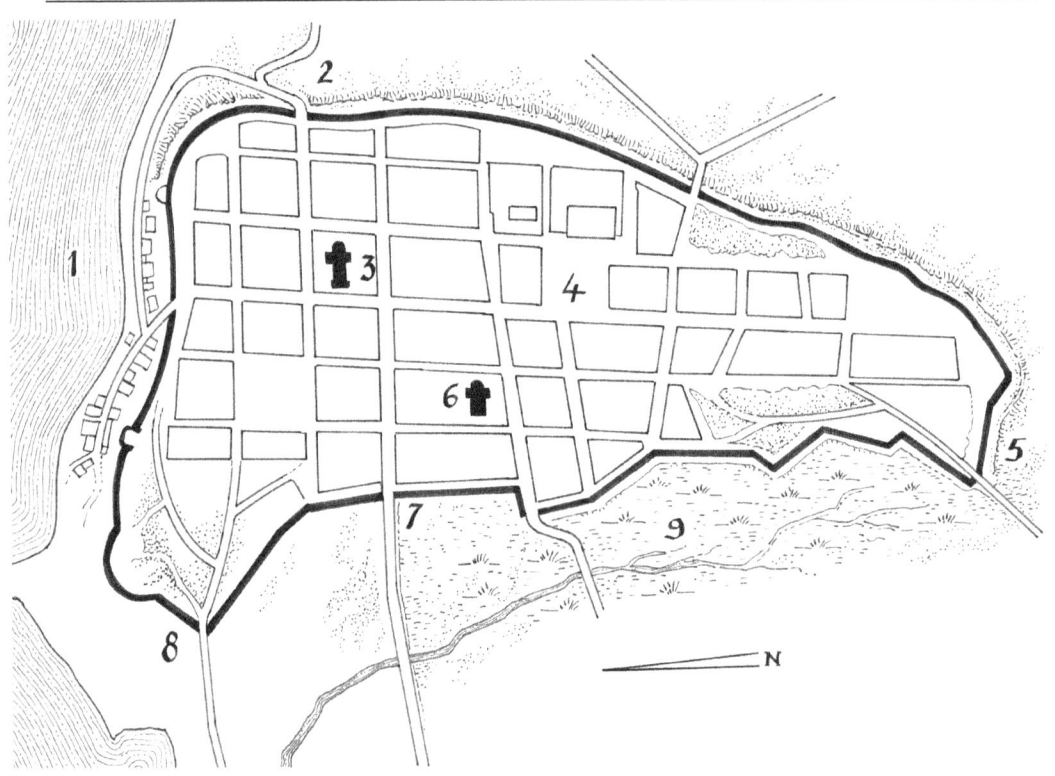

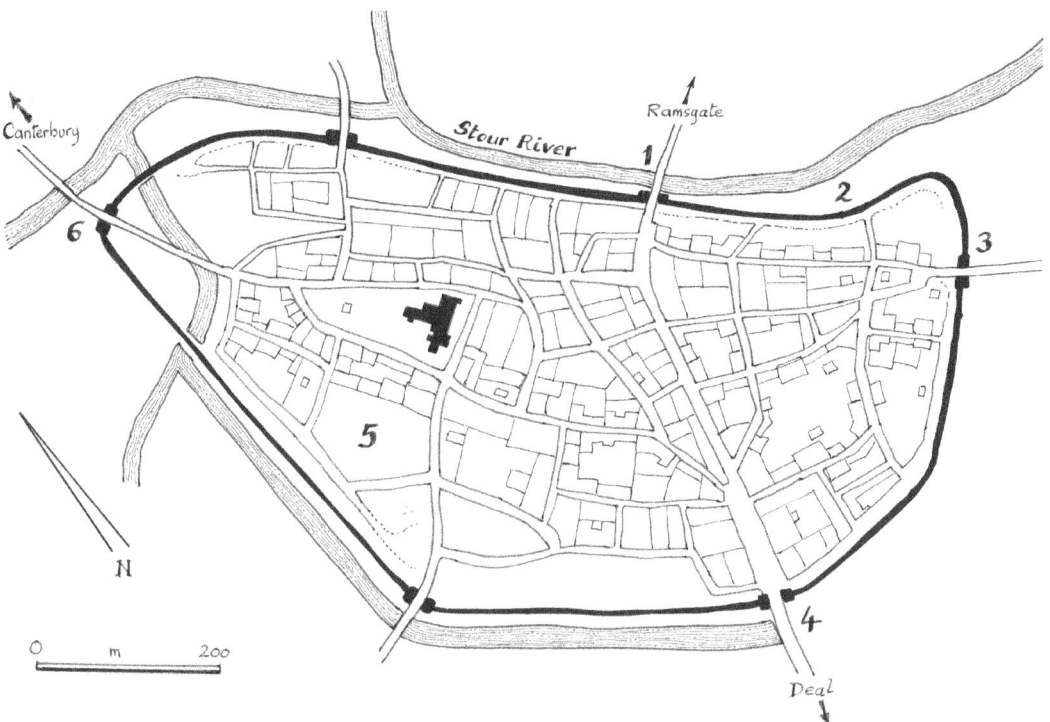

Above: *Plan of Sandwich.* Today Sandwich in Kent is best known for having given its name, via the fourth Earl of Sandwich, to a snack made from slices of bread with a filling, but it is in fact one of the finest historic towns of England with readily visible medieval buildings. The town was established in the middle of the 7th century close to the ancient site of the Roman fleet base at Richborough. By the 9th century it was a thriving port but between the 9th and 11th centuries it was frequently raided by the Danes. One of the five original Cinque Ports, Sandwich, however, declined in the 14th century, partly because of the silting up of its harbor. A stone town wall (probably replacing a palisade and a ditch) was built in the years 1274–1275. This was improved in 1321, and again in 1385 under Sir Simon Burley, constable of Dover Castle. Further work was done in 1404 and 1412, and in 1451 a bulwark armed with guns was built at the southeast corner of the town. This proved effective in defending against the French attack of 1457. Work on the urban fortifications continued through the second half of the 15th century, and large sections of walls have been preserved to this day. The plan shows: 1: Davey's gate; 2: The quay; 3: Sandown Gate; 4: New Gate; 5: The Butts (archers' practice ground); 6: Canterbury Gate.

Opposite bottom: *Plan of Winchelsea (14th c.).* Winchelsea, located approximately two miles (3 km) southwest of Rye and seven miles (12 km) northeast of Hastings in East Sussex, was founded by King Edward I in 1288. It actually replaced an earlier port which had been destroyed by a massive flood a year before. New Winchelsea and its port had in the 1300s a considerable trade in wine from Guyenne, France, and it was also a fishing port. King Edward I, an inveterate town planner, may well have taken a hand himself in the grid design, which resembles some of his French bastides (notably Monsegur) in southwest France, then a part of his kingdom. The streets were laid out to cross each other more or less at right angles and, within the squares formed, suitable plots were laid out for each householder by name. The new town inherited from Old Winchelsea its affiliation with the Cinque Ports League, together with Rye and the five headports. The town suffered a terribly destructive French raid in 1360, after which recovery was painfully slow. Winchelsea remained prosperous, although reduced in size, until the 1520s, when the silting up of the harbor ultimately destroyed its significance as a port. The map shows. 1: Tidal Harbor on the River Brede; 2: Strand Gate; 3: St. Thomas Church; 4: Market; 5: New Gate; 6: St. Giles Church; 7: Gate; 8: Gate; 9: Marshes.

London was becoming a substantial city, most present-day cities were well established, and in England the ten largest towns were in this order: (1) London; (2) York; (3) Bristol; (4) Norwich; (5) Plymouth; (6) Coventry; (7) Lincoln; (8) Salisbury; (9) King's Lynn; and (10) Colchester.

Merchant guilds and trading fellowships joined forces, founding associations and consortia (like the famous German Hansa) in order to regulate trade, spread the risks, supervise prices, and fight piracy. In the 13th century such an organization appeared in Britain, known as England's League of the Cinque Ports. Originally the Cinque ("five" in French) Ports included the five English ports of Dover, Hythe, Hastings, Romney and Sandwich with Rye and Winchelsea as later additions. This coastal confederation of English traders and seamen reached a total of 42 towns at its medieval peak. The Cinque Ports cities were granted extensive powers of self-government and in the administration of justice, and freedom from tax and toll by a charter in the 1200s. The fortunes of the Cinque Ports varied a lot. Dover, with its excellent coastal harbor, prospered. Others fared less well. The sea receded over the medieval period, and rivers silted up, leaving Winchelsea and Tenterden totally isolated from the coast. Rye transformed from a coastal port into a river one, with subsequent loss of trade. Once bustling, prosperous towns dwindled into villages of little significance.

England was growing increasingly nationalist in the second half of the 14th century and fortifying the southeastern cities exposed to French raiders was something of a national effort, as well as one dictated by self-interest. The prosperous cities of Kent, Sussex and Hampshire did not want to share the fate of Rye and Winchelsea (devastated in the 1370s). So citizens played their part, alongside the Crown, in strengthening their town walls.

CITY FORTIFICATIONS

Despite the great diversity to be found among British towns, they had many fundamental features in common. Some towns grew entirely within the protection of the outer bailey of a castle, whilst many town walls effectively formed an extension to the defensive system of a fortress (e.g., Caernarvon and Denbigh). Towns increasingly tended to become independent of castles as the need for defense declined, but even so the first care of a free city was to build a wall in order to protect inhabitants and their wealth, but also to demonstrate its political importance, independence and pride. The city walls indeed fulfilled several functions. The walled enclosure defined the urban area and indicated the space to be populated. The wall was an object of pride and prestige, a sign of union, a source of confidence and self-consciousness, the expression of physical and moral solidarity, the reflection of the spirit of the citizens, who despised peasants. In many cases, the city wall was a civic status symbol rather than a military defensive structure. It was the legitimate conclusion of the process of emancipation making the inhabitants no longer villains but a recognized social group. The urban wall also constituted a juridical border, as the town had tutelage over the surrounding countryside, which furnished raw materials, food and manpower. The town's authority spread around, and certain particularly important cities dominated the villages in their vicinity, sometimes a whole region. Once established, a town had geographical limits. It was important that peasants living outside the town did not share its privileges and liberties. Although England was united, regional particularism and local privileges were still strong and urban fortifications put a physical barrier between "them" and "us." Also when a town had its own legal jurisdiction it was important to know how far the authority of its court extended. Thus a town's boundaries were known, documented and perambulated. The bounds of some Welsh boroughs were very large; Conwy's measured some 18 miles (30 km). Others were very small: Boroughbridge was 95 acres (40 hectares), and Bishop's Castle only 11 acres (5 hectares).

Evidence shows that town wall construction started in earnest in the early 13th century when the threat of invasion from both France and Wales led to renewed activity. During the following two centuries construction was continued with a steady build-up in complexity, particularly with regard to walltowers and gateways. By 1500 many towns of any importance were surrounded by defensive walls of some sort. Construction and maintenance were financed by the municipality and the citizens themselves. As can be imagined, the construction of urban walls was a costly undertaking. Every extension of the town diameter and every foot of masonry implied greater building costs, greater maintenance expenses, and a larger garrison for adequate defense. Therefore the wall's strength and perimeter were extremely various. When the edification of a castle was due to the lord's private initiative, construction of a city wall was a collective undertaking. The urban wall, therefore, resumed the ancient concept of public interest, which had disappeared since the collapse of the Roman Empire. The large amount of money needed was usually raised by a murage grant, which enabled taxes or tolls to be levied specifically for the construction of a town wall. Urban defenses were in some cases vestiges of ancient Roman enceintes or improvised fortifications dating from the time of Viking invasions. Fortifications were built or reconstructed according to the wealth and strength of the city. The outline of a town wall depended on many factors. It could follow the line of any earlier defenses; it might simply surround the town; or it might leave some space for expansion. Some towns, unable to afford a complete circuit of wall, simply constructed gates across the main accesses in order to levy tolls and taxes (e.g., Chesterfield, Henley-in-Arden and Tewkesbury). Stone walls were by far not universal, many cities could not afford strong defenses and retained earthwork defenses until quite late in the medieval period (e.g., Cambridge, Lichfield, St. Albans and Salisbury). At Coventry, for example, such fortifications were replaced by stone walls only in the 15th century. A few towns had fortified bridges (e.g., Monmouth, Warkworth, Bedford, Oxford, and Durnham). Royal boroughs tended to be walled, whilst those controlled by the Church were not. Most Midlands and southeast England lesser towns were not defended, and most of those towns which did acquire urban fortifications did not do so until the 13th century, having thus grown for centuries without them. The construction of the urban enceinte was a long process lasting for years, and depended on budgets as well as population growth, lurking danger and the probality of a war. Certain enceintes were never completed.

While a private castle housed a tiny group of combatants in a small space, a town grouped a rather large number of non-combatant inhabitants living and working in a relative large space. The urban enceinte was an ensemble of comprehensive military constructions established around a place of life and work intended to provide security. Its configuration resulted in a difficult compromise between defensive necessities which demanded inaccessibility (possibly as strong as those of a castle) and the requirements of living and trading conditions which tended on the contrary to establish the city near a commercial road, to develop the area and to multiply accesses. To fortify with efficiency a large city was thus a difficult task. The evolution of urban military architecture was directly connected to castral fortification and practically all elements of the former were applied to the latter, including ditches, walls, brattice, turrets and towers with variable height, strength and shapes. Those elements were fitted with the same combat emplacements such as crenels and merlons, loopholes and crosslets, hoarding, later machicolation, and later firing ports and embrasures adapted to the use of firearms.

While one tends to think of the city walls in terms of siege, with defenders behind the crenellation casting down projectiles on ascending invaders, the peacetime everyday and even more important purpose of walls must not be neglected: control of entry. The particularity of urban fortification was, therefore, the importance given to the access, by definition the most vulnerable place in a fortified unit. Urban gatehouses on the whole had the same structure as those of castles. They included a wide arched portal deeply recessed in one tower (or between two strong flanking towers), heavy doors, a drawbridge, a portcullis and a chamber for the windlass on the first floor, completed with active combat emplacements such as firing chambers, a guardhouse, loopholes, crosslets, murder-holes, and brattice and machicolation. Beside military defensive elements, the city gatehouse also included a custom-office where taxes and tolls were levied on all persons and all goods coming in or going out of the city. The urban gatehouse also played a prestigious and symbolical role. Its imposing defenses displayed the city's strength and many ornaments showed with ostentation to visitors and travelers its wealth and importance. For security reasons entry points for the town were as limited as possible, resulting on many occasions in annoying traffic-jams, particularly on market days. Therefore secondary accesses—called posterns—were arranged and opened in peacetime. From dusk to dawn, all drawbridges, gates and posterns were closed.

Towns located on waterways were generally prosperous with intense fluvial and commercial activities, and fluvial accesses were defended by watergates fitted with defensive elements rather similar on those of a landgate. Also a chain was extended across the entry into a harbor or river in part to prevent access by smugglers, or enemy or hostile vessels. In reality the main function of such chains was to control trade and ensure the collection of tolls. The mechanism housing the chain and allowing it to be raised and lowered was housed in a defensive tower, often a small fortress in its own right. Chain towers were built, for example, at Dartmouth (Devon), East Cowes (Isle of Wight, Hampshire), Kingston-upon-Hull (East Riding, Yorkshire).

The urban fortifications were manned by a militia composed of all physically able male citizens, recruited from the wealthiest of them—the only ones who could afford weapons and equipment, had time to train, and had strong motivation to defend their family, property and wealth. As time went by the wealthy burghers considered fighting too perilous for themselves and their sons, and they found training a waste of their precious time, and the condition of soldier unworthy of their rank. Instead they paid for professional and mercenary replacement.

Suburbs

Towns were growing, which in turn attracted more and more people. The story of medieval cities is of people trying to get into towns, not out of them. Only towns with their special legal status offered freedom, the conditions and facilities for an existence based on the production and exchange of goods and services as opposed to the rural life on the land outside. In peacetime, townsmen were allowed to cultivate strips of ground right up to the town's enclosure. Outside the town, in front of the gatehouse, there were generally one or more inns for travelers who had arrived after nightfall when the gates were closed. A few artisans, traders and shopkeepers might move alongside, and after a while economic activities just outside of the main gates were mushrooming. A new settlement was created, called a suburb. The suburb often resulted from new settlers and growing populations who found no place left inside the saturated town, and who built houses there, where the ground was available and cheaper. A suburb might also come into existence because of the installation of a convent outside the walls. The development of a suburb was always dangerous, though, because it was outside the protection of the walls, and therefore exposed to theft in peacetime and destruction and looting in wartime. Municipalities tried to regulate, sometimes to forbid, those illegal and spontaneous occupations, but after a while the temporary settlement became a permanent part of the town. The suburb often turned into a major satellite nucleus of economic life in competition with the older and usually smaller markets within the walls. In most cases, the economic pressure of the suburbs and of the growing population could not be denied, and the risks and fiscal burden of a new wall had to be accepted. Suburbs were then integrated into the town and fortified with new walls, towers, moats and gatehouses. By the end of the Middle Ages, many British towns had reached a layout, which they would generally keep until the Industrial Revolution in the 19th century. For the most part town walls and gates have been dismantled over the centuries in order to make way for new neighborhoods, new streets or improved access. The sum total of what survives, both complete circuits and otherwise, is only a fraction of the hundreds or more towns in Britain which are known to have had enclosing walls. Where the original walls do not survive intact their course can often be traced on old maps, in the present-day layout of the town, and even in street names. The most impressive remaining walls and gates in Britain include, for example, those at Caernarvon, Chepstow, Conwy, Chester, Denbigh, Newcastle, Norwich, Southampton, Tenby, Yarmouth and York.

PRIVATE FORTIFICATIONS

Private fortified townhouses also existed. They were somewhat similar in status to rural fortified manor houses but built within the walls of a town or city. Some of these were the houses of wealthy merchants with high social status who could hold considerable sums of precious goods and money at home, so their houses were strongly built. Other private urban fortified dwellings were owned by those who were wealthy, but had modest social status, such as civil servants (usually clerics). Because towns were so heavily redeveloped, very few of these buildings have survived and even contemporary medieval documents only rarely mention or describe these houses. Examples are still to be seen, though, like Hutton Hall (Cumberland), Isaacs Hall and Wensum Lodge, both in Norwich (Norfolk).

Monasteries, priories, churches and other ecclesiastical properties like bishops' castles and priests' towers were private residences often defended against intruders and thieves. Monastic communities were made up of mainly high-status people, and most abbots would be the close relatives of castle-owning lords. Monasteries were also often used as stop-over residencies for traveling lords. Many monastic fortifications such as walls and gatehouses were actually status displays rather than really defensive, although urban and peasant riots (and Scottish raids in the north) did occasionally put such defenses to the test. Churches were an important resource for the local peasant community, having many functions beyond spiritual succor. In unsafe areas like the Marches, this included short-term defense against raiding bands. The later Middle Ages in England were marked by rising anti–Catholicism. The pope was hated because it was thought he sided with the French. Clerical wealth and privileges aroused endless resentment and, on the whole, high ecclesiastics were identified with government mismanagement and intolerable taxation. The murder of Becket in 1170 had been universally unpopular, but from the 14th century such crimes against prelates brought public rejoicing. For example, Bishop Stapleton of Exeter was murdered by a mob in 1326. Archbishop Sudbury of Canterbury was assassinated in 1381, and Bishop Ayscough of Salisbury, secretary to King Henry VI, suffered the same fate. So to defend themselves, prelates fortified their residences. Hence a great many of the surviving late-medieval fortifications are ecclesiastical sites. These buildings were not defendable against an army, but they provided some degree of safety against rioting mobs or gangs of marauders. Examples of fortified ecclesiastical sites are at York Abbey (Yorkshire), Wetheral Priory (Cumberland), Ewenny Priory (Glamorgan), Butley Priory (Suffolk), and Wells Cathedral Precinct (Somerset), to name a few.

(Continued on page 277.)

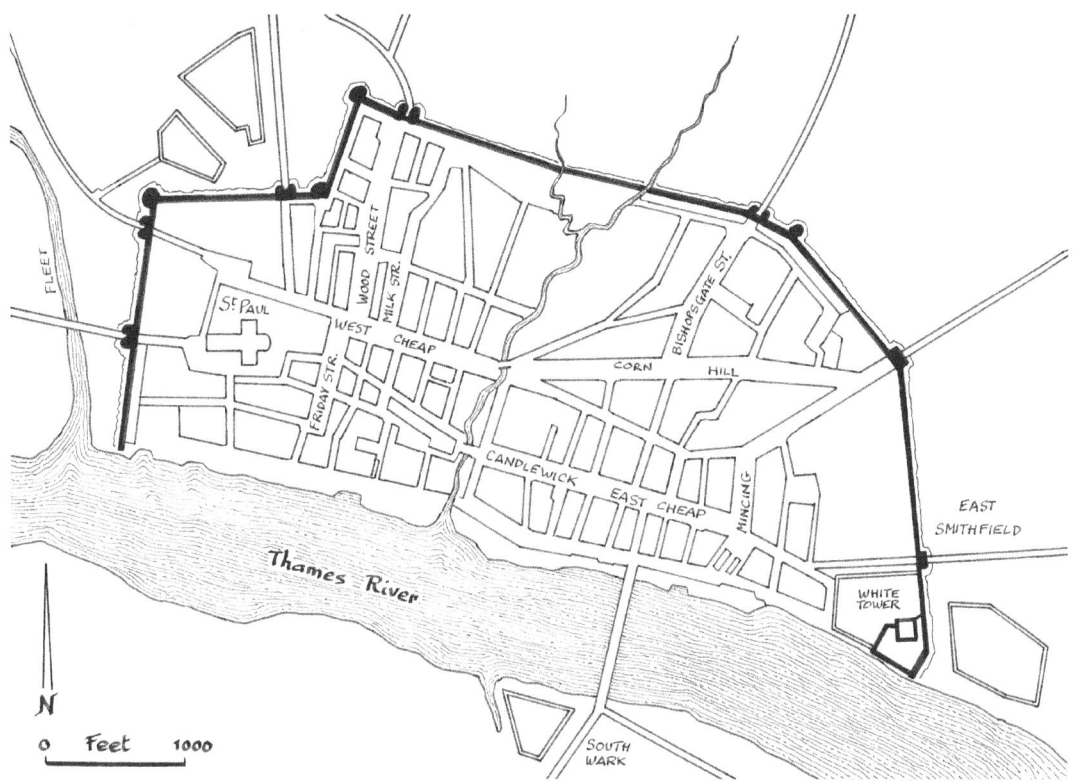

London in the 12th c. After the Norman conquest in 1066 the city fortifications dating from Roman times were reinforced, as much to protect the Normans from the hostile inhabitants as to protect London from outside invaders. King William I had two fortifications built: the White Tower, the first part of the Tower of London to be built, was constructed in 1078 to the east of the city, between Aldgate and the river Thames; and Baynard's Castle, to the southwest, next to the River Fleet, near present day Blackfriars station. A third fortification, Montfichet's Castle, was built to the northwest by Gilbert de Monfichet, a native of Rouen and relative of William's. This tower was demolished by King John in 1213, after he banished Richard, successor to Gilbert, the actual owner. The site of Monfichet's Castle more or less corresponds with today's Blackfriars Thameslink station on Ludgate Hill. Later in the medieval period the walls were redeveloped, with the addition of crenellations, gates and stronger towers. There were six main entrances through the wall into the city, five built by the Romans at different times in their occupation of London. These were, going clockwise from Ludgate in the west to Aldgate in the east: Ludgate, Newgate, Aldersgate, Cripplegate, Bishopsgate and Aldgate. A seventh, Moorgate, was added in medieval times between Cripplegate and Bishopsgate. The gatehouses were multistory buildings with one or two archways through the middle for traffic, protected by gates and portcullises. They were often used as prisons, or to display executed criminals to deter passers-by. Beheaded traitors often had their head stuck on a spike on London Bridge, then their body quartered and spread among the gates. The gates were used as checkpoints, to control people entering and leaving the city, and to collect tolls that were being charged for the upkeep of the wall, or any other project that might require money. Collecting taxes was in fact an important source of revenue. The gates were repaired and rebuilt many times. After the restoration of the monarchy in 1660 all of the city gates were unhinged and had their portcullises wedged open, rendering them defenseless, but they were retained as a visible sign of the prestige of the city. Most of the gates were demolished after 1760 due to traffic congestion.

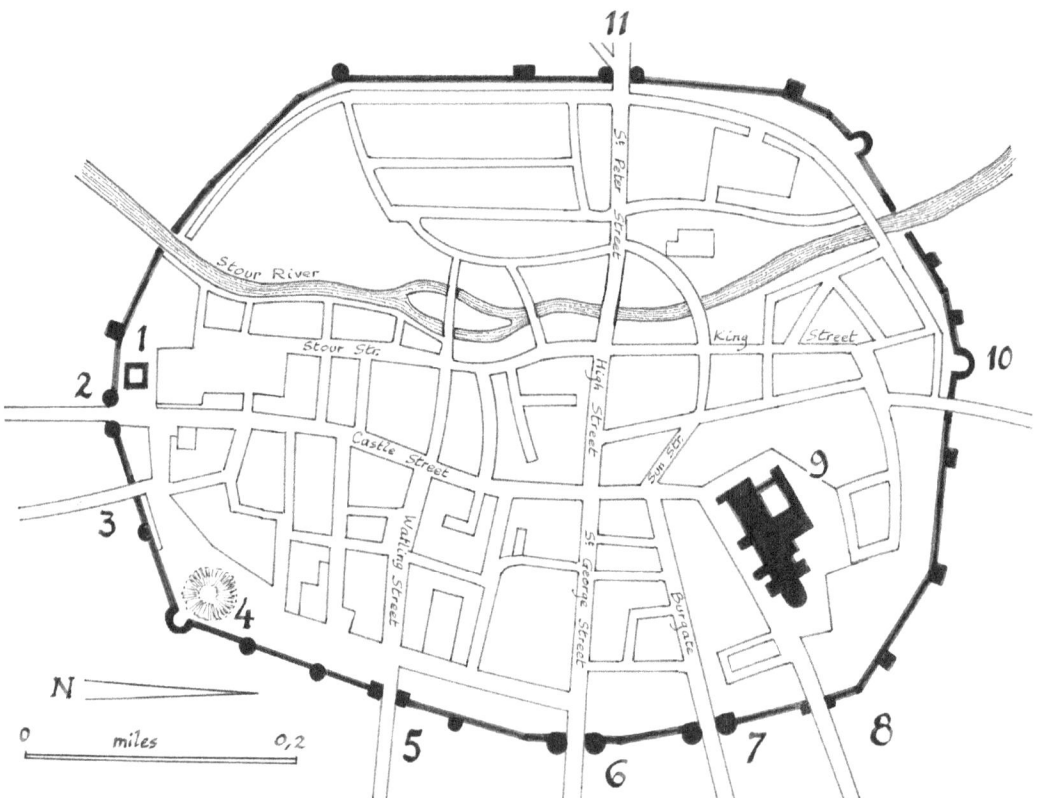

Canterbury in east Kent, one of the major historic cities of Christendom in Europe, originated from an Iron Age oppidum, then a Roman fort established in A.D. *43, which was abandoned in* A.D. *70 Not until the end of the 3rd century did the town become Roman Durovernum Cantiacorum. The Roman defense, built between* A.D. *270 and 290 included a masonry wall, an earthen rampart behind, a ditch in front and seven gates. From early Anglo-Saxon times Canterbury was the royal center of the kingdom of Kent, and St. Augustine established England's first bishopric here in 597. In the 9th century the walled town was a refuge against the threat of the Vikings who wintered on the Isle of Thanet in 850, and made several raids between 991 and 1016. They besieged Canterbury in 1011 but were repulsed. Right after the Norman conquest William I ordered the construction of a motte-and-bailey castle utilizing an earlier Romano-British burial mound for the motte. Soon afterwards a new castle with a massive keep was built. The end of the 14th century saw considerable work on the refurbishment of the defenses, notably gates were reinforced and mural towers added. Further work took place at the end of the 15th century, probably as a matter of civic pride rather than defense. The Norman keep was purchased by the city council in 1928 and the remaining parts of the defensive circuit (about 3 km in perimeter) are now a part of the city's historical heritage. The map shows: 1: Ruins of the Norman keep; 2: Worth Gate (originally giving access to the keep's bailey), demolished in 1791; 3: Wincheap Gate; 4: Dane John Mound (emplacement of Norman motte-and-bailey castle); 5: Riding Gate; 6: St. George Gate, built in the late 9th century; 7: Burgate; 8: Roman Queningate, built in the late 3rd century; 9: Cathedral; 10: North Gate, refurbished between 1390 and 1396; 11: West Gate, built in c. 1380 on the site of a former Roman gate, used as city prison until 1829.*

Burgate, Canterbury. Originally a Roman construction, this gate was the principal entrance of the burh in Anglo-Saxon times. The Burgate was refurbished in 1475 and entirely rebuilt in 1525 in an up-to-date style incorporating brick.

264　British Fortifications

Town Gate at Chepstow. The urban fortifications were built in the 1270s. The wall were 2 m (7 feet) thick, up to 6 m (20 feet) high, and ran the length of 1,200 yards (1.1 km) around the town, enclosing an area of over 110 acres (45 hectares). Chepstow Town Gate was originally the only gate in the 13th-century Port Wall, founded by Roger Bigod, Earl of Norfolk. The two-story stone gatehouse was remodelled in the late 15th century and in 1524 the upper story was made into a prison by Charles Somerset, Earl of Worcester. It is now sadly hemmed in and hidden by other buildings and the windows, battlements and internal archways are 19th- and 20th-century replacements.

6. Late Plantagenet Fortifications 1327–1485   265

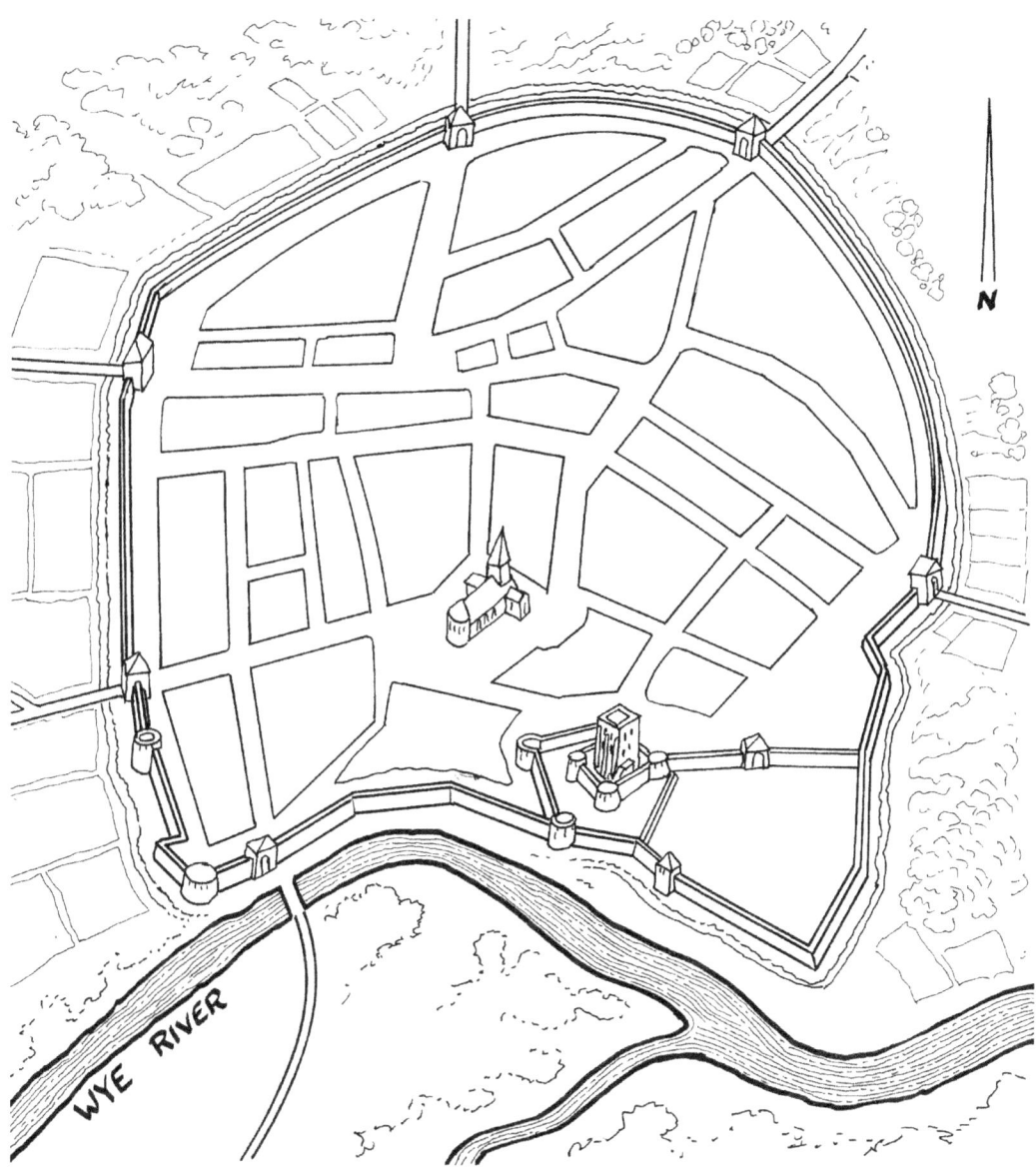

The county town of Herefordshire, Hereford, lies on the River Wye, approximately 16 miles (26 km) east of the border with Wales, 21 miles (34 km) southwest of Worcester, and 23 miles (37 km) northwest of Gloucester. Hereford was founded in around A.D. 700 and became the Saxon capital of West Mercia. Hereford, a base for successive holders of the title Earl of Hereford, was once the site of, Hereford Castle, which rivalled that of Windsor in size and scale. This was a base for repelling Welsh attacks and providing a secure stronghold for English kings such as King Henry IV when on campaign in the Welsh Marches against Owain Glyndŵr. The castle was dismantled in the 1700s and landscaped into Castle Green.

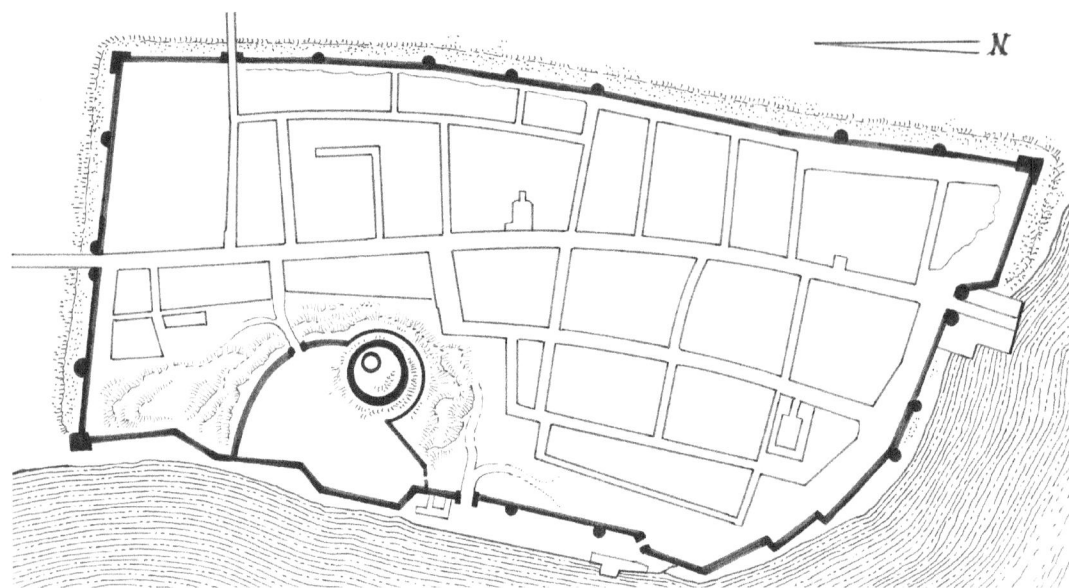

Southampton was created by the Romans in about A.D. 70 on a bend in the River Itchen. The Roman town, called Clausentum, was fortified in the 2nd century with an earth rampart, a wooden palisade and a ditch. In addition an inner area of 8 acres was given its own ditch, rampart and palisade. In the 4th century the inner area was strengthened and given stone walls. The Roman army left Britain in A.D. 409 and the town of Clausentum was abandoned soon afterwards. The Saxon King Ine built a new town on the other side of the Itchen about A.D. 690–700 It stood where St. Mary's Church is today. The new town, called Hamwic or Hamtun, soon became a large and important port (later this name changed into Southampton). It is estimated that the population of the Saxon town was 4,000–5,000, which was very large by Saxon standards. The new town was laid out with streets on a grid pattern like the old Roman town, but all the buildings in it were of wood. Saxon Southampton suffered severely in the Danish raids of the 9th and 10th centuries. The Danes sacked the town several times. In the 10th century Southampton went into decline. This may have been partly due to the Danish raids but it was probably also due to the silting up of the Itchen River. As the first Southampton declined many people probably moved to Winchester, but at least some moved to a new settlement beside the Test. This new settlement was also called Hamtun. It was much smaller than the old town. At the time of Domesday (1086) it may have had about 1,000 inhabitants. The Normans also built a wooden castle in Southampton. In the 12th century the castle was rebuilt in stone. Southampton grew rapidly and probably had about 3,000–4,000 inhabitants by the 14th century. By the 13th century there was a small suburb north of Southampton where Above Bar is today. By 1250 another little suburb, Newtown, had grown up outside the East Gate on the road to St. Mary's church. By the 13th century Southampton was fortified with an earth rampart with a wooden palisade and a ditch. In the years 1260–1300 a stone wall replaced it. Unfortunately the wall only protected the landward side of the town. The wall did not extend along the shore, and this proved a dire weakness in 1338 when a force of Frenchmen and Sicilians made a deadly raid. In 1339 the king visited Southampton and ordered improvements to be made to the fortifications. The work went on for decades and was a huge burden on the town. The cost of the new fortifications was immense. Several new towers were added to the walls and in 1378–1380 the keep of the castle was rebuilt. The Bar Gate was given a new facade with machicolations. This time the walls of Southampton were extended along the seafront.

In the late Middle Ages the prosperity of Southampton partly depended on trade with the Italians. Southampton also benefited from the Hundred Years' War, which dragged on from the middle of the 14th to the middle of the 15th centuries. Ships were built for the navy in Southampton and the town was used as a departure point and supply base for armies on their way to France.

Bargate, Southampton. Constructed in Norman times in c. 1180 as part of the fortified walled city, the Bargate was the main point of entry and exit for the north of the town. Further alterations were made to the building around 1290, and additional archways were added in 1764 and 1774.

Above: *Westgate, Winchester. Standing at the upper end of High Street, the Westgate was built in the 12th century, with later additions in the 13th and 14th centuries. When the defensive needs of the city declined, the Westgate was put to use as a jail and debtors' prison. From the late 19th century it has been used as a town museum and secure storage for city archives.*

Opposite: *The Westgate, built in 1338, was the only access to the quay from the town. Inside the gate was a double portcullis and murder-holes.*

1
2
3
4
5
6
River Dee
N

0 m 150
N
1
2
3
4
5
6
7
8
River Teme
Castle
Bailey
Market

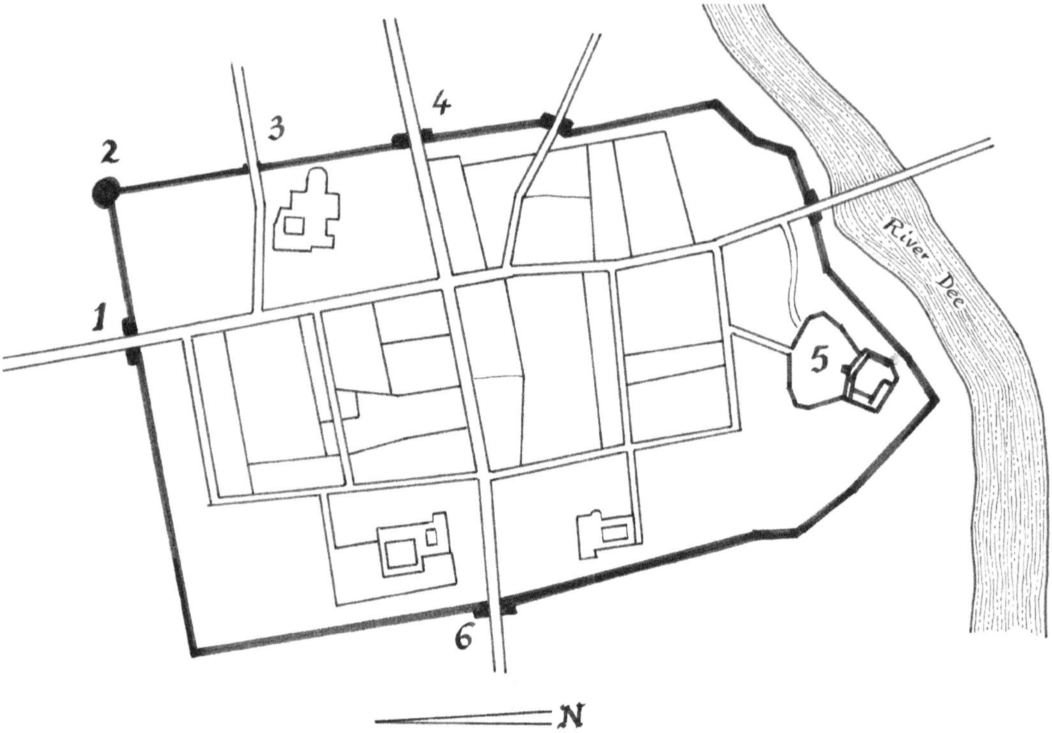

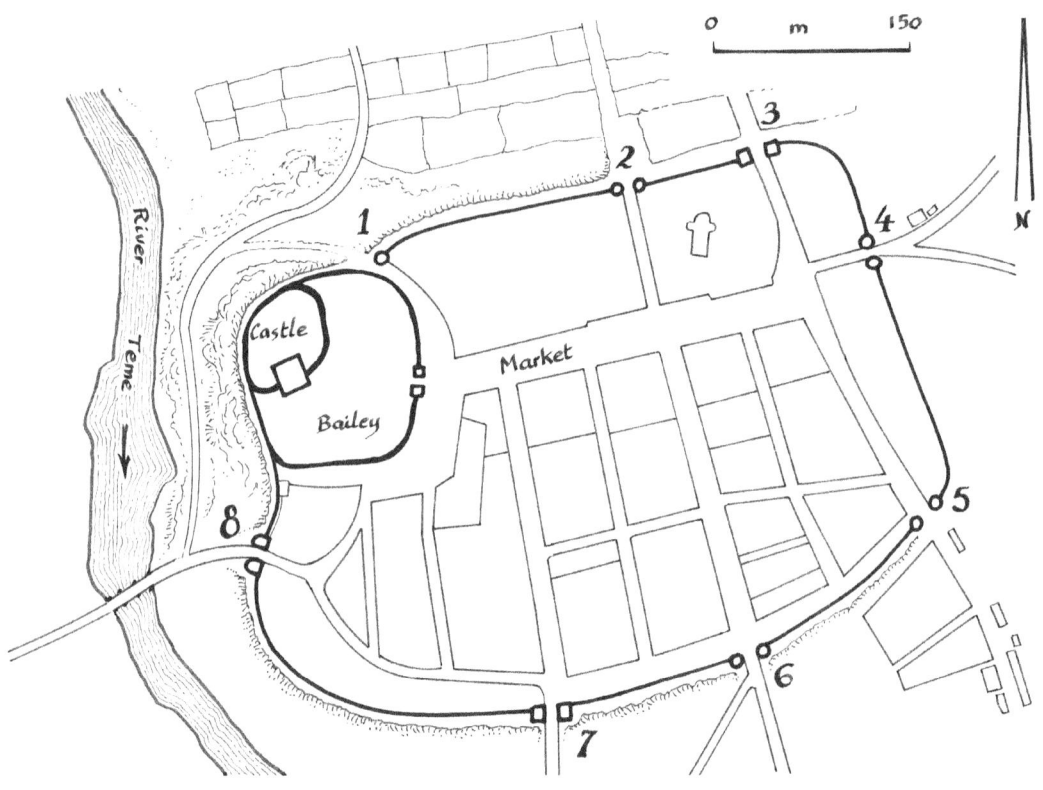

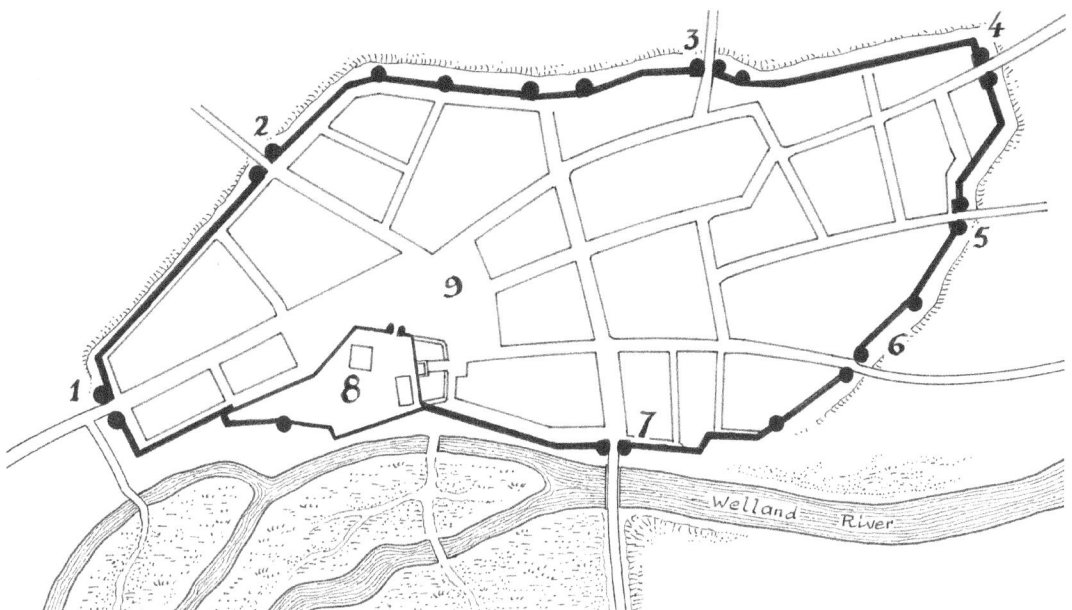

Above: *Stamford, located on the River Welland between Rutland and Peterborough in southwest Lincolnshire, originally grew as a Danish settlement. A walled town, Stamford became an inland port on the Great North Road, and it became famous for its production of wool and woolen cloth. A Norman castle was built about 1075 and apparently was demolished in 1484. The map shows the situation in the Middle Ages: 1: St. Peter's Gate; 2: St. Clement's Gate; 3: New Gate; 4: St. Paul's Gate; 5: St. George's Gate; 6: Water Gate; 7: Bridge Gate; 8: Norman castle (with keep and hall); 9: Market.*

Opposite top: *Situated in Cheshire south of Liverpool, Chester originated from a castrum created by the Romans in a meander of the river Dee. For about 200 years, Chester was garrisoned by the XXth legion Valeria Victrix, whence its Roman name Deva Victrix. The Roman fortifications were re-shaped in the beginning of the 10th century by Aethelflaeda, king Alfred's daughter. The map shows the fortifications which are today well preserved: North Gate; 2: King Charles Tower; 3: Kalevards Gate; 4: East Gate; 5: Castle; 6: Water Gate. The walls encircle the medieval city and constitute the most complete city walls in Britain, the full circuit measuring nearly 2 miles (3 km). The only break in the circuit is in the southwest section in front of County Hall. Of the medieval city another surviving structure is Chester Castle, particularly the Agricola Tower. Much of the rest of the castle has been replaced by the neoclassical County Court and its entrance, the Propyleum.*

Opposite bottom: *Ludlow, one of the most famous English medieval towns, is located in Shropshire close to the Welsh border and the Welsh Marches. It lies within a bend of the river Teme and originates from a Norman manor built in about 1090. With many later additions in the following two centuries, Ludlow Castle is one of the most interesting strongholds in the Marches, in a dominant and imposing position high above the river Teme. It features examples of architecture from the Norman, medieval and Tudor periods. The original Norman castle was part of a series of fortified points along the Welsh border, strategically placed on an important river crossing halfway between Hereford and Shrewsbury. The building of the castle led to the development of the town itself, at first grouped in the outer bailey and around the castle. The street layout seems to be a grid, but it remains unclear whether there ever was a deliberate urban plan. The first defenses were probably a ditch, earthwall and palisade, and these were replaced with a stone wall built between 1233 and 1304. The walls were joined to the castle's outer bailey taking advantage of breaks in the slopes, particularly on the northern side of the ridge, and were surrounded by a ditch elsewhere. Of the following gates, only the massive Broad Gate survives. 1: Portal (leading to the fields); 2: Linney Gate (leading to the fields); 3: Corve Gate; 4: Galdeford Gate; 5: Old Gate; 6: Broad Gate; 7: Mill Gate; 8: Lower Corve Gate.*

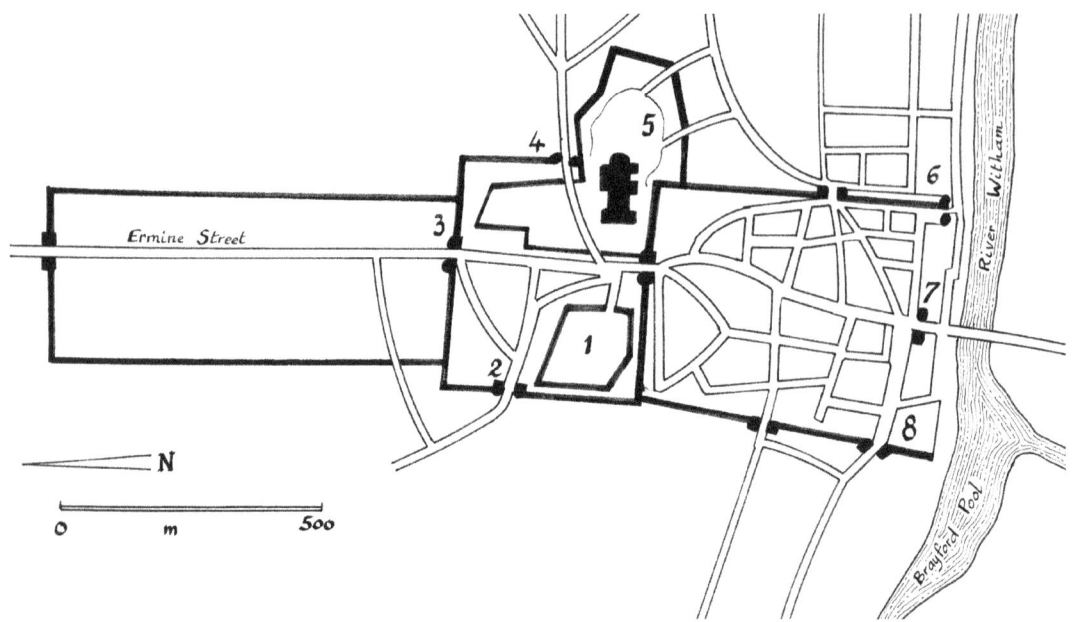

Above: *Plan of Lincoln. The Romans conquered what later became Lincolnshire in* A.D. *48 Shortly afterwards they built a fort on the site of Lincoln. In the late 1st century* A.D. *the area was pacified, the fort was abandoned and a new town named Lindum Colonia was created on the site. Roman Lincoln grew into a large and prosperous town, also an inland port, surrounded with walls and having streets laid out in a grid pattern. Roman Lincoln reached a peak of prosperity in the early 4th century. It declined as Roman civilization was breaking down and the last Roman soldiers left in* A.D. *407 By the 5th century most or all of the town's inhabitants had fled, the Roman buildings gradually fell into ruins, and Lincoln had ceased to be a town. It revived when the Danes conquered the area in the late 9th century. In the 10th century it was captured by Alfred the Great's son, but the Danish influence lingered on. Lincoln grew slowly to be a large and important town again, and by the time of the Domesday Book (1086) Lincoln probably had a population of around 6,000, which by the standards of the time, was a large town. In 1068 William the Conqueror built a wooden motte castle (replaced with a stone castle in the 12th century) to control the townspeople. In the late 11th century a new suburb called New Port grew up with its own market. After a fire that destroyed many buildings in 1123, the town was granted a charter in 1157 giving privileges to rich citizens whose prosperity was based on the export of cloth and wool in the 12th and 13th centuries. In the 14th century Lincoln's prosperity declined. Its wool trade faced increasing competition from abroad and also from Boston and the new port of Hull. The map shows the city walls with 1: Castle; 2: West Postern; 3: Newport Arch; 4: East Gate; 5: Cathedral with walled precinct; 6: Thorne Gate; 7: Stonebow; 8: Newland Gate.*

Opposite top: *Berwick-upon-Tweed. Located in the county of Northumberland on the east coast at the mouth of the River Tweed, Berwick is England's most northerly town, being only 2.5 miles (4 km) from the Scottish border. There is no doubt that Berwick-upon-Tweed can claim the distinction of being the Border Town, as it has had an eventful history inextricably tied up with the struggle for the Anglo-Scottish frontier. Berwick began as an Anglo-Saxon settlement, in the Kingdom of Northumbria, and for four hundred years it regularly changed hands—no fewer than thirteen times between England and Scotland. In the fourteenth century Berwick became a real walled town when King Edward I fortified it against Scottish attack. His defensive walls supplemented the stronghold of Berwick Castle, which stood on the site of the present railway station. Berwick has always been a traditional market town, and a wealthy trading port, but it also boasts some notable architectural features, particularly remarkable bastioned fortifications still to be seen today, dating mainly from the later Elizabethan period. They are among the best preserved and finest of their kind in Europe.*

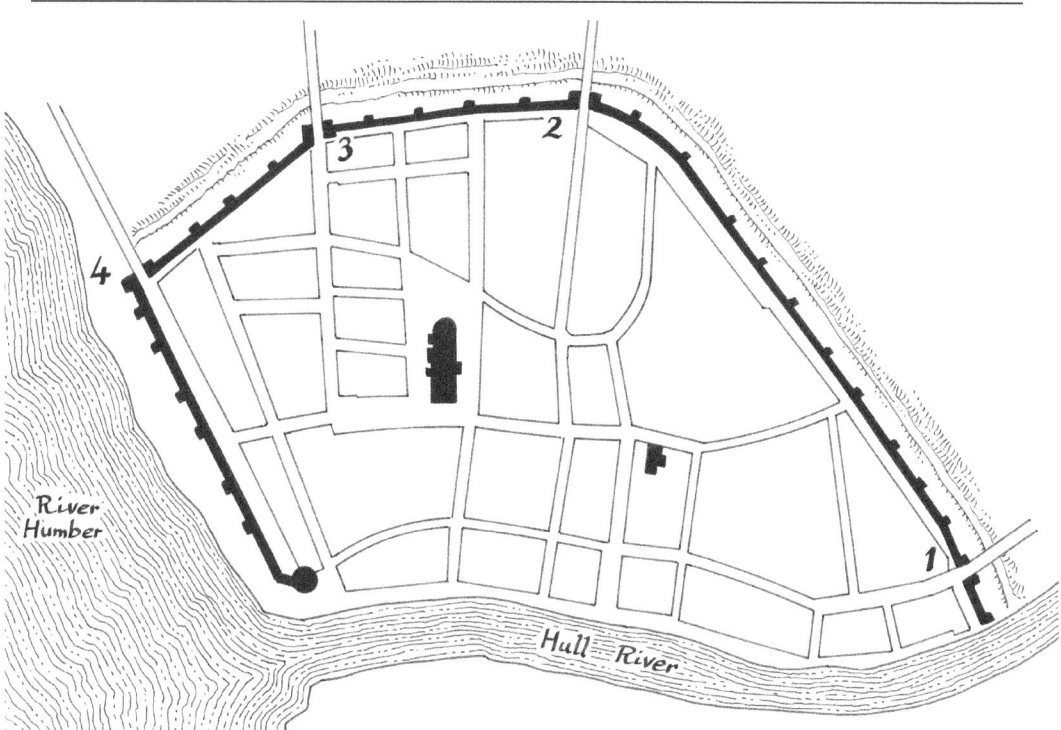

Plan of Hull. The town of Hull in East Yorkshire was founded late in the 12th century. Some local monks needed a port where the wool from their estates could be exported. They chose a place at the junction of the rivers Hull and Humber to build a port. The exact year Hull was founded is not known but it was first mentioned in 1193. It was called Wyke on Hull. In 1279 Hull was granted the right to hold a market and a fair. In 1293 King Edward I acquired Hull, and the city was renamed Kingston (king's town) upon Hull. The king wanted a port in northeast England through which he could supply his army when fighting the Scots. The king set about enlarging Hull. He gave it the right to hold two weekly markets and an annual fair lasting for 30 days. The king also established a mint there about 1300. The same year he built an exchange where merchants could buy and sell goods. The main export from Hull was wool. Much of it was exported to towns in what is now Holland and Belgium, where it was woven and dyed. Some salt was also exported, as well as grain and hides. The chief import into Hull was wine (the drink of the upper classes). Other imports were wood and iron from Scandinavia and furs, wax and pitch. The only other substantial industries were brick-making and tile-making, and fishing. In the early 14th century Hull was given a stone wall and a ditch. There were four main gates: North Gate (1); Beverley Gate (2); Myton Gate (3); and Hessle Gate (4).

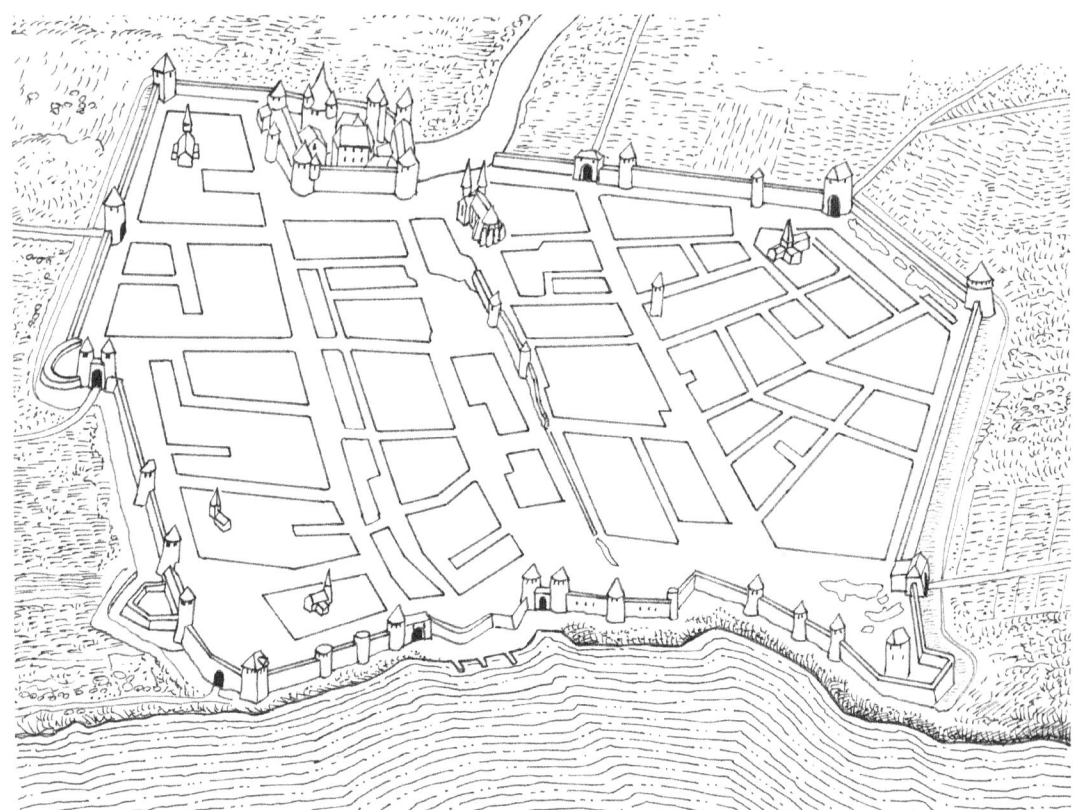

Plan of Bordeaux. The first traces of the town of Bordeaux date from the 1st century B.C. Called Burdigala, it was founded by the Gallic tribe Biturgies Vivisques and soon became a prosperous town. This prosperity was upset by a succession of barbaric invasions by the Vandals, Wisigoths, Franks and Normans until the 12th century. With the marriage of Alienor of Aquitaine to Henri II Plantagenet in 1152, Bordeaux returned to peace, and remained under English control for three centuries. During this long period the town began to grow. The exportation of wine to England in the 13th century gave Bordeaux its reputation in the wine trade. English ownership in Aquitaine gradually dwindled, and by 1453 represented only a small band which extended from Bordeaux to Biarritz. After the Hundred Years' War, as a result of the battle of Castillon, Bordeaux fell back under the authority of the king of France. The citizens felt more English than French and their loyalty to France was put to the test. The town only regained its sovereignty in 1462, and eventually Louis XIV gave Bordeaux the definitive status of a town in the kingdom of France.

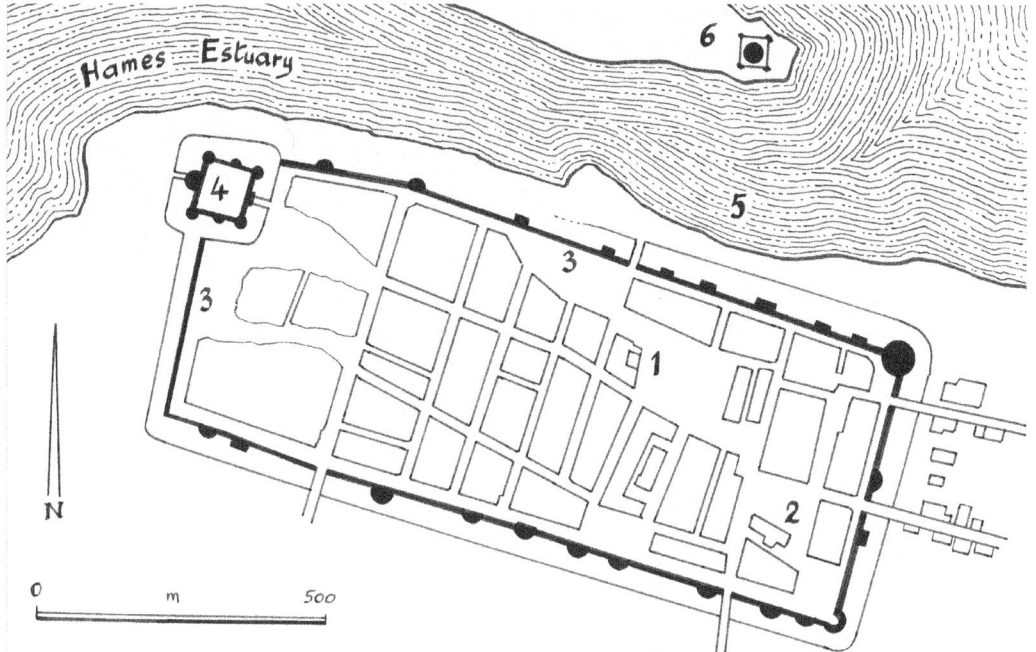

Plan of Calais (15th century). Calais in the ancient county of Artois in northern France, famous for its lace and its six burghers immortalized in bronze by the sculptor Auguste Rodin, is now continental Europe's largest passenger ferry port. The site of Calais has been populated since ancient times, and it started as a fishing place. The Romans developed the settlement as a port called Caletum. As the centuries passed Calais grew in importance as a port under the protection of the counts of Boulogne in the 12th century. While sovereignty over Calais passed from one authority to another, the people were Flemish and spoke Dutch. In 1228 Count Philippe Hurepel, the son of King Philippe Auguste of France, built a castle and had the town enclosed with a stone wall. Calais's position as the point in continental Europe closest to England led the English King Edward III, who believed himself the rightful king of France, to cross the Channel and capture the city in 1347, starving the place into submission after an eleven-month siege. The English cut the town off from supply ships by building a wooden tower, known as the Lancaster Tower, at the entrance to the harbor. The Treaty of Brétigny in 1360 ceded officially the city to England. For two centuries Calais remained an integral part of England, and several fortified advanced posts (Sangatte, Marck, Oye, Fretun, Hames, Guines and Balinghem) were built to protect the important English bridgehead. In the 15th century as artillery grew in importance, the Lancaster Tower (later known as Fort Risban) was surrounded by a perimeter wall and two low towers mounting guns. At the same time Calais's urban walls and towers were re-inforced with fortifications able to support artillery. To the west of the town sluices and watergates were built in order to control the river Hames. When these sluice gates were closed, the river water was diverted to flood the land to the south of the town. This inundation system (designed by Flemish engineers) could be used to prevent an attack on Calais from the land. In the early 16th century the English built a fort to protect these vital sluices. This fort, called Fort Nieulay, was square with four stone towers. In 1556, as the threat of a French attack was looming over Calais, the military engineer John Rogers (d. 1558) was ordered by King Henry VIII to construct bastioned fortifications at Boulogne and Ambleteuse, which were briefly held by England in the 1540s. Calais, regarded as invincible, was besieged, captured and returned to France in 1598. Although its military role declined, the fortified city remained a key French check against British invasion. The plan shows: 1: Tour du Guet (watchtower); 2: Notre Dame Church; 3: Town walls (late 13th century); 4: Hurepel's Castle (late 13th century); 5: Harbor; 6: Lancaster Tower (later renamed Fort Risban).

Left: *The Tour du Guet (watchtower), located near the Place d'Armes in the center of Calais, is one of the town's oldest monuments. It is 35 m high, and legend has it that it was constructed in c. 810 by the Carolingian Emperor Charlemagne (742–814) as a lighthouse and a defense against Viking raiders. More probably it was built by Philippe Hurepel together with the town fortifications. The tower was damaged in 1580 by an earthquake, and reconstructed in 1606. It was transformed into a lighthouse between 1818 and 1848, and until 1905 it housed firemen and watchmen (whence its name). The Tour du Guet, listed as a Historic Monument since 1931, has survived heavy bombardments in 1940 and 1944.*

Right: *Wetheral Priory Gatehouse. The Benedictine Priory in Wetheral (diocese of Carlisle, Cumbria) was founded in 1106 by its motherhouse of St. Mary's Abbey, York. The fortified gatehouse, built in the 15th century, is virtually the only standing remnant of the much grander priory buildings, and was the main entry into the monastic outer court. The gatehouse has a pair of domestic chambers on two floors above the main entranceway. The rest of the priory, which included a chapel, administrative offices, service buildings and a school, was demolished following Henry VIII's dissolution of the monasteries in the 1530s. The gatehouse survived as the vicarage to the local church, and it is now in the care of English Heritage.*

British Bastides in France

A bastide was a type of newly built village or small town, largely in the 13th and 14th centuries during the reigns of Henry III, Edward I, Edward II and Edward III in England and in Aquitaine (comprising Guyenne and Gascony in southwest France), as the king of England was also duke of Gascony. Bastides were founded for security as a part of the English defensive system in the south, but also for colonization and economic purposes, and many of them were dependent on the production and exportation to England of grain and wine. The bastide's founder, the English king or his representative — seneschal or count or other vassal — gave land and each bastide was founded on the basis of a charter. A charter was an official document specifying the grant of rights, stating that the granter formally recognized the prerogative of the recipient to exercise the rights specified. Attractive legal and economic privileges were granted to new settlers who came to build the town and work and develop the bastide. The charter guaranteed their freedom, safety and property ownership. In return, the Crown could raise taxes and levy troops in the event of war. The lord of a successful bastide could expect an increase of revenue from the rents, fairs and market tolls, justice profits, and trade tariffs. However, not all bastides flourished and a number have vanished.

With allowances made for local terrain, bastides were laid out according to a rectangular grid (with streets, as much as possible, meeting at right angles) derived from ancient Roman town design. The grid-plan presented two main advantages. First it allowed entire blocks of buildings to be dedicated to a specific use, for example public buildings or marketplaces could be grouped together. Second it made the bastide easier to defend, as soldiers could move rapidly to the point of attack. The bastide was often built on a hilltop, with the streets — usually 8 m wide — dividing the town into rectilinear Roman-like *insulae* (blocks), which, in turn, were divided into *placae* (house and garden lots). Between houses there were *andrones* (narrow separating gaps or back alleys) intended to limit the spread of fire and enable rain and wastewater disposal. A church was obviously always built, as well as a marketplace with *cornières* (arcaded shops) and often a market hall. Fortifications around the bastides varied from a modest enclosing earthwall topped with a palisade to a circuit of stone wall reinforced with towers and stone-fortified entrances with gatehouses. Most bastides have been rebuilt, transformed and enlarged over the centuries. Sadly, many fortifications were dismantled in the course of history, notably at the beginning of the 17th century by order of Cardinal Richelieu, who no longer tolerated private strongholds. As a result very few bastides still have their original characteristics, but in several cases, a few medieval buildings, a section of defensive wall, a gatehouse and the grid-plan are still visible.

In all over 300 bastides were built by the English in fifteen départements in southwest France. Ownership, of course, often changed following the strained relation between England and France, and more particularly when the Hundred Years' War raged back and forth. The bastide of Fleurance in the Gers département, founded

Left: *The bastide of Beaumont-du-Périgord was founded in 1272 by Lucas de Thaney, Seneschal of Guyenne, by order of King Edward I. In 1277 the king granted a charter to the citizens. Beaumont-du-Périgord remained an English possession until 1442, when it was taken by the Viscount de Turenne, lieutenant to Charles VII, King of France. From its medieval past Beaumont-du-Périgord had kept its typical street layout, some remnants of stone wall, the depicted Luzier Gate, and several medieval house façades (notably in the rue Féliciane).*

Bottom: *The village of Saint-Clar, situated in the Lomagne in the département of Gers, originally developed as a castelnau, built in 1274 near a small castle built by the Bishop of Lectoure, Géraud de Monlezun. Following an agreement (and the grant of a charter) between the bishop and Edward I of England in 1289, Saint-Clar became a bastide.*

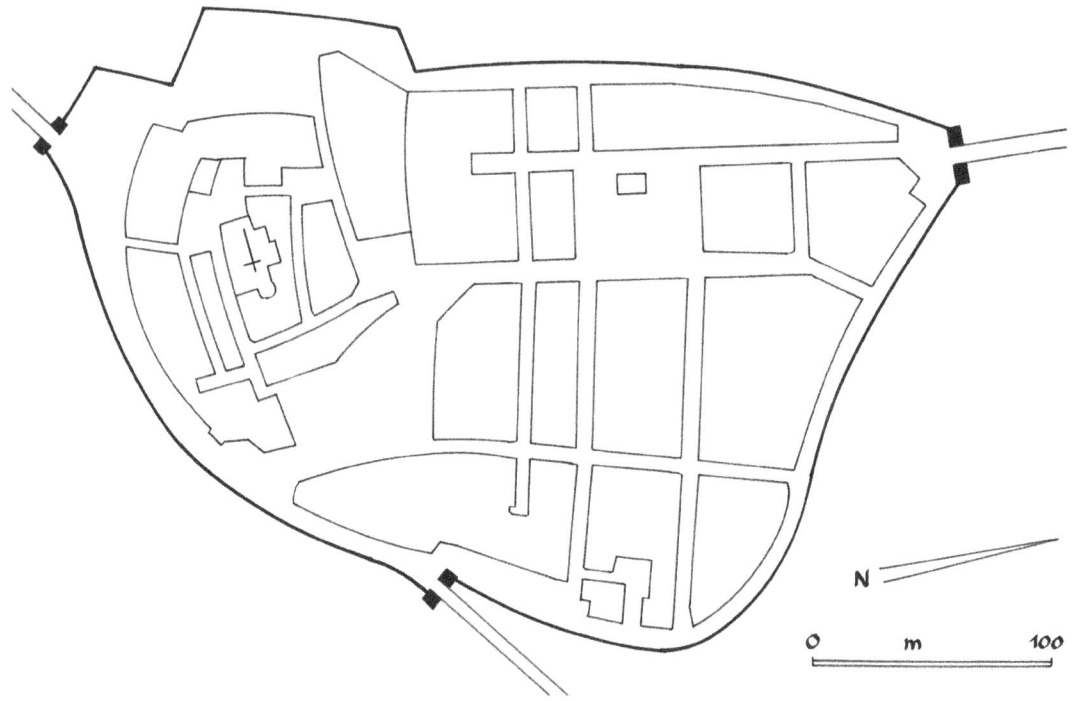

in 1274 by Géraud de Cazaubon, Count of Gaure, was yielded to the king of England in 1279, and returned to France in the 14th century. The bastide of Montreal-du-Gers, founded in 1255 by Count of Toulouse Alphonse de Poitiers, passed under English control in 1279, French in 1324 and English again in 1360. The bastide of Monguilhem, created in 1319 by the English Seneschal William of Montaigut, was captured by the French in 1337 and eventually changed hands. British-built bastides in Gascony include, amongst other examples Lalinde (established in 1267), Libourne (1270), Beaumont-du-Périgord (1272), Cadillac (1280), Villefranche-de-Queyran (1280),

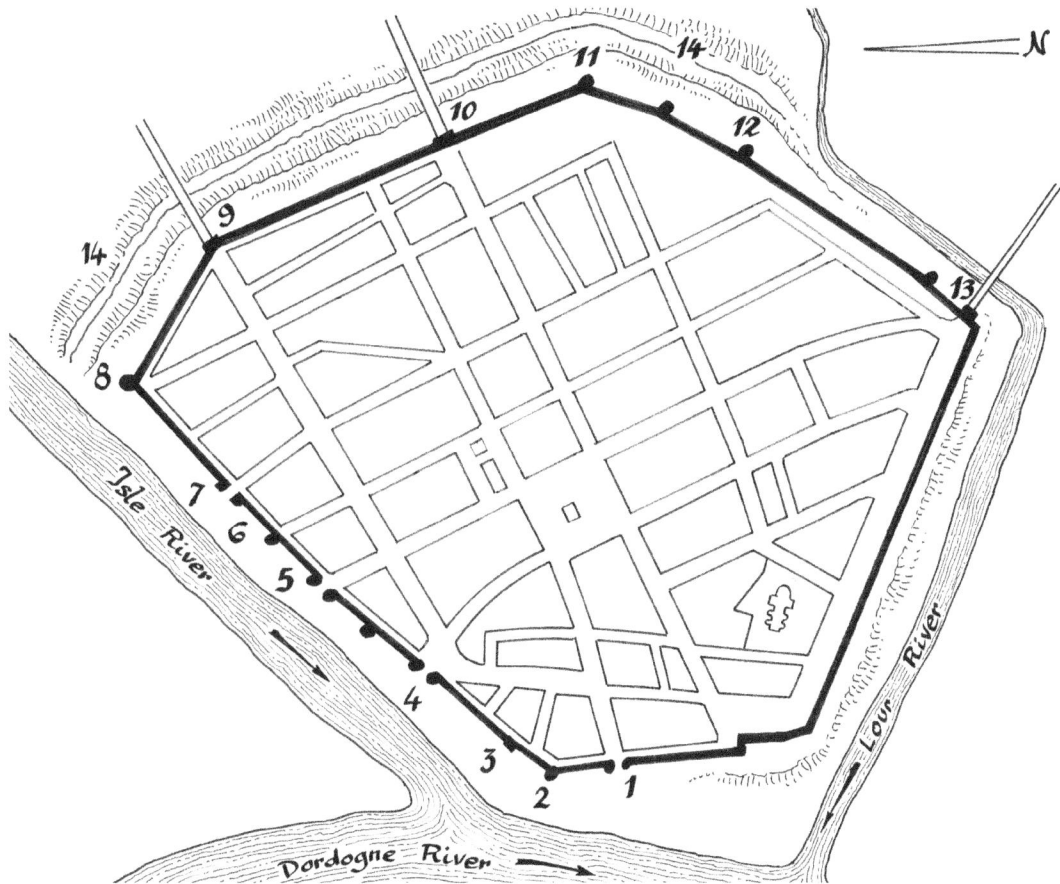

Libourne, in the Aquitaine region in southwestern France, is a sub-prefecture of the Gironde département. Located at the confluence of the Isle and Dordogne Rivers, it was founded in 1270 as a bastide (called Leybornia) by Roger de Leybourne of Kent, then English seneschal of Gascony, under the authority of King Edward I of England. Libourne was defended by a stone wall with towers and gatehouses, a double ditch and, in the south, by the little river Lour acting as a moat. The bastide suffered considerably in the struggles of the French and English for the possession of Gironde in the 14th century, and was finally captured by the French in the 15th century. Today the town is the wine-making capital of northern Gironde and lies near Saint Emilion and Pomerol. 1: Bédignon Gate; 2: Gringalette Tower; 3: Lou Portau Postern; 4: Grand Port Gate; 5: Porte Neuve; 6: Salinières Gate; 7: St. Jacques Gate; 8: Grenouillère Tower; 9: Guitres Gate; 10: Terre Gate; 11: Terreyre Tower; 12: Lour Tower; 13: St. Emilion Gate; 14: Double ditch.

Left: *Hastingues, located near Dax in the Landes département in the Aquitaine region, was a bastide built on a hill in 1292 by the English Lord John Hastings (hence its slightly gallicized name).*

Bottom: *Plan of Monpazier Bastide. The well-preserved bastide of Monpazier (Montis Pazerii, meaning "mount of peace") in the Dordogne is often considered the most typical example of a bastide in the entire southwest of France. Monpazier was founded in 1284 by King Edward I of England with the help of Pierre de Gontaut, Lord of Biron, and it changed ownership several times—English in 1285, French in 1327, English again in 1345—and it was only during the reign of King Charles V of France (1366–1380) that the bastide became definitively French. Despite the ravages of time and war (the Hundred Years' War and the French Wars of Religion) Monpazier has remained remarkably unchanged during its seven-hundred-years existence. Four hundred by two hundred and twenty meters, Monpazier is perfectly quadrilateral and the streets run parallel to the longest sides from one end of the town to the other. These are crossed by transversal streets thus dividing the town into rectangular sections.*

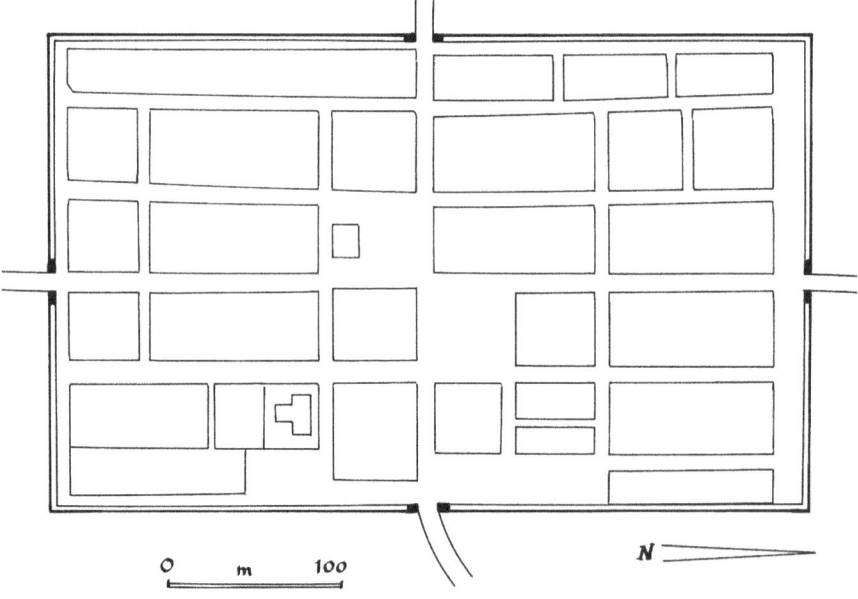

Sauveterre-de-Guyenne (1281), Molière (c. 1284), Monpazier (1284), Roquepine (1285), Beauregard-en-Dordogne (1286), Saint-Clar (1289), Labastide d'Armagnac (1291), Hastingues (1292), Sarron (1315), Montguilhem (1319), Grenade-sur-Adour (1322), Londres (1327), Port-de-Lannes (1330), and Labastide-Chalosse (1342).

Tower Houses in the North

Throughout the Middle Ages life in the country was hazardous and only a castle or fortified town was safe from predatory raids or armed invasions. When conditions improved governments became stable the need to maintain high standards of defensive feature was relaxed, and there emerged the semi-fortified manor. In many cases machicolated walls, towers and gatehouses were retained, but the aristocratic villa was the symbol of the martial traditions of an arrogant ruling upper class. Stokesay Castle in Shropshire, built in the 1290, displays how a fortified manor could already, at the end of the 13th century, provide security but also a reasonable level of comfortable accommodation and privacy with a spacious hall, fine timber roof, shuttered gable windows with a pleasant view across the wooded countryside, wall painting, tiled floor, richly carved fireplace and flowered courtyard.

When England was pacified by a centralized government, the situation was, however, quite different in the north of the main British Isle, where a state of insecurity still reigned during the 14th, 15th and 16th centuries. Until the union of England and Scotland in 1603, the northern countries were very much an unsafe frontier zone. The roots of these troubles lay in the times from 1296 onwards, when King Edward I of England attempted to take control of the Scottish throne. From that time on, although long periods of peace existed, the lives of those on the borders were affected by invasions, raids, burnings, blackmail and murder perpetrated by the so-called Border Reivers, whose heyday was the 15th and 16th centuries. A violent way of life based around strong families and clans developed. Raids and counter-raids led to quarrels and vendettas between them. The feuds, which were often carried on over many years, could be across the border or even between clans of the same nationality. Many borderers indeed wore their nationality lightly, and there were many marriages between Scottish and English families. Protection money or extorted tribute in kind was paid by small farmers and peasants to the Reivers in return for freedom from molestation, and to prevent raids and theft. Some rulers, particularly Henry VIII, encouraged the troubles on the Anglo-Scottish border both to cause problems for the opposite side, and to develop troops skilled in guerrilla warfare for use overseas. Once the Crowns of England and Scotland were united in 1603, a determined effort was made to stop the activities of the Reivers. Many were banished to Ireland, many were hanged, and others were forced to join the army for service abroad. The chances of the remaining troublemakers escaping the law were greatly reduced, but reiving activities died out slowly, with incidents occurring well into the 17th century, notably carried out by small gangs of bandits known as Moss-troopers during the Royalist rising of 1651–1654.

There was thus a considerable amount of private military building at the Anglo-Scottish border region involving fortified towers, manors, and castles of various kinds.

In this context of endemic violence, a particular type of fortification was used, known as *pele* (also spelled "peel" — small fortified dwelling keep) and *bastle* (fortified farm), commonly designated under the generic term of tower house. Unlike the semi-fortified manor and the residential palace, the 16th-century Scottish towerhouse had military defensive features not as symbolic and ornamental display but out of necessity. Built by clan chiefs, small lords, and fairly wealthy farmers, they were, however, humble structures of only local importance. They were primarily designed for private living but also had to safeguard the owner, his family, and his retainers against the ever-present threat of a sudden attack. They were also used in the Anglo-Scottish wars although their purpose was not so much defense against a regular army equipped with artillery, for which they would have been useless anyway, as defense against sporadic attack by small armed bands intent on cattle raiding and looting. Tower houses were private buildings, thus there is no such thing as a standard design but instead there was a wide range of layouts, and many additions and alterations. Inevitably there were developments within the basic tower formula to provide additional and more varied accommodation. There were, however, many similarities, as all towers were designed for the same defensive purpose. Pele towers and bastles were built in fairly large numbers on both sides of the Scottish border for about 300 years, basically from 1300 to 1600. Fundamentally border towers were of the same vertical type, simple in plan (a rectangle) and internal arrangement (a single room on each floor). They were high and narrow buildings but nevertheless cleverly designed for defense. In certain more elaborate and complex cases, groundplans conformed to the shape of a Z or an L by staggering turrets, towers or parts of the building so that overlapping fields of fire and flanking fire could be poured from gunports pierced in the ground and upper floors. This way an all-round defense was maintained with minimum expenditure on a few light handguns. These designs also allowed at least some of the rooms to be alongside each other rather than superimposed. Tower houses were made of stone, always with thick walls about one meter thick, and had no opening on the ground floor except the entrance. This could also be on the first floor and reached by an outside staircase. The roof was usually made of stone slate to improve the building's resistance to fire. Sometimes they were provided with an adjoining enclosure bailey or barmkin containing ancillary buildings, and also used for the protection of tenants and their livestock during raids. Sometimes there was a moat (crossed by a drawbridge) surrounding the tower and bailey. So with improvement, additions and enlargement a towerhouse could take the shape of a small castle. Of course, the landowner who one day was sheltering in his pele tower from the depredation of his neighbor, was the next day riding out on his own robbing and blackmailing expedition. Some towers, however, functioned entirely

Right: *The well-preserved Amisfield Tower, also known as Hempisfield Tower, located about 5 miles north of Dumfries, Dumfries and Galloway, Scotland, was built by the Charteris family around 1600. It has a height of approximately 90 feet, and although its basic plan is a simple square (30 × 30 feet) with four stories and an attic, its richness in corbelling and turrets, dormer windows, steeply-pitched roof, stonework imitating logs and rope, and dog-toothed motifs around the armorial panels give it a quite impressive and romantic guise. Three corners have double-storied turrets while the fourth is decked. These upper features are built in warm, red ashlar in contrast to the rubble walls below. Gunports were arranged in the upper level, and the entrance was defended by a machicolation. Within the castle there is a vaulted basement, the rooms have fine fireplaces with evidence of tempera wall-painting, and the first floor is arranged as a hall and a garderobe.*

Bottom: *Claypotts Tower, located near Dundee (Tayside), was built on the Z-plan between 1569 and 1588, and it presents a splendid example of a Scottish tower house: a rectangular main tower block (c. 33 × 22 feet) with two additional round towers (20 feet in diameter) at two diagonally opposite corners. As circular rooms do not provide the most convenient spaces for living accommodation, the upper rooms in the round towers were turned into rectangular spaces by corbelling. This feature gives Claypotts much of its striking appearance.*

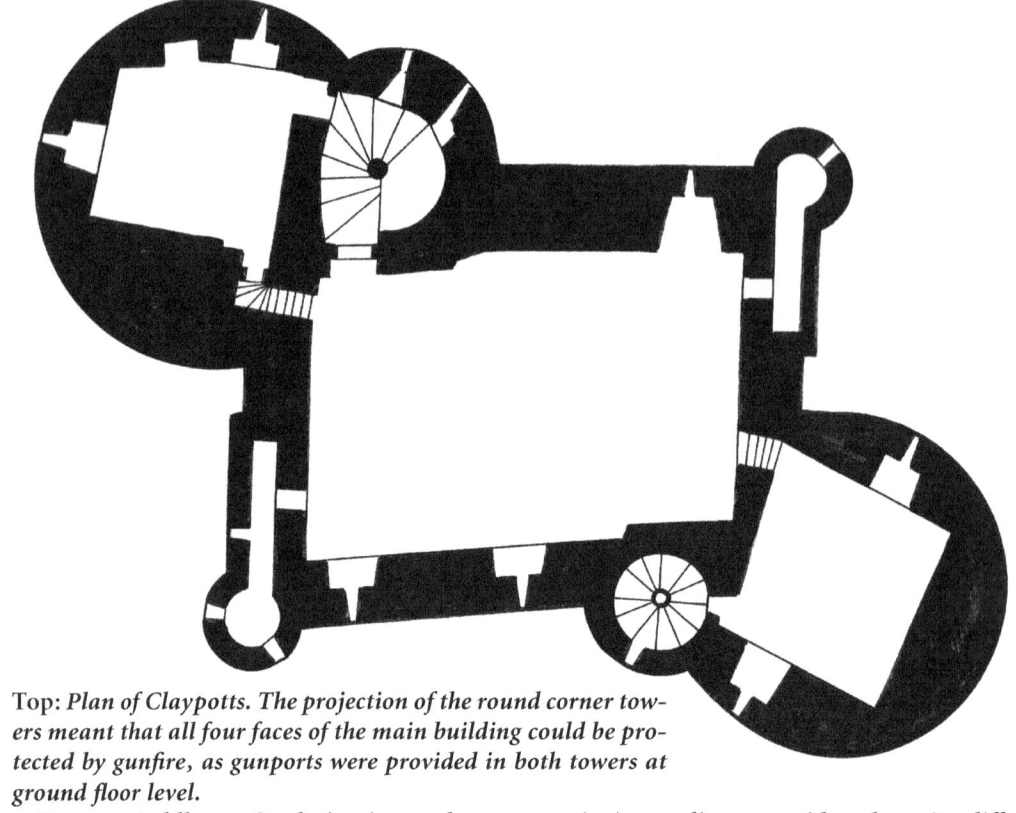

Top: *Plan of Claypotts. The projection of the round corner towers meant that all four faces of the main building could be protected by gunfire, as gunports were provided in both towers at ground floor level.*

Bottom: *Auldhame Castle (conjectured reconstruction), standing on a ridge above Seacliff beach, about 3 miles east of North Berwick in East Lothian, is a ruined L-plan tower house with round corner turrets. The castle was built in the late 16th century, probably by Adam Otterburn of Reidhall, Lord Provost of Edinburgh. It consists of a three-story main block with a projecting stair-tower. Part of a vaulted basement remains, but the upper floors are mostly gone. The building had a yellow harling wash over its mixed rubble construction, which would have given it a bright yellow appearance against the steel grey waters of the North sea below.*

Auchindoun Castle, located about two miles southeast of Dufftown, Scotland, an L-plan tower house, stands on a hilltop within the earthworks of an Iron Age hill fort. The castle was built in the mid–15th century for John Stuart, Earl of Mar. In 1480 the estates and titles were given to the king's favorite, Robert Cochrane, master mason turned architect. In 1482, Scottish nobles captured many of the King's favorites, including Robert Cochrane, and hanged them from Lauder Bridge. Ownership of the castle passed swiftly through the hands of many people. In 1571 it was the home of Adam Gordon, a staunch supporter of the ousted Mary, Queen of Scots. That year he marched to Corgarff Castle to confront his enemy, John Forbes, but finding the menfolk away he set fire to the building, killing John's wife, Margaret, and 27 other women, children and servants. Auchindoun Castle was sacked and burnt in 1591 by the Mackintoshes in revenge for the murder of the Bonnie Earl O'Moray by the Marquis of Huntly and Sir Patrick Gordon of Auchindoun. The castle was restored but by 1725 it had been abandoned and partly demolished to provide building material. The illustration is a conjectured reconstruction.

as refuges. In some cases churches were fortified so that the local villagefolk could shelter there until the lord to whom they normally paid blackmail came to their rescue.

Tower houses, which were a late medieval version of the ancient broch, were also constructed in Ireland where well over 2,000 of them are still extant. Some estimate that there were as many as 8,000 built during the Middle Ages. They, of course, also existed in Northern England. English castles of the courtyard type, such as Bodiam and Herstmonceux, described above, were not the only ones built during the 14th and 15th centuries. In this type of castle quarters and service buildings had one or two floors and were placed laterally, side by side in the yard. In another group of castles, however, built or added to during the same period, the rooms were arranged vertically, one above the other, forming a tower four or five stories high, and therefore could be termed a tower-house. As discussed above, tower houses form one of

Left: *Preston Tower (conjectured reconstruction) is a ruined L-plan keep in the ancient village of Preston, southeast of Prestonpans and southwest of Prestongrange in East Lothian, Scotland. The original structure, some of which may date from the 14th century, had four stories. A further two stories were added above the parapet in 1626, with Renaissance windows. The entrance to the tower was defended by a lean-to hoarding from which projectiles could be dropped. The tower was damaged by Oliver Cromwell's troop during the English Civil War in 1650. After being restored it burnt again, accidentally, in 1663 and was abandoned for the nearby Preston House, East Lothian. Preston Tower was purchased by the National Trust for Scotland in 1969. It is currently under the guardianship of East Lothian Council.*

Above: *Ballencrieff Tower, located three miles northwest of Haddington, and one mile south of Aberlady, East Lothian, Scotland, was built in 1507 when King James IV ordered his private secretary James Murray to build himself a fortified house. The stronghold was destroyed in around 1545, and was rebuilt by his son, John Murray, in 1586. The house burnt down accidentally in 1868, and stood roofless until it was restored between 1992 and 1997. It is now privately owned. The long, rectangular tower had extensive accommodation over three stories, including a vaulted basement, with a near-symmetrical north front. The tall, narrow southeast wing has crow-step gables, and gun holes.*

Opposite bottom: *Dalkeith Castle, located in Dalkeith, Midlothian, Scotland, originates from an early castle built in the 12th century, and was home to Sir James Douglas (the Black Douglas). The castle was strategically sited in an easily defensible position above a bend in the River North Esk. In 1543, the castle was besieged. It was taken and destroyed by the English in 1547. Around 1585 it was rebuilt in the form of an L-plan keep with a curtain wall, for James Douglas, the fourth Earl of Morton. In 1642 Dalkeith Castle was bought by Francis, the second Earl of Buccleugh, and between 1702 and 1710 it was extensively remodelled for Anne, the Duchess of Buccleuch, with part of the existing castle demolished, and the rest incorporated into a new palace, named Dalkeith House, designed by James Smith. The palace was later enlarged and embellished over the years by the celebrated Scottish architects John Adam, James Playfair and William Burn. Dalkeith House is now a European study center for the University of Wisconsin, and the centerpiece of the Dalkeith Country Estate. The illustration shows how the castle might have appeared by the end of the 16th century.*

Above: *The now ruined Berriedale Castle, located on a rocky promontory projecting into the mouth of the Berriedale River in Caithness, was originally a stronghold constructed by order of Sir Reginald Cheyne in the 14th century. It was later developed into a larger castle by the Sutherlands clan. The castle passed from the Sutherlands to the Oliphants clan before it was handed to the Earl of Caithness in 1606. The walls and foundations represent the remains of a courtyard castle, which including a rectangular keep, and various domestic buildings, and date from the 15th or 16th century. The landward side was protected by a deep ditch, which would once have been crossed by a drawbridge.*

6. Late Plantagenet Fortifications 1327–1485 289

Above: *Warkworth, situated in a loop of the River Coquet in Northumberland, is one of the most unusual and elaborate of all tower houses in England. It was rebuilt in c. 1390 from an earlier 12th-century keep. The castle consists of three main sections: The outer bailey is a roughly square section at the southern end of the castle. The inner bailey is roughly triangular and is to the north of the outer bailey. The depicted keep is situated on a mound at the extreme northern end of the inner bailey. It was basically square in plan (80 by 80 feet) with a tower-like projection (25 by 15 feet) in the middle of each face. Externally the contrast with the great Norman keeps of the earlier period is demonstrated by the ample provision of windows. The internal space includes an intricate pattern of rooms, passages and staircases. The ground floor provides space for storage, a guardchamber and a prison. On the first floor are the hall, kitchen, and chapel, and on the second floor private chambers, a parlor and bedrooms. Today the reasonably well-preserved castle is managed by English Heritage.*

Opposite bottom: *Dudley Castle, located in West Midlands, originated from a motte-and-bailey timber stronghold built after the conquest of 1066 by one of William I's barons named William FitzAnsculf. After FitzAnsculf, the castle came into the possession of the Paganel family, who built the first stone castle on the site. However, after Gervase Paganel joined a failed rebellion against Henry II in 1173 the castle was demolished by order of the king. The Somery's dynasty was the next to own the site and they set about building the castle in stone starting in the second half of the 13th century and continuing into the 14th. The castle was oblong in plan with four round corner-towers and was two stories high. A Royalist stronghold during the English Civil War, the castle was surrendered to Cromwell's forces in 1646. Parliament subsequently ordered that Dudley be partly demolished and the present ruined appearance of the keep resulted from this decision.*

Above: *Penrith Castle (conjectured reconstruction), located at Penrith, south of Carlisle in Cumbria, was built at the end of the 14th century by Ralph Neville (c. 1364–1425), who played a key role in the defense of the Scottish border. Contrary to what might be expected, the castle was not built at the highest point of the hill, which lies 170 meters away. Its location was chosen because it was probably the site of an old Roman fort, the banks and ditches of which could be conveniently reused for their defensive function. The castle was improved and added to over the next 70 years, becoming a royal fortress for Richard, Duke of Gloucester before he became King Richard III in 1483. Richard added a new gatehouse and an impressive range of lodgings around the courtyard. The castle and the town remained part of the Crown Estate until the reign of William III, who gave it and most other Crown property in Cumberland to his friend Hans Wilhelm Bentinck, first Earl of Portland. The castle eventually passed from the Earls and Dukes of Portland to the Dukes of Devonshire. The layout of the castle can still be seen, but, sadly, only parts of the curtain wall and towers stand to any height. The ruined castle is now in the care of English Heritage. The illustration shows how the castle might have looked in c. 1430, after alterations made by Richard Neville, Earl of Salisbury.*

Right: *Seafield tower. Located between Kinghorn and Kirkcaldy on the North Sea coast of Fife in Scotland, Seafiels tower was built in c. 1542. Abandoned since 1733, the tower is now in ruins. Constructed in sandstone, it was probably five stories high, its internal dimensions were 20 feet (6.1 m) by 14.3 ft (4.4 m), with walls 5 feet (1.5 m) thick. Since 1973 the ruins have been designated a Category B listed building by Historic Scotland.*

Opposite bottom: *Waughton Castle (conjectured reconstruction). On a rough rock outcrop some two miles west of the village of Whitekirk in East Lothian, clings a few fragmented remains of the ancient castle of Waughton. The earliest tower of Waughton is said to be of Saxon construction, but it was replaced by medieval works including a small chapel, an enclosing wall and a lean-to tower. Waughton first appears during the reign of King David II of Scots (1329–1371), when it was held by the family Hepburns. By the 18th century the castle was being used as material for building walls and cottages in the area. The illustration shows how the castle might have looked in the 15th century.*

the major types of Scottish fortification, but there are a few in England. The English instances are distinct from the Scottish ones but they observe the same vertical principle. One of the earliest examples of an English tower-house is Dudley Castle in West Midland, built in c. 1320; Nunney in Somerset, built in c. 1373; Warkworth in Northumberland, rebuilt in the 1390s; and the already described Tattershall Castle in Lincolnshire.

Conclusion

Both England and France emerged from the troubles, horrors and desolations of the Hundred Years' War stronger than ever before. In both countries the kings had overcome the menace of feudalism by destroying or greatly reducing the power of the great noble families. The royal government was constantly becoming more powerful. Commerce and industry increased the national wealth and supplied the monarchs with the revenue necessary to maintain government officials and a sufficient armed force to execute the laws and keep order throughout their realms. They were

Tantallon Castle, located some 3.1 miles (5 km) east of North Berwick, in East Lothian, Scotland, stands on top of a promontory opposite the Bass Rock, looking out onto the Firth of Forth. The castle was built in the mid–14th century by William Douglas, first Earl of Douglas, and passed to his illegitimate son, later created Earl of Angus, and despite several sieges, it remained the property of his descendants for much of its history. The last medieval curtain wall castle to be constructed in Scotland, Tantallon comprises a single wall with gatehouse and two large corner-towers blocking off the headland, with the other three sides naturally protected by sea cliffs. It was besieged by King James IV in 1491, and again by his successor James V in 1528, when extensive damage was done. Tantallon saw action in the First Bishops' War in 1639, and again during Oliver Cromwell's invasion of Scotland in 1651, when it was once more severely damaged. It was sold by the Douglases in 1699, and the ruin is today in the care of Historic Scotland.

no longer forced to rely upon the uncertain pledges of their vassals. In short, the French and the English were both becoming nations, each with a strong national feeling and a sovereign whom everyone, both high and low, recognized and obeyed as the head of the government.

The Wars of the Roses too had important results. Nearly all the powerful noble families of England had been drawn into the fierce struggles, and a part of the nobility, whom the kings had formerly feared, had perished on the battlefield or lost their heads in the ruthless executions carried out by each party after it gained a victory. This had greatly weakened the nobility and left the king far more powerful than ever before. He could now dominate Parliament, if he could not dispense with it. For a century and more the Tudor kings enjoyed almost absolute power. England ceased for a time to enjoy the free government for which the foundations had been laid under the Edwards and the Lancastrian kings, whose embarrassments at home and abroad had made them constantly dependent upon the aid of the nation.

With the restoration of public order under the strong government of the Tudor monarchy, the history of the English castle hurried to its close. The techniques of military engineering had started to outrun its uses, a state of affairs that was more marked in the 16th century, when castles were erected for effect and show, indeed almost for fun. The Renaissance movement was afoot. Henceforth military building would be the concern no longer of local barons and feudal magnates but exclusively the prerogative of the state. Since the 12th century feudalism had been declining, and artillery brought a definitive end to the Middle Ages. Technically the adaptations of existing fortifications to the use of the artillery were nonetheless only improvised and hastily constructed makeshifts. In essence 15th-century castles remained predominantly vertical and medieval-spirited in design. They still used an ill-suited method of defense when the characteristic effects of artillery fire became clearly understood. It was only during the reign of Henry VIII (1509–1547) that remarkable coastal forts totally designed for artillery fire were designed and constructed along the shores of the English Channel. However, the history of castellar construction in England may be said to have come to an end by the 1480s—but by no means the history of castles. For during the series of armed conflicts and political machinations known as the English Civil War (1641–1651) the stout old walls and towers of many a royal and baronial fortress (e.g., Conwy, Bodiam, Donnington, Corfe, Scarborough, Ashby-de-la-Zouch, Wardour, Kenilworth, Warwick, Raglan and many others) still played a military role, although in many instances they proved unable to resist the siege artillery of the Parliamentarian and Royalist belligerents.

Appendix 1

Maps of the Main Castles in the British Isles

(NB: Maps are not to scale)

Appendix 1

Main Castles in England

1: Penzance
2: Launceston
3: Plymouth
4: Exeter
5: Corfe
6: Southampton
7: Portsmoutth
8: Portchester
9: Arundel
10: Brighton
11: Pevensey
12: Bodiam
13: Dover
14: Rochester
15: London Tower
16: Windsor
17: Nunney
18: Bristol
19: Berkeley
20: Oxford
21: Colchester
22: Ipswich
23: Orford
24: Framlingham
25: Cambridge
26: Warwick
27: Worcester
28: Ludlow
29: Birmingham
30: Kenilworth
31: Petersborough
32: Great Yarmouth
33: Nottingham
34: Chester
35: Liverpool
36: Manchester
37: Conisborough
38: Hull
39: Leeds
40: Middleham
41: Bolton
42: Richmond
43: Carlisle
44: Newcastle-upon-Tyne
45: Warkworth
46: Alnwick
47: Dunstanburgh
48: Bamburgh
49: Norham

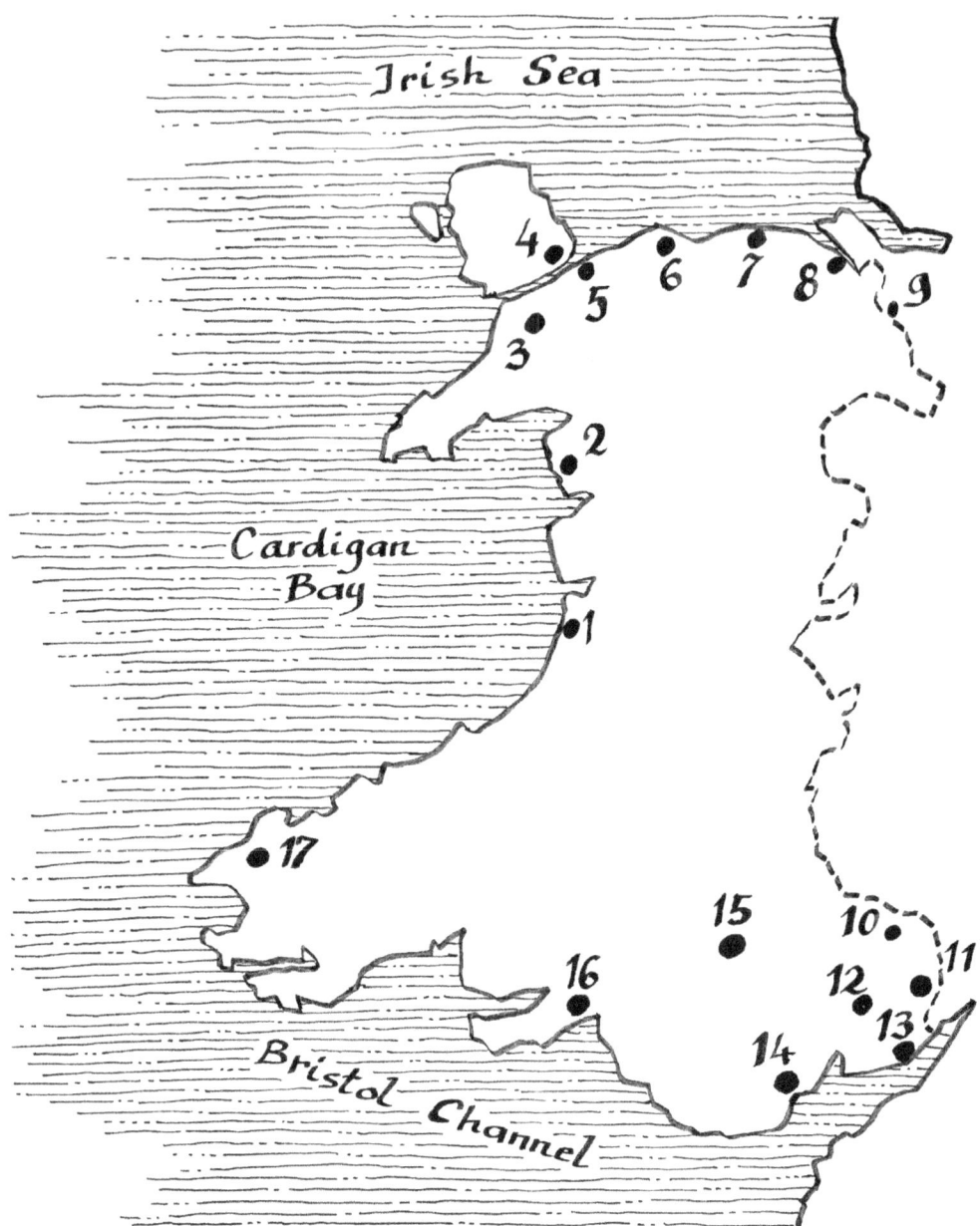

Main Castles in Wales

1: Aberystwyth
2: Harlech
3: Caernafon
4: Beaumaris
5: Bangor
6: Conway
7: Ruddlan
8: Flint
9: Chester
10: Grosmont
11: Skenfrith
12: White Castle
13: Chepstow
14: Caerphilly
15: Merthyr Tydfil
16: Swansea
17: Fishguard

Maps of the Main Castles in the British Isles 299

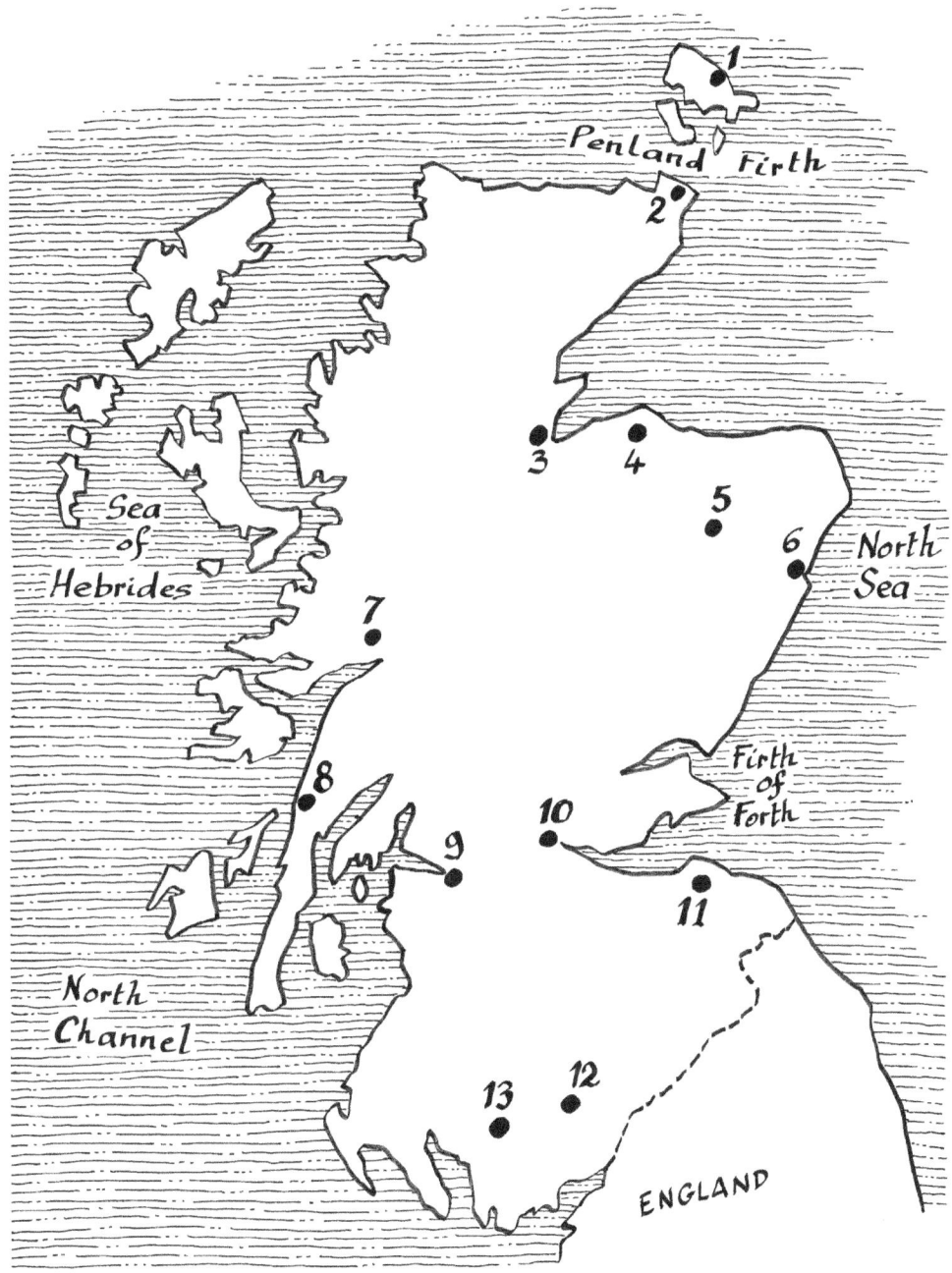

Main Castles in Scotland

1: Cobbie Row's Castle
2: John O'Groats
3: Inverness
4: Duffus
5: Kildrummy
6: Aberdeen
7: Fort William
8: Castle Sween
9: Glasgow
10: Stirling
11: Tantallon
12: Caerlaverock
13: Threave

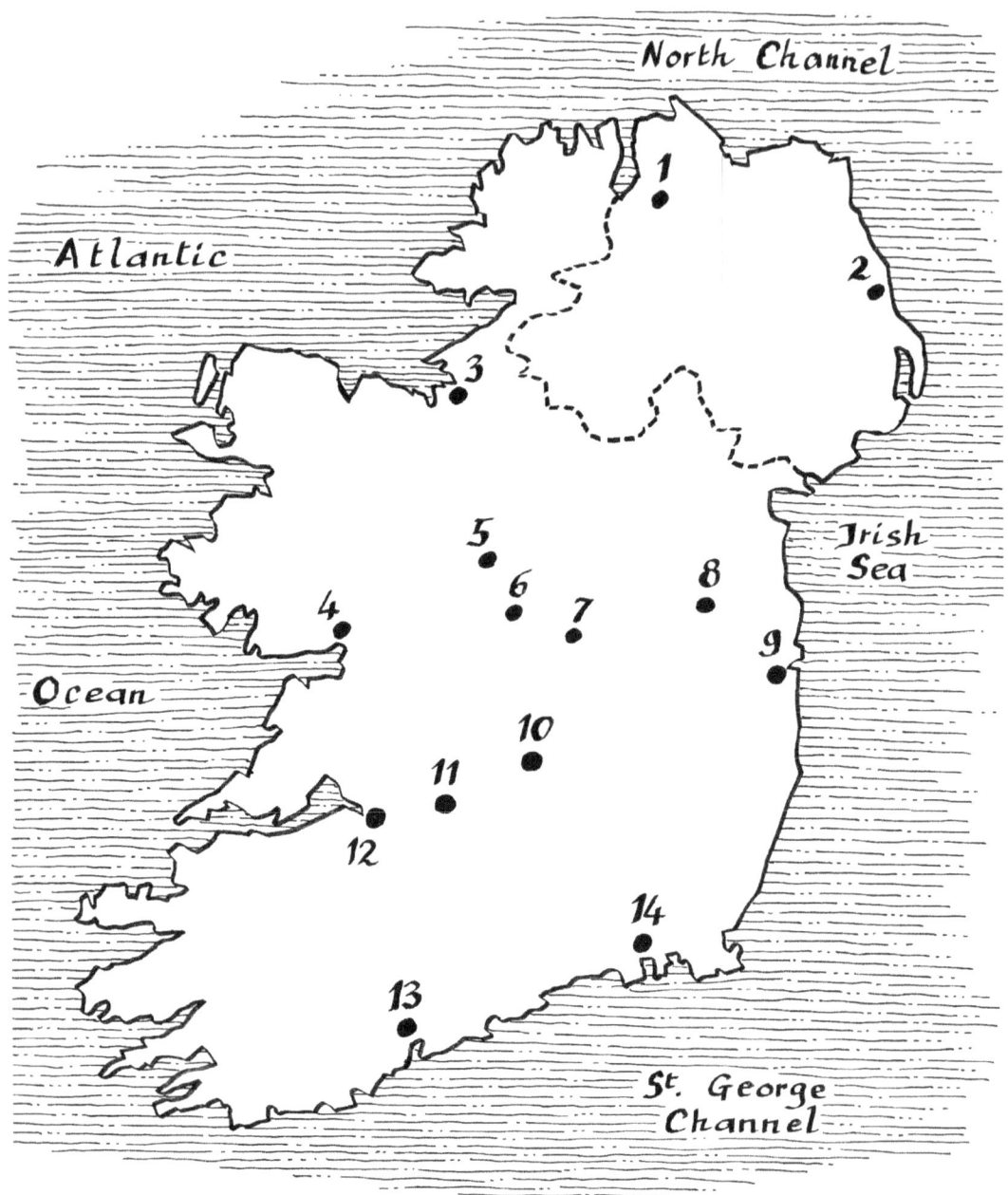

Main Castles in Ireland

1: Londonderry
2: Carrickfergus
3: Sligo
4: Galway
5: Roscommon
6: Athlone
7: Castledown Geoghgan
8: Trim
9: Dublin
10: Roscrea
11: Nenagh
12: Limerick
13: Cork
14: Waterford

APPENDIX 2

Conservation Organizations

There are three types of listed status in the United Kingdom.

Grade I: buildings "of exceptional interest, sometimes considered to be internationally important";

Grade II: "particularly important buildings of more than special interest";

Grade III: buildings that are "nationally important and of special interest."

In England and Wales the authority for listing is granted by the Planning (Listed Buildings and Conservation Areas) Act 1990 and is presently administered by English Heritage, an agency of the Department for Culture, Media and Sport, and by Cadw in Wales (where it is a devolved issue). Listed buildings in danger of decay are listed on English Heritage's Buildings at Risk Register.

Below are listed some of the most important organizations charged with the conservation of British historical buildings.

English Heritage

English Heritage is the government's statutory adviser on the historic environment. Officially known as the Historic Buildings and Monuments Commission for England, English Heritage is an executive non-departmental public body sponsored by the Department for Culture, Media and Sport (DCMS). Its powers and responsibilities are set out in the National Heritage Act (1983) and the organization reports to Parliament through the Secretary of State for Culture, Media and Sport. English Heritage was created by Parliament in 1984 and charged with the protection of the historic environment and with promoting public understanding and enjoyment of it. English Heritage is the government's official advisor on all matters concerning heritage conservation, conservation areas, and the repair of historic buildings. English Heritage's principal aims are: to secure and enhance the conservation of England's historic sites, monuments and buildings; to promote people's access to, and enjoyment of, this shared heritage; to raise the understanding and awareness of this heritage to increase commitment to its protection. English Heritage is located at 23

Savile Row, London, WC1H 1AB, United Kingdom. The website is http://www.eng-h.gov.uk.

National Trust

The National Trust was founded in 1895 by three Victorian philanthropists—Miss Octavia Hill, Sir Robert Hunter and Canon Hardwicke Rawnsley. Concerned about the impact of uncontrolled development and industrialization, they set up the Trust to act as a guardian for the nation in the acquisition and protection of threatened coastline, countryside and buildings. As a charity society, independent of government, the Trust relies on the generosity of its supporters, volunteers and members. The National Trust runs a huge range of historic buildings, including traditional vernacular, industrial and polite forms of architecture. Today National Trust is Britain's largest landowner and the greatest guardian of historic sites, protecting over 200 houses, 47 industrial monuments and mills, 12 lighthouses, 35 pubs and inns, the sites of many factories and mines, 19 castles, 49 churches and chapels, 57 villages and 25 medieval barns. The National Trust's adress is PO Box 39, Warrington WA5 7WD, United Kingdom, and website is http://www.nationaltrust.org.uk.

Historic Houses Association

The Historic Houses Association (HHA) represents 1,500 privately-owned historic houses, castles and gardens throughout the UK. These are listed buildings or designated gardens, usually Grade I or II, and are often outstanding. Many are considered to be iconic symbols of Britain's unique heritage. Around 300 HHA houses open to the public for day visitors, attracting between them about 14 million visitors each year. Others open for special visits, weddings, corporate events or short breaks. The address is Historic Houses Association, 2 Chester Street, London SW1X 7BB, and the website is http://www.hha.org.uk.

Historic Scotland

Historic Scotland is an executive agency of the Scottish government charged with safeguarding the nation's historic environment and promoting its understanding and enjoyment on behalf of Scottish Ministers. Historic Scotland is located in Longmore House, Salisbury Place, Edinburgh EH9 1SH, United Kingdom. The website is http://www.historicscotland.gov.uk.

Architectural Heritage Society of Scotland

The Architectural Heritage Society of Scotland (AHSS) originated from a group formed in 1956 to respond to the threatened demolition of Edinburgh's George

Square. It became the Scottish Georgian Society in 1959, and the present name was adopted in 1984 to reflect the broader scope of the society's activities. The society is committed to encouraging public understanding and appreciation of the built environment, and it supports the thoughtful and meaningful preservation and restoration of historic buildings. The society publishes both a journal and a twice-yearly magazine for its members. The AHSS is located in Glasite Meeting House, 33 Barony Street, Edinburgh, EH 3 6NX, United Kingdom. The website is http://www.ahss.org.uk.

Cadw

Cadw is a Welsh word which means "to keep." Created in 1984, with headquarters in Nantgarw, just north of Cardiff, Cadw is the Welsh Assembly government's historic environment division, whose aims are to protect and sustain, promote, encourage community engagement in, and improve access to the historic environment of Wales. This includes historic buildings, ancient monuments, historic parks, gardens and landscapes, and underwater archaeology. Working with partners in the public, voluntary and private sectors, Cadw produces a range of publications that cater to all levels of interest in the built heritage of Wales, runs a photo library located in Cardiff, and organizes visits, events and reinactments in historical places. More information can be found on the website: http://www.cadw.wales.gov.uk.

World Heritage Sites

A World Heritage Site is a place (such as a forest, mountain, lake, desert, monument, building, complex, or city) that is listed by the United Nations Educational, Scientific and Cultural Organization (UNESCO, funded in 1945) as of special cultural or physical significance. The list is maintained by the international World Heritage Programme administered by the UNESCO World Heritage Committee. The program catalogues, names, and conserves sites of outstanding cultural or natural importance to the common heritage of humanity. Under certain conditions, listed sites can obtain funds from the World Heritage Fund. Each World Heritage Site is the property of the state on whose territory the site is located, but it is considered in the interest of the international community to preserve it.

APPENDIX 3

Kings and Queens

(from A.D. 802 to 1485)

Saxon

Egbert 802–839
Ethelwulf 839–855
Ethelbald 855–860
Ethelbert 860–866
Etherred 866–871
Alfred the Great 871–899
Edward the Elder 899–925
Athelstan 925–939
Edmund 939–946
Edred 946–955
Aedwig 955–959
Edgar 959–975
Edward the Martyr 975–978
Ethelred Unraed 978–1016
Edmund Ironside 1016

Danish

Cnut 1016–1035
Harold I 1035–1040
Harthacnut 1040–1042

Late Wessex Saxon

Edward the Confessor 1042–1066
Harold II Godwinson 1066

Norman

William I 1066–1087
William II 1087–1100
Henry I 1100–1135
Stephen 1135–1154

Plantagenet

Henry II 1154–1189
Richard I (The Lionheart) 1189–1199
John Lackland 1199–1216
Henry III 1216–1272
Edward I 1272–1307
Edward II 1307–1327
Edward III 1327–1377
Richard II 1377–1399

Plantagenet-Lancaster

Henry IV 1399–1413
Henry V 1413–1422
Henry VI 1422–1461

Plantagenet-York

Edward IV 1461–1483
Edward V 1483
Richard III 1483–1485

Bibliography

Beda Venerabilis (also known as Saint Bede or Bede the Venerable). *Historia Ecclesiastica Gentis Anglorum (Ecclesiastical History of the English People)*. Translated by Leo Sherley-Price. Harmondsworth: Penguin, 1955.
Beresford, M. W. *New Towns of the Middles Ages.* Cambridge: Lutterworth Press, 1967.
Boon, G. C. *Segontium Roman Fort.* London: Her Majesty's Stationary Office, 1963.
Bragard, Philippe, Johan Termote, and John Williams. *A la Découverte des Villes Fortifiées (Kent, Côte d'Opale et Flandre Occidentale).* Dunkerque: Syndicat Mixte de la Côte d'Opale, 1999.
Braun, Georg, and Franz Hogenberg. *Civitas Orbis Terrarum (Steden van de Wereld, Europa-Amerika).* Amsterdam: Atrium, 1990.
Breasted, James Henry. *Ancient Time. A History of the Early World.* New York: Ginn, 1916.
Brøndsted, Johannes. *The Vikings.* Baltimore: Penguin Books, 1960.
Campbell, Duncan, and Brian Delf. *Roman Legionary Fortress 27 B.C.–A.D. 378.* Oxford: Osprey, 2006.
Clayton, Hugh. *Royal Faces, 900 Years of British Monarchy.* London: Her Majesty's Stationary Office, 1977.
De Bouard, Michel. *Guillaume le Conquérant.* Paris: Presses Universitaires de France, 1958.
Delderfield, Eric R. *Kings and Queens of England and Great Britain.* Newton Abbot (Devon): David & Charles Publishers, 1972.
D'Haucourt, Geneviève. *La Vie au Moyen Age.* Paris: Presses Universitaires de France, 1987.
Dupuy de Clinchamps, Philippe. *La Chevalerie.* Paris: Presses Universitaires de France, 1961.
Eyre, A. G. *An Outline History of England.* Harlow: Longman Group, 1971.
Fields, Nic, and Donato Spedaliere. *Rome's Saxon Shore. Coastal Defences of Roman Britain A.D. 250–500.* Oxford: Osprey, 2007.
Génicot, L., and P. Houssiau. *Le Moyen Age.* Paris: Casterman, 1959.
Gravett, Christopher, and Adam Hook. *The Castles of Edward I in Wales 1277–1307.* Oxford: Osprey, 2007.
_____ and _____. *Norman Stone Castles (1) The British Isles 1066–1216.* Oxford: Osprey, 2003.
Hamilton-Thompson, A. *Military Architecture in England during the Middle Ages.* Oxford: University Press, 1912.
Heer, Friedrich. *The Medieval World, Europe from 1100 to 1350.* London: Weidenfeld & Nicolson, 1961.
Heers, Jacques. *Le Travail au Moyen Age.* Paris: Presses Universitaires de France, 1975.
Janson, H. W. *History of Art.* New York: Harry N. Abrams, 1969.
Keegan, John. *A History of Warfare.* London: Hutchinson, 1993.
Koch, H. W. *Middeleeuwen. Het Krijgsbedrijf in de Middeleeuwen.* Amsterdam-Brussel: Elsevier Nederland BV, 1988.

Konstam, Angus, and Peter Bull. *The Forts of Celtic Britiain.* Oxford: Osprey, 2006.

Lavelle, Ryan, Donato Spedaliere, and S. Sulemsohn Spedaliere. *Fortifications in Wessex c. 800–1066.* Oxford: Osprey Publishing, 2003.

_____. *Hadrian's Wall* A.D. *122–410.* Oxford: Osprey, 2003.

Lewis, Archibald R. *Emerging Medieval Europe* A.D. *400–1000.* New York: Alfred A. Knopf, 1967.

Libal, Dobroslav. *Châteaux Forts & Fortifications en Europe du Ve au XIXe Siècle.* Paris: Ars Mundi, 1993.

Lilley, K. D. *Urban Life in the Middle Ages, 1000–1450.* London: Palgrave, 2002.

Lobel, M. D. *Historic Towns.* Volume 1, Oxford: Lovell Johns, 1969; Volume 2, Oxford: Scoler Press, 1975; Volume 3, Oxford: Oxford University Press, 1998.

Maurois, André. *Histoire d'Angleterre.* Paris: Fayard & Cie, 1937.

McEvedy, Colin. *The Penguin Atlas of Medieval History.* Baltimore: Penguin Books, 1971.

Merian, Matthaeus. *Die Schönsten Europäischen Städte.* Hamburg: Hofmann und Campe Verlag, 1963.

Neubecker, Ottfried. *Gids van de Heraldiek.* Amsterdam: Elseviers Uitverij, 1981.

Newark, Tim. *Celtic Warriors 400* B.C.–A.D. *1600.* Poole: Blandford Press, 1986.

Nossov, Konstantin. *Ancient and Medieval Siege Weapons.* Staplehurst: Spellmont, 2005.

Painter, Sidney. *A History of the Middle Ages 284–1500.* London and Basingstoke: Macmillan, 1972.

Paluzie de Lescazes, Carlos. *Castles of Europe.* Barcelona: EGC S.A (date unknown).

Penoyre, John, and Michael Ryan. *British Architecture.* London: Frederick Warne, 1951.

Platt, C. *The English Medieval Town.* London: Martin Secker & Walburg, 1976.

Reid, Stuart, and Graham Turner. *Castles and Tower Houses of the Scottish Clans 1450–1650.* Oxford: Osprey, 2006.

Reynolds, A. *Later Anglo-Saxon England: Life and Landscape.* Stroud: Tempus, 1999.

Robinson, John. *Windsor Castle Official Guide.* London: Royal Collection Enterprise, 1995.

Roe, Derek. *Prehistory.* London: Paladin-Granad, 1970.

Rumble, A. R. "The Manuscript Evidence: The Known Manuscripts of the Burghal Hidage." In *The Defence of Wessex: The Burghal Hidage and Anglo-Saxon Fortifications,* edited by D. Hill and A. R. Rumble. Manchester: University Press, 1996.

Saint John Parker, Michael. *Britain's Kings and Queens.* Hants Pitkin Pictorials, 1990.

Salamagne, Alain. *Les Villes Fortes au Moyen Age.* Paris: Editions Jean-Paul Gisserot, 2002.

Stier, Hans-Erich. *Grosser Atlas zur Weltgeschichte.* Braunschweig: Georg Westermann Verlag, 1956.

Strayer, Joseph R. *Feudalism.* New York: Van Nostrand Rheinhold, 1965.

Taylor, A. J. *Caernarvon Castle and Town Walls.* London: Her Majesty's Stationary Office, 1953 (reprinted and amended 1972).

_____. *The Welsh Castles of Edward I.* London: Hambledon Press, 1986.

Unknown. *Roman York from* A.D. *71.* York: Ebor Press, 1971.

Viollet-le-Duc, Eugène-Emmanuel. *Histoire d'une Fortresse.* Paris: Berger-Levrault, 1978 (reprint of the 1874 edition).

_____, and M. MacDermott. *An Essay on the Military Architecture of the Middle Ages.* London: J. H. and J. Parker, 1860.

Wilkinson, Frederick. *Wapens en Wapenuitrusting.* London: Hamlyn Publishing Group, 1980.

Wood, Marguerite, and J. S. Richardson. *Edinburgh Castle.* London: Her Majesty's Stationary Office, 1953.

Index

Aberystwyth Castle 209
Agger 65
Aisled roundhouse 49
Alcantara 56
Alesia 56, 58
Alfred the Great 102, 103, 109, 111, 112
Amisfield Tower 283
Amphitheater 72, 74
the Anarchy 129, 159
Androne 277
Anglo-Saxon Chronicle 103, 104, 159
Antonine Wall 75, 80, 81, 105
Apron 185
Aquitaine 163, 166, 274, 277, 279, 280
Architectural Heritage Society of Scotland 302
Arletta 118
Armentaria 69
Armoricae 101
Arrow loop 142, 143, 145, 193, 223, 239, 245
Arrow slit 142
Arthur, king 99
Arundel Castle 151
Ashby-de-la-Zouch 249, 293
Ashlar 138
Assault tower 176
Auchindoun Castle 285
Auldhame Castle 284

Bacon, Roger, friar 235
Badbury Rings 28
Ballencrieff Tower 287
Balliol, Robert (king) 203
Ballista 61, 175
Bamburgh Castle 152
Bannockburn, battle of 205, 230

Barbican 193, 194, 195, 241, 242
Barrack (Roman) 70, 74
Bartizan 189
Basilica 69, 90
Bastide 206, 225, 255, 277
Bastle 282
Bath (Roman) 64, 70, 71, 72, 74, 95, 97
Bathampton Down 11, 13
Batter 39, 179
Battering ram 24, 137, 177, 179
Bayeux 83, 117
Bayeux Tapestry 120, 126, 127
Beaumaris Castle 212, 218, 220, 221, 222, 223
Beaumont-du-Périgord 278
Becket, Thomas 167, 260
Beffroy 176
Belfrey 176
Belvoir Castle 199
Berkhamsted Castle 128
Berm 16, 66
Berriedale Castle 288
Berwick-upon-Tweed 272
Bibracte oppidum 10
Bindon Hill 11
Black Death 234
Blockade 24
Bodiam Castle 241, 242, 243
Bolton Castle 238
Bombard 236
Bordeaux 274
Border Reivers 281
Bothwell Castle 176, 181, 188, 189, 225, 227
Boudica, queen 90, 91
Bramber Castle 130
Brattice 191
Breizh 101
Bretasche 191
British Camp 27

Brittany 15, 163
Broch 42, 43, 44, 45, 49, 285
Bronze Age 6, 8, 9, 11, 14, 25, 29, 38, 48, 51, 163
Broom flower 161
Bruce, Robert (king) 203, 205
Builth Castle 230
Burghal Hidage 109, 113
Burghead 35
Burgus 109, 252

Cadbury Castle 12, 18, 25
Cadw 208, 219, 247, 301, 303
Caen 122, 135, 138, 145, 154
Caer Alyn 14
Caer Drewyn Castle 31
Caer Luel 97
Caerlaverock Castle 226, 227
Caerleon 73
Caernarvon 209, 211, 214, 215, 217, 220, 256
Caerphilly Castle 197, 198, 199
Caesar, Julius 1, 6, 8, 9, 16, 57, 58, 63
Cairn 33
Calais 234, 275, 276
Camera 139
Canterbury 262, 263
Canterbury Castle 154
Cardiff Castle 153
Cardo maximus 65
Carisbrooke Castle 132, 194
Carlisle 96, 97
Carloway broch 45, 46
Carreg Cennen Castle 224, 225
Cashel 38, 42
Castell-y-Bere 224
Castellum 65
Castrum (castra) 2, 56, 60, 90, 253, 258, 271
Cat 177

307

Catapult 175
Celts 5, 6, 8, 51, 52, 62, 97, 124, 203
Centuria 70, 77
Ceorl 114
Cervi 59
Chain tower 259
Chambois Casle 135, 166
Chaplain 139
Charlabhaigh 45; see also Carloway
Charlemagne (emperor) 105
Charles III the Simple 117
Charter 277
Château Gaillard 167, 168, 169, 170
Chedworth villa 89
Chemise 129, 136
Chepstow 264
Chepstow Castle 184, 185
Chester 72, 75, 92, 270, 271
Chester Castle 133, 271
Christianity 53
Cinque Ports 254, 255, 256
Cippe 59, 66
Citadel 35, 90
Civitas 30, 89, 90, 148, 213
Classis Britannica 82
Clavicula 65
Claypotts Tower 283, 284
Clickhimin broch 48
Clifford's Tower 181, 183, 184
Clopi 237
Cnut 103, 304
Coeur de Lion 167; see also Richard I
Colchester 91, 92, 93, 147
Colonia 72, 89, 90, 92, 93, 147
Command 52, 199
Conisbrough 178, 179, 180, 181, 297
Conwy Castle 210, 211, 212, 213, 215
Corfe Castle 170, 293, 297
Cornière 277
Counterscarp 16, 208
Craggaunowen crannog 51
Crannog 50, 51
Cricklade 111, 114
Cromlech 9
Cromwell, Oliver 170, 209, 210, 246, 286, 289, 292
Cross-and-orb 240
Crosslet 142
Crusades 167, 169, 173, 178, 191, 194, 197, 199, 205, 206, 211, 253
Culverine 237
Czech hedgehog 60

D-shaped 46, 132, 189, 218, 223
Dalkeith Castle 287
Danebury 26
Danelaw 100, 103, 113
Danish dynasty 103, 304
Dark Age 31, 104, 105, 108, 115
Daw's Castle 12, 112
De Bello Gallico 16
Deblai 65
Decumanus maximus 65
Defense in depth 8, 52
Denbigh Castle 207, 223, 256, 260
Dinan 126
Dirleton Castle 187
Dolmen 9, 51
Domesday Book 121, 158, 253, 266, 272
Domus 124, 129
Donnington Castle 246, 293
Doune Castle 228, 229
Dover 2, 83, 95, 255, 256
Dover Castle 163, 164, 165, 166, 177
Dowsborough Camp 26
Drawbridge 143, 190, 244, 245
Dry stone 16, 40
Dudley Castle 289
Duffus Castle 128, 299
Dun 33, 38, 39, 40, 41, 42, 49, 64
Dun Mhulan 44, 46

Edward I 134, 157, 171, 176, 202, 203, 205, 214, 215, 225, 226, 230, 272, 273, 277, 304
Edward II 230, 231, 277
Edward III 230, 231, 234, 304
Edward the Confessor 118, 121, 304
Eilean Donan Castle 228
Embrasure 240, 258
Emeriti 72
Emmotted keep 137
Enaim Macha 37
Enceinte-castle 195
English Heritage 131, 132, 157, 178, 180, 249, 276, 289, 301
English longbow 232

Fabri 55
Fabrica 71, 75
Featherwood West 65
Feudalism 2, 103, 104, 118, 121, 203, 291
Fire stick 237

Firing port 240
Flint Castle 206, 207, 209, 212
Forebuilding 136, 146, 148, 155, 163, 183
Fortlet 64, 77, 78, 80, 81
Fossa 59, 65, 90, 91
Foulque Nerra 134
Frizzy horse 60
Fulk the Black see Foulque Nerra
Fyrd 114

Gaff 244
Gask Frontier 79, 80
Geoffrey of Anjou 161
Glacis 16, 18, 80
Glastonbury 51
Gloucester 72, 73, 90, 95, 112, 153, 235, 265
Gothic style 171, 190, 199, 200, 202, 244
Greek fire 176
Grianan of Aileach 38, 39
Grid-plan 209, 253, 277
Groma 60
Grosmont Castle 189, 200, 298
Guienne (Guyenne) 231, 234, 255, 277, 278, 2281
Guillaume le Bâtard 118, 145, 305; see also William I the Conqueror
Guisarme 237
Gunport 240, 241, 242, 244, 245, 248, 250, 282, 283, 284

Hadrian's Wall 2, 33, 75, 77, 80, 81, 82, 85, 93, 97, 106, 306
Hall keep 146
Hallstatt culture 11
Hammer of the Scots 203
Harald Hardrada 120
Harlech Castle 2, 198, 207, 212, 218, 219, 221, 298
Harold Godwinson 118, 119, 120, 121, 304
Hastings 113, 121, 123, 154, 255, 256
Hastingues 280, 281
Hauberk 114, 129, 167
Hedingham Castle 136, 150
Henge 11
Henry I Bauclerc 148, 151, 159
Henry II 132, 152, 161, 163, 166, 167, 231, 274, 304
Henry III 170, 171, 177, 277
Henry IV 234
Henry V 234
Henry VI 234, 235

Henry VII 235, 247
Henry VIII 203, 293
Hereford 265
Herepath 13, 109
Herstmonceux Castle 243, 244
Hill, Octavia 302
Hill forts 8, 9, 10, 11, 15, 19, 22, 23, 25
Hill of Tara 36
Historic Houses Association 302
Historic Scotland 187, 227, 292, 302
Historica Ecclesiastica 104
Hoarding 136, 140, 141, 145
Hod Hill 21, 56
Horrea 70, 74, 75
Huchette 191
Hull 259, 273, 297
Hundred Years' War 232, 234, 235, 238, 245, 266, 272, 274, 277, 280, 291
Hunter, Sir Robert 302
Hunting 8, 15, 140, 228, 232
Huscarl 114

Imager 138
Inchtuthil 72
Iron Age 5, 11, 25, 49, 51, 93, 105, 110, 125, 147, 152, 224, 262
Isca 72, 73, 74, 95
Ivanhoe 181, 249

Jarshof broch 46
Jericho 1
Joan of Arc 234
John Lackland 169

Kelheim style 18
Kildrummy Castle 225, 227
Kingdom of Great Britain 205
King's Tower 183, 184
Kirby Muxloe Castle 240, 250
Knife stand 60

L-plan 282, 284, 285, 287
Lake village 50
Lanfranc, bishop 118, 121
Langeais Castle 134
Lanthorn Tower 172
Largest British medieval towns 256
Late Wessex dynasty 304
Laughton-en-le-Morthen 127
Libourne 279
License to crenallate 123, 124, 196
Lilium 59
Limes 79, 108

Lincoln 72, 131, 272
Litus Saxonicum 82, 83
Liverpool Castle 171
Loch Leven Castle 205
Loch Tay crannog 50, 51
Loches Castle 135
Londinium 90, 91, 92, 95
London 90, 121, 261
London Tower 144, 145, 146, 147, 167, 171, 172, 205, 225
Longshanks 202
Loophole 2, 142, 239, 244, 248, 258
Lorica 59, 67
Ludlow 270, 271
Ludlow Castle 195, 196

Machicolation 140, 166, 192, 242, 247, 258
Magna Carta 170
Maiden Castle 21, 22, 25, 29, 30, 56
Mare Nostrum 53
Marines 83
Masada 56
Matilda, queen 118, 151, 159, 161, 163
Maurice l'Ingénieur 163
Maxstoke Castle 238, 239
Merlon 2, 59, 67, 136, 141, 176, 186, 191
Milecastle 80, 82, 106
Milimete, Walter of 236
Militia 53, 54, 259
Mining 176, 177, 181, 237
Moel Y Gaer 20
Monpazier 280, 281
Mooghaun 35
Mortar 237
Mortimer of Wigmore, Roger 195, 219, 230, 231
Moss-troooper 282
Motte 125
Moucharabieh 191
Mousa Broch 43, 46
Multivallate 13, 15, 19, 28, 33, 38, 39
Murage grant 257
Murder-holes 190, 193, 218, 223, 258, 269
Murus Gallicus 16, 17, 18

National Heritage Act 301
National Trust 246, 286, 302
Nenagh Castle 186, 300
Neolithic 8, 9, 11, 29, 36, 51
Norman dynasty 304
Normandy 83, 117, 118, 120, 134, 138, 166, 169, 170, 203
Normans 117, 118, 119, 121

Offa 105, 106, 107, 108, 109
Oilette 142
Operation Sealion 114
Oppidum (oppida) 8, 10, 11, 16, 18, 33, 56, 58, 262
Orford Castle 180, 181, 297
Oswestry 33, 107

Papilio 71
Pax Romana 53, 92
Peel tower 229, 282
Pele 282
Pembroke Castle 182, 183
Penrith Castle 290
Pentaspastos 61
Peregrini 74
Perpendicular style 244
Petard 237
Petronel 237
Pevensey 83, 84, 86, 120, 136, 149, 297
Pfostenschlitzmauer 16, 18
Pinna 59
Plantagenet dynasty 161, 304
Plantagenet empire 163, 164, 231
Plantagenet-Lancaster dynasty 304
Plantagenet-York dynasty 304
Playing-card form 64, 65, 74, 83
Plinth 179, 182
Plunging fire 237
Pontefract Castle 181, 233
Portchester Castle 87, 88, 148
Portcullis 143, 182, 190, 193, 206, 218, 242, 261, 269
Postern 87, 97, 149, 213, 237, 258
Praetorium 69, 70, 71, 73, 74, 75, 90
Preston Tower 286
Pretani 62
Prince of Wales 203, 214
Principia 69, 73, 74
Privacy 139
Privy 139
Processional castle 211
Propugnacla *see* Hoarding
Provisions of Oxford 171
Ptolemy 8
Purbeck marble 138

Quatrefoil 181, 183
Queenborough Castle 232

Raedikes 65, 68
Raglan Castle 240, 247, 248, 293

Rathgall 37
Rawnsley, Hardwicke 302
Rayleigh Mount 134
Reculver Castle 82, 83, 88
Reivers 281
Remblai 65
Restormel Castle 131, 132
Rhuddlan Castle 206, 207, 208, 209, 212
Richard I the Lionheart 167, 169, 177
Richard II 233, 234
Richard III 2, 161, 235, 246, 249
Richborough 85,
Richmond 137, 156, 253, 297
Ringfort 33, 36, 38, 39, 41, 42, 48, 51
Rising Castle 157, 158
Robert the Magnificent 118
Rochester Castle 155, 156, 177, 181
Rollo 117, 169
Roman army 53, 54, 55
Roman cities in Britain 95
Romanesque architecture 137
Rouen 83, 117, 169, 261

Saint-Clar 278
Saint George, Master James of 206, 208, 210, 211, 214, 218, 220, 223
Salic Frank Law 231
Sandwich 255, 256
Sapping 177, 179, 185
Saxon dynasty 304
Scarp 16
Scopet 237
Scott, Sir Walter 181, 226, 229, 249
Seafield Tower 291
Senlac Hill, battle of 121
Severan Wall 81
Shirt 129, 136
Shutter 191, 240
Siege warfare: ancient 24; early medieval 115;
 medieval 145, 146, 173–177; Roman 58, 59
Silchester 96, 97
Skenfrith Castle 192, 193, 253, 298
Smailholm Tower 229
Snowdon mountain 202
Solar 139
Solsbury Hill 10
Southampton 260, 266, 267, 297
Spangenhelm 114
Springal 175
Staigue ringfort 42
Stamford 103, 271
Stamford Bridge, battle of 120
Stephen (king) 129, 151, 158, 159, 161, 177, 304
Stimulus 59
Stirrup 119
Stonea Camp 28
Strigae 65, 70
Sudes 60, 65
Surcoat 167

Tacitus 7, 92
Talus 179
Tantallon Castle 292, 299
Tattershall Castle 246
Taunton Castle 158
Thegn 114
Titulus 65, 68
Totnes Castle 132
Tower house 2, 52, 187, 205, 225, 249, 252, 281, 282, 283, 284, 285, 289, 306
Traprain Law 32, 33
Trebuchet 175
Trevelgue Head 14
Tudor kings 292
Turma 70, 71
Turris 59

Unesco 303
Univallate 13, 15, 23, 25, 26, 31, 33, 37, 39

V-shaped 16, 66, 78, 80
Valetudinarium 70, 74
Vallum 59, 65, 91
Vertical flanking 191
Via principalis 65, 69, 73
Vicus 76, 245
Villa 89, 91, 92, 281
Villains 256

Wallingford 112, 114
Wareham 113, 114, 170
Warkworth Castle 289
Wars of the Roses 2, 218, 224, 230, 234, 238, 240, 249, 292
Warwick Castle 242, 250, 251, 252
Watchtower 58, 64, 68, 77, 78, 79, 80, 81, 82, 88, 189, 275, 276
Waughton Castle 290, 291
Westminster Hall 189
Wetheral Priory 276
Wheelhouse 46, 47, 49
White Tower *see* London Tower
William I (the Conqueror) 1, 118, 121 122, 123, 202
William II Rufus 158, 304
William III 290
William of Orange 1
Winchelsea 234, 241, 253, 255, 256
Winchester 268, 269
Winchester Castle 189
Windsor Castle 129
Witan 102, 118, 119, 121
Wolf's pit 59
World Heritage Sites 213, 214, 303

Yett 228
York 72, 183, 276

Z-plan 282, 283

www.ingramcontent.com/pod-product-compliance
Lightning Source LLC
Chambersburg PA
CBHW081539300426
44116CB00015B/2690